# The Islamic Lineage of American Literary Culture

# The Islamic Lineage of American Literary Culture

*Muslim Sources from the Revolution to Reconstruction*

JEFFREY EINBODEN

OXFORD
UNIVERSITY PRESS

## OXFORD
UNIVERSITY PRESS

Oxford University Press is a department of the University of Oxford. It furthers
the University's objective of excellence in research, scholarship, and education
by publishing worldwide. Oxford is a registered trade mark of Oxford University
Press in the UK and certain other countries.

Published in the United States of America by Oxford University Press
198 Madison Avenue, New York, NY 10016, United States of America.

© Oxford University Press 2016

Library of Congress Cataloging-in-Publication Data
Names: Einboden, Jeffrey.
Title: The Islamic lineage of american literary culture : Muslim sources from
the Revolution to Reconstruction / Jeffrey Einboden.
Description: New York, NY : Oxford University Press, [2016] | Includes
bibliographical references and index.
Identifiers: LCCN 2015050061| ISBN 9780199397808 (hardback : alk. paper)|
ISBN 9780190612931 (epub)
Subjects: LCSH: American literature—19th century—Islamic influences.
Classification: LCC PR129.I75 E46 2016 | DDC 810.9/38297—dc23 LC record available
at http://lccn.loc.gov/2015050061

1 3 5 7 9 8 6 4 2
Printed by Sheridan Books, Inc., United States of America

*For*
*Hillary,*
*Ezra & Eve*

راهیست راه عشق که هیچش کناره نیست
Muḥammad Shamsuddīn Ḥāfiẓ

The way of love is unlimited
R. W. Emerson (trans.)

# CONTENTS

# ACKNOWLEDGMENTS

Although a monograph—a "single-author study"—*The Islamic Lineage of American Literary Culture* received vital support from multiple institutions and individuals. Culminating a decade of research conducted at a dozen sites—from Cambridge, England, to Cambridge, New England—the book is indebted especially to the National Endowment for the Humanities, whose award of a 2014 Fellowship funded a full year of final research and writing. During 2013–2014, the book benefitted too from my tenure as a fellow at the Boston Athenaeum, where I gained access not only to essential archives, but also to the generous expertise of Mary Warnement and Stanley Cushing. For nearly a decade, I have also received regular aid from Northern Illinois University, including a 2012–2013 sabbatical, which proved critical to the book's completion. This institutional support allowed for the time, but also the travel, necessary for such a book based on primary source research and manuscript recovery. In addition to the Boston Athenaeum, I am deeply grateful to the following libraries for welcoming my repeated visits, and for permitting images and quotations from their collections to appear in the book: the Houghton Library, Harvard University, and the Harvard University Archives; the Boston Public Library; the Concord Free Public Library; the Digital Collections and Archives at Tufts University; the Phillips Library at the Peabody Essex Museum; the Berg Collection, and the Manuscripts and Archives Division, of the New York Public Library; Cornell University's Carl A. Kroch Library; the Redwood Library and Athenaeum in Newport, Rhode Island; Yale University's Beinecke Rare Book and Manuscript Library, as well as the Yale University Art Gallery. Finally, I express especial thanks to the American Antiquarian Society in Worcester, whose rich collections inform much of this book's research, and where I have profited from the gracious guidance of Tom Knowles, Lauren Hewes, and Jaclyn Penny.

Beyond financial support at Northern Illinois University, I have enjoyed much moral support from NIU colleagues and students since 2006; I thank, in particular, Betty Birner, for her ceaseless help, as well as Lara Crowley, Tim Crowley, Ryan Hibbett, Amy Levin, Kathleen Renk, Jessica Reyman, Luz Van Cromphout, and

Mark Van Wienen. Colleagues at a host of other institutions have offered gener-ous aid and encouragement in recent years; I am grateful especially to Fr. Sidney Griffith, David Jasper, Timothy Marr, Walid Saleh, Mustafa Shah, Fr. Isaac Slater, Shawkat Toorawa, Brian Yothers, and Eric Ziolkowski. My research into Islamic influence and the American canon was warmly welcomed at conferences on the Qur'ān hosted at London's School of Oriental and African Studies in 2009 and 2011, as well as by SOAS's *Journal of Qur'anic Studies*, whose pages first featured essays that are expanded upon in Chapters 3, 4, and 5, namely "The Early American Qur'an: Islamic Scripture and US Canon" 11:2 (2009): 1–19, and " 'Minding the Koran' in Civil War America: Islamic Revelation, US Reflections" 16:3 (2014): 84–103. Finally, also in London and Cambridge, I offer profound thanks to Tamara Follini, who supervised with such care and wisdom my Cambridge University dissertation on Emerson's Islamic translations—"Ralph Waldo Emerson, Persian Poetry and the German Critical Tradition"—which informs and is further devel-oped in this book's fifth chapter.

I am indebted to Oxford University Press—and especially, to my outstanding editor, Cynthia Read, and to Gina Chung—for consistent support through the writ-ing process and production. For reviewing the book in manuscript, in whole or in part, and for offering generous corrections and suggestions, I thank Mustafa Shah and the anonymous readers at Oxford University Press. All errors or inadequacies that remain in the book are, of course, entirely my own.

As implied by its title, this book is conceived as a *lineage*, its contents forming a genealogy of Islamic influence; however, this book's contexts are equally contoured by lineage, shaped by the loving support of my own family members and friends. As always, I have received inspiration and unwavering encouragement from my parents—Ed and Pam—and from Becky, Steve, Avery, Josh, and Rachel; Syd and Lily; Shelley and Mike; as well as from cherished lifelong friends, Andrew, Brad, James, Matthew, and Richard. My deepest gratitude is due to my wife, Hillary, whose love and labors have sustained this project from its distant beginnings, and to our children, Ezra and Eve, who have spent much of their young lives in trips to New England, and who enliven each of our days with immeasurable joy. With a love beyond limit, this book is dedicated to them.

# INTRODUCTION

Arguing that Muslim sources exercised a formative impact on U.S. literary origins, this book traces a genealogy of Islamic influence that spans America's critical century of self-definition, unfolding from the 1770s to the 1870s. Focusing on celebrated writers from the Revolution to Reconstruction, I excavate Arabic and Persian precedents that shaped U.S. authorial lives and letters, newly exposing neglected witnesses to American literary engagement with Islamic texts and traditions.

An act of historical recovery, this book's subjects are solidly grounded in the nation's earliest years. However, like all such acts of recovery, *The Islamic Lineage of American Literary Culture* not only addresses a historical period, but also inevitably reflects its own period of authorship, offering a portrait of the past that is conversant—explicitly or implicitly—with contemporary interests and anxieties. The present study is calibrated to its own time in at least two tandem ways, self-consciously intersecting specific critical trajectories, as well as broader cultural concerns. Reflecting the increasingly transatlantic and hemispheric perspective of American Studies, this book builds upon recent remappings of U.S. literary origins, defining early American authorship as a dynamic site of global exchange, rather than as an integral outcome of national exceptionalism.[1] Pioneered by prominent Americanists including Wai Chee Dimock, Lawrence Buell, Paul Giles, and Susan Manning, this transnational approach to early U.S. literature has included a rising interest in the Middle East in general, and Islam specifically; exceptional studies authored recently by Brian Yothers (2007) and Jacob Rama Berman (2012), for instance, have advanced a twenty-first-century trajectory of Americanist engagement with the Muslim Middle East that was heralded by Timothy Marr's foundational *The Cultural Roots of American Islamicism*—a 2006 study that superbly mapped an expansive "critical history of cultural imagination."[2] Reaching beyond the academy, this mounting Americanist historiography of Islamic influence itself, of course, reflects a wider "cultural" currency, intersecting the geopolitical climates and concerns that have defined the first decades of this century. Published in an era that continues to be shaped by 9/11 and its succeeding conflicts, *The Islamic Lineage of*

*American Literary Culture* treats historical topics that nevertheless hold a distinct twenty-first-century resonance, synthesizing national and religious identities that form the urgent polarities of much modern debate.

However, if broadly reflective of contemporary concerns, my study's specific interests also resist recent trends, diverging from the theoretical accents that increasingly typify "transnational" criticism, as well as the combative paradigms that continue to plague more popular discourse addressing Islam and America. Rather than an abstract appraisal of American literature's transnational contexts, *The Islamic Lineage of American Literary Culture* emphasizes the practical and the private, exposing the Islamic interiors and interiority of early U.S. authorship. Domesticated in a double sense, literal and literary, Muslim sources are seen to permeate the personal lives and labors of iconic American writers, inhabiting their home environs and household writings. Extracting Muslim threads woven into the familiar fabric of U.S. letters and sermons, journals and journalism, memorials and marginalia, I argue that the identities and idioms of foundational American authors were catalyzed through creative, and occasionally covert, acts of Islamic engagement. My study's emphasis on personal moments of Muslim source reception is sustained, moreover, by the unpublished materials it unearths, recovering tangible witnesses to writers' individual interests in Islamic texts. Instead of a novel theoretical frame, it is fresh evidence that supports this study's critical intervention, uncovering manuscripts that reveal private American readings of Islamic precedents, or gesture to personal contexts for American authors' published texts on Islam. Distinct from prior treatments, the present study situates physical "artifacts" as clues to cultural significance, pursuing a literary retrieval of Islamic influence in America that embraces priorities that partially overlap "Material Culture Studies"—an interdisciplinary field that explores, in the words of Mary Brooks, "the multi-layered meanings of objects and the way they evoke, contain and reflect human concerns or 'material memories.'"[3] While recent transnational readings of Islamic influence in the West have helpfully moved beyond the totalizing dichotomies associated with Saidean "Orientalism," *The Islamic Lineage of American Literary Culture* seeks to advance our understanding further by retreating back to primary sources, advocating a more minute concentration on material legacies, which, I argue, form the neglected sites of instructive nuance.[4]

This study's recovery of original sources offers a renewed focus not only on the *familiar*, however, but also on the *familial*, excavating documents of Islamic interest that have descended across American generations, either bequeathed through actual blood relatives or artistically inherited by later acts of authorship. Frequently inscribed privately, in solitude, or shared within intimate coteries, the Islamic engagements of early American authors also spawn personal lineages, leading to the present study's own lineal structure. Addressing global influences on icons of U.S. culture, *The Islamic Lineage of American Literary Culture* also pursues a domestic family history, its five body chapters arranged in overlapping chronologies, stretching from revolutionary beginnings to the aftermath of the Civil War, treating successively Ezra Stiles (1727–1795); William Bentley (1759–1819); Washington Irving (1783–1859); Lydia Maria Child (1802–1880); and Ralph Waldo Emerson (1803–1882). Nationally implicated, these five figures have been traditionally framed in terms of their "American" achievements, recognized as U.S. precursors in their respective pursuits, from theology to fiction, Abolitionism to Romanticism. Surprisingly, however, it is *The Islamic Lineage of American Literary Culture* that marks the first study to synthesize these authors of American renown, their shared appeal to Muslim sources ironically forging new links between these national literati.[5]

It is this study's earliest two authors whose critical neglect has proved most acute, and it is my first two chapters that therefore bear the heaviest evidentiary burden. Ezra Stiles and William Bentley uniquely embody the generational continuities and contrasts that cross the Revolution and the early Republic. Celebrated as their eras' leading intellectuals, even while authoring daily diaries that index the nation's progress, Stiles and Bentley occupy opposite poles in New England religious life, the former upholding Calvinism in revolutionary Newport and New Haven, the latter pioneering American Unitarianism in Salem at the turn of the century. Juxtaposed in their Christian commitments, Chapters 1 and 2 reveal these American diarists to be joined in their successive "Eastern" interests, sharing an Islamic literacy expressed in personal writings and epistolary exchanges. Chapter 1 argues that the public profile of Ezra Stiles, friend of founding fathers and polymath president of Yale, shields his private devotion to Arabic; even while recording his nation's patriotic struggles for independence, Stiles himself personally struggled to read the language of the Qur'ān. Relying on eighteenth-century marginalia and manuscripts never before published, Chapter 1 explores the Islamic interventions that emerge throughout Stiles' domestic writings, uncovering parallel revolutions of country and creed embedded in his eighteenth-century Arabic inscriptions. Chapter 2 argues that William Bentley, the successor to Stiles as America's diarist, also surpassed Stiles in his personal appeal to Muslim sources, Bentley fostering familiarity with Islamic precedents even while forging an American Unitarianism. Exploring the Arabic and Persian inscribed in his student notes, as well as the Islamic echoes scattered through his more mature journals, Chapter 2 also exposes for the first time William Bentley's newly uncovered cache of Arabic correspondence and his collection of Islamic manuscripts, situating these transatlantic traces as a forgotten early chapter in U.S.–Middle Eastern relations.

Shifting genres, my study's genealogy advances in Chapter 3 from America's religious foundations to its Romantic fictions, reaching up from the Republic's beginnings to the brink of the Civil War. Celebrated as the "Father of American Literature," famed especially for his "Rip Van Winkle" and "The Legend of Sleepy Hollow," Washington Irving is freshly defined in Chapter 3 as America's pioneer of Qur'ānic translation, with neglected manuscripts evidencing his private refashioning of Muslim scripture.[6] Reproducing select pages from Irving's unpublished journals, including his New York Public Library "Arabic Notebook," Chapter 3 indexes the domestic contexts that surround Irving's Islamic interests, stretching from his Andalucían travels in the 1820s to his late *Mahomet and his Successors* (1850)—a biography that bequeaths Irving's Muslim renditions to diverse literary descendants, even while blurring his own interventions and identity. This complex afterlife for Irving's Islamic interests is also the concern of Chapter 4, which mirrors his Muslim engagements in the career of Lydia Maria Child, whose private renditions of Islamic sources reflect Irving's methods, yet reverse his motives. A "household name in America," acclaimed as "the first woman in the republic," Lydia Maria Child's widespread renown arose from her career's wide authorial range, producing not only historical novels and children's periodicals, but also feminist chronicles and antislavery polemics.[7] However, Chapter 4 suggests that underneath her "household" writings Child fostered a domestic Islamicism, personally refashioning Muslim precedents even as she pursued her progressive reforms. Reviving print sources now ignored, while also recovering Child's manuscript renditions from George Sale's *Koran*, Chapter 4 traces the lifelong Islamic interests of "the most celebrated American woman author of the day," her revisions of Muslim sources paralleling both her political activism and her personal religiosity, culminating in the private Qur'ānic adaptations that underlie Child's final book, her 1878 *Aspirations of the World: A Chain of Opals*.[8]

Complementing Chapter 4 in its span of the nineteenth century, my study concludes with its fifth chapter dedicated to Ralph Waldo Emerson, mapping the wide expanse between his public American image and his private practice of Islamic reception. Stretching from Emerson's student quotation of the Qur'ān in 1819 to the Islamic endowments that emerge at his 1882 death, Chapter 5 is centered on Emerson's decades of daily reading and rendition of Persian poetry, generating hybrid translations of medieval Muslim lyricists, especially the "prince of Persian poets," Muḥammad Shamsuddīn Ḥāfiẓ.[9] Chapter 5 reveals Emerson, an icon of American exceptionalism, nevertheless to be early America's most prolific translator of Islamic verse, rendering more than two thousand lines of Persian poetry from German sources—a campaign of translation that continues to be underestimated in Americanist scholarship. Scribbled through diaries, letters, even on the backs of envelopes, I highlight the private sites of Emerson's Islamic quotations and Persian poetry translations, arguing that they offer instructive insights into an Islamic interiority that echoes to the end of his life and beyond, reaching posthumously forward to descendants, familial and national.

In closing with the death of Emerson, America's Romantic pioneer, near the end of the nineteenth century, Chapter 5 concludes far from Ezra Stiles at the outset of the Revolution in Chapter 1, not only crossing the span of a pivotal century, but also progressing across periods of immense religious, intellectual and social change. However, even while fusing divergent generations, *The Islamic Lineage of American Literary Culture*, like all genealogies, arises from core bonds of kinship, detecting a family likeness expansive enough to embrace Calvinist Stiles in the 1770s and Transcendentalist Emerson in the 1870s. Diverse in their concerns and outcomes, the Islamic interests of each of the five authors treated in this book share not only a personal identity, but reflect a personal imperative to render and revise Middle Eastern sources, adapting the essential expressions of a supposedly "foreign" religion into idioms and environs that are most familiar. In the introduction to his 2012 *American Arabesque: Arabs, Islam and the 19th-Century Imaginary*, Jacob Rama Berman noted that "If American Studies is truly to take its much-advertised global turn, its scholars must cultivate an appreciation for the languages from which foreign references are pilfered."[10] This is certainly correct; however, unlike preceding studies, the present book argues that the early American "imaginary" was itself infused and inspired by "an appreciation for [Middle Eastern] languages," with figures from Ezra Stiles, to William Bentley, to Washington Irving, engaged in transcribing and translating actual Arabic and Persian. Indeed, it is the authentic character of American interests in Islam that has ironically served to keep such interests hidden, with sources neglected by modern scholars due precisely to their inscription in Middle Eastern languages. In the manuscript witnesses recovered and reproduced in *The Islamic Lineage of American Literary Culture*, I seek to show that the "global turn" now "much-advertised" in "American Studies" has been partially inhibited by the global languages "cultivated" during the nation's first years, prompting our neglect of an early tradition of adaptive translation that echoes from Ezra Stiles in the eighteenth century to later figures less interested in Middle Eastern philology, such as Lydia Maria Child and Ralph Waldo Emerson. By excavating archival sources that exhibit U.S. authors' adoption of Arabic and Persian idioms, this study seeks not to take a new "global turn" merely, but to trace arcs in early America that anticipate our contemporary interests, while implying too the wealth of neglected sources that await circulation in twenty-first-century "American Studies."

# The Islamic Lineage of American Literary Culture

# 1

# "Blessed be Allāh, Most Fair"

## Ezra Stiles' Arabic Revolutions

September 1774 was a pivotal month for America—and for Ezra Stiles. Minister of the Second Congregational Church in Newport, Rhode Island, Stiles spent his September eager for turbulent news sent north from Philadelphia, where the First Continental Congress had convened on the first of the month. Filling his diary with dates and delegates, with reports of British affront and Boston resistance, Stiles charts with excitement the unfolding "scene of remarkable Occurrences in New England and thro' America," championing the "Members of the Congress" committed to standing "firm in the cause of LIBERTY."[1] Closer to home, September 1774 also proved a month of domestic upheaval for the Stiles family, with Ezra and his wife, Elizabeth, bidding farewell to their eldest son—Ezra Jr.—sending him off to New Haven, where he was enrolling as a first-year college student. Poignant for any parent, the departure of Ezra Jr. was particularly meaningful for Stiles, as his namesake was entering Yale—not only where Stiles himself had been an undergraduate and a tutor, but where he would soon become college president, guiding Yale through the tumultuous years of the Revolution and its aftermath, up to his own death in 1795.

A revolutionary month for nation and family, September 1774 signaled for Stiles the start of both colonial Congress and his son's college career, witnessing delegates assemble as well as a domestic disruption. It was during this same month, however, that Ezra Stiles also sketched the most revolutionary religious document to survive among his copious cache of manuscripts (Fig. 1.1).[2]

Dated September 6, 1774—the day before Stiles embarked "on a Journey to Connecticutt to enter my son Ezra into Yale College"—this document's sum total is a single sheet of paper, single-sided; its contents, however, are multiple and complex.[3] Picturing four outer circles, orbiting a fifth in the middle, and enclosed by yet another, perimeter circle, the exotic design of Stiles' diagram is matched by its exotic diction, synthesizing various Semitic texts and traditions. Featuring Hebrew as its radiant center, Stiles' circles revolve around a shining sacred word: "יהוה"— "Jehovah," the Hebrew Tetragrammaton, the four-letter divine name. Dilating outward

*Figure 1.1* Ezra Stiles, *"Linguarum orientalium specimen quadrilinguale"* (1774). Image courtesy of the Beinecke Rare Book and Manuscript Library, Yale University.

from this hallowed core, each of Stiles' satellite circles is composed in an allied Near Eastern language, distinct bodies in a constellation of scriptural tongues. Reflecting his engagement with ancient Judaica, and with Newport's own historic Jewish community, Stiles dedicates his top and bottom circles to languages and literary sources based in the Hebrew Bible. With subtle self-reference, Stiles quotes "Ezra VII:10" in his "HÆBRAICA" sphere at the top; at the bottom, Stiles inscribes "Micha VI:8" in "CHALD[EE]," quoting this verse from an ancient Aramaic translation, the *Targum of Jonathan*.[4] A Christian balance to these Judaic centers is found in Stiles' right-hand circle. Composed in Syriac—an Aramaic dialect vital to the New Testament's early transmission— Stiles reproduces the theologically tendentious query of 1 John 5:5: "For who is he that overcometh the world, but he that believeth that Jesus is the Son of God?"

("ܡܢܘ ܓܝܪ ܕܙܟܐ ܠܥܠܡܐ ܐܠܐ ܐܝܢܐ ܕܡܗܝܡܢ ܕܝܫܘܥ ܒܪܗ ܗܘ ܕܐܠܗܐ").[5]

It is the sphere that occupies the left of Stiles' global sketch, however, that seems most surprising; featuring not a biblical tongue and text, Stiles' left-hand circle is inscribed instead entirely in Arabic. Distinct in script and scriptural association, this circle is distinct too in its lack of citation; while Stiles' other circles confess their sacred sources, his "ARABICA" acknowledges no clear precedent, concluding merely with a stellar symbol:

بسم الله
الرحمن الرحيم
من سر الله تعاله
الله الملك الحق المبين
وتبارك الله احسن
الخالقين ✴

[In the name of *Allāh*
the Merciful, the Compassionate.
Of the secret of *Allāh*, exalted be He
*Allāh*, the King, the Real, the Manifest
And blessed be *Allāh*, most fair
of the creators ✴]

If silent as to its textual origins, the opening phrase of this Arabic sphere yet announces a distinct religious identity. The leading lines of Stiles' circle reads "بسم الله / الر حمن الر حيم"—"In the name of *Allāh* / the Merciful, the Compassionate"— the precise formula that also serves as the standard prelude to all Muslim prayer and liturgy, claiming origins in the Qur'ān itself. Confirming his Qur'ānic commencement, the brief text of Stiles' "ARABICA" also evinces specific echoes of Muslim scripture. Line four, for instance, describes "*Allāh*" as "الحق المبين"—"the Real, the Manifest"— divine epithets that derive from the Qur'ān 24:25 and 27:79. This phrase from Islam's scripture also lends a stylistic coherency to Stiles' circle, establishing a euphony between its lines four and six, which each conclude with a shared syllable—"*īn*"—pairing together in rhyme "*al-mubīn*" ("the Manifest") and "*al-khāliqīn*" ("the creators").[6]

In September 1774, witnessing the dissolution of national borders and family ties, Ezra Stiles fuses a fresh family and nation in his circular manuscript, forging a family of Semitic philology, and a nation of Abrahamic religions, which encompasses not only the Judaic and the Christian, but also the Islamic. Obliquely reflecting its revolutionary date, Stiles dedicates September 6 to reconciling Middle Eastern traditions, even as his own homeland, the Western Colonies, moves toward fractious revolt. Mapping a new world through redrawing the old, forming a more perfect union by shifting ancient borders, Stiles posits a private universe in which the Qur'ān belongs in the same orbit as the Bible, charting a cosmic harmony above transatlantic ruptures and domestic departures. Consistent with his own Christian allegiance, Stiles' circles clearly privilege the Hebraic; not only does Hebrew occupy Stiles' divine center, but it is also Hebrew script that parses his Syriac and Arabic spheres, Stiles supplying transliterations immediately below these side circles. Alone and positioned on the left periphery, Stiles' Arabic circle with its Islamic appeal does not, however, seem peripheral in his celestial scheme; solitarily on the margins, Muslim expression nevertheless occupies the center of its own autonomous globe, independent from biblical siblings, yet navigating within the same compass.

This private interplay of interiors and exteriors—of inscribed circles within inscribed circles—invites particular attention due to the public profile of its author. Straddling the last decades of British America, and the first decades of the United States, the career of Ezra Stiles charts the volatile transition from colony to nation, while indexing also the cultural tensions of eighteenth-century New England life. Widely celebrated as "the most learned man of his time," or "one of the most learned men in America," Stiles' capacious intellect left few fields of inquiry untouched.[7] Spanning commitments conventionally understood as opposed, Stiles was author of didactic sermons and political histories; library charters and silkworm studies; metaphysical lectures and local maps. Congregationalist pastor and college president, circulating between Newport and New Haven, Stiles also moved in more cosmopolitan circles, corresponding with American founders and European elites. Exchanging ideas with Benjamin Franklin and books with Thomas Jefferson, Stiles received an honorary doctorate from Edinburgh in his early career, and at the end of his life, three decades later, wrote to Calcutta, sending a lengthy letter to the eighteenth century's leading philologist and Orientalist, Sir William Jones.[8]

It is not Stiles' public prominence, or his contact with renowned personalities, that has proved his most recognized achievement, however, but rather his personal memorials—Stiles' multivolume *Diary*, which spans dozens of years and hundreds of pages, forming an indispensable witness to the origins of national life. Begun on New Year's Day 1769, Stiles' *Diary* offers a rich source of reference for a surprising range of scholarly histories, garnering regular mention in recent studies of early America, helping to chronicle cultural exchange across race and religion, intersecting the discrete histories of Native Americans, African Americans, and Jewish Americans in the eighteenth century.[9] Celebrated in particular for his intimacy with Newport's Touro Synagogue, Stiles' friendship with Rabbi Haim Isaac Carigal, which included a sustained correspondence conducted in Hebrew, is perhaps the most recognized of early America's interreligious relationships, portrayed as a precedent for New World pluralism in belief and practice.[10]

These rival elements that build Stiles' reputation each seem expressed in his September 1774 manuscript. Penned at a moment of political anxiety, this document is yet a vision of cosmic order, its mystic circles forming a geometric map, charting personal Christian faith while expressing interfaith outreach. However, this 1774 document also witnesses an element of Stiles' life that has escaped our eclectic portrait of America's "most learned man": namely, Stiles' private appeal to Islamic idioms, integrating Muslim language into his domestic reading routine and informal acts of authorship. Remaining outside the periphery of contemporary scholarship, Stiles' circles in September 1774 help to recenter the Muslim margins of his personal literacy, hinting at the Islamic interiors of his private writings. While Stiles' familiarity with Arabic merited frequent mention, though cursory, in the earliest studies—including *The Life of Ezra Stiles* (1798), authored by Stiles' former student and son-in-law, Abiel Holmes—this familiarity has lately been ignored, or dismissed as mere philological diversion.[11] Edmund Morgan's otherwise comprehensive *The Gentle Puritan: A Life of Ezra Stiles* (1962), for instance, neglects Stiles' Arabic interests altogether.[12] More typical of recent trends is Shalom Goldman's assessment in his 2003 *God's Sacred Tongue: Hebrew and the American Imagination*, which briefly acknowledges Stiles' "reading of Arabic," but quickly concludes that "unlike the Hebrew reading [it] was a secular pursuit."[13]

The present chapter will chart, for the first time, Stiles' increasing investment in Arabic through the core years of his career, relying on unpublished manuscripts and previously unrecovered marginalia. This chapter will also, however, find Stiles' broad Arabic interests leading to specific Islamic engagements, with Muslim sources impacting—directly and indirectly—his private literary life. As the first figure to be addressed in *The Islamic Lineage of American Literary Culture*, Stiles will also offer an illuminating point of departure, forming a predictive precedent, as well as an ironic mirror, for national successors. Fostering facility with Islamic language during the final years of the 1760s, Stiles anticipates a century to come, launching a tradition of private appeal to Muslim sources that punctuates pivotal moments of American self-definition, from the Revolution to Reconstruction. However, Stiles' Islamic engagements are also distinct from U.S. descendants. Unlike subsequent New England generations—from Unitarians such as William Bentley to Transcendentalists such as Ralph Waldo Emerson—Stiles will find little in common with Islam's disavowal of the Trinity and its embrace of a strictly human Christ. Haunted by increasing evangelical anxiety as the eighteenth century nears its end, Stiles' late concern with

America's waning Calvinism makes his constructive engagement with Muslim sources all the more surprising.[14] As suggested by his oscillating circles in 1774—revolving spheres that converge, yet do not overlap—Stiles' Islamic interiority offers an oblique pattern and early parallel for later American expressions, touching but not transgressing New World circulations to come. ✹

Held at Princeton's Rare Books and Special Collections are several valuable volumes dating from New England's first decades; barely visible on the endleaf of one such volume is an autograph, thinly traced in faded ink, that reads "Isaak Chauncy." The very name borne by the eldest son of Charles Chauncy—Harvard's second president (d. 1672)—it may seem unsurprising to find Isaak's signature etched in a book surviving from colonial America. This specific autograph, however, is remarkable due to the particular item it inscribes. Fusing two texts, Isaak's signed volume is a *sammelband* combining a 1572 grammar of Syriac, and a slightly later primer of Arabic—the 1592 *Alphabetum Arabicum*. Inscribed indistinctly, the distinguished name of "Isaak Chauncy" offers a nominal witness to a facet of New World philology often overlooked; while Puritan devotion to Hebrew is widely acknowledged, Arabic's role in early America has received little attention.[15] Literally stitching together distinct languages, this *sammelband* owned by "Isaak Chauncy" stands as material symbol of colonial ties to this sibling Semitic tongue, binding Arabic and its *Alphabetum* to New England's biblical literacy.

Of all Puritan patriarchs, it seems apt that Princeton's volume bears the family name of "Chauncy" in particular. President of New England's own "Cambridge college," Isaak's father, Charles Chauncey, had first studied "Oriental Languages" at the University of Cambridge in England, where his years as a student and young tutor coincided with Arabic's recognition as an autonomous discipline at the university. Arriving in Massachusetts in 1638, Charles Chauncy led Harvard from 1654 to 1672, integrating Arabic into the fledgling college's curriculum during his presidency.[16] However, even before Chauncy's early leadership, Arabic had already found a home at Harvard. The college's first president, Henry Dunster, would anticipate Chauncy not only in studying at the University of Cambridge, but also in advocating Semitic studies at Harvard. Transporting Eastern philology to America's East Coast, President Dunster especially sought to acquire language resources for his colonial students; writing to the famed European Orientalist, Christian Ravis, in 1648, Dunster appealed "to you, and them, who shall procure us" books, petitioning in particular for

> what soever Hebrew, Caldee, Syriack, or Arabick-authors, Gods providence shall enlarge their hands, and hearts to procure us: A wonderfull impulse unto these studies lyes on the spirits of our students [. . .][17]

Bound again to the biblical languages, Dunster ties Arabic not only to the godly tongues—"Hebrew, Caldee, Syriack"—but also to God Himself, with "Gods providence" and "Arabick-authors" immediately juxtaposed. Commissioning the help of European "hearts," as well as "their hands," Dunster links Oriental literacy— including Arabic "studies"—with the "spiritual" welfare of "our students" at Harvard, arising from their own "wonderfull impulse."

A linguistic parallel to Hebrew and Aramaic, Arabic's key value for Puritan founders was, of course, its exegetical potential, promising to help parse their faith's biblical roots. Reflecting a commitment to scriptural primacy essential to Puritanism, American interest in Arabic matures through the eighteenth century, with an Ivy League tradition of Arabic transplanted to Yale at its 1701 foundation.[18] The century's most celebrated American theologian—Jonathan Edwards—received his early training at Yale from Harvard graduates, and would himself eventually include Arabic in his private readings of sacred writ. Begun in 1730, Edwards' "Blank Bible" comprises his personal commentary on scripture, occasionally appealing to Arabic in explaining arcane Hebrew diction. Defining "Gopher wood" as mentioned in Genesis 6:14, for example, Edwards quotes Arthur Bedford and his *Scripture Chronology*, writing:

> The word in Hebrew גֹּפֶר [*gopher*] may perhaps signify the cypress by an easy variation of the same into Greek, and Latin, and other languages. And the Arabic شمشار [*shamshār*] signifies the same [. . .][19]

A tool of comparative philology, "Arabic" contributes to Edward's biblical interpretation, tracing its Semitic script in the wake of Europe's classical tongues, "Greek, and Latin." Inscribing Arabic's fluid lines into the interleaved pages of his biblical commentary, Edwards also discovers Arabic implied in the Bible itself; explaining the mysterious final word of Deuteronomy 2:20— the Hebrew "זמזמים" ("*Zamzummīm*")—Edwards again relies on Bedford, asserting that

> Zamzummims is a word that in Arabic signifies "thundering fellows," being taken from a word that signifies "a rattling like thunder" [. . .][20]

Not a Hebrew comparative merely, Arabic is seen as inhabiting Hebrew scripture itself, covertly surfacing in passages from the Pentateuch, challenging Puritans such as Edwards to foster at least some familiarity with Arabic's root "significances."

A close contemporary of Jonathan Edwards, and his fellow student at Yale, Isaac Stiles owed much of his early education to the Edwards' family, schooled initially by Jonathan's prominent father, Timothy Edwards. Both born in East Windsor, Connecticut, and only six years apart, Isaac Stiles and Jonathan Edwards would, however, pursue divergent paths, opposed in both fame and theology; while Edwards earned celebrity as a "New Light" champion, Isaac Stiles remained conservative, enjoying a humble and quiet career.[21] Assuming the pulpit in North Haven, Connecticut, it would be here that Isaac's first son—Ezra—was born in

1727. Following his father's lead, Ezra Stiles entered Yale in 1742, graduated in 1746, and obtained his license to preach in 1749. However, the line that extends from Ezra Stiles' early Yale education and his later ministry—and his Near Eastern linguistics—is neither smooth nor straight. Plagued by doubts, and questioning Calvinist doctrines, Stiles avoided ministerial appointment until offered the pulpit of Newport's Second Congregational Church in 1755. More than a decade then elapsed before Stiles turned to "Oriental" tongues, having "neglected" all but the Hebrew alphabet during his early years at Yale.[22]

And yet, by the time Stiles launched his celebrated *Diary*, it is clear that not only Hebrew, but also Arabic, had earned an intimate place in his intellectual routine; the first entries of Stiles' *Diary*, beginning on New Year's Day, 1769, read as follows:

January, 1769.

1. Lord's day. Preached forenoon & afternoon. Fine mild New Years day.
2. Read a chapter in Hebrew, & some Arabic.
3. Read two chapters in Hebrew, & Arabic.
4. Read two chapters in Hebrew. I begun to write my Ecclesiastical History of New England & British America 22[d] of last month. Wrote some upon it.
5. Mr. Ephraim Judson came to preach on the Hill (late M[r] Vinal's).
6. Read five chapters in Heb. & some Arabic.
7. Finished Esther in Heb.
8. Lord's day. Preached. Mr. Judson preached on the hill.
9. Wrote history; finished first three sheets. Ezra began to learn hebrew about this time, Æt. 10.
10. Read two chapters. Begun Joshua in Hebrew; & read some Arabic.[23]

Recalling Puritan beginnings more than a century before, Stiles binds together Hebrew and Arabic at the beginning of 1769, with priority ascribed to the former, Hebrew meriting first mention in his New Year's entries. Reaching back in genealogy to New England forebears, this initial page of Stiles' *Diary* also reaches forward to succeeding generations; even while immersed in his own Arabic reading, Stiles records passing "hebrew" on to his eldest son, recalling that "about this time" his namesake—"Ezra [Jr.]"—had begun "to learn" the language at age "10." However, it is simply Arabic's inclusion in the researches of a committed Calvinist that seems most striking. Casually intersecting both his sacred duties and his secular observations, Arabic is firmly at home amid Stiles' "Ecclesiastical" writing and scripture reading, with "some Arabic" imprecisely recorded between informal remembrances of daily life.

At the forefront of Stiles' verbal *Diary* in 1769, Arabic will also form a backdrop for Stiles' visual portrait, begun the next year. Commissioned in 1770, Samuel King's iconic painting of Ezra Stiles depicts not only his physical likeness, but also his intellectual formation, illustrating shelves of books behind its primary subject, suggesting Stiles' eclectic interests, spanning religion, philosophy, and science (Fig. 1.2). Detailing this self- designed portrait in his *Diary*, Stiles confesses that he "selected the Books to my Taste" for these background shelves, including "Plato" and "Newtons Works," along with the "N Engld Fathers." From this latter group, Stiles elects to distinguish a single Puritan Patriarch above all: "President Chauncy"— the "most truly & extensively learned" of America's "Fathers," Stiles insists, possessing "Knowledge of the learned Languages," not only "Hebrew," but "its several Dialects"— including "Arabic."[24] Foregrounding Arabic as he sits for his portrait in 1770, Stiles not only traces the language's

*Figure 1.2* Samuel King, "Ezra Stiles Portrait, 1770–71," with Arabic on book spine (picture right). Image courtesy of the Yale University Art Gallery.

influence abstractly, however, but graphically in his portrait's background. Conspicuous in Samuel King's painting is a shining orb of Hebrew over Stiles' right shoulder, featuring again the divine Tetragrammaton: "יהוה" (i.e., "Jehovah"). Easily overlooked, however, is the painting's inclusion of another Middle Eastern script above Stiles' left shoulder as well, not imprinted in Hebrew, but in Arabic. Inscribed unsteadily in deep gold, the spine of a volume at Stiles' left- hand reads: "משה אבן מימון מורה נבוכים" ("*Mosheh ibn Maymūn Moreh Nabūkīm*")—that is, "Moses Maimonides, *The Guide for the Perplexed*." Recording this rabbinic title in Arabic transliteration, Stiles faintly traces the Islamic contexts for this classic Jewish text, gesturing to Maimonides' original land and language— Andalucía and Arabic—while also suggesting Stiles' aspirational lineage, etching his efforts with "learned Languages" into his visual autobiography. Posterior in his portrait, and grounded in an American posterity, Arabic arises in Stiles' own self-representation, visibly gilded on the left margins of his likeness.[25]

Artistically invoking "Arabic" and its prior New World experts—including "President [Charles] Chauncy"—Stiles situates himself within an American legacy of Arabic in 1770 that will surface again at the end of this same decade, even as Stiles assumes his own college presidency. Returning in 1778 to lead Yale, Stiles will take a moment to recall in his *Diary* the college's storied past of scholarship, remembering especially Timothy Cutler—Yale's early "rector," and his own father's teacher:

> Rector Cutler was an excellent Linguist — he was a great Hebrician & Orientalist. He had more Know. of the *Arabic* than I believe any man ever in N. England before him, except President Chauncy and his Disciple the first M$^r$ Thatcher [. . .][26]

Distinguished broadly as "an excellent Linguist," Cutler's specific distinction is his "Know. of the *Arabic*," an achievement that reminds Stiles again of "President Chauncy." Recalling his father's college days with "Rector Cutler," Stiles is prompted to retreat further, reaching the academic roots of New England "Arabic" with Charles Chauncy, as well as "M$^r$ Thatcher," his "Disciple." Although the current president of Yale, Stiles gravitates back to Harvard history and its early president, sketching an "Orientalist" heritage whose imprint was first hinted by the "Chauncy" autograph inscribed within Princeton's *Alphabetum Arabicum*. Bridging generations and institutions, Stiles embraces a genealogy of American Arabic that is intimately patriarchal—inherited by sons from fathers—but which seems tinged too with spiritual initiation—passing from masters to "Disciples." ✿

Although reverencing a "Know[ledge] of the *Arabic*" centered in New England's emergent universities, Stiles had graduated from Yale without Arabic, and yet returns to Yale three decades later, now familiar with this "Oriental" language. If not at Yale, then, where did Stiles acquire his Arabic?

The call to lead Newport's Second Congregationalist Church in 1755 attracted Stiles' attention partly due to Newport itself—and, more particularly, Newport's Redwood Athenaeum. America's oldest circulating library, the Redwood offered Stiles a rich store of rare books, promising to feed his eclectic intellectual appetite. Appointed the Redwood's "Librarian" only a year after his arrival in Newport, Stiles helped publish the *Laws of the Redwood-Library Company* in 1765, defining the library's aim as "diffusing Light and Truth to Places far and wide"—a global imperative reflected too in the catalog appended to the Redwood's *Laws*.[27] Fusing foreign and domestic, the library's collection in 1765 boasted an inventory that included "Quarto Volumes" such as the following, alphabetically arranged on the catalog's page 7:

> Price's British Carpenter.
> Robins on the Strength of the Navy.
> Rowe on Wheel Carriages.
> Sale's Koran.
> Saunderson's Algebra, 2 Vols.[28]

Amid volumes on mathematics and the military, grappling with common concerns from the "Carpenter" to "Wheel Carriages," a copy of the "Koran" also emerges, with George Sale's 1734 English translation listed amid the Redwood's diverse registry. It would not be "Sale," however, but a name just further along in the Redwood's catalog that catalyzed Stiles' first engagements with Arabic and Islamic studies: John Selden. Prominent jurist and prolific Orientalist in Britain's tumultuous seventeenth century, Selden earned the label of "the chief of learned men reputed in this land" from John Milton himself, a label anticipating Stiles' own "repute" in revolutionary America.[29] And although separated by a century and the Atlantic, the careers of Selden and Stiles do overlap in broad outline, each witnessing their nation's war to end monarchic rule at home, while fostering interests in foreign languages. Perhaps detecting a kindred mind, Stiles was drawn especially to the Redwood's six-volume set of John Selden's works, the posthumously published *Opera Omnia* (1726). Composed primarily in Latin and English, Selden's *Opera* also includes generous selections in Hebrew and Arabic, appealing to Oriental antiquity while addressing issues critical to contemporary Britain.[30]

Although intrigued by the *Opera Omnia*, Stiles' ignorance of Arabic impeded his full enjoyment of Selden, prompting him to seek domestic help to decipher this transatlantic source. Uniquely aware of America's own Arabic legacies, Stiles also naturally knew where to turn: Harvard. Once home to Charles Chauncy, the

*Figure 1.3*  Stephen Sewall, "Specimen of an Arabic Grammar" (1768), pages 1 and 4, featuring the Arabic alphabet and "the first Psalm in Arabic" respectively. Image courtesy of the Beinecke Rare Book and Manuscript Library, Yale University.

colony's "most truly & extensively learned" linguist, Harvard had coincidentally appointed its very first "Hancock Professor of Hebrew and Other Oriental Languages" in the same year Stiles became the Redwood's librarian, naming Stephen Sewall to this unprecedented post in 1765.[31] Charged with a remit beyond merely "Hebrew," the "Other Oriental Languages" of Sewall's professorship included not only Syriac and Aramaic, but also Arabic, prompting Stiles to write Sewall in 1768, seeking aid in his own philological efforts. Responding to Newport from Cambridge in an unpublished letter dated July 29, 1768, Sewall offers Stiles perhaps the most striking material witness to Arabic's epistolary exchange in Colonial America. "Agreeably to your desire," Sewall declares in the initial lines of his 1768 note, "I have inclosed the first Psalm in Arabic, expressed in Roman letters, as I should read it"—an introduction that describes a four-page pamphlet whose first and last leaves are reproduced as Figure 1.3.

Opening with the alphabet on its initial page, Sewall's pamphlet treats Arabic declensions and grammar on its pages 2 and 3, concluding on page 4 with Psalm 1 in Arabic, his last page offering a transliteration of this Psalm not only in "Roman letters," as Sewall suggests, but also in Hebrew, furnishing Stiles with a sense of Arabic's kinship with this language of the Bible. Although preparing his pamphlet "[a]greeably to your desire," Sewall expresses concerns in his accompanying letter, seeming anxious that Stiles might be overwhelmed by such material. Apologizing for his pamphlet's extended transliterations, Sewall closes his cover letter by excusing his attempts to make Arabic "explicit" for Stiles, concluding:

Perhaps I have been too explicit,—have left nothing for the exercise of your own invention.—It is my profession, & inclination too, to propagate the knowledge of Oriental literature in this Western world. If the inclosed shall have the least tendency to this desirable end, it will give the highest satisfaction to,

> Sir,

> > your obedient &

> > > humble Servant,

> > > > *Stephen Sewall*[32]

Confessing his own pedantic "tendency," Sewall concludes with his pedagogic mission, reflected not only in his Harvard "profession," but also his personal "inclination." A source of intimate "satisfaction," Sewall internationally frames his efforts to "propagate" Arabic, synthesizing the Near East and New England by seeking to spread "knowledge of Oriental literature in this Western world." Balancing Orient and Occident, individual pleasure and public imperative, Sewall's letter anticipates his pamphlet's linguistic precision as well as its inscribed beauty. Aiming to engage Stiles' imagination—anxious that Stiles may not have room to "exercise [his] invention"—Sewall's careful calligraphy seems stylized as well as studious, both academic and artistic in concern. Advising correct pronunciation in his paratexts to page 1, for instance, Sewall parses the sound of *"Sad"*—that is, Arabic letter "ص"—as possessing "the power of ʃ as in pleasure, measure, &c.," a pairing of aesthetics and accuracy that seems to embody Sewall's own approach to Arabic overall.[33]

The meticulous "measure," as well as "pleasure," offered in Sewall's Arabic pamphlet matched precisely Stiles' own motives and methods. Slow to receive Sewall's letter and enclosed pamphlet, not opening them until well into October, Stiles quickly responds to Sewall's kindness, writing to Cambridge on October 24:

> Three days ago I rec'd your agreeable Letter with the Specimen of an *Arabic Grammar*; for wᶜ please to accept my hearty Thanks. I shall be able by it to make somthing of the *Arabic Quotations* in Books, & particularly in the Writings of the learned *Selden*. I am truly obliged & greatly gratified with the pains you have taken to give me your Idea of the Arabic.[34]

Acknowledging his gratitude, while confessing his "gratification," Sewall's personal *"Arabic Grammar"* aptly inspires Stiles' own "hearty" sentiments, his first reply forecasting the intimate friendship that develops between the two men, grounded in their shared "Idea of the Arabic." Building from these "explicit" beginnings, Stiles informs his new teacher of his next project, promising to pivot from Sewall's "Specimen of an *Arabic Grammar*" toward "the *Arabic Quotations* in Books," specifying in particular "the Writing of the learned *Selden*"—a promise Stiles fulfills in the following six weeks, writing Sewall again on December 9, 1768, reporting that "Upon receiving your Letter in October last, I set myself to look into the Arabic," and boasting that

> [I] have read most of the Arabic interspersed thro the third volume of the learned Seldens Works: particularly Eutychius Origines of the Chh of Alexandria, & Seldens Notes thereon. I am famished for want of the oriental Authors.[35]

Justifying his friend's faith in him, Stiles becomes a precocious Arabic student, imbibing Sewall's own passion to "propagate" Eastern "knowledge." Unsatiated by his new Arabic "read[ing]," Stiles' hearty "gratification" has turned to insistent hunger, declaring himself to be "famished for want of the oriental Authors." Expressing visceral desire, Stiles offers details too of his Arabic investments, reporting not only his wide reading in "Seldens Works," but also his "particular" attraction to the writings of "Eutychius" (i.e., Saʿīd ibn Baṭrīq, mediaeval North African patriarch [ca. 877–940]), whose Arabic chronicle on the "origins" of "the Ch[urch] of Alexandria" is offered to Stiles, with ample annotations, in the "third volume" of Selden's *Opera*.[36]

Reporting from Newport his interest in ancient "Eutychius," it is in Newport that material traces survive of Stiles' reading of Eutychius, secluded in the original holdings of his beloved Redwood Athenaeum. Preserving the very copy of Selden's *Opera* used by Stiles, the "third volume" of this edition evidences Stiles' Arabic appetite, featuring marks of his repeated reading of Eutychius in particular. Although predating Stiles' celebrated daily *Diary*, which only begins in January 1769, Stiles' reported encounter with "Eutychius Origines" in 1768 may be dated precisely due to his own timekeeping, with Stiles' copy of Selden's *Opera* indexing his Arabic studies. Only a week after initially responding to Sewall's letter and acknowledging receipt of his "Specimen of an *Arabic Grammar*," Stiles records his reading of Eutychius' "Origines" in the margins of the Redwood's edition of Selden, penciling "Oct 31. 1768" to the left of Eutychius' initial Arabic lines.[37] And reflecting his keen hunger, such quick progress with Eutychius will also lead to Stiles' sustained investment, reviewing this same Arabic history repeatedly through the following year.[38] Indeed, by the summer of 1769, Stiles is no longer content to read merely, but instead renders and reproduces Eutychius' Arabic *Origines*, as recorded in consecutive *Diary* entries from the end of August:

> August 28. This day I translated into English *Eutichii Origines Ecclesiæ Alexandrinæ* from the original Arabic.
> August 29. Copied the Arabic of Eutychius.[39]

Two August days, dedicated solely to two Arabic acts, Stiles first translates then transcribes Eutychius' *Origines*, speaking and scripting his ancient source anew. "Exercising" his "own invention" with Eutychius, Stiles' creative engagements with Arabic in 1769 will be precious enough to preserve, his own "copies" surviving among papers at Yale's Beinecke Library. Reproduced as Figure 1.4 is the first page of Stiles' "The Antiquities of the Church of Alexandria"—his six-page rendition from Eutychius, plainly dated "Aug.28.1769," and proudly subtitled "Translated from the Original Arabic 1769 By Ezra Stiles."[40]

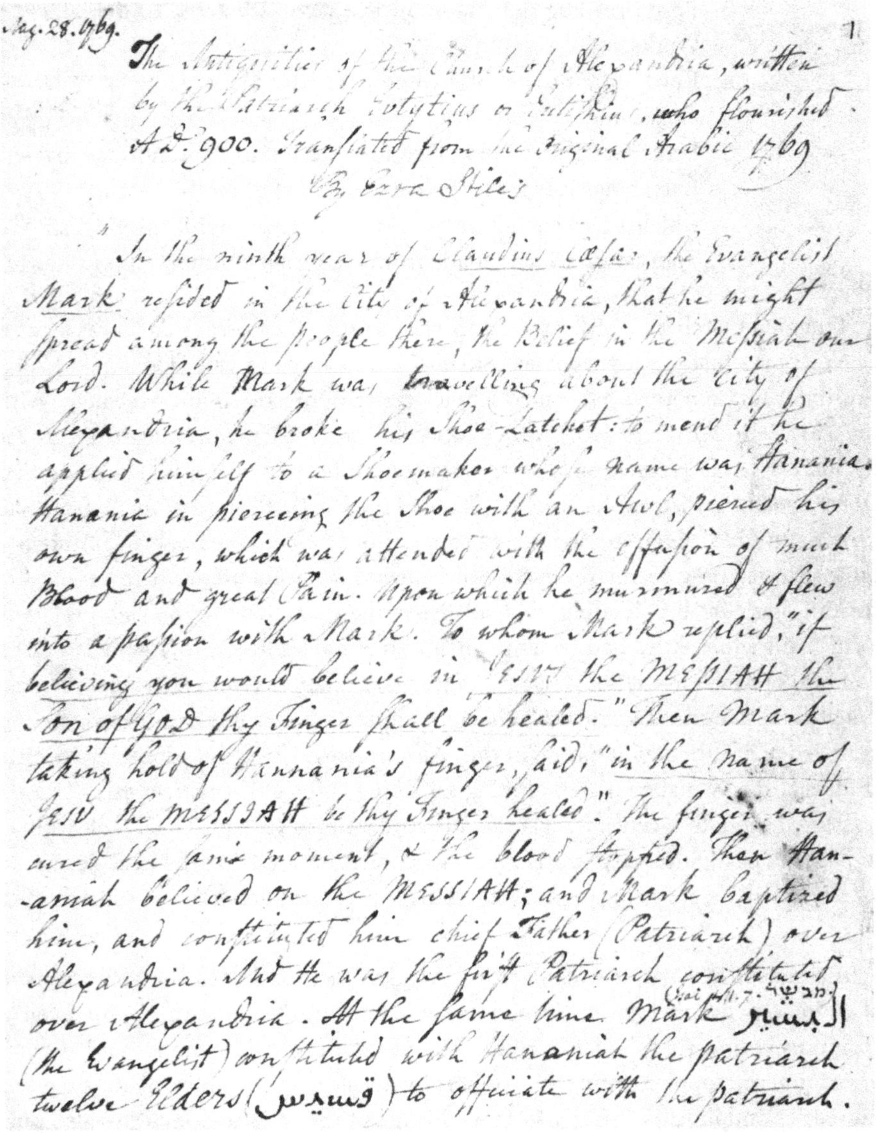

Aug. 28. 1769. 1

The Antiquities of the Church of Alexandria, written by the Patriarch Eutychius or Eutichius, who flourished A.D. 900. Translated from the Original Arabic 1769 By Ezra Stiles

In the ninth year of Claudius Cæsar, the Evangelist Mark resided in the City of Alexandria, that he might spread among the people there, the Belief in the Messiah our Lord. While Mark was travelling about the City of Alexandria, he broke his Shoe-Latchet: to mend it he applied himself to a Shoemaker whose name was Hanania. Hanania in piercing the Shoe with an Awl, pierced his own finger, which was attended with the effusion of much Blood and great Pain. Upon which he murmured & flew into a passion with Mark. To whom Mark replied, "if believing you would believe in JESU the MESSIAH the Son of GOD thy Finger shall be healed." Then Mark taking hold of Hannania's finger, said, "in the Name of JESU the MESSIAH be thy Finger healed". The finger was cured the same moment, & the blood stopped. Then Hanamiah believed on the MESSIAH; and Mark baptized him, and constituted him chief Father (Patriarch) over Alexandria. And He was the first Patriarch constituted over Alexandria. At the same time Mark מבשר الـبشير (the Evangelist) constituted with Hananiah the patriarch twelve Elders (قسيس) to officiate with the Patriarch.

*Figure 1.4* Ezra Stiles, "The Antiquities of the Church of Alexandria" (1769), page 1. Image courtesy of Beinecke Rare Book and Manuscript Library, Yale University. Note Stiles' transcript of original Arabic terms near page bottom (e.g., "البشير" [*al-bashīr*, "the Evangelist"]).

Privately penned in August 1769, Stiles' rendition and reproduction of Eutychius' Arabic history would reach an intimate audience by October, becoming a performance piece for select spectators. At the opening of the month, Stiles' *Diary* reports circulating his Arabic exercises among fellow American enthusiasts:

October 2.  New Year's day at the Synagogue.
> 3.  Began reading the Arabic in the second Volume of Selden's Works, folio.
> 4.  Revd. Mr. Brown of Killingly & Mr. Tutor How of Yale Coll. came.
> 5.  Lent Mr. Tutor How, Origines Ecclesiae Alexandrinae by Eutychius, Patriarch of that Chh. in the Tenth Century;— which I had copied in the Arabic Letter;—with the English Translation which I made from the Original Arabic.[41]

Opening October by observing Rosh Hashanah—"New Year's day"—as a guest at Newport's historic "Synagogue," Stiles also welcomes guests from "Yale Coll.," shifting from hometown Hebraic celebration to a domestic Arabic exchange. With the arrival of "Mr. Tutor How" on October 4, Stiles finds a communal context for his interests in Eutychius, but also an occasion for his personal pride, insisting that "the English translation" he lends to "Tutor How" is that "which *I* made from the Original Arabic." Again posing sacred tongues in tandem—Hebrew and Arabic— their priority now seems reversed, Stiles devoting more attention to his Arabic "reading" and Arabic "lending" than all else in these first days of the Hebrew "New Year." And while Stiles had benefited from an Arabic gift in 1768 from Sewall— Harvard's professor—it is now a Yale "Tutor" who benefits from Stiles' own Arabic donation. Domesticating Sewall's collegial imperative—striving to "propagate the knowledge of Oriental literature in this Western world"—Stiles promotes Semitic studies at his own alma mater, offering his home college that which Stiles himself neglected there to receive. Redeeming his student disregard of "Oriental learning" in decades past, Stiles also subtly reaches forward, anticipating the next decade in which he will indeed bring precisely this language "learning" to Yale's presidency. ✿

Witnessed in his marginal dating and detailed memoirs is Stiles' characteristic passion for chronicling. Renowned as an "indefatigable measurer"—or even a "compulsive measurer"—Stiles avidly charts his personal economy and natural environment, supplementing his voluminous *Diary* with a miscellany of other itineraries and indexes.[42] Eager to gauge his life's times and season, Stiles also purchases and preserves yearly almanacs, many of which survive in his collected papers. Synthesizing his diverse interests—from meteorology to astronomy, from cosmic cycle to societal calendar—Stiles' pocket almanacs track the annual progress, while also serving as domestic companions in his daily affairs. Localized and regional,

Stiles' almanacs also suggest, however, his more foreign interests, with the very etymology of "Almanac" evoking "Eastern" atmospheres. Scribbling on the first page of his *New York Pocket-Almanack* in 1759, for instance, Stiles himself observes these verbal associations, asserting simply that

> *Almanack* is a word brot into Europe by the Arabians.
> *Zenith, Nadir, Azimuth, Al de baran*[43]

Inscribing the linguistic origins of "Almanack" into the opening pages of his own almanac, Stiles uncovers an old "Arabian" source for his *New York* pocketbook, finding this familiar "word" in "Europe[an]" tongues to be Arabic in origin.[44] Befitting its service as an astronomic guide, Stiles also adds a host of other Arabic etymologies; not only is "*Almanack*" offered to the West by "the Arabians," but also "*Zenith, Nadir, Azimuth, Al de baran*"—stellar terms dear to Stiles, the amateur astronomer. Imported from far geographic distance, Stiles' "Arabian" vocabulary also reaches cosmic heights, with "Oriental" vocabulary "brot" westward also helping to orient his gaze upward to the stars.

Considering Stiles' lexical link between "Almanack" and the "Arabians" in 1759, it is perhaps fitting that Stiles' own almanacs witness his initial steps toward Arabic literacy a decade later. First scribbling in Selden's scholarly margins, Stiles will also inscribe Selden's scholarship into the margins of his own almanacs during 1768 and 1769, reciprocally charting his Arabic reading in pocketbook pages. For example, adjacent to November 9 in his 1768 copy of *Mein and Fleeming's Register for New-England and Nova Scotia*, Stiles scrawls, "I finished reading the Origines Eccl. Alex. by Eutychius Patriarch written in Arabic"—an entry followed a few pages later with these scribbled sentences:

> Arabic Name for Patriarch البطريرك the first Father
> *al* is a praefix or particle like *ille*—*Biter* or *Bater* is πατερ—
> *Irk* or *jrch* may be αεχοσ
> In Arabic بَ or B is for P or π thus بطرس Petrus; بولس Paulus[45]

A scattered primer of "particles" and "praefixes," Stiles parses the "Arabic Name for Patriarch" as well as the Arabic "P," finding familiar analogies in Latin and Greek for these more foreign elements. Noting the "Arabian" etymology of "Almanack" itself in 1759, Stiles recruits his almanac a decade later in 1769 for the study of Arabic etymologies, seeking to scaffold Eastern script and sounds onto Western equivalents, aligning the "Arabic بَ or B" with "P or π," as well as Arabic's definite article "*al*" with the Latin "praefix" "*ille*."

Covertly scribbled inside his almanacs, Stiles' Arabic jottings eventually emigrate outside as well, erupting on the front cover of his daily calendars. Figure 1.5 reproduces the facade of Stiles' 1770 copy of *The New-England Almanack or the*

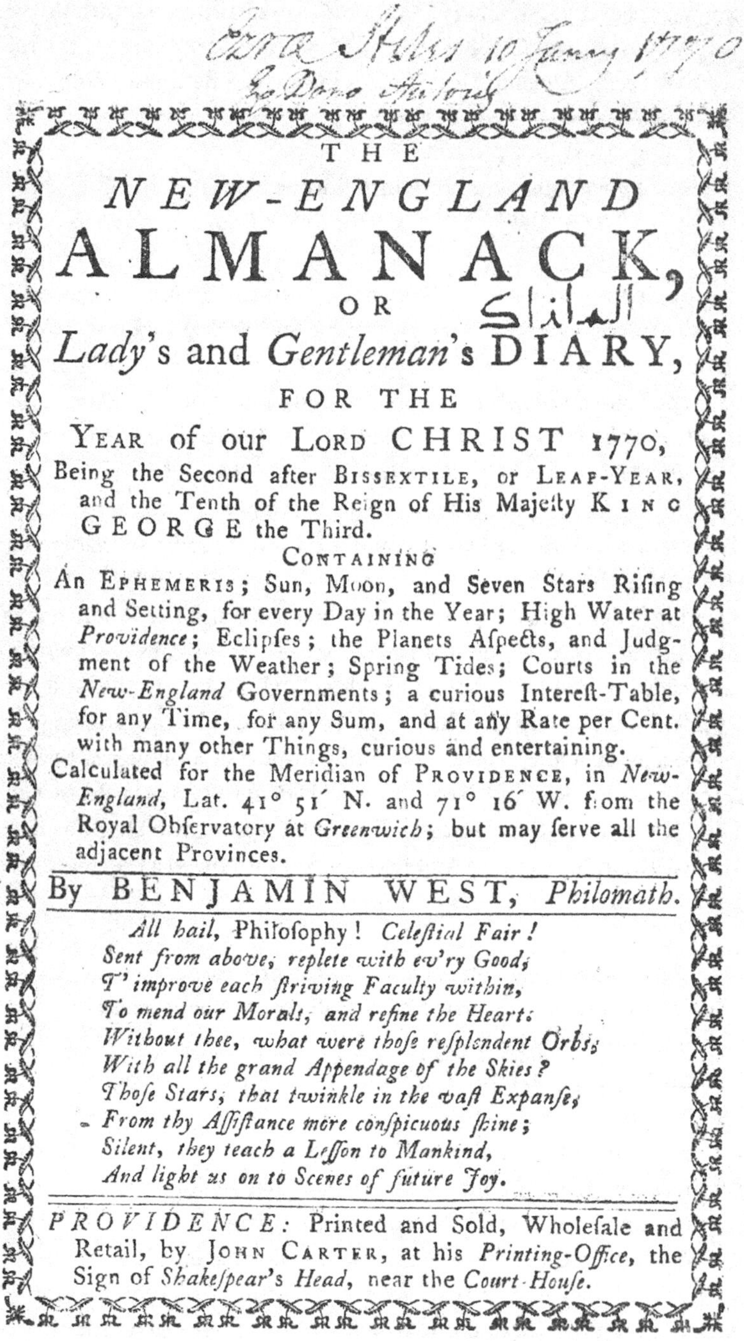

*Ezra Stiles 10 Jany 1770.*
*Ex Dono Autoris*

THE

## NEW-ENGLAND

# ALMANACK,

OR الالمناك

*Lady's* and *Gentleman's* DIARY,

FOR THE

YEAR of our LORD CHRIST 1770,

Being the Second after BISSEXTILE, or LEAF-YEAR,
and the Tenth of the Reign of His Majesty K I N G
GEORGE the Third.

CONTAINING

An EPHEMERIS; Sun, Moon, and Seven Stars Rising
and Setting, for every Day in the Year; High Water at
*Providence*; Eclipses; the Planets Aspects, and Judgment of the Weather; Spring Tides; Courts in the
*New-England* Governments; a curious Interest-Table,
for any Time, for any Sum, and at any Rate per Cent.
with many other Things, curious and entertaining.
Calculated for the Meridian of PROVIDENCE, in *New-
England*, Lat. 41° 51′ N. and 71° 16′ W. from the
Royal Observatory at *Greenwich*; but may serve all the
adjacent Provinces.

By BENJAMIN WEST, *Philomath.*

*All hail*, Philosophy! *Celestial Fair!*
*Sent from above, replete with ev'ry Good;*
*T' improve each striving Faculty within,*
*To mend our Morals, and refine the Heart:*
*Without thee, what were those resplendent Orbs,*
*With all the grand Appendage of the Skies?*
*Those Stars, that twinkle in the vast Expanse,*
*From thy Assistance more conspicuous shine;*
*Silent, they teach a Lesson to Mankind,*
*And light us on to Scenes of future Joy.*

PROVIDENCE: Printed and Sold, Wholesale and
Retail, by JOHN CARTER, at his *Printing-Office*, the
Sign of *Shakespear's* Head, near the *Court-House.*

*Figure 1.5* Cover of *The New-England Almanack* (1770), with Stiles' signature and Arabic inscription of "الالمناك" (*almānāk*). Image courtesy of the Beinecke Rare Book and Manuscript Library, Yale University.

*Lady's and Gentlemen's Diary*—an almanac produced by Stiles' own friend, Benjamin West, a bookseller and publisher based in Providence, Rhode Island.[46] As with his previous almanacs, Stiles autographs the cover of this 1770 daybook, while noting too the details of its acquisition, recording the date—"10 Janry 1770"—and identifying this copy to be a gift from West himself, labeling it to be "*Ex Dono Auctoris*" ("from the author's gift"). It is not these mundane details, but a single word inscribed on its facade, that sets this almanac apart. Nestled aptly under the word "*Almanack*" and above "*Diary*" in West's wordy title is Stiles' inscription of a single Arabic term: "الماناک," i.e., "*almānāk*".

Reaching back a decade to the same Arabic etymology noted first in his 1759 *Almanack*, Stiles by 1770 elects to retitle his own *Almanack* in Arabic, labeling this familiar work through lines of foreign script. Reversing the direction of linguistic migration, Stiles no longer notes Eastern backgrounds for a Western word, but returns this Western word eastward, orienting his own American *Almanack* by (re) covering it as an Arabian "*almānāk*". Interrupting English type with Oriental handwriting, Stiles rebrands this printed gift from his Providence friend, marking it as unmistakably his own. Autographed as property of "Ezra Stiles," this almanac's acquired idioms from the East equally serve as a unique signature for Stiles, indexing his own evolving "Arabian" identity.[47]

Received in January 1770, Stiles' *New-England Almanack* elevates Arabic to the cover of his daily calendar, initiating a new year by suggesting the advances in Arabic made by Stiles throughout 1769—a year that had itself begun with an act of Arabic timekeeping. Opening 1770 with his almanac's Arabic façade, it is the previous New Year that saw the opening of Stiles' *Diary* on January 1, 1769, with his first mention of Arabic on the very next day, his January 2 entry recording that he "Read a chapter in Hebrew, & some Arabic," as noted above. However, "January 2 1769" is a date found not only at the beginning of Stiles' *Diary*, but in the side margins of his edition of Selden, with the first pages of the *Opera*'s third volume featuring precisely this date, inscribed alongside a pivotal passage (Fig. 1.6).[48]

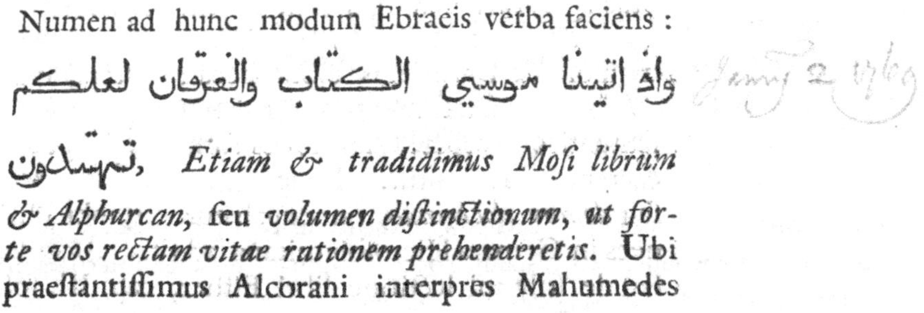

Numen ad hunc modum Ebraeis verba faciens :

واذ اتينا موسي الكتاب والفرقان لعلكم

تمسكون, *Etiam & tradidimus Mosi librum & Alphurcan, seu volumen distinctionum, ut forte vos rectam vitae rationem prehenderetis.* Ubi praestantissimus Alcorani interpres Mahumedes

*Figure 1.6* Stiles' marginalia in the Redwood Library's copy of Selden's *Opera*, Volume 3, recording "January 2 1769" beside the Arabic of the Qur'ān 2:53. Image courtesy of the Redwood Library and Athenaeum.

Coinciding with the beginnings of a new year, Stiles' peripheral date confirms his *Diary*'s first mention of Arabic on January 2, 1769. However, rather than the imprecision of his personal memoirs—which mentions merely "some Arabic"—Stiles' marginalia specifies the exact Arabic that he reviews at the opening to 1769, showing Islam's sacred source to be the subject of Stiles' New Year's studies. Writing in stylized English cursive beside supple Arabic characters, Stiles marks the second day of 1769 immediately adjacent to a line from the second chapter of the Qur'ān:

واذ اتينا موسى الكتاب والفرقان لعلكم تهتدون
[And when We (God) gave Moses the Book,
and the means to distinguish, so that you might be guided][49]

A brief selection with broad significance, Stiles highlights foreign scripture that nevertheless reflects ideas and interests that are most familiar to him. Invoking a biblical precedent—"Moses"—this Qur'ānic quote also emphasizes bibliographic precedence, celebrating "the Book" as a divine endowment, God's "gift" for human "guidance." Reading this sacred verse in the first days of 1769, Stiles discovers a verse about sacred reading, extolling a literary "means to distinguish," even as Stiles distinguishes his own literacy through recording its precise date on "January 2." Finding the Qur'ān in original Arabic, as well as Selden's Latin translation, Stiles also finds the Qur'ān itself gesturing to a cosmic moment of "*translatio*" ("crossing over"), with the "Book" bestowed across elemental barriers, a text transmitted from God to man, from transcendent to immanent.[50] A decade earlier, at the opening to his 1759 almanac, Stiles had marveled at "the Arabians" who carried "words" to the West; at the opening of 1769, Stiles marks actual Arabic words describing scripture carried from heaven to earth, crossing the line that divides here from hereafter. Rather than transcribe Muslim textuality into his pocket calendar, Stiles here grafts his own calendar onto the Muslim text, this Qur'ānic quotation aligned with a pivotal date and year from Stiles' life, coinciding with the very opening of his own personal "Book" of "guidance": his *Diary*. Although a text conceived to be timeless, the Islamic scripture is newly calibrated within Stiles' ordinary routine, his daily reading now anchored in this extraordinary source. Traditionally conceived as beyond the confines of human history, the Qur'ān is yet concretely situated in an American's own chronology, accruing biographical time and place, this holy text serving as a surprising "means to distinguish" the private phases of Stiles' unfolding Islamic literacy. ✵

Merely reading Stiles' scribbles in narrow scholarly margins, it is easy to forget that his personal encounter with Islamic sources will have broader, interpersonal dimensions as well. As first suggested by his loan of Eutychius to "Tutor How" in 1769, Stiles' private progress with Arabic in the 1770s increasingly forms the center of public exchanges, shifting from individual study to social circulations. A year after his visit from Yale's "Tutor," Stiles entertains his professor friend from

Harvard, welcoming Stephen Sewall to Newport near the end of October, as noted in his *Diary*:

> October 23.   Yesterday came here Mr. Stephen Sewall Professor of Hebrew & the other Oriental Languages at Harvard College, Cambridge, & Mr. Andrew Eliot Jun. one of the Tutors.
>
> October 24.   Went to Synagogue &c. Mr. Sewall is well acquainted with Hebrew & its Dialects as Samaritan, Ethiopic, Syriac, Arabic, Chaldee—but not with the Armenian, Persic, & Coptic. We examined the Inscriptions on the Mountains at Mt. Sinai as given Bp. Pococke. And we could find some hebrew & Arabic. I think they were antient Arabic.[51]

Exactly two years after responding gratefully to Sewall's Arabic pamphlet—on October 24, 1768—Stiles here responds personally to this same "Professor of Hebrew & the other Oriental Languages." Now more peer than pedagogue, Sewall's 1770 stay in Newport provides Stiles a sympathetic partner in his Semitic studies, visiting together the local Jewish congregation, as well as deciphering overseas "Inscriptions." Traversing sacred spaces in tandem—first at Newport's physical "Synagogue," and then Palestine's "Mt. Sinai" texts—Stiles is careful to map his own friend's sacred philology, lauding Sewall's possession of "Hebrew & its Dialects"—including "Arabic"—but noting too the Professor's boundaries, his lack of "Armenian, Persic, & Coptic." And while Sewall and Stiles collaborate to decipher Bishop Pococke's "Inscriptions" from Sinai, this alliance also makes room for Stiles' increasing independence. Although he begins by recalling that "*we* could find some hebrew & Arabic" in the inscriptions, Stiles quickly shifts to his own first-person singular: "*I* think they were antient Arabic," he concludes.[52]

Pairing together "hebrew & Arabic" in his hospitality, visiting a modern Jewish congregation while scrutinizing "antient Arabic," Stiles recalls the initial gift he received from Sewall, parsing Arabic through Hebrew parallels. And, fittingly, it will be Stiles' own social visits to the Newport synagogue that will soon offer him living contact with the Arabic language and Arab lands. As early as 1768, Stiles befriended Isaac Touro—Newport's resident *ḥazzan*, and leader of the Jewish community— who supplied pivotal aid to Stiles in his preliminary Hebrew studies.[53] It would be the 1773 arrival of Rabbi Haim Isaac Carigal, however, that initiates Stiles' most meaningful relationship with the local synagogue. The "first rabbi to visit the Colonies," Carigal would bring traditional Jewish learning to America in 1773. Carigal would also bring, however, his personal experiences with Islam, being a native of Palestine and veteran traveler of Ottoman territories.[54] First encountering Carigal at Purim services on March 8, 1773, Stiles begins to foster a private friendship with the rabbi by the end of the month, inviting him to his home on March 30. Launching an iconic episode in early American ecumenism, Stiles' account of his

initial interview with Carigal quoted below not only implies Jewish–Christian relations, however, but also involves essential Islamic elements:

> This Afternoon the Rabbi came to visit me in Company with Mr. Lopez.
> The Rabbi is æt. 39, a large Man, neat and well dressed in the Turkish Habit.
> We conversed largely on the Gemara, the 2 Talmuds (of which he pre-
> ferred the Babylonish) the Changes of the Hebrew Language in different
> Ages &c. &c. He was born in Hebron, where he says are only 107 Families
> of Jews. From æt. 7, has followed his Studies. He says, one may breakfast
> at Hebron and dine at Jerusalem, which are but six hours apart. He has
> been at Samaria, Tiberias, and thro' the Holy Land, at Constantinople &c.
> &c. He spake of Aly Bey, and shewed me a passage in the *Zohar* which he
> said predicted that the *Russians should conquer the Turks.* I observed that in
> the Original it was that *Edom* should conquer the *Ismaelites*—he replied
> that Edom there denoted a Northern Power, and the Ismaelites those of
> their Religion. He said he did not understand *Arabic* to read it, upon my
> showing an Arabic Extract from Eutychius. Yet he said it was the common
> Tongue now in the Holy Land, only the Jews were not allowed to learn the
> Writings. I shewed him the first Psalm in Arabic but in Hebrew Letters—
> he read it off freely—and I suppose I then for the first Time heard the true
> pronunciation of Arabic. He did not perfectly understand it. He said the
> vernacular Arabic now was different from the antient. We talked upon the
> difference of the Dialects of the Chaldee, Syriac, and rabbinical Hebrew, on
> the Targums &c. Evening coming on he took Leave in a polite & friendly
> manner.[55]

Initially "conversing largely" on ancient Judaica—an expected topic of shared
interest for both rabbi and minister—Stiles quickly passes over rich subjects such
as the "Gemara," "the 2 Talmuds," "the Changes of the Hebrew Language," abbreviating these interests with an elliptical "&c. &c." The core of Stiles' report is
devoted not to Hebrew, but instead to Arabic, exploring this sibling Semitic language and its Muslim milieus—a substitution that seems to arise from Stiles' own
suggestion. Of the three actions that Stiles attributes to himself in his account, two
involve his "showing" Arabic—"showing" both "Eutychius" and "the first Psalm
in Arabic"—while his first act is to voice an "observation" regarding "Ismaelites,"
a group interpreted by Carigal as Muslims ("those of their Religion"). Outlining
Carigal's character and conversation, Stiles also remarks especially on his "Turkish
habit" and his Middle Eastern travels, not only his sojourns from the "Holy Land"
to "Constantinople," but also his mention of "Aly Bey"—Egypt's famed Mamluk
leader, and Muslim rebel against Ottoman rule.[56] Intersecting these interreligious
engagements is "Eutychius" once again, with Stiles' own "Extract" allowing him to
test Carigal's varying levels of Arabic literacy. And while he "did not understand

Arabic to read it," Carigal does nevertheless recite "the first Psalm in Arabic but in Hebrew Letters"—an oral performance that occasions a unique rupture in Stiles' private writing. Shifting from narrated memory to personal epiphany in the present, Stiles spontaneously reflects in his *Diary* that "I suppose I then for the first Time heard the true pronunciation of Arabic." An original and interior experience, this striking sound of "Arabic" is amplified by its precedence and its authenticity, Stiles' "first Time" hearing "true pronunciation" distinguished from the rest of his remembered account, surfacing as a sudden "supposing" in the first person, and in the present tense.

While a spontaneous experience and an unexpected discovery, this poignant moment of Arabic performance in 1773 has a long foreground, catalyzed by Sewall himself, whose 1768 pamphlet provided Stiles with this "first Psalm in Arabic but in Hebrew Letters," which is now "shown" to Carigal five years later. And again recalling Sewall, Stiles will enjoy a rich correspondence with Carigal, which equally features Arabic intersections. Concluding this intimate episode in March 1773 with his guest's "friendly manner," Stiles will indeed spend the following months in friendship with Carigal, forming a fast bond with the rabbi before he departs for South America in July 1773. Moreover, consistent with Arabic's pronunciation at their initial interview, Arabic also echoes to the very end of Carigal's time with Stiles. Diary entries penned by Stiles in the days before the rabbi's departure suggest a dense interplay between individual study and personal interactions, with sporadic activities such as the following, recorded over an eight-day span in June 1773:

> June 12. Reading Selden's Opera. Finished the travels of Chevalier D'Arvieux into Arabia.
> June 14. [ . . . ] In the Forenoon I went to visit the Rabbi—discoursed on Ventriloquism & the Witch of Endor & the Reality of bringing up Samuel. He had not heard of Ventriloquism before & still doubted it. He shewed me a Hebrew Letter from Isaac Pinto a Jew in N. York, in which Mr. Pinto who is now reading Aben Ezra desires R. Carigals Tho'ts. upon some Arabic in Aben Ezra. But the Rabbi says he supposes Aben Ezra wrote in the Coran Arabic which he doth not understand. [ . . . ]
> June 19. Hot day, Thermo 88 at XI A.M. Finished reading the Description of Arabia by *Sultan Ismael Abulfeda*.[57]

Various elements in these entries now seem familiar, with Stiles again reading "Selden's Opera," as well as "discoursing" on an eclectic range of biblical *esoterica*, including "Ventriloquism & the Witch of Endor & the Reality of bringing up Samuel." Amid this miscellany, however, a consistency emerges in the "Arabian" atmosphere that envelops Stiles' conversations with Carigal. Surrounding their "Forenoon" discussion on June 14 is Stiles' own reading of "travels [. . .] into Arabia" (on the 12th), and a "Description of Arabia" (on the 19th), even while Stiles himself marvels at the heat of the Newport summer, its "Hot" weather serving to complement the arid climates of his Eastern studies. Intersecting Stiles' Arabian "readings" is his own "visit" with the Palestinian rabbi, a visit that itself is interrupted by Arabian interests. Emerging at the center of their conversation in Newport is a piece of correspondence from New York, a friendly petition from "Mr. Pinto" for "Carigals Tho'ts. upon some Arabic in Aben Ezra"—a petition that Ezra Stiles quickly notes is complicated by the kind of Arabic implied: the language of "the Coran." Surfacing in an overheard exchange between two Jewish scholars, Muslim idioms ironically impact compre-hension of the Judaic past, even while Stiles pushes forward with "finish[ing]" his review of the "Description of Arabia by *Sultan Ismael Abulfeda*"—a "Description" itself "wrote in the Coran Arabic," featuring Qur'ānic idioms and allusions.[58]

Only one month after recording these intertextual entries, Stiles' friend will embark again on his own international travels. On July 18, Stiles notes in his *Diary* that "In the Evening Rabbi H. I. Karigal came to take his Leave of me and my Family, which he did very affectionately"—a record that suggests the growing intimacy be-tween the men, their farewell now qualifying as a familial concern, no longer merely "polite" as in March, but fully "affectionate." Moreover, Stiles' ecumenical exchanges with Carigal will not be suspended, but strengthened, with the latter's departure, their relationship sustained through a unique series of letters in Hebrew and English, a correspondence carried on until Carigal's 1777 death. The very day after "Karigal" took "his Leave" of the Stiles family, Ezra Stiles finished his first Hebrew letter to the rabbi; dated "July 19th 1773," this Hebrew letter's conclusion is reproduced as Figure 1.7—a conclusion which Stiles himself renders into English as follows:

> May God bless thy seed, that there may always be a light unto thee in Israel. And when thou send a letter to thy wife at Hebron, salute her and thy house in my name, for I love all thy friends for thy sake. And may thy father and thy mother rejoice, when thou shalt be exalted and shine among the Chosen ones of Righteousness & among the Seraphim: *then may thy Light break forth as the morning; and thine Health spring forth speedily, and thy righteousness go before thee, the Glory of the Lord be thy reward [Isai LVIII.8].* These are my words, written at Newport, Rhode Island in America, the 28th day of the month Tammuz, in the 5533 year of the Creation. I am the least of the Disciples of JESUS of Nazareth.[59]

Fusing personal intimacy and celestial prophecy, Stiles concludes his Hebrew letter with a stunning rhetorical flourish. Equally affectionate and apocalyptic, Stiles' finale offers familial love to the "house" of Carigal and his "wife," while envi-sioning the future joy of Carigal's "father and mother" as they witness him enter the eternal abode "among the Seraphim." In a dizzying traversal of space and time,

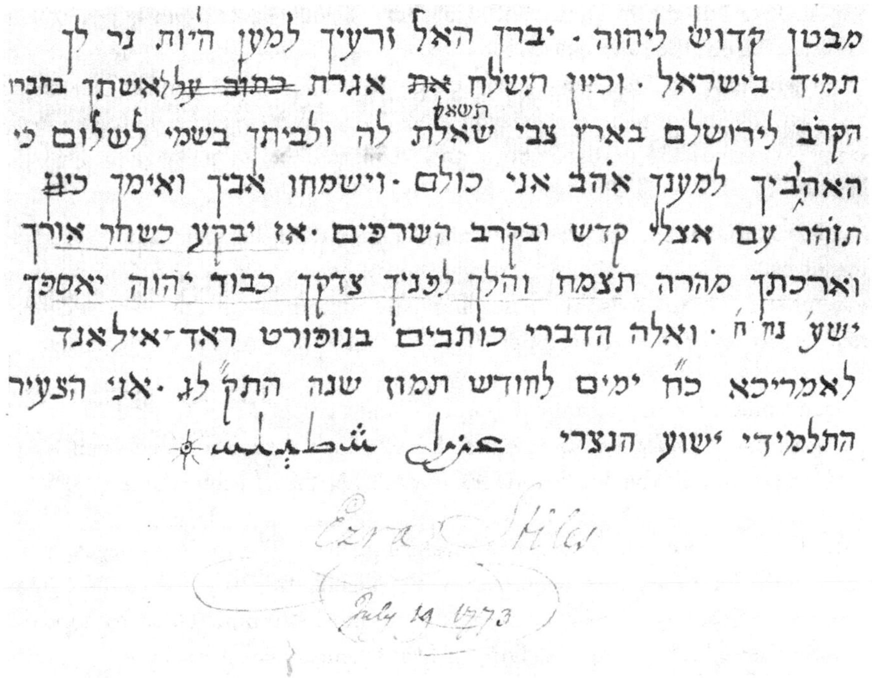

מבטן קדוש ליהוה · יברך האל ורעיך למען היות נר לך
תמיך בישראל · וכיון תשלח את אגרת כתוב על־לאשתך בחנו
הקרב לירושלם בארץ צבי שאלת לה ולביתך בשמי לשלום כי
האהביך למענך אהב אני כולם ·וישמחו אביך ואימך כעץ
תזהר עם אצל קדש ובקרב השרפים ·אז יבקע כישחר אורך
וארכתך מהרה תצמח והלך לפניך צדקך כבוד יהוה יאספך
ישע נ"ח · ואלה הדברי כותבים בנופורט ראד־אילאנד
לאמריכא כ"ח ימים לחודש תמוז שנה התק לג ·אני הצעיר
התלמידי ישוע הנצרי    عزرا شطيلس

*Ezra Stiles*

*July 19 1773*

*Figure 1.7* Hebrew letter from Ezra Stiles to Isaac Carigal, dated July 19, 1773, concluding with Stiles' Arabic signature: "عزرا شطيلس". Image courtesy of the Beinecke Rare Book and Manuscript Library, Yale University.

these dramatic lines stretch from Newport to Hebron, from the Creation to the Resurrection, while also spanning spiritual traditions, exalting the Jewish rabbi as a "Chosen one of Righteousness," while humbly characterizing Stiles himself as "the least of the Disciples of Jesus of Nazareth" ("הצעיר התלמידי ישוע הנצרי"). Among all these startling shifts in identity and idiom, however, it is the final shift performed by Stiles that is most climactic and conspicuous. Immediately after confessing his Christian discipleship, Stiles offers his farewell signature, inscribing his own autograph not merely in English or Hebrew, but rather in Arabic, naming himself as "عزرا شطيلس"—that is, *'Izrā Shṭīls* ("Ezra Stiles").[60]

Breaking from the style and sounds of his foregoing letter, Stiles' most intimate and essential marker of identity is offered in Arabic, his name traced not in angular Hebrew script, but in the fluid lines of its Semitic sister language. While his adopted hometown ("Newport") and his emergent nation ("America") are both inscribed in Hebrew, "Ezra Stiles" is uniquely set apart, this biblical and British name emerging as a linguistic stranger, an Arabic exile isolated at the end of this letter to an itinerant rabbi from Palestine. Completing a process of familiarizing himself with this foreign language initiated five years earlier, Stiles no longer secludes Arabic beneath the covers of his memoirs, or behind the painted profile of his portrait; rather, Arabic now emerges as the American's own façade, this language invoked to spell "Ezra Stiles" himself. Instead of authoring documents subtitled proudly as "Translated from the Original Arabic [. . .] By Ezra Stiles," this 1773 letter terminates by translating "Ezra Stiles" into "Original Arabic," the American "exercising [his] own invention" to advance beyond the "Western World," rendering an iteration of his native identity that is thoroughly "Oriental." ☼

It will be at the end of the year following Carigal's 1773 departure that Stiles sees himself truly at home in Arabic. Tracing the outlines of his "ARABICA" circle in September 1774, Stiles also traces his linguistic attainments as the year concludes, recording in his *Diary* on December 10, 1774, that he has successfully fostered

> acquaintance with the antient learned Languages of *Latin Greek Hebrew Samaritan Chaldee Syriac & Arabic* in all which I have attained such a Competency as to be able to read & examine any Authors freely in them [. . .][61]

Bold in its scope, Stiles' boast of mastering these "learned Languages" aptly begins with "Latin," but also culminates with "Arabic," this language of the Qur'ān positioned at the very climax of Stiles' proud and hyperbolic claim to universal "Competency." Perhaps most striking is Stiles' emphasis on his *easy* familiarity, professing a relaxed "acquaintance" with such languages, now able to "examine any Authors freely in them." Accenting his linguistic liberty in 1774, just months before the first skirmishes in the nation's "cause of LIBERTY," Stiles aptly recalls the revolutionary contexts for his language efforts, pursuing Arabic studies even as America advances toward political fracture. It is, of course, his charting of America's rebellion against British rule for which Stiles is most known, his *Diary* characterized as a unique register of New England patriotism, offering "invaluable accounts of the particulars of (and participants in) the American Revolution."[62] However, even while historians regularly excavate Stiles' detailed *Diary* for their revolutionary research, the concurrence of Stiles' "freely" reading Arabic and his advocacy for American freedoms has been entirely neglected.

This scholarly neglect is due, in part, to specific acts of editorial suppression, with Stiles' later publishers stifling the Eastern atmosphere of his *Diary* during the critical years leading up to the Revolution. For instance, during the very first summer of Stiles' *Diary*, it is clear that "Liberty" was much on his mind; on July 31, 1769, Stiles records the "burn[ing]" in Newport of the "Sloop *Liberty*," the ship owned by John Hancock, whose seizure for customs violations became a cause célèbre for Boston patriots. Two weeks later, Stiles would mark the "Annivers$^{y}$ of Repeal of the *Stamp Act*," noting that "14 Aug$^{t}$." was clandestinely "celebrated at Liberty Tree in Dorchester"—a dinner hosted by the "Sons of Liberty," the society of patriots that included John Adams, Samuel Adams, and Paul Revere.[63] Such pivotal moments of Stiles' political interest are readily evident in the Scribner edition of his *Diary*, first published in 1901, and edited by Franklin Bowditch Dexter. The standard resource for more than a century of Americanist scholarship, the Scribner edition reliably reproduces Stiles' nationalist jottings through this summer of 1769; however, this edition also omits small slices of Stiles' writing, and occasionally entire entries. A week after recording the "Liberty Tree" dinner "in Dorchester," the published version of Stiles' *Diary* features entries for August 21 and August 23, but nothing for August 22, 1769, suggesting perhaps that Stiles skipped this day in his memoirs.[64] When reading Stiles' *Diary* in manuscript, however, it becomes clear that August 22 was a day he considered worth recording—indeed, a day that witnesses perhaps the most striking interreligious intervention in any early American diary. Silently excluded from the Scribner edition, Stiles' unpublished entry for August 22, 1769, in his *Diary* reads in full:

> Heb. Arab. The Alcoran calls Jesus Christ كلمته
> the *word* the *Logos*. Mahomet in a Letter which he
> wrote to the King of Abyssinia (which had been christianized
> about an hundred years before) calls Jesus Christ
> وكلمته　الله　روح　　*Spiritum Dei & Verbum ejus*
> וכלתה　אלה　רוּח　　*Seldini Opera* V3 p. 815[65]

Linguistically complex, Stiles' omitted entry is suffused with Arabic, Hebrew, and Latin, reflecting broadly his philological pursuits in 1769, and specifically his reading of Selden's *Opera Omnia*, which receives explicit reference in this entry's final words. Verbally diverse, this entry's concern is nevertheless verbal unity, centered on "*Verbum*" itself, defining "Christ" as God's "*word*." An expected interest for a Christian minister, it is the Islamic source and speech of Stiles' meditation that seems distinctive, appealing to "the *Logos*" in light of both the Qur'ān and Muḥammad. Citing a single Arabic term from the "Alcoran," Stiles opens by marveling at the definition of "Jesus Christ" as "كلمته"—"His word"—a characterization original to the Qur'ān 4:171. This citation of Muslim prophecy finds support too from the Muslim Prophet, whose own "Letter" to the "King of the Abyssinia" is discovered by Stiles also to define "Jesus" as "روح الله وكلمته"—"the spirit of *Allāh* and His word."[66] A surprising parallel to his own faith, Stiles literally parallels this phrase with dual languages, electing to transcribe this Islamic teaching in triplicate, supplying not only the original Arabic, but also his own Hebrew transliteration, together with Selden's Latin translation ("רוּח אלה וכלתה"/ "*Spiritum Dei & Verbum ejus*").[67] Merging a "Letter" of "Mahomet" with the memorials of Ezra Stiles, this triad of lines caps a meditation on "the *word*" that marries discrete media, human and divine, while also finding a home for Qur'ānic quotation and prophetic correspondence within Stiles' own "invaluable accounts" of revolutionary America. Inscribed during days of increasing New World "Liberty," breaking from monarchal rule and authority, Stiles appeals to a revolutionary "Letter" to an ancient

"King," citing a communication whose "spiritual" diplomacy builds common ground upon the verbal character of "Jesus Christ."

Excised due to its alien scripts and scripture, suppression of such entries in Stiles' *Diary* has helped ensure that his Islamic interests and Arabic inscriptions have not interrupted Western scholars as they scan his pages for domestic American politics. However, the Scribner edition's omissions are not always so dramatic, often suppressing seemingly minor material—material which nevertheless significantly refigures our understanding of Stiles' revolutionary records. Eight months after his quotation of "Mahomet" in August 1769, for example, Stiles excitedly heralds the event now known as the "Boston Massacre."[68] A primary catalyst of the Revolution, news of this British firing on unarmed Americans on March 5, 1770, resounded rapidly throughout New England; reaching Newport on March 9, Stiles relays the incoming "news" of the "Massacre," writing in his *Diary*:

> This day news from Boston, that an Affray had happened there between the Inhabitants & the Army, wherein the Soldiery fired & killed three men & wounded others: upon which the Bells all rang & the Town thrown into most alarm$^g$ confusion.[69]

Contrasting "the Inhabitants & the Army," Stiles forges new language to chart new divisions between "Boston[ians]" and British "Soldiery," seeking to account accurately for this "most alarming confusion" gripping the Colonies, calmly describing the cacophony in "which the Bells all rang." At least, this is how Stiles' entry appears in the Scribner edition. Compared with his *Diary* in manuscript, it becomes clear that this published edition silently suppresses two fragments that stand at the start of Stiles' March 9 account, whose text actually begins:

> Heb. Arab. This day news from Boston, that an Affray had happened there [ . . . ][70]

Before summarizing the incendiary "news from Boston" just arriving "this day," Stiles records his own daily studies, reading not only "Hebrew," but also "Arabic," using the same two contractions that appeared in tandem at the head of Stiles' August 22, 1769, entry, namely "Heb. Arab." There is, of course, no great surprise to find Stiles recording his Semitic studies in the spring of 1770, a full year after initially noting his reading of "Hebrew, & some Arabic" in his 1769 *Diary*. However, in abbreviating entirely Stiles' own abbreviations—excising "Heb. Arab." from entries such as March 9, 1770—the standard edition of Stiles' *Diary* has helped hide the Near Eastern contexts for his experience of New England's "confusion." Returning to the manuscript *Diary*, Stiles' final word before reporting the first "martyrs" of the Revolution is found to be "Arab[ic]," this sacred language of Muslim antiquity previewing a fresh language of secular politics, preceding Stiles' own remarks on the unprecedented "Affray" in America.[71]

Remaining hidden at the Revolution's opening year, Stiles' Arabic interests would, by the Revolution's end, find occasion to be publicized, with Stiles himself confessing openly his allied interests in Arabic reading and American nationhood. Delivered as an "election sermon" to the Connecticut State Assembly in the spring of 1783, "The United States Elevated to Glory and Honor" witnesses Stiles at his most patriotic, championing the Revolution that now nears completion, and the unlimited prospects of the Republic to come. Envisioning New World freedom as foretold in biblical antiquity, Stiles' sermon frames America itself in prophetic terms, predicting a coming era in which

> the *religious* as well as *civil* patriot will shine in the faces of the future *Moses's* and *Joshuas* of this land. So shone it in the first governor WINTHROP, and so shineth it in a WASHINGTON.[72]

Marrying the "religious" and the "civil," Stiles aligns New World leaders with Near Eastern patriarchs, mapping a biblical background for historic governor ("WINTHROP") as well as contemporary general ("WASHINGTON"). Hebraic in its religious tenor, Stiles' nationalist sermon also extends to other Eastern climes; justifying Puritan rejection of Anglican episcopacy, Stiles offers his audience a familiar North African precedent for New England Congregationalism, declaring a little earlier in his sermon that

> The church of alexandria, founded by St. Mark, retained presbyterian ordination, exclusive, for 300 years, as appears from *Eutychius*, the patriarch there in the ninth century, who wrote the originals of that church in *arabic*, from which I have translated the following extract, viz. [ . . . ][73]

Intersecting his sermon's "elevation" of America, Stiles introduces an "extract" of his own "arabic" translation, with "*Eutychius*" recruited to prove that the earliest church "retained presbyterian ordination, exclusive, for 300 years"—an apostolic model for America's own simple ecclesiasticism, free from British bishops and their bureaucracy. Privately fashioned and personally exchanged in 1769, Stiles' rendered Arabic reaches beyond friends and family in 1783, surfacing in a forum more public and more political, enunciated triumphantly and endowed with a surprising currency. Stiles' invocation of Arabic in his revolutionary address reflects not only his longstanding interest in Eutychius, however, but his Islamic interests as well. Viewing American liberty through the lens of the nation's linguistic promise, Stiles asserts even earlier in his "The United States Elevated to Glory and Honor" that

> The rough sonorous diction of the english language may here [in America] take its athenian polish, and receive its attic urbanity; as it will probably become the vernacular tongue of more numerous millions, than ever yet spake one language on earth. It may continue for ages to be the prevailing

and general language of north-america. The intercommunion of the united states with all the world, the *travels, trade,* and *politics,* and the infusion of letters into our infancy, will probably preserve us from the provincial dialects, risen into inexterminable habit before the invention of printing. The greek never became the language of the alexandrine, nor the turkish of the ottoman conquests; nor yet the latin that of the roman empire. The saracenic conquests have already lost the pure and elegant arabic of the *koreish* tribe, or the family of *Ishmael,* in the corrupted dialects of egypt, syria, persia, and indostan. Different from these the english language will grow up, with the present american population, into great purity and elegance, unmutilated by the foreign dialects of foreign conquests.[74]

Opening with classical precedents well known to his Connecticut audience, Stiles asserts the "athenian" and "attic" promise of "the english language"; equally implied, however, is English's unprecedented potential, forecasted for a larger population "than ever yet spake one language on earth." Arguing America's immunity from "provincial dialects," Stiles laments the "corruption" that previously befell "greek," "turkish," "latin," and, finally, "arabic." This last language of Stiles' list is also distinguished by meriting a more extended description, with the "saracenic conquests" blamed for spoiling "the pure and elegant arabic of the *koreish* tribe, or the family of *Ishmael.*" Emphasizing its essential "purity" and its aesthetic "elegance," the "arabic" eulogized by Stiles is both tribal and biblical, descending in a single "family" from "*Ishmael*" to "the *koreish.*" As Stiles in 1783 is also well aware, however, this "arabic" is unmistakably the language of Islamic origins; the Prophet Muḥammad is himself "of the *koreish* tribe," while the Qur'ān is this dialect's most "pure and elegant" exemplar.[75] These covert associations with Islam become more significant as Stiles smoothly shifts from Quraysh Arabic to American "english"—a "language" that he hopes "will grow up, with the present american population, into great purity and elegance." Repeating the exact adjectives for "arabic" in his aspiring nouns for "english," Stiles implicitly links the "pure and elegant" idiom of Islamic pasts with the projected "purity and elegance" of the "present american population"—a telling echo in Stiles' own diction, even as he maps Muslim precedents for his new nation's "prevailing and general language."

If the Revolution provides occasion for Stiles to publicize his efforts in Arabic, these same Arabic efforts would be preempted by the Revolution too. Assuming the presidency of Yale at the war's height in 1778, Stiles authors an address for this year's college commencement, dedicated to his most recent attainments in "Oriental Learning." Yale's public commencement would, however, be a casualty of the war, suspended not only in 1778, but also for the two years following. Even in 1781, Stiles was unsure if ceremonies could proceed; on September 11, he notes in his *Diary* that "The Corporation of Yale College assembling, altho' we greatly fear that Commencement will be interrupted by the Enemy."[76] The next day, however, Stiles notes victoriously: "Public Commencement here. (The first public Commencement in my Presidency.)." This September 12 entry also concludes with Stiles' "account" of Yale's "Commencement," including his own contribution, described as "An Oration upon the Oriental Learning, in *Hebrew, Chaldee* and *Arabic*, by the President."[77] Recommencing his public career at his home college in 1781, Stiles returns to Yale as "President," but also as an "orator" of "Arabic," this "elegant" idiom meriting a place of prominence in his opening address, paired with the other Semitic languages, sacred and scriptural. The third in a holy triad—listed only after "*Hebrew*" and "*Chaldee*"—"*Arabic*" nevertheless occupies the position closest to "the President" himself, Stiles' report of his "Oration" concluding with this "pure" tongue, as well as his college title, closing with the words "*Arabic*, by the President." ✾

Arabic's participation in both college commencement and national Revolution returns us to this chapter's own revolutionary commencement, recalling the September of seven years previous, the month that gave rise to Stiles' 1774 circles (see Fig. 1.1). Tracing the repetitions and returns of Stiles' Islamic studies, it is apt to cycle back to this circular opening, the moment that had opened the Yale career of his adolescent namesake—Ezra, Jr.—as well as America's own embryonic Congress. However, in returning to Stiles' circles after surveying his capacious career, it is fresh and more fulsome meaning that also emerges, his circles seeming more profound and predictive. Spiraling outward in significance, Stiles' intersecting circles appear to chart his own biography, which itself crosses perimeters of language and religion, gesturing back to Stiles' earliest private studies pairing "Hebrew, and some Arabic," while also anticipating his late "Oration," in which "*Arabic*" will be publicly preached by "the President." Dilating yet wider, Stiles' circles also seem involved in a more extended biography of the nation, centering America's own genealogy of "Oriental learning," stretching back to alphabetic primers in Puritan New England, and promising the Islamic investments that culminate in later American expressions through the Civil War. Returning to Stiles' circles, it is not their centers merely that seem newly amplified, however, but also their peripheries, with elements emerging in this manuscript that were initially overlooked. At the very bottom of the page, immediately below his multilingual circles, Stiles inscribes several multilingual lines, signing off in Arabic, Latin, and Hebrew:

الله    تعاله    الله  سر  من    الرحيم    الرحمن  الله    بسم
*Deus  exaltatus  Deus  ergo  sit  maxime  misericordis  Dei  In nomine*

الخالقين             احسن        الله        وتبارك        المبين  الحق  الملك
*Entium omnium pracellentissimus Deus benedictus laudandus verus Rex Seldeni Opera* v.2. p.1701.

עזרא שטילס לבנו עזרא שלום

Sept. 6. 1774.[78]

Spelling out his left-hand sphere into straight and simple lines, Stiles unravels his "ARABICA" circle, transporting its Arabic text into a new form, while also translating it into a new language. Supplying Latin immediately below his two rows of Arabic, Stiles provides an interlinear rendition for "ARABICA," translating its Qurʾānic phrases into a Western classical idiom, parsing for instance its opening Arabic invocation— "بسم الله / الرحمن الرحيم" ("In the name of *Allāh*, the Merciful, the Compassionate")—with the Latin "*In nomine Dei misericordis maxime.*" And while his interlinear rendition is not entirely accurate—Stiles parses this Arabic's final phrase as "*pracellentissimus omnium entium*" ("most fair of all beings"), rather than correctly as "most fair of creators"—even such inaccuracies are telling, suggesting this Latin translation to be Stiles' own. Although "Selden" is the familiar source that Stiles acknowledges for his foreign text (citing "*Seldeni Opera* v.2. p.1701."), Stiles innovates a new and original rendition for his copied Arabic, advancing shakily toward his own autonomy in Islamic studies, independent from his British benefactor, even as America too resists British influence, moving unsteadily toward its own independence.

A first in American literary life, Stiles translates fragments of Muslim scripture within his informal writings, rendering Qurʾānic quotations into the ecclesiastic language of his Christian forefathers. This hybrid paternity of Stiles' multilingual document deepens, however, in his final words; again pairing sibling and sacred tongues, Stiles' document ends with a valediction that shifts from Arabic to Hebrew, even while retaining a strong sense of legacy and lineage:

עזרא שטילס לבנו עזרא שלום
[Ezra Stiles, to his son, Ezra: *Shalom*]

Not merely a first-person autograph, but a second-person address, Stiles' last line of text finally reveals his circular document to be a gift to his son, passing forward in paternal cycle, from "Ezra [Sr.]" to "Ezra [Jr.]."[79] Inscribed above a date that evokes national crisis—"Sept. 6. 1774"—this document's concluding dedication recalls not the opening of Congress, however, but rather college initiation, penned at a time of familial transition, as well as national formation. A farewell bequest, Stiles sends "his son" off into a world of conflict with a single, pivotal word: "שלום"—"*Shalom.*" Drafted in advance of war, in revolutionary expectation, these interreligious circles are nevertheless intended to forward "peace" and "salutation" to the next American age. An intimate moment that enriches the entirety of Stiles' cosmic map, this fatherly dedication is positioned, however, most closely to his Latin translation of the Qurʾān, with his Hebrew signature situated immediately below Arabic inscriptions, Stiles' private line to his son copied underneath praises to *Allāh*. Advancing from parent to child, from domestic present to future descendants, Stiles transmits the "great Goodness" of Qurʾānic "guidance" as part of his son's own inheritance, enclosing an Islamic endowment within circles of national revolution and familial generation.

# "I most sincerely wish an Arabic Manuscript of the Koran"

## William Bentley's Islamic Archives

By the spring of 1794, Ezra Stiles had entered his final months of life, his death in May 1795 only a year away. However, despite his increasing age, Stiles shows no sign of slowing in 1794, his spring *Diary* recording vigorous pursuits, personal and professional. Consider, for example, the following entry, scribbled on the first day of March 1794:

> Rec$^d$ Lett. fr. Mr Holmes & Betsy of 22$^d$ ult. Polly stationary. Betsy a few weeks past made a pub. profession of Religion, and was admitted in the Chh at Cambridge; where on Ldsdy 16th Ins$^t$ she partook of the Sacram$^t$ for the first time. Read$^g$ Sales Koran. Also rec$^d$ a Letter from M$^r$ Adams of Medfield inclos$^g$ at my Desire a Profile of his Daughter Miss Hannah Adams the Historian.[1]

Punctuating Stiles' catalog of correspondence is his "read$^g$" of the Muslim revelation, the "Koran" finding place amid family communications and the news of a first communion. Leading with a letter from "Mr [Abiel] Holmes"—his former student, current son-in-law, and future biographer—Stiles initially learns that his own daughter, Betsy, has "made a pub[lic] profession of Religion."[2] This cause for paternal pride anticipates the end of Stiles' entry, which concludes with another father's "Profile of his Daughter," Stiles receiving a report from "M$^r$ Adams" on "Miss Hannah Adams"—a pioneering "Historian" of comparative religion, whose *An Alphabetical Compendium of the Various Sects* had appeared a decade earlier in 1784.[3] Intersecting these letters of public proclamation and filial piety is Stiles' private interests, his own religious "Read$^g$" complementing his daughter's "profession of Religion," her Christian "Sacram$^t$" followed immediately by his review of the "Koran." A domestic act nestled in communal contexts, Stiles' reading also gestures beyond regional borders, reaching to Arabian antiquity via a familiar British intermediary: George Sale's *Koran* translation, which Stiles had first encountered in the catalog of the Redwood Library three decades previous.[4] Perhaps most reminiscent in Stiles' entry is simply the imperfect and individual tenor of his Islamic interests. While other events recorded on March 1, 1794, are performed by other people and in the "past," Stiles' own encounter with the "Koran" is personal and progressive, unfolding as an abbreviated act of "Read$^g$." Such enduring energy and familial intimacy of Stiles' Islamic interests seems particularly poignant in 1794— a year that marks not only the last full year of Ezra Stiles' own life, but also a full decade since the premature death of his eldest son, Ezra Jr. Receiving news in 1794 of his daughter's Christian confession, sent from his son-in-law, Abiel Holmes, from nearby Cambridge, Stiles' own son—for whom he had drafted his 1774 circles with Qur'ānic quotations—had died ten years before and far away, succumbing to deteriorating health while traveling in North Carolina on August 22, 1784.[5]

Stiles' own looming death in the spring of 1795 will bring an abrupt end to his "invaluable" records of American life, as well as his Islamic "Read$^g$," his *Diary* breaking off just before his May illness and sudden decline. However, this loss of the nation's revolutionary diarist in the last decade of the eighteenth century would also coincide with the rise of the "journalist of the early Republic"—a "journalist" whose interests are equally enriched by Islam.[6] Born in 1759, three decades after Ezra Stiles, William Bentley's life broadly mirrors Stiles' own, with echoes and inversions unfolding across American generations. Native to neighboring colonies (Connecticut and Massachusetts) and educated at rival colleges (Yale and Harvard), Stiles and Bentley both become leading Congregationalist minsters at bustling New England ports, the former at Newport, Rhode Island, the latter at Salem, Massachusetts. Distinguished from their respective contemporaries by a shared scholarly prowess, Bentley succeeds Stiles too in intellectual acclaim, labeled his own generation's "most learned man in America."[7] The academic precedence enjoyed by both men would, moreover, equally bring them into contact with early America's political elite; like Stiles before him, Bentley too exchanges ideas with Founding Fathers, becoming a correspondent and fervent champion of Thomas Jefferson especially. It is not their national profiles, however, but their intimate records that most urgently unite Stiles and Bentley. Begun in April 1784, and pursued until the day before his death at the close of December 1819, Bentley will author a capacious diary that rivals Stiles' own, meticulously recording Salem life in the years following the Revolution.[8] A successor to Stiles' *Diary*, Bentley's personal journal too has served as a touchstone for historians of the early Republic; published in a multivolume edition between 1905 and 1914, Bentley's *Diary* has won the same labels attributed to Stiles' *Diary*, referenced regularly as an "invaluable source" by chroniclers of U.S. origins.[9]

Public intellectuals celebrated for their private accounts, the careers of Stiles and Bentley straddle the historic and the prosaic, dramatizing iconic American moments and men, while also cataloguing the quotidian details of American life.

However, such continuities between Stiles and Bentley—each having an impact on early national history, while shaping later national historiography—have also over-shadowed a continuity whose implications are more global, and less predictable. Approaching the final year of his life and literary *Diary*, Stiles records his reading of the Qurʾān in between his familial correspondence on March 1, 1794. During the same season, Bentley also documents his own epistolary life in his *Diary*, penning the following entry a few weeks later, dated May 3, 1794:

> Mʳ Gibaut furnished me with several Arabic & Persia[n] letters written by Merchants, & has promised me a specimen of the Peguan language & writ-ing. The letters I have received are written on the paper in various direc-tions. Some parts obliquely, others in columns, &c.[10]

Recalling Stiles two months prior, Bentley here lists the arrival of "letters," "furnished" by his Salem friend and former student, John "Gibaut." It is the Near Eastern foregrounds to this New England receipt, however, that seems most fa-miliar; as Stiles' own Islamic "Readˢ" in March 1794, Bentley reads messages in May sent from Islamic lands, opening transatlantic texts inscribed in "Arabic and Persia[n]." Intersecting his literary life at "oblique" angles, Bentley's own Islamic "Readˢ" in 1794 too seems idiomatic and imperfect; not only "written" in "various directions," these Arabic and Persian letters also gesture forward to future poten-tial. Noting that he is "promised" further "specimens" from the East, Bentley ends his own entry informally and inconclusively, closing simply with a tentative "&c."[11] Ending in informal abbreviation, Bentley's 1794 entry not only reaches forward to his own later Islamic receptions, however, but also anticipates the abbreviation of his Islamic interests from present-day scholarship. Again recalling Stiles, Bentley's encounter with Muslim "language & writing" has been ironically forgotten despite leaving behind a myriad of material witnesses—witnesses that are physically "writ-ten on the paper," but that have nevertheless been entirely abridged from our ac-counts of early U.S. literary culture.[12]

Establishing a Middle Eastern correspondence between discrete American di-aries, this overlap between entries penned by Stiles and Bentley in the spring of 1794 is, moreover, no coincidence, but instead hints at a shared lineage of Islamic investment that unfolds hemispherically and historically, reaching from the Near East to New England, and from the Revolution to the Republic. Celebrated as Stiles' successor in professional scholarship and personal journaling, Bentley also covertly extends a generational tension between American interiority and Islamic invest-ment, with the nation's premier "man of letters" again qualifying as its most eager connoisseur and collector of "Arabic & Persia[n] letters." Suggesting a family like-ness, the overlapping diary entries of Stiles and Bentley also help draw the "various directions" that these two men, separated by three decades, will pursue. Broadly parallel in their public profiles and private practices, the national careers of Stiles and Bentley follow divergent trajectories—a split made obvious, surprisingly, in the character of their Islamic engagements. While Stiles will ultimately vacate his Newport pulpit to assume the presidency of Yale, Bentley doggedly refuses to quit the port of Salem for higher office, reportedly rejecting Jefferson's own offer to lead the incipient University of Virginia.[13] Rather than climb ladders of national advancement, Bentley will explore further channels of global exchange, benefitting from the foreign currents uniquely circulating through Salem itself—the Republic's richest trading port with India and Arabia at the turn of the nineteenth century. Rejecting political advancement at American institutions, Bentley also differs from Stiles by rejecting traditions of American religion, electing to spurn New England's Calvinist past. Although it is Bentley who remains a Congregationalist minister until his death in 1819, it will also be Bentley who interrupts and reimagines the Congregationalist ministry, becoming one of New England's first clergy to embrace Unitarianism openly, preaching its "post-Puritan" doctrines as early as 1785.[14] Situated on the perilous edge of the new Republic, surveying its physical and theological coasts from his Salem pulpit, Bentley's Islamic interests also progress beyond what seemed possible for Stiles in Revolutionary America. As anticipated by his diary entry in 1794, Bentley's interest in the languages of Muslim antiquity will develop into lively exchanges with living Muslim "Merchants," ultimately allowing Bentley to trade letters, and to cultivate a library, in "Arabic & Persia[n]"—letters and a library that together represent the most substantive, yet now most neglected, cache of Muslim literary culture in the early Republic. Acquiring Islamic epistles and archives, Bentley advances the interreligious exchanges initiated by Ezra Stiles; however, reflecting the generational overlaps between Stiles and Bentley, it is fitting that their personal engagements with Islam also claim a common source in a singular person: Stephen Sewall. ✡

> In the last discourse I began with the Arabic language, & pursued the subject so far as to point out its origin, changes & duration. Its genius & idiom still remain to be treated of. The Arabic, as I have hinted before, is so exceedingly useful in sacred philology, that I shall omit nothing, purposely, which may serve to give one the best idea of the language he can attain to without actually studying it. But I would not be understood to insinuate, that such a speculative knowledge of the Arabic will alone answer any valuable purposes in criticism. It is an intimate, &, if I may be allowed the expression, an experimental acquaintance with it, [that] can do this. And I wish the former kind of knowledge, which I shall now attempt to give, might excite the curiosity of some to gain the latter.[15]

These were the first words addressed to William Bentley and his college classmates on November 25, 1776, as they attended the fortnightly lecture of Harvard's "Hancock Professor of Hebrew and other Oriental Languages," Stephen Sewall.

Proposing to address Arabic's "genius and idiom," Sewall begins by recalling his topic's genesis, linking this present lecture to his previous "discourse" that had traced the "origin, changes & duration" of the "Arabic language." Situated in his broader curriculum, Sewall also provides a biblical context for Arabic study, citing its "usefulness" as a supplement for "sacred philology."[16] Echoing Ezra Stiles' own introduction to the language, Sewall introduces Arabic to Bentley and his Harvard classmates as an exegetical aid, framing this "other Oriental Language" as ancillary to the "Hebrew" scriptures. And yet, even while invoking Arabic as "exceedingly useful," Sewall's approach to the language seems more inspirational than instrumental. Opening with Arabic's past contexts, Sewall quickly pivots to its future potential, expressing a "wish" to see his students surpass mere "speculative" distance, aspiring instead for direct "acquaintance" with Arabic. Although this lecture aims to supply only his "best idea of the language," Sewall's primary hope is to "excite curiosity," prompting his students to engage with Arabic personally and practically, developing a rapport with the language that is both "intimate" and "experimental."

Inspirational in approach, Sewall's Arabic lecture seems tailored to his impressionable audience, appealing to the dawning ambitions of his young listeners. A member of Harvard's senior class, Bentley himself was only seventeen years old in November 1776, having entered college at the tender age of fourteen in the fall of 1773.[17] If aware of his audience's age, however, Sewall's Arabic address seems equally aware of his country's own coming of age. Immediately after his introductory words quoted above, Sewall's lecture shifts from the personal to the patriotic:

> And this I wish not only for their own private benefit & satisfaction, but for the honour and reputation of this Society. It is the oldest upon the Continent, & the only one endowed with a Professorship of this kind; & by the munificence of its benefactors, it is perhaps as well furnished with means [. . .] to attain the knowledge of the Arabic as any University in Europe. And there is no University, I believe, in all Europe, of equal note with this, where the Arabic is not more or less studied. What pity, not to say disgrace, is it then that we, who equal most, & surpass some, of the Universities of Europe, in this means, should fall short of them all in the application to attain the end? What a satisfaction would it afford to the living friends & patrons of this Society, to find their benefactions have had the effect they designed, that is, as some of them have expressed it, have produced some prime Scholars in the oriental languages. If any are [emulative] of glory & reputation which in a degree are commendable here is a fair opportunity of gaining them: For the same attainments in these studies in an American will you may depend upon be looked upon as so much the more extraordinary than in others, by how much the further he is removed west, & so from the fountain of Oriental knowledge.[18]

Recommended first as an intimate experiment, Arabic is now envisioned as a national enterprise, no longer promising "private benefit," but rather "satisfaction" for public "benefactors." Raising the stakes of Arabic study, Sewall suggests both its risks and rewards, threatening "disgrace" for this language's neglect, while guaranteeing "glory" for its "attainment." Delivered just weeks after the Declaration of Independence was ratified, Sewall challenges his students to demonstrate their own independence in Arabic "attainment," rousing this "oldest" college of the American "Continent" to prove its "equal" or "surpassing" worth against "the Universities of Europe." Refracting America's political rise in its Arabic potential, Sewall seems especially anxious for New World "reputation," sensitive to how Harvard's "Society" and its students will be "looked upon." However, Sewall also cleverly translates current American weakness into incipient Arabic strengths. Although New England scholars are "further removed" from Near Eastern origins, their home in the far "west" itself makes progress in "oriental languages" all the more "extraordinary." Echoing his mission as expressed to Ezra Stiles—"to propagate the knowledge of Oriental literature in this Western world"—Sewall again finds the remoteness of Western frontiers as ironic incentive for Eastward errand, equating America's thirst for the "fountain of Oriental knowledge" with improbable "glory."[19]

Bridging American Republic and the Atlantic World, political duty and private pleasure, Sewall's early lecture on Arabic seems predictive of Bentley's own maturing career, forecasting polarities that will later inform his future linguistic "attainments." Sewall's influence on Bentley's "oriental" interests is not merely "speculative," however, but has left more material traces. The same semester that sees Sewall frame Arabic studies as both personal and patriotic, Bentley will be roused by his teacher's rallying cry, seeking "acquaintance" beyond the lecture hall with both Semitic philology and Sewall himself. Expanding his horizons of "Oriental knowledge," Bentley begins in the fall of 1776 to copy out his professor's own private researches—an act uniquely witnessed in one of Bentley's student notebooks, now housed at Tufts University's Digital Collections and Archives.[20] A testimony to Bentley's Semitic studies during his senior year, the cover page of this notebook is headed "*A Chaldee Grammar*," under which Bentley immediately adds: "This Grammar is founded upon the writings of Daniel and Ezra composed by the learned Stephan Sewall, Professor of the oriental languages at Cambridge."[21] Spanning the next forty-one pages, Bentley transcribes not only Sewall's own *A Chaldee Grammar*, but also his *A Lexicon of the Chaldee Language* and *A Compendious Syriac Grammar*—three unpublished works arising from his professor's Eastern philology.[22] Copying down Sewall's manuscript drafts into his own notebook, Bentley also precisely dates his transcripts, anticipating his later repute as a meticulous chronicler. Below the heading of his notebook's first page—*A Chaldee Grammar*—Bentley briefly explains that this was "Copied from the original/A. 1776/Cal. Sept. 24th." Similarly, concluding Bentley's transcript of *A Lexicon of the Chaldee Language*, he inserts a final line that reads "Copied from Professor Sewall's in the winter vacation of the Senior year

1777—Jan.—Bentley."[23] Lastly, on page 41 of Bentley's notebook, his attribution that concludes Sewall's *A Compendious Syriac Grammar* notes that "Feb. 24th 1777 copied from the original by William Bentley, under-graduate." Supplying his own agenda and autographs to Sewall's "originals," young Bentley fills the spaces that surround such Eastern studies with his personal signature, superimposing his "under-graduate" calendar over his professor's antique Orientalism.[24]

Recalling the "Arabic Grammar" he prepared specifically for Ezra Stiles in 1768, it is Stephen Sewall again who supplies Bentley with material support, offering his student privileged access to his private Semitic manuscripts. Implying a new sense of intimacy and initiative, however, Bentley not only reviews Sewall's resources, but manually reproduces them over many months, costing countless hours of delicate handiwork in copying. Spanning much of his "Senior year," Bentley begins to transcribe from Sewall's grammars on "Sept. 24th" 1776 and continues to copy through the first weeks of the New Year, concluding on "Feb. 24th 1777." Perhaps most impressive is Bentley's persistence, despite interruptions to the Harvard term; entrusted to take Sewall's *Lexicon of the Chaldee Language* home for the holidays, Bentley pushes on through "the winter vacation," carrying his Semitic studies from the halls of academe to his family's house.[25] Copied through January 1777, Bentley's inscription of Sewall's *Lexicon* moves outside college rooms and semester rhythms; however, this *Chaldee Lexicon* also prompts Bentley to move outside the closed circles of biblical language as well, experimenting for the first time with actual Arabic. Transcribing Sewall's *Lexicon* into his notebook's fifteenth page, Bentley arrives at an entry for "דחון"—*dachavān*—a "Chaldee" term that Sewall parses in both English and Latin, while also invoking a sibling Semitic word for comparison. As shown in Figure 2.1, Bentley's copied entry for "דחון" (*dachavān*) is intersected by his own shaky inscription of a single Arabic term: "دخن" (*dakhan* [i.e., "fume," "vapor"]).[26]

Musing first that the Aramaic "דחון" signifies "instruments of music," Bentley's copied entry suggests too that "perhaps it means perfume as the Arabic دخن," citing the famed British philologist Edward "Castell," who associates this Arabic word

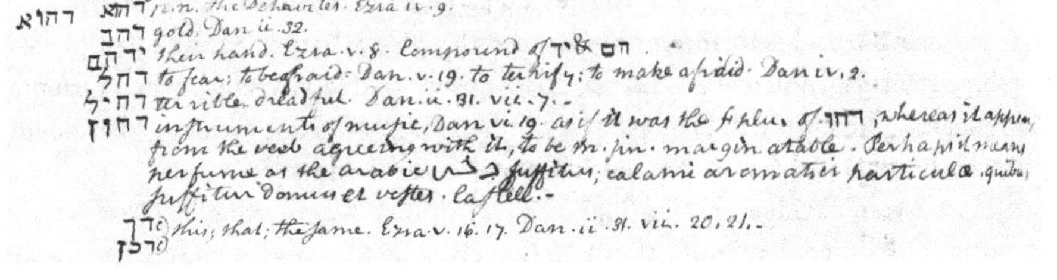

*Figure 2.1* William Bentley, "Middle Eastern Languages Notebook," page 65, featuring his inscription of a single Arabic term: "دخن" (*dakhan*). Image courtesy of Tufts University, Digital Collections and Archives.

with an "aromatic reed" that freshens "home and clothes" ("*calami aromatici* [. . .] *domus et vestes*").[27] Justifying Sewall's portrait of this language as "exceedingly useful in sacred philology," Bentley's professor borrows Arabic for biblical exegesis, invoking "*dakhan*" to define a "*Chaldee*" word from "*Daniel*." And recalling Sewall's Arabic lecture in November 1776, this entry as transcribed by Bentley appeals to an Arabic word through aesthetic "intimacy," offering a sensual intervention in Sewall's sacred *Lexicon*. Visibly traced for the first time in Bentley's own hand, Arabic characters suggest a sweet atmosphere of sound and smell, with "the Arabic دخن" marking a transition from "music" to "perfume." Paralleling Bentley's own domestic environs— copying at home and on holiday—Arabic emerges for the first time from his pen with distinctly domestic associations, tracing a term that fragrantly imbues both household environs ("*domus*") and personal attire ("*vestes*").

Witnessing his inaugural moment of Arabic literacy during the last months of his Harvard degree, Bentley's "under-graduate" notebook, containing copies of Sewall's "originals," will remain a close companion long after Sewall's personal instruction drifts far out of reach. Completing his senior year in the spring of 1777, Bentley's early career leads him back to Harvard, hired as a university tutor in 1780.[28] As President Stiles in New Haven, Bentley finds refuge at his alma mater through the last years of the Revolution, rising in rank from mere "under-graduate" to an instructor of undergraduates during this tumultuous time. However, these same years of academic elevation for Stiles and Bentley also witness the fatal decline of their shared teacher of "Oriental Languages." Overtaking his thirst for the "fountain of Oriental knowledge," Sewall's worsening alcoholism in the 1780s leads Harvard to charge him with "intemperance," ultimately removing Sewall from the faculty. Judging him "unfit to continue at the college" due to his inability "to control his drinking," Sewall was dismissed by the Harvard Corporation in 1785—a firing that troubled Bentley, as implied by a diary entry penned early the following year, soon after Sewall's successor, Eliphalet Pearson, took up the Hancock Professorship.[29] "On Tuesday attended the induction of Professor Pearson into the Oriental Chair in the room of S. Sewall, ungenerously dismissed," Bentley notes in his *Diary* on February 12, 1786.[30] A decade after his domestic "acquaintance" with Sewall, copying his scholarship through the "winter vacation" of 1776, Bentley bemoans Sewall's own forced vacation, "ungenerously" evicted from his rightful "room" at Harvard. Sympathizing with his former professor, Bentley also renames Sewall's lost professorship, referring not to the "Hancock Professor of Hebrew and other Oriental Languages," but simply to Harvard's "Oriental Chair"—an abbreviation that deemphasizes biblical Hebrew in favor of "the East" more broadly.[31]

This Eastern abridgement in Bentley's *Diary* suits his environs in 1786, having recently settled in Salem, ministering to this city's historic East Church. Two years before Sewall's forced departure from Harvard, ending his college career in 1785, Bentley himself had departed the college voluntarily, launching his own career by joining Salem's Second Church, known more simply as "the East."[32] Leaving Harvard behind, it would be Bentley's Harvard beginnings that nevertheless helped gain him the pulpit in Salem. Preaching his ordination sermon on September 24, 1783, Reverend James Lathrop explicitly references Bentley's years as a university scholar and tutor, reminding the East's congregation that "It is no small favor to obtain a young minister of such accomplishments." Bentley was, in the Rev. Lathrop's words, a minister "full of youth and activity," willing to offer "his time and talents—his natural and acquired abilities to God, and the service of your souls."[33] If Bentley's Harvard "accomplishments" were uppermost in the mind of his new congregation, these "accomplishments" would not be forgotten by the "young minister" himself either. Even while dedicating himself to ministerial duties at the East Church, Bentley nevertheless reserves much of his "time and talents" in the years following 1783 to his own "abilities" in Eastern languages. And although Bentley was doubly removed from Sewall's influence—having departed Harvard himself, while also witnessing Sewall "dismissed" from Harvard "ungenerously"—the young minister would re-begin his Oriental studies in Salem with the help of a familiar source: the very same "under-graduate" notebook he had begun in September 1776.

Accompanying him to Salem in 1783, Bentley's student notebook opens with transcripts from his professor's "originals" as mentioned above, extending to the end of Sewall's *A Compendious Syriac Grammar* on "Feb. 24th 1777." However, in the pages and years that follow, Bentley continues to use this same notebook as an index of his Eastern interests, filling its remaining sixty leaves with new linguistic advances. Initiated as a juvenile "under-graduate" at revolutionary Harvard, the second half of Bentley's notebook records his maturing Orientalism in the young Republic, acting as a linguistic register through the early 1800s.[34] Spanning national and personal progress, pushing across centuries and vocations, Bentley's notebook also pushes further East as it unfolds, leaving behind the languages of biblical study and moving into explicitly Islamic regions. While Arabic appears as a single term in Bentley's eighteenth-century transcripts from Sewall, his notebook's later entries at the dawn of the nineteenth century find Arabic occupying entire pages. Copying into his notebook the works of a range of British and European Orientalists— borrowing from the grammars of luminaries such as John Gilchrist, Georg Otho, and most conspicuously Sir William Jones—Bentley fosters familiarity with the mechanics of Muslim idioms.[35] Figure 2.2 reproduces two representative pages from the latter half of Bentley's notebook—pages 70 and 83—the first forming an outline of Arabic pronouns, and the second a paradigm of a Persian verb.

Marking a new level of "Oriental" independence, Bentley advances his own "intimate" relationship with Arabic and Persian, these languages no longer scrawled as a single term, nor invoked merely as an exegetical aid.[36] A departure from his student days, these middle-age efforts yet recall Bentley's undergraduate years, not only literally filling the last pages of his Harvard notebook, but also fulfilling his Harvard professor's literary hopes. Personally "experimenting" with Arabic, Bentley here indexes Arabic's personal pronouns, the "singular" and "plural" forms of page 70

*Figure 2.2* William Bentley, "Middle Eastern Languages Notebook," pages 70 and 83. Images courtesy of Tufts University, Digital Collections and Archives.

obliquely mirroring both the individual and "communal" implications of his own Arabic explorations. Refracting the solitary "I" of Bentley's private studies, while gesturing to a global "they" abroad, his outline of Arabic pronouns is followed by a "Paradigm" of the Persian "verb" on page 83, Bentley's Oriental literacy shifting into new territory, as well as new tenses and times. Reaching beyond the "past" tutelage of his university career, and expressing his "present" efforts of Muslim philology, Bentley's adolescent notebook begun under Sewall serves too as a preview, presciently forecasting the Eastern "futures" soon to be traced by Bentley's own unfolding career. ☼

> *Divitis Indiae usque ad ultimum sinum*
> ["To the farthest port of the rich East"]
> Nineteenth-century motto of the City of Salem[37]

Assuming leadership of Salem's East Church in 1783, William Bentley became a resident of a town whose own prospects and perspectives were defined as Eastern. Founded as a refuge for religious conscience in the seventeenth century, Salem had become a haven of commercial wealth by the end of the eighteenth, acclaimed as "[p]robably the nation's richest community per capita in 1800."[38] At Bentley's arrival in 1783, Salem was fast becoming America's wealthiest port, its prosperity derived from its maritime reach, procuring products for New World sale from India, China, and Arabia. As suggested by the city's nineteenth-century motto, Salem understood itself through affluence and the "Orient," prioritizing the former, with "*Divitis*" ("rich") preceding *"Indiae"* ("East") at the open to Salem's slogan. Pastoring the East Church of America's most Eastern outpost, Bentley himself was drawn to the city's global range, fascinated by the "farthest port[s]" to which Salem sailors ventured, recording in his diary the *"ultimum sinum"* from which ships regularly returned. As Bentley was neither merchant nor mariner, but the city's most scholarly minister, his interests tended, however, toward the cultural capital available via Salem's commercial exchange. Realizing the potential for imaginative and intellectual travel offered by its trade routes, Salem's impact on Bentley's intellectual development is perhaps best witnessed in a series of commonplace notebooks, which he began soon after settling at the East Church. Unlike Bentley's *Diary* started in Salem, his "Octavo Notebooks" remain unpublished, housed in manuscript at the American Antiquarian Society (AAS) in Worcester, Massachusetts. However, recalling his *Diary*, Bentley would arrange these miscellaneous journals in careful sequence, offering an invaluable index of his interior and intellectual life, stretching from his first years in Salem to his last.[39]

Recording his eclectic reading and researches, Bentley's notebooks are penned in Salem but also reflect Salem priorities, embracing the town's global horizons at the turn of the century. Transatlantic in focus, the Octavo Notebooks suggest Bentley's particular interest in Middle Eastern travel, the young minister experiencing through secondary literature the same exotic lands encountered by many of his parishioners first hand. Attracted to accounts that mix foreign discovery with foreign dialects, Bentley transcribes into his notebooks, for instance, generous selections from *The History of Nadir Shah*, a colorful chronology of Persian conquest authored by Scottish adventurer James Fraser in 1742.[40] Cribbing substantive chunks from Fraser's *Nadir Shah*, Bentley's quotations address Islamic politics, as well as Islamic prophecy, selecting for instance the following "note" concerning the Muslim creed from Fraser's *History*, which Bentley copies on page 146 of his Octavo Notebook 18:

> The note tells us Ali the friend of God is always annexed
> in this manner لا اله الا محمد رسول الله وعلي ولي الله
> There is no God but God, & Mahommed the prophet of God, & Ali the
>    friend of God[41]

No longer single terms, Bentley copies in Arabic an actual sentence testifying to God's singularity—a sentence penned first in Arabic, with Bentley's English following. Selecting from Fraser's scattered "notes" in his *History*, Bentley quotes the Muslim creed in its distinctly Shi'a expression, adding "& Ali [is] the friend of God" to "There is no God but God, & Mahommed [is] the prophet of God." Including this "annexed" phrase, Bentley also inadvertently abbreviates the *shahāda*, providing a defective transcript of its very first phrase. Cited correctly in English—"There is no God but God"—Bentley's Arabic strangely omits "*Allāh*," opening merely with the words "لا الله لا" (i.e., "There is no god but").[42] Seemingly a mere slip, likely the fault of fallible eye and hand, Bentley's omission of the *shahāda*'s prime presence— *Allāh* Himself—also intriguingly performs the incomplete and informal character of Bentley's own first inscription of Islam's initial declaration, witnessing to the personal and provisional nature of Bentley's incipient Arabic literacy. Perhaps more instructive than Bentley's unconscious omission, however, is simply his deliberate inclusion of the *shahāda* in his 1790s notebook—an act replete with interreligious resonance and irony. During the very decade that sees Bentley publicly break with his own faith's Trinitarian traditions, he also privately pens Islam's departure from Trinitarianism, tracing this Arabic testimony to God's unity even while delivering English sermons in Salem on the "Unity of God."[43] In the same years that mark New England Unitarianism's imperfect first steps, Bentley also imperfectly scripts Islam's Unitarian declaration, seeking to foster in eighteenth-century America a belief in divine oneness while finding this same belief also articulated in seventh-century Arabia. A coincidence of theological commitments, Bentley's own unique position in U.S. religious history amplifies the significance of his 1790s appeal to the *shahāda*, lending his Arabian transcript a certain American timeliness. Rather than a foreign statement of Islamic antiquity merely, Bentley's inscription of "There is no God but God" echoes a statement of urgent relevance to his own Salem situation, quoting a spiritual conviction reflective not only of an Eastern *History*, but also Bentley's own Western currency.

If timely in expression, Bentley's appeal to Islam in his Octavo Notebooks will feature spatial interventions as well, with Eastern discourse pushing Bentley in Eastern directions, not only mapping Middle Eastern literatures, but reproducing literal maps of the Middle East. Even while copying Fraser's *History*, more contemporary authors will also attract Bentley's attention, including one of his own century's most influential Orientalists, Carsten Niebuhr. Published first in 1772, Niebuhr's famous account of Arabian topography—his *Beschreibung von Arabien*—soon appeared in French, published as *Description de l'Arabie*, an edition that Bentley begins to read early in the 1790s.[44] Like Fraser, Niebuhr familiarizes Bentley further with Middle Eastern travel and tongues, sprinkling his work with ample selections in Arabic. However, unlike Fraser, Niebuhr's concern is not the Persian past, but rather the present place of Arabia, outlining not a temporal *History*, but a spatial *Description*. Replete with detail and design, the Eastern vocabulary of Niebuhr's *Description* stretch out in Eastern vectors, prompting Bentley not only to experience Arabia vicariously second hand, but to trace Arabia's topographic outlines in his own hand. Figure 2.3 shows a page from Bentley's Octavo Notebook 27, authored in the late 1790s—a page witnessing the American's reproduction of Niebuhr's sketch of North Africa, his bare lines extending from Egypt's Nile and Cairo in the West (at the top) to Suez in the East (at the bottom).[45]

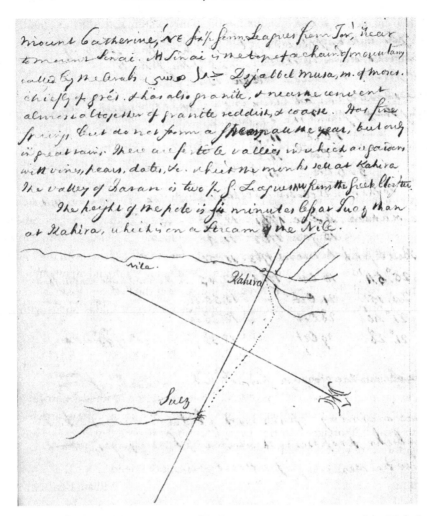

*Figure 2.3* William Bentley, Octavo Notebook 27, page 40, copying a map from Niebuhr's *Description of Arabia* and inscribing in Arabic "جبل موسى" (*"jabal Mūsā"*; "Moses' Mountain"). Image courtesy of the American Antiquarian Society.

Stark in shape, yet complex in its content, Bentley's map merges languages and lands, reaching eastward to Mt. Sinai—not only the sacred site of Hebraic revelation, but also home to the first Christian monastery (i.e., the community of "St. Catherine," which Bentley names at the top of his page). It is not merely Sinai's Judaic and Christian pasts, however, but its Muslim present that is here implied, with Bentley shifting languages in the third line of his page, recording that this summit is "called by the Arabs جبل موسى *Dsjabbel Musa*, M. of Moses."[46] A locus of religious crossing, Bentley's description of Mt. Sinai itself crosses languages, his diagrammatic lines surveying historic environs, even while his description serves to align authentic Arabic sounds with actual Arabian spaces. Straddling diverse spiritual markers—Judaic covenant, Christian cloister, and Muslim country—Bentley's "M[ountain] of Moses" implies religious intersections embodied in his map's intersecting lines, its skeletal compass suggesting more irregular borders of culture.

Charting Muslim lands, while helping to chart Bentley's interest in Muslim languages, Niebuhr's *Description* offers smooth surfaces merely, its mountainous contours leveled to flat lines on Bentley's notebook page. And yet, it will also be Niebuhr's *Description* that motivates Bentley to move beyond two-dimensional diagrams, reaching transatlantically to initiate three-dimensional exchanges with the Muslim world. Pursuing spatial trajectories traced first by Niebuhr, Bentley reaches laterally across to actual Arabian lands through Salem trade routes, no longer copying maps domestically at the end of the eighteenth century, but fostering friendships in foreign regions during the first decade of the nineteenth century. Writing in the winter of 1804, Bentley first petitions a friend who is most familiar with the Middle East, seeking aid from Captain Henry Elkins, a Salem mariner and merchant whose commerce regularly took him to Arabia. Deposited at the Peabody Essex Museum's Phillips Library, Bentley's previously unpublished letter to Elkins opens with the following plea:

> Salem 14. Feb 1804
>
> Captain Henry Elkins,
> Sir [as per] our request, I give you the following memoranda, knowing your disposition to our queries, & your success in gaining curious articles in Asiatic, & foreign countries. Every attention will merit & will receive the gratitude of your devoted
> > Servant & Friend.
> > William Bentley.[47]

Dated Valentine's Day 1804, Bentley aptly appeals first to his friend's sympathy; citing his "disposition to our queries," Bentley flatters Elkins' commercial prowess, praising his prior success in "gaining curious articles" abroad. Balancing camaraderie and commodities, Bentley's familiar entreaty is, however, concerned with "foreign countries," comprising a cover letter to "the following memoranda" that itemizes "Asiatic" curiosities requested by Bentley. Turning over the page, Bentley begins this "memoranda" on the back of his cover letter, citing a "celebrated" source before listing the desired "curious articles":

> The celebrated Niebuhr, in his *Description of Arabia*, says he was shewn several Arabian Histories, & observes, "perhaps a European merchant, trading at Mocha, might purchase them. They are to be had at the shops of Constantinople & Cairo."

Books he directly mentions are:

| | |
|---|---|
| *Berk al Yemen* | برق اليمن |
| *Kurrêt al gnuyûn* | قرة العيون |
| *Nefaîs al gueraïs* | نفايس العرايس |
| *Tarikh al avelin, u al cherin* | تاريخ الاولين والاخرين |
| *Dsjemheerêt al guerreb* | جمهرة العرب |
| *Rûh al Rûh* | روح الروح |
| *Tarikh al charredjî* | تاريخ الخررجي |

He says the two first are said to contain the History of Yemen.
The first of the two, the Turkish Conquest, & the second a later period.
Mr Forskâl mentions also,

| | |
|---|---|
| *Ketâb molûk hemjîr* | كتاب ملوك حمير |
| *Burdje al Deêb* | بروج الذهب |
| *Bedûhê al khalk* | بدوي الخلق |
| *Durr al manûr* | در المنور |
| *Bodgnîêt aben Hadjâh* | بدعية ابن حجاه |

I most sincerely wish an Arabic Manuscript of the Koran. In the Arabian *Nessich*, or Persian *Talik* character, would be preferred. Specimen of different writings would be acceptable.[48]

Addressed to Elkins, an American merchant, it is European exploration that Bentley mentions first in his "memoranda," opening with "the celebrated Niebuhr," while quoting specifically his *Description of Arabia*. Confined no longer to his notebook's compass, Bentley's interest in Niebuhr leads to composed lines dispatched eastward with Captain Elkins. However, the mention of Niebuhr's single book also anticipates a bibliographic miscellany in Bentley's "memoranda," petitioning Elkins to secure a variety of Muslim "manuscripts." Opening with European citation and American commerce, it is Arabic sources that forms the heart of Bentley's "request"; aided by his Western resources, Bentley seeks to transcend Western intermediaries, cutting across circuitous routes to the East through this appeal to acquire actual Islamic sources. Targeting Yemen's capital of culture and commerce— Mocha— Bentley begins by translating from Niebuhr, quoting his belief that a "merchant, trading at Mocha, might purchase" a whole host of Arabic books, these materials equally available in this Yemeni city as in famed "Constantinople & Cairo." Transatlantically triangulated— merging European travelogue, American trade, and Middle Eastern texts— most striking in Bentley's "memoranda" is its lines of parallel languages, providing Arabic script and imperfect transliterations to help Elkins procure specific sources in Mocha's "markets."[49] Proving himself no average antiquarian, Bentley's American "memoranda" is globally linguistic; its bibliographic detail, however, is somewhat deceptive. Characterizing his "two first" books ordered as "History," Bentley neglects to mention that the majority of his requests represent not Muslim historiography but Muslim hermeneutics, concerned not with "Turkish Conquest" but with Qur'ānic exegesis. Immediately after his initial two requests, Bentley asks Elkins to procure "نفايس العرايس" ("Nafā'is al-'Arā'is")—a text whose full title translates as *Gems of the Brides respecting the Narratives of the Glorious Qur'ān and the Lives of the Prophets* (*Nafā'is al-'Arā'is fī Qiṣaṣ al-Qur'ān al-'Aẓīm wa-Siyar al-Anbiyā'*).[50] In this "precious" biography of the prophets, Bentley also anticipates the sacred luster of his second section of requests—a list derived from "Mr Forskål," Niebuhr's traveling companion in Arabia, which includes *The Scattered Pearls* ("در المنذ[ة]ور"), a classic compendium of Qur'ān interpretation by the celebrated fifteenth-century Egyptian scholar, as-Suyūṭī.[51]

Witnessing his initial efforts to build an Islamic archive in early America, Bentley's 1804 "memoranda" concludes by reaching Muslim beginnings, with the Islamic character of his requests climaxing by identifying a final "article" that he desires: the Qur'ān itself. Breaking from his book list, Bentley also breaks into his own voice, expressing original ideas as he approaches Islamic origins. Shifting from Niebuhr's prescribed register, it is Bentley's first-person "wish" that emerges at the end, no longer passively identifying books that "are to be had," but actively expressing his own heart's yearning, exclaiming emphatically that "I most sincerely wish an Arabic Manuscript of the Koran." If more simple and "sincere," it is the specificity of Bentley's Qur'ānic confession that lends it emphasis, stipulating that "In the Arabian *Nessich*, or Persian *Talik* character, would be preferred. Specimen of different writings would be acceptable."[52] Balancing discretion with discrimination, Bentley expresses care and concern for the Muslim scripture's own script, designating two styles above others, privileging "*Nessich*," or "*Talik*" as "preferable" while relegating all other "writings" as "acceptable." Articulating his subjunctive desire for this "Arabic Manuscript," Bentley's engagement with the Qur'ān shifts from the solitary to the solicitous, no longer inaccurately citing the Muslim creed in his notebooks near the end of the eighteenth century, but sending a neighborly note at the beginning of the nineteenth century, specifying the exact "character" of the "Koran" in this Valentine's Day request for "Asiatic" curiosities. Writing in February 1804, Bentley seems "wishful" rather than confident, submitting his epistolary appeal for Muslim materials in friendship and hopeful faith. However, despite his trust in Elkins' personal "disposition" and past "success," it is unlikely that Bentley could have predicted the fruits that would return from "foreign countries." Although he would have to wait until the following year, Bentley's 1804 "memoranda" ultimately "merited" more than Elkins' "attention" merely, but would instead inspire a series of acquisitions that reach from the Arab world to the Indian subcontinent, with

Bentley's improbable request provoking generous responses that far exceeded its author's "most sincere" expectations. ☼

1805 marked a year of extraordinary exploration and expansion for Jeffersonian America. Opening with news of Jefferson's own reelection, and witnessing his second inauguration in March, the first months of 1805 prompted the president to turn attention from national politics to national perimeters, heralding the success of his most iconic effort of exploration, the Lewis and Clark expedition. Glimpsing Pacific coasts by year's end, the continental crossing sends its first fruits of discovery back East in April, finally reaching Jefferson at the White House by the autumn of 1805.[53] Comprising "four boxes, two large trunks, and three cages," Jefferson unpacked these Lewis and Clark curiosities "in the first days of October 1805," discovering not only fossilized relics, but also live specimens of flora and fauna, hinting at the vast riches, natural and cultural, of the American expanse.[54] During these same first days of October 1805, William Bentley also received a curious package at home in Salem—a package dispatched not from America's Pacific edge, but across America's Atlantic waters. Delivered on October 2, 1805, Bentley's small brown envelope was handed to him by his neighbor, Thomas Bancroft, who had recently returned from Mocha, Yemen. Master of the ship *Commerce*, Bancroft's ship was the seventh to arrive in Salem from Arabia since the beginning of the year, contributing to American's import of "two million pounds of Mocha coffee" in 1805 alone.[55] Carrying home its heavy bags of caffeinated beans for public consumption, Bancroft's *Commerce* carried home also a slender piece of private correspondence, addressed specifically to Bentley. Opening this small brown envelope on October 2, Bentley found the letter reproduced as Figure 2.4—a letter that greets Bentley with the following first words:

الحمد لله
اقرب مودتا للذين امنو الذين قالوا انا نصارا ذالك بان
منهم قسيسين ورهبانا وان هم لا يستكبرون
الله ولي الذين امنو يخرجهم من الظلمات الى النور

[Praised be *Allāh*
Closest in love to those who believe are those who say: "we are Christians." That is because among them are priests and monks and they are not arrogant. *Allāh* is the ally of those who believe. He brings them forth from the shadows into the light.][56]

Silent as to its author's identity and intentions, the initial lines of Bentley's letter loudly signal a surprising certainty: in the autumn of 1805, America's founding Unitarian minister received a letter composed entirely in Arabic—a letter whose first words voice "praise" of "*Allāh*."

*Figure 2.4* 1805 Arabic letter from Sayyid Aḥmad as-Saqqāf to William Bentley (Mss. L452). Image courtesy of the Boston Athenaeum Special Collections.

The irony of this foreign letter's introduction is heighted by its familiar intimacy, Bentley's epistle from the Muslim world initiated with an appeal to Christian "closeness." Despite speaking across religious difference and regional distance, this Arabic letter stresses neighborly nearness; sent from afar, its opening accents confidential companionship, beginning with nothing less than "love," while figuring *Allāh* Himself as humanity's "Ally." Balancing its friendly intimacy is the elegant form of Bentley's letter, its introduction infused with Arabic cadence, featuring elevated rhyme and rhythm—a high style that hints at a most holy source. These first lines of William Bentley's October 1805 letter are, in fact, quotations: quotations from the Qur'ān. After its initial doxology—"Praised be *Allāh*"—this letter's Arabic opening edits and adjoins two distinct verses from Islam's sacred book: the Qur'ān 5:82 ("Closest in love [. . .] are not arrogant"), and the Qur'ān 2:257 ("*Allāh* is the ally [. . .] into the light").[57] Even before acknowledging its human identity—before naming both its author and its addressee—this letter appeals to a divine identity, approaching its Christian correspondent through the words of Muslim revelation. Ironic in its interreligious appeal, these first words are also surprisingly apt, forming a fit reply to Bentley himself. In the winter of 1804, Bentley had ended his request for Middle Eastern materials by "sincerely" soliciting a copy of the Qur'ān; in the fall of 1805, he receives a sensitive Qur'ānic response, opening a letter that not only leads with selected verses from this scripture, but also articulates a reciprocal solicitude.

Received at the very same time as Jefferson's good news from the far West, Bentley's evangelical letter arrives from the Near East, an act that not only bridges continental frontiers but breaches cultural façades. Dispatched from opposing directions, the dual packages opened by Jefferson and Bentley in October 1805 also enjoy opposing legacies in the national memory. Jefferson's receipt of Lewis and Clark curiosities marks a step in America's most iconic exploratory expedition; Bentley's receipt of an Arabic epistle at exactly the same time has remained wholly hidden from scholarly and popular attention. Although a letter of historic significance, signaling an unprecedented act of Islamic outreach to the early Republic's pioneering intellectual, Bentley's Arabic epistle has been entirely lost to American history. Amplifying the irony of this persistent hiddenness is this letter's own opening insistence on ultimate disclosure. Closing its prelude with a revelatory urgency—celebrating God's bringing "forth from the shadows into the light"—Bentley's letter itself has remained shrouded, its own imperative illumination entirely overshadowed, receiving no notice in modern scholarship. This contemporary neglect is even more surprising considering that Bentley's correspondence with the Arab world was a source of his celebrity in the nineteenth century, bolstering his credentials as America's "most learned" man. Capturing the imagination of his contemporaries, Bentley's knowledge of "Oriental languages" and his epistolary exchange with Muslims in particular were even publicized in the pages of newspapers, as I emphasize below. Recognized as marking his exceptional intellect, Bentley's Eastern epistles were also remembered posthumously by his Salem neighbors, including the town's jurist, Joseph E. Sprague, who characterized Bentley three decades after his death as "reputed to have understood twenty-one languages. He corresponded in Arabic, through the shipmasters in his parish, with some of the petty chiefs in Arabia and Eastern Africa."[58] When the initial histories of American Unitarianism began to appear at the close of the nineteenth century, Bentley's Arabic exchanges again received mention, his "Oriental" interests linked with his Unitarian innovations. "Dr. Bentley corresponded with scholars in Europe, as he also did with Arab chiefs in their own tongue," asserts George Willis Cooke in his 1902 *Unitarianism in America*, adding too George Batcher's view that "the two potent influences shaping the ancient Puritanism of Salem into Unitarianism were foreign commerce and contact with the Oriental religions."[59]

This trail of anecdotal evidence testifying to Bentley's Arabic correspondence begins to fade at the beginning of the twentieth century, ultimately falling off altogether, unnoticed in contemporary accounts, remaining beyond the remit, for instance, of the most recent study of Bentley, J. Rixey Ruffin's pioneering *A Paradise of Reason: William Bentley and Enlightenment Christianity in the Early Republic*.[60] The continued neglect of Bentley's correspondence with "petty chiefs in Arabia" is especially remarkable in light of contemporary American concerns. A historic witness of Islamic intersections in the literary life of early America, the letter pictured in Figure 2.4 seems also to possess twenty-first-century resonance, engaging current preoccupations with America's relations with the Muslim world. Ironically, however, it is the very distinctiveness of Bentley's letter that has ensured its disregard; historically exceptional due to its Arabic composition, it is this letter's Arabic that has helped it remain hidden from subsequent historians. Illegible to the majority of Americanists, Bentley's Arabic letters, including the one pictured above, were not collected as part of the primary cache of his correspondence deposited at the AAS, but were instead classed as "Oriental" and ultimately collected in a manuscript box at the Boston Athenaeum ("Mss. L452")—a box housing uncataloged materials in Middle Eastern languages that has long eluded scholarly notice.[61] It is in this box that I first located Bentley's Arabic letters, uncovering in October 2012 the precise pieces of Arabic correspondence that were initially reported by his own contemporaries but were entirely misplaced since Bentley's death.

If first made public by Bentley's admirers in the nineteenth century, it was Bentley himself who first recorded his Eastern correspondence in private, registering these letters from the Arab world in his own diary. As noted above, Bentley first records his receipt of unattributed and unaddressed letters in "Arabic and Persia[n]" from John Gibaut in 1794; however, it would be a full decade later that he received the personally addressed letter pictured in Figure 2.4. Opening his entry for October 2, 1805, in his diary, Bentley notes, "This day a letter from an *Arabian Chief Said Ahmed* by Mr. Bancroft, a Salem Factor in those Seas."[62] Rather than generic "letters" written in various directions, as those from Captain Gibaut in 1794, Bentley receives from Captain Bancroft more than a decade later a single "letter," personally addressed and authored. Specified in his region and rank— "Arabian" and "Chief"—it is the religion of Bentley's correspondent that is also subtly implied in his diary entry. The "Said" prefix that precedes "Ahmed" is an epithet of distinctly religious resonance, indicating the sacred lineage of Bentley's new friend. Raising the stakes of his epistolary receipt from Arabia, the person who writes America's foundational minister in 1805 is a "*Sayyid*"—namely, "a direct descendant of the prophet Muhammad."[63]

This significant identity of Bentley's correspondent is also stressed in his 1805 Arabic letter itself, the name of its writer emphasized immediately after its Qur'ānic opening as quoted above. Transitioning from divine authority to human author, the lines that follow this letter's scriptural preface not only specify the sender's name, however, but also characterize Bentley himself, continuing with these words:

> From Sayyid Aḥmad bin Sayyid ʿAbd al-Qādir as-Saqqāf to the right honor-
> able, the most exemplary and exalted, the learned priest and noble monk,
> our beloved and dear, the minister, Mr. Bentley, the American, may *Allāh*
> protect him, and sustain him, and avail him of good, and guide him. Amen.
> Peace be upon he who follows guidance.[64]

Revealing the full name of his "Arabian Chief," Bentley's "Said Ahmed" self-identifies as "السيد احمد بن السيد عبد القادر السقاف"—"Sayyid Aḥmad bin Sayyid ʿAbd al-Qādir as-Saqqāf"—a personal name enveloped by patriarchal qualifiers, suggesting lineages both immediate and extended. Characterizing himself as a "Sayyid," as well as a son ("bin") of another "Sayyid," Aḥmad's identity is tied to his father, "Sayyid ʿAbd al-Qādir as-Saqqāf." Defined doubly through his descent, Aḥmad's name begins with prophetic antiquity, descending from the Muslim founder as a "Sayyid," and ends with his own present-day family, a son of "as-Saqqāf"—a "highly influential Hijazi family" prominent in Yemen during Aḥmad's day.[65] Rather than the established identity of this letter's Arabian author, it is the acquired identity of its American addressee, however, that may seem most striking in this opening. Designated as "مستر بينتلي"— (*"Mistir Bīntlī"*), "Mr. Bentley"— Aḥmad expresses Bentley's name in transliteration, innovating an Arabic signature for the American minister. Recalling a moment three decades earlier, in which Stiles himself had adopted Arabic script to spell his own name for Rabbi Carigal (see Fig. 1.7), this Arabic autograph in 1805 also seems the mirror opposite. Rather than "Arabicizing" himself at the end of his own letter, "Bentley" is rendered into Arabic at the opening of a letter addressed *to* him. Ezra Stiles had actively projected his own name into Arabic arenas, even while addressing a familiar Jewish acquaintance; Bentley, however, acquires his Arabic autograph passively from correspondence freshly received from the Muslim world. Perhaps more significantly, Bentley's new Arabic name does not stand alone, but is enveloped by epithets, preceded by a host of assonant adjectives that inscribe "*Mistir Bīntlī*" into an Arabian tradition of reciprocal "honor." Denominated as "the learned priest and noble monk," Bentley is contextualized through Arabic composition, offered a stylized portrait framed by rhyming qualifiers of respect—"*al-ʾadīb*"/"*an-najīb*"; "learned"/"noble"—praising Bentley's own position through Arabic poetics.[66] Despite its foreign form, however, Aḥmad's approach is again intimately familiar, prefixing the name "Bentley" with "beloved," echoing the Qurʾān's own opening accent on ever "closer" proximity. Extending this privilege further, Bentley's suffixes merge also region and religion, characterizing him nationally as "the American," while consecrating him Islamically, Aḥmad offering Bentley the following benediction: "may *Allāh* protect him, and sustain him, and avail him of good, and guide him. Amen."

Trailed by both "America" and "*Allāh*," the epithets for Bentley build as Aḥmad transitions to the primary purpose of his letter, citing his addressee's Western reputation as cause for this epistle from the East:

> Know, O Great Minister and Humble Priest, that our beloved Captain Elkins, the American, has reached us at the Port of Mocha, and has described to us thy states, and explained to us thy words, and we have seen thy writing, and thus we conclude that there is no one that exists like you today, and that you are of those who *Allāh* said "among them are priests and monks and they are not arrogant." And so we have responded that we may correspond with you, and so that there may be a line of communication between us and between you, if *Allāh* wishes.[67]

A "minister" portrayed as modest, Bentley is also elevated as extraordinary, Aḥmad relaying a report heard from "Captain Elkins" that "there is no one that exists like you today." Embodiment of American exceptionalism, Bentley is not only nationally superior, but also scripturally implied, translated into a figure from the Qur'ān itself, qualifying as one of the "priests and monks" who are "not arrogant"— phrases original to the Qur'ān 5:82, one of the verses Aḥmad quotes also in his letter's introduction.[68] An "American" who merits mention by *Allāh*, Bentley not only finds Qur'ānic quotations in Aḥmad's letter, but finds himself characterized by the Qur'ān; requesting Islamic scripture from abroad in 1804, Bentley by 1805 is situated within the scripture itself. Framing Bentley through high and sacred phraseology, these Arabic lines also accent the humble and the humane, revealing the personalities and purposes that prompt Aḥmad's letter. Bridging Mocha and Massachusetts, it is "Captain Elkins" who serves as intermediary, with coffee's transatlantic trade supporting Aḥmad's energetic appeal to Bentley in Arabic. It is not the merchandising of caffeine merely that catalyzes this exchange, however, but Bentley's own "memoranda"; testifying that he has read Bentley's "writings," it is the American's written request that engages Aḥmad's attention, catalyzing their prospective correspondence, "if *Allāh* wishes." Exalted in his language, Aḥmad's letter is, moreover, no empty gesture. Not only confirming his receipt of Bentley's "memoranda," Aḥmad demonstrates himself responsive to its specific requests, signaling that he has procured for the American one of his desired Muslim manuscripts. Reportedly purchased "for forty four riyal," Aḥmad brags that he has "bought" for Bentley *Nafā'is al-'Arā'is* (i.e., *Gems of the Brides*), one of the classic texts of Qur'ānic exposition that Bentley had requested in his 1804 "memoranda."[69] Facilitated through the coffee trade, it is not material commerce that Bentley receives from Arabia, but rather a Qur'ānic *Gem*, this jewel of Islamic exegesis marking just one of the two dozen Muslim manuscripts passed to America's pioneering Unitarian beginning in 1805, eventually building to a budding library of Islamic materials that was unparalleled in early America.[70]

At the close of his letter, Aḥmad circles back to the benediction that had con-cluded his letter's introduction, repeating his sacred salute now as a farewell, ending with:

السلام على من اتبع الهدى وخشي عواقب الردى

*as-salām* [i.e., peace] upon he who follows guidance and fears
the results of the ruin

Sending to Salem another "*salām*," Aḥmad's epistle to the "city of peace" ends with a last irenic act, mirroring the verbal root of Bentley's Hebraic hometown in his Arabic valediction (Salem/*salām*).[71] Returning to his letter's opening, Aḥmad's fare-well also reflects an ever "closer" relationship unfolding between him and Bentley provoked by the latter's 1804 "memoranda," with gifts crossing the Atlantic between Salem and Yemen in both directions. In exchange for desired books of Islamic spiri-tuality, Bentley dispatches eastward donations more scientific and stellar, including, for example, his own telescope; amid New England's craze for a comet designated "C/1807 R1," Bentley reports in his *Diary* the excitement triggered by this celestial phenomenon, but also notes on September 29, 1807:[72]

Having sent my Dolland to Sheik Ahmet, I have no telescope. Several are in town, not of large magnifying powers, & I hear of no one who is observ-ing the motions of the Comet which is said from Cambridge to be in Virgo. Many are star gazing.[73]

Reporting on the "Comet" as tracked from nearby "Cambridge," Bentley laments his own inability to "observe," remaining blind to the "motions" in the Massachusetts skies as he has "sent" his telescope to Mocha. Inhabiting the assumed foreground to this American entry is Bentley's Arabian friend; abbreviated in name, while of-fered a new honorific, "Sheik Ahmet" is mentioned in parenthetic passing by 1807, forming the casual condition of Bentley's opening clause. A personal act of dona-tion, Bentley's gift of his own "Dolland" helps to "magnify" a global phenomenon, merging astronomic interests across continents and hemispheres. "Many are star gazing," Bentley muses at his entry's end, a summary statement that is aptly generic and plural, equally applicable to professors in "Cambridge" as well as to "Sheik[s]" in Arabia. In exchange for metaphysical texts clarifying ancient revelations, Bentley sends to Arabia a physical instrument that points toward future progress; however, in this trade of the scientific for the spiritual, a stellar symmetry also emerges. While Aḥmad opens his 1805 letter to Bentley by directing his attention heavenward—foregrounding *Allāh* and His cosmic mercy—Bentley supports his new friend's own gaze to the heavens, offering fresh means of celestial speculation. And while Aḥmad's epistle had traversed the immense Atlantic by offering a message of religious "close-ness," opening with sacred words that collapse spiritual distance, Bentley offers a gift equally capable of transcending cosmic divides, its "large magnifying powers" spanning the space between remote stellar regions. ☼

Intervening between his 1804 appeal to Arabia and the answer received from Arabia in 1805, Bentley opened another religious communique, reflecting not the fruits of foreign commerce, but rather politics in the domestic capital. On November 16, 1804, Bentley learned from Washington that he had been elected "Chaplin to the Congress," with the "majority of the votes of the whole House [. . .] found in favor of the reverend William Bentley."[74] Even while awaiting answer to his Arabian inquiries, Bentley had been nominated the pastor of America's political elite. Inverse in direction and denomination, Bentley's reaction to this U.S. invitation also contrasts with his enthusiasm for Yemeni exchange. "Upon a moment's reflection," Bentley admits, "I found a compliance impracticable, & wrote an answer accordingly," refusing immediately the Congress' call.[75]

The reasons for Bentley's refusal to leave Salem were many; it is, however, his congregation that is most often cited as Bentley's incentive to stay in the city until his death in December 1819. As Joseph G. Waters asserts in his early biography, Bentley supposedly believed that "he had been so long wedded to the East Church, he could not think of asking a divorce from it."[76] Bentley's decision not to abandon his local congregation for national office may be attributable, however, to more international motives as well. Even while "wed" to Salem's "East Church," it would be the Eastern assets available uniquely through Salem that also kept Bentley enamored with the city. Faithful to his ecclesiastic "bride," Bentley's decision to stay in Salem was soon followed by the arrival of desired Arabic manuscripts, including Aḥmad's bequeathed *Gems of the Brides*—this nuptial volume of Qur'ānic exegesis delivered to Bentley soon after he declines to "divorce" his domestic church for congressional honors. Initiating a decade of Muslim manuscript collection, 1805 will witness Bentley's receipt of several such items requested in his 1804 "memoranda," with the first packet of Muslim manuscripts reaching him at the very opening of the year, more than nine months before Aḥmad's October letter. Writing in his Book Accounts, Bentley records the arrival of a "Gift from Capᵗ Henry Elkins" on January 15, 1805; comprising seven "folios" as well as "other Mss.," this massive donation from Arabia would include "a Copy of the *KORAN*" as Bentley notes, isolating the Qur'ān's title in emphatic capitals.[77] Seeming to satisfy his "most sincer[e] wish" to acquire the Islamic scripture, Bentley yet extends his search for Muslim manuscripts as 1805 unfolds, moving beyond materials listed in his initial "memoranda," while also involving other intermediaries. Assembling a support network of Westerners in the Arab world—such as John Pringle, a surgeon for the East India Company—Bentley would ultimately secure more than two dozen Muslim manuscripts, including *ḥadīth* collections and Arabic literary classics, as well as standards of Islamic exegesis, ethics, and jurisprudence.[78] Successes in Arabic acquisitions even led Bentley to expand attention beyond the Arab world, reaching farther East in land and language; securing items from as far away as India, Bentley managed to procure, for instance, exquisite Persian manuscripts, comprising classics of Sufi poetry. A full three years after opening Aḥmad's letter in October 1805, Bentley continued to obtain copies of sacred Islamic writ, recording in his private accounts the following unpublished entry, dated October 18, 1808:

> Oct. 18   Received of Capt T Welman son of Adam from Moka
>     An Arabian MSS. الجز الثلثون M. 26 pages [. . .][79]

Recording his newly received "Arabian MSS," Bentley first offers details of its acquisition, opening his entry with a genealogy, tracing a paternal lineage before either tracing Arabic lines or enumerating manuscript pages. Conveyed from a port now familiar to Bentley—"Moka"—by a Salem friend, Timothy Welman—who is defined as the "son of Adam"—Bentley "receives" a single volume of "26 pages," designated simply as "الجز الثلثون" (i.e., "The Thirtieth Part").[80] A generic title that itself implies a textual genealogy, identifying this "MSS" as a later "part" taken from a larger whole, the book that arrives under Bentley's understated label again carries sacred significance, representing the final section of the Muslim scripture itself: "The Thirtieth Part" of the Qur'ān.[81]

It is Bentley's own antiquarian tendencies that make it possible, even two centuries later, to learn the provenance of his Islamic acquisitions, including the precise days on which Arabic copies of "the *KORAN*" were received by the early Republic's pioneering Unitarian. Despite Bentley's own efforts in documentation, however, his library of Muslim manuscripts, as his letters from the Muslim world, have gone entirely undocumented by modern scholarship. Thomas Jefferson's single copy of the *Koran*—his widely available edition of George Sales' English translation—has inspired multiple scholarly studies and attracted copious public attention; Bentley's Islamic archives, including his authentic Qur'āns in Arabic, have never received critical notice, despite representing the richest collection of Muslim manuscripts assembled in Jeffersonian America.[82] If overlooked by professional academics since his death, Bentley's personal exchanges with the Islamic East ironically did inform, however, his own professional life of Christian ministry in the early nineteenth century. The fall of 1808—which witnessed the latest arrival of the Muslim scripture from "Moka," conveyed by "Capt T Welman"—was the same season in which Bentley was engaged in writing his own "Commentaries on the Scriptures," a scattered two-volume compendium of Bentley's biblical exegesis.[83] In entries penned in 1808 and 1809, Arabic increasingly appears as part of Bentley's interpretations. For example, in parsing the fourth chapter of Galatians—a chapter that features Paul's association of Hagar with the Mosaic covenant on "Mount Sinai"—Bentley concludes his entry by invoking an "illustration of Hagar from the Koran," which he quotes as follows:

> Cap. 2.57 When [Moses] sought water for the people, we spoke to him smite *the rock* (الحجر) *El Hajar,* with thy staff.[84]

Abbreviated and informal, Bentley offers an incomplete English version of a Qur'ānic verse, recounting God's command to Moses as he seeks water for the Israelites—a verse that offers Bentley an etymologic echo of the name "Hagar" in "*El Hajar*"—the "rock" that Moses strikes on Mt. Sinai. An "illustration" that he attributed to prominent exegete J. D. Michaelis, Bentley's exposition of the New Testament leads him to Qur'ānic transcription, this single verse of the Muslim scripture synthesizing complex strands from Galatians 4, weaving together Hagar, Moses, and Mt. Sinai.[85] An act that recalls Bentley's career origins, Arabic is shown to be "exceedingly useful in sacred philology," as predicted by Professor Sewall. However, rather than merely invoke Arabic as a linguistic aid to parse Hebrew roots, it is now Arabic scripture that grounds the American's exegesis. At the same time that an "Arabian MSS." arrives to him across Atlantic waters in 1808, comprising the Qur'ān's "Thirtieth Part," Bentley himself partially quotes the Qur'ān and its "illustration" of "water [. . .] from the rock," manually inscribing its Arabic—"الحجر"—into his own scriptural meditations.

The significance of Islam's substantive intervention in Bentley's private studies is perhaps outweighed, however, by interventions that also emerge in his public sermons during this same time. Supporting his informal biblical interpretations, Eastern languages also infuse Bentley's evangelization, appearing in his notes for Sunday homilies delivered formally to his beloved East Church. Paralleling his detailed diary, Bentley preserved over a thousand pulpit orations, sequentially organized into a dozen discrete volumes, representing "one of the largest extant collections of manuscript sermons of one minister from that period," as Ruffin has recently noted.[86] Exceptional in expanse, Bentley's sermons are entirely unique in expression, incorporating not only expected biblical tongues, but also Arabic terms. In the volume of his sermons that opens in November 1808—the very month after he received "The Thirtieth Part" of the Qur'ān from Mocha—Bentley begins a sermon with "Our feet shall stand within thy gates O Jerusalem," a quotation from Psalm 122:2, which Bentley contextualizes by invoking Arabic cognates, citing "عمود" "عماد" ("'imād, 'umūd") as kindred terms to the Hebrew word for "stand" in this psalmic sentence ("'oməḏōt," "עמדות").[87] Marveling at Arabic parallels, even while instructing his American parishioners, Bentley's regular citations of Middle Eastern precedents will unfold from single terms to entire sentences in the following years. For example, on February 1, 1814, Bentley dedicates his Sunday message to Mark 14:8—"She hath done what she could"—a verse that commends the woman who anoints Jesus' body at Bethany. First quoting Mark 14:8 in both original Greek and traditional Syriac, the second line of Bentley's sermon shifts to Arabic, asserting that this gospel verse's meaning is:

More simply the Arab. فعلته لها كان والذي The best in her power.[88]

Heading this familiar lesson with foreign languages, Bentley's sermon to the East Church at the opening of February 1814 becomes a vehicle for his own east-ward interests, lecturing to his American audience from a page topped with Arabic. Offering exegesis of a verse that exalts "the best" of human efforts, Bentley's bibli-cal selection itself becomes a venue to praise Arabic's superlative "simplicity," this complex Middle Eastern language ironically offering a "more" concise impression of Mark 14:8.

It is not the appeal to Arabic in Bentley's late sermons, however, but rather their Islamic echoes that seem most audacious, citing Muslim precedents even while ex-plaining Christian parables. Reproduced in Figure 2.5 is the opening to a sermon delivered on September 2, 1812, dedicated to expounding Mark 4 and its "Parable of the Sower." Opening again by quoting the Greek of his chosen passage (i.e., Mark 4:14: "the sower soweth the word"), Bentley follows the Bible's original language with another linguistic intervention from the Middle East; however, rather than supply an Arabic version for his biblical citation, Bentley provides a Persian parallel, writing in the second and third lines of his sermon:

> A fondness for this image particularly in Oriental Literature & works lately published. Says the Gulistan of Sadi "Grain groweth not unless it be scat-tered." Seed دانه افشاندن Sprinkled[89]

Sharing a single "image," Bentley mirrors the Gospel in the *Gulistan* (*The Rose Garden*), this medieval poem of Muslim spirituality invoked as context for Mark's parable. Bridging genres of "Literature," it is "Oriental" language that also emerges

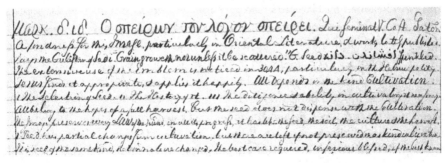

*Figure 2.5* William Bentley, Sermon 3042, Octavo Notebook 35, quoting the "Gulistan" of "Sadi." Image courtesy of the American Antiquarian Society.

as Bentley cites "Sadi," infusing his sermon with a gloss on his *Gulistan* quotation, inscribing original Persian as a means of explaining a biblical parable, and its concern with "Seed دانه افشاندن Sprinkled." A seminal "image" that grafts Islamic canon onto Christian scripture, Bentley's oration betrays his own reading "lately" of "Oriental Literature," and especially of Sufi poetry, a verse tradition celebrating mystic love, both erotic and esoteric.[90] Presenting his own ecclesiastic "bride" with an interreligious bouquet, Bentley offers his Salem congregation a sermon rooted in *The Rose Garden*, cultivating lithe lines of Persian poetry in Unitarian soil. Knowing that "Grain groweth not unless it be scattered," Bentley's dissemination of "Sadi" in 1814 seems to embody the very imperative it expounds, broadcasting to Bentley's New England parishioners his own Islamic engagements, looking toward a future in which such exchanges will bear fruitful increase. ✿

> By the sudden and lamented decease of my uncle the Rev. Wm. Bentley of Salem, it has become my duty to inform you that by his will a considerable part of his Library will become the property of the Institution under your care. You probably have seen in the newspapers the particulars of Dr. Bentley's death. While in familiar conversation with his aged landlady he fell backward & expired almost instantly.[91]

It was Bentley's nephew and namesake—William Bentley Fowle—who received the charge to announce the "sudden and lamented decease" of his uncle on December 29, 1819. Writing on January 6, 1820 to Timothy Alden—founder of the newly formed Allegheny College—the first words of Fowle's letter above reflect his role as both Bentley's closest relative and his legal executor, blending institutional and intimate details. Informing Alden of Bentley's bequest of books to "the Institution under your care"—Allegheny College—Fowle also reveals the domestic atmosphere of Bentley's last moments, his uncle perishing "instantly" while engaged in "familiar conversation with his aged landlady."

Receiving this news of intimate grief, and yet institutional gain, Bentley's death and donation would signal a "sudden" windfall for Alden and his fledgling "College." Long disillusioned by Harvard's disregard for his own accomplishments, Bentley elects to rebuff his alma mater, bequeathing instead his vast "Library" to Allegheny—or, at least, a "considerable part of his Library," as Fowle stipulates equivocally.[92] Gesturing obliquely to books owned by Bentley not included in Allegheny's inheritance, these details omitted from the opening to Fowle's private letter would receive a public airing in local papers the following week, with articles appearing in the *Salem Register* and *New-England Palladium* dedicated to dissecting "Dr. Bentley's Will." Reporting Allegheny's gain, these newspapers also reveal the fate of more rare volumes, informing their readers that it is the American Antiquarian Society in Worcester that will receive Bentley's manuscripts, including

His manuscripts not of his own hand-writing [which] comprise some of the richest Oriental manuscripts sent him by some of the wise men of the East with whom he *corresponded in their own languages.* His Koran and Persian and Chinese manuscripts are [the] richest and most splendid specimens of excellence in the art of writing, in the world.[93]

A postmortem of Bentley's property, it is Islamic prophecy that is itemized in this newspaper account, the "Koran" named as part of the American's corpus. Published in the neighborhood press, this *New-England* account is also global in scope, ending with "the world" itself while claiming Bentley's "specimens" to be superlative, exemplifying "excellence in the art of writing." Inscribed with value, these manuscripts are also environed with italicized vernaculars, Bentley acquiring these treasures while he reportedly *"corresponded"* in Eastern *"languages."* Published just days after Bentley's death, his private trafficking in "Oriental" tongues forms a part of his own obituary, Salem readers mourning their learned Christian minister as they learn more of his Muslim archives and epistolary exchanges. Disclosing the domestic bequest of Bentley's manuscripts, it is their foreign provenance that is also accented in this newspaper account. Although owned by Bentley, his Eastern books are nevertheless "not of his own hand-writing," received remotely from "men" speaking *"in their own languages."* This elusive foreground of Bentley's Muslim materials also forecasts their hybrid and hidden futures, largely escaping public notice and, eventually, Bentley's own original site of bequest. Willed initially to the AAS in Worcester, Bentley's manuscripts will lay dormant there for three decades, rediscovered only midway through the nineteenth century by Yale professor Edward Elbridge Salisbury, who produced a partial index of Bentley's Arabic acquisitions. Publishing his cursory catalog under the generic title "Valuable Arabic Manuscripts, at Worcester, Mass" in an 1851 issue of the *Journal of the American Oriental Society,* Salisbury's three-page article omits all mention of Bentley himself, helping to distance these manuscripts "not of his own hand-writing" even farther from association with Bentley.[94]

The last published notice of Bentley's "valuable" items, Salisbury's article also marked the last witness to their deposit at "Worcester." When I began my own search for Bentley's manuscripts, it became clear that they no longer formed part of the AAS's vast holdings of Bentley materials. After months of search, I finally located Bentley's collection, still uncataloged, at the Peabody Essex Museum's Phillips Library near Salem; transferred quietly to this library sometime in the twentieth century, Bentley's Muslim manuscripts have arrived again to his beloved hometown, their sweeping transatlantic circulation, from Mocha to Massachusetts, ending with a small circuit within the state itself, moving from Salem to Worcester in the nineteenth century, and back again to Salem in the twentieth.[95] Despite their unique transfers across distant spaces and domestic sites, the items now held at the Peabody Essex Museum are remarkably preserved, representing twenty-eight discrete items classed together by

Bentley as his "Oriental Manuscripts." Featuring Bentley's own numbering system, marked on their first or final pages in his "own handwriting," these manuscripts housed as part of the Peabody Essex collection substantiate Aḥmad's claim to have sent specific items, including works such as ath-Thaʿlabī's *Nafāʾis al-ʿArāʾis* (*Gems of the Brides*), procured for Bentley in 1805. However, the Peabody Essex collection also boasts titles not immediately obvious from Bentley's own personal papers, including substantial Arabic volumes that represent classics of Qurʾānic interpretation, such as

> al-Wardī's *The Pearl of Wonders and the Uniqueness of Things Strange*
> (*Kitāb kharīdat al-ʿajāʾib wa-farīdat al-gharāʾib*)
> al-Anṣārī's *The Opening of the Glorious in the exposition of "The Lights of Revelation"*
> (*Fatḥ al-Jalīl bi-Bayān Anwār at-Tanzīl*)
> al-Bayḍawī's *The Lights of Revelation and the Secrets of Interpretation*
> (*Anwār at-Tanzīl wa Asrār at-Taʾwīl*)[96]

Grouped alongside such texts of scriptural exegesis are literary and spiritual standards, including works by al-Hamadānī, Qāḍī ʿIyāḍ, al-Ḥarīrī, and al-Bukhārī, whose canonical *ḥadīth* collection is represented by two weighty volumes, spanning hundreds of pages. And preserved quietly among Bentley's items at the Peabody is also a text that bears the simple title "الجز الثلاثون" ("The Thirtieth Part"), forming a single volume of "26 pages"—the precise volume Bentley had received on October 21, 1808, a beautifully inscribed copy of the final section of the Qurʾān, spanning its chapters 78 through 114.[97]

Enjoying an afterlife, circuitous and covert, Bentley's Muslim books begin a new itinerant life at his December 1819 death, appearing first in the New England press during January 1820, and finally resurfacing nearly two centuries later near his own Salem home. Beginning their fluid travels again just weeks after Bentley's "sudden and lamented decease," his Islamic archives aptly remain in dynamic formation just weeks before his death, with items still arriving from transatlantic passage immediately before the American's own "instant" passing. Less than two months before his demise, Bentley penned an entry in his "Account of Books" (Fig. 2.6), recording yet another acquisition from abroad. Inscribed near the unforeseen summit of his own biography, Bentley's record of this bibliographic arrival also summarizes the diverse strands that reflect his life's Middle Eastern intersections. Again arriving through the agency of another Salem captain and neighbor—"Capt Samuel Briggs"—it is not an Arabic book from Arabia, but rather a Persian book from "Pondicherry" that Bentley here records, receiving a copy of Niẓāmī Ganjavī's *Khusraw va Shīrīn*—a Sufi romance recounting Khosrow's fatal and frustrated quest for the beloved Shīrīn.[98] However, recalling Bentley's initial "memoranda" requesting Arabic scripture, this import of Persian poetry forms not only literary exchange but a linguistic opportunity, prompting Bentley to practice his Middle Eastern literacy by scripting selections from his newly arrived item. Writing out the title of this

*Figure 2.6* William Bentley, Octavo Notebook 55, page 141, recording his receipt of Niẓāmī's "Chosru & Schereen," inscribing its Arabic *basmala* in black ink and the poem's Persian opening in red. Image courtesy of the American Antiquarian Society.

manuscript's initial episode in red—"اغاز داستان خسرو شیرین" (i.e., "The Beginning of the Story of *Khusraw* [and] *Shīrīn*")—Bentley also prefixes to this Persian preface a larger Arabic inscription in black ink. Drawing the doxology that opens this item acquired from India, Bentley writes the *basmala* itself—"بسم الله الرحمن الرحیم" (i.e., "In the name of God, the Merciful the Compassionate")— tracing this Qurʾānic opening in stylized script. Reproducing this multilingual beginning to a Muslim love poem even as his own American life of intellectual labor comes to a close, Bentley's dual inscription embodies the tensions of his prior Islamic investments, spanning a career that leads from idealist undergraduate to mature antiquarian. Writing an Arabic scriptural verse that prefaces verses of a Persian romance, Bentley's last act of Islamic literacy straddles familiar and foreign, transcendent and imminent, offering a sacred introduction to a poem of Sufi passion. Recording this Muslim elegy to tragic love at the end of his own life of bachelorhood, Bentley's final Islamic inscription supplies too a foretaste of unfulfilled genealogies. Inscribing this line in both "Arabic & Persia[n] letters," quoting from a fatal poem of ecstatic love, Bentley expresses his own enduring love for Islamic traditions, even while hinting at its failure to procreate future legacies, his commitment to Muslim traditions remaining as hidden and hindered as the star-crossed romance of *Khusraw* and *Shīrīn*. And yet, in merging his prosaic "accounts" with erotic poetry, Bentley seems also in his last moments to embody the youthful mission received three-and-a-half decades earlier, his relationship with Middle Eastern languages reaching a heartfelt "intimacy" at his untimely end. Mirroring his own sudden death while in "familiar" exchange with his "landlady," Bentley's late Islamic appeals are domestically implied, but interrupted midsentence; planted through years of passionate investment, Bentley's Qur'ānic archives, cultivated until days before his death, are yet covered over by posthumous neglect, leaving "scattered" seeds sowed underground, still yearning for new American "growth."

# 3

# *"Intermingled with Texts of the Koran"*

## Washington Irving's Moorish Renovations

William Bentley's death at the end of 1819 deprived the East Church of its celebrated minister, and Salem of its "learned" genius of "Eastern tongues." At the opening of 1820, however, the city's commerce with the East continued apace, its escalating trade with India and Arabia increasingly situating Salem as "the center of America's multicultural consciousness," in the words of Robert Booth.[1] Trafficking in the same regions where Bentley had traded letters, the next generation of Salemites not only personally sojourned in Arabia, however, but also published accounts of their experiences, selling tales of exotic travel alongside their exotic commodities. For example, Salem's Osgood family—well known to Bentley through the family patriarch, Captain William Osgood—doubly capitalized on their Arabian commerce by publishing *Notes of Travel: Or, Recollections of Majunga, Zanzibar, Muscat, Aden, Mocha, and Other Eastern Ports*, a lively narrative of Arabian sea trade that appeared on Salem shelves in 1854.[2] A fraternal collaboration between two of William Osgood's sons, Joseph Barlow Felt Osgood and John Felt Osgood, *Notes of Travel* is anchored in John's actual experiences in "Eastern ports," but is brought to press by his elder brother, Joseph—a Harvard graduate, who would became mayor of Salem a decade later, elected to lead the city through the tumultuous final months of the Civil War in 1865.[3]

Appearing in Salem precisely a half-century after Bentley had dispatched his "memoranda" to Yemen on Valentine's Day 1804, the Osgoods' 1854 account of foreign adventure covers familiar ground, this text of Eastern "travels" again spanning America and Arabia, Massachusetts and Mocha. International in scope, *Notes of Travel* recalls Bentley too in its informal and intimate style; rather than an objective survey, the Osgoods supply subjective "*recollections*," fashioning a personal memoir from global exploration. And as Bentley fifty years earlier, it is Islamic interests that again infuse this first-person account of the Osgoods, aptly foregrounded even as their narrative arrives at Yemen's principal port city. In the last paragraphs of Chapter 32, Mocha sets the scene for the following vivid description, the Osgoods recounting the last rites and rituals performed for the dead in Arabia's capital of coffee:

> The mode of burial is as follows. The corpse, covered with a white shroud and placed on a bier, is raised upon the shoulders of four men, who, bearing it to the grave, are followed by a crowd of persevering mourners, whose cries summon to the door the occupants of each dwelling along their path, who intermingle their cries of "*Yalla hi l' Allah,*"—God lives always," till the procession has passed. The burial yard reached, the corpse is deposited in the grave on the right side, with the face toward Mecca, covered with a board, and the earth is filled in. The crowd disperses, and the deceased is left till the last day, "when," in the sublime description of the Koran, "the sun shall be shrouded and the stars shall fall from the heavens; when the camels about to foal will be neglected and the wild beasts will herd together through fear; when the waves of the ocean will boil and the souls of the dead be again united to the bodies; when the female infant that has been buried alive will demand, for what crime was I sacrificed?—and the eternal books be laid open; when the heavens shall pass away like a scroll and hell will burn fiercely and the joys of paradise will be made manifest."
>
> Over the grave of those who can afford the expense, a mound of stone and plaster is raised. The bier on which males are borne to the grave is in shape like that still used in the New England villages, the legs being dispensed with. That used for females has a slatted roof. The deceased often leaves a will, in which some fakeer, or schoolmaster, is remembered, on condition that he will read prayers over the grave on Sundays. Such persons as leave children behind to pray for them are superstitiously believed to be happier while waiting in "*Bere al Warma,*"—"The Well of Life," in which all souls are thought to remain till the resurrection, and which is supposed to have been once opened, when pilgrimages were made thereto, and relatives conversed with their dead friends' spirits. The Arabs make no change in their dress on the death of a relative.[4]

It is familial commemoration that concludes this chapter from the Osgoods' own fraternal "*recollections,*" with "the death of a relative" ending this exploration of Muslim memorials for the deceased. Traversing not only life and death, but also East and West, reflections of rural America are glimpsed in Arabia, with the "bier on which males are borne to the grave" in Mocha mirroring the one "still used in the New England villages." This sudden transfer between Arabia and "New England" is accompanied too by sudden transfers between Arabic and English; signaled in italics, splinters of imperfect Arabic survive in this morbid American account, with lively phrases offered in the original, including "*Bere al Warma*" (rendered as "The

Well of Life") and *"Yalla hi l' Allah"* (rendered as "God lives always").[5] It is not fragmentary transliterations, however, but an effusive translation that forms the center of this chapter conclusion. Invoking a "description of the Koran" to clarify what awaits "the deceased," the first paragraph above closes with a lengthy quotation from the Qur'ān's eighty-first chapter, recounting a vivid eschatological vision that balances the "fierce" punishments of "hell" and "the joys of paradise."

Reaching across to a foreign East, and reaching forward to an apocalyptic future, this Qur'ānic quotation from the Osgoods seems to echo a hometown precedent, revealing in print an Islamic interest cultivated previously and privately in Salem by Bentley himself. Expressing his "sincere" request in 1804, sending from Salem his "memoranda" across the seas, Bentley had solicited his own personal "Arabic manuscript of the Koran"; a half century later, "sublime" verses "of the Koran" surface openly in Salem, voiced in a stylized English for a broader New England audience.[6] And yet, even while elevating the Qur'ān's "sublime" speech for public notice, *Notes of Travel* also leaves the source for its Qur'ānic quotation submerged. Describing "the last day" when all "will be made manifest," the rendition cited by the Osgoods itself remains mysterious, this translation from Arabic offering no hint as to its English translator. Lacking all citation, readers of *Notes of Travel* might reasonably ascribe this "sublime" version "from the Koran" to the Osgoods themselves—an ascription that would, however, be incorrect. Instead, "buried" beneath this Qur'ānic borrowing is another, more unexpected, American identity. Although neither acknowledged by the Osgoods nor recognized by later scholarship, this anonymous Qur'ānic quotation originates from perhaps the most recognizable writer in the early nation: Washington Irving.[7]

Acquired quietly by America's first Unitarian minister from Salem in 1804, the Muslim scripture reappears in Salem five decades later, covertly rendered by Irving, America's "first bona fide best-selling author"—a Qur'ānic continuity between two U.S. luminaries whose careers are otherwise contrastive.[8] Embodying the differing possibilities and polarities that define the early Republic, both Bentley and Irving claim the last year of the Revolution as a pivotal opening in their lives. Marking the first year of Bentley's Salem ministry, 1783 marks Irving's first year of life, born not in colonial New England, however, but in cosmopolitan New York, a city inextricably linked to his early authorship. Fashioning a fanciful chronicle of his hometown, Irving's *A History of New-York*, written under the pseudonym "Diedrich Knickerbocker," begins to build his reputation in 1809, launching a career based in aesthetic belles-lettres, rather than academic learning.[9] Unlike Bentley's Enlightenment precision, or his prosaic recordkeeping, Irving will win renown for his romantic tales infused with subtle irony, blending "fact and fiction" in future classics such as his 1819–20 *The Sketch Book of Geoffrey Crayon, Gent.*[10] And while Bentley stays settled at home in Salem, engaging transatlantically only through epistolary exchange, Irving's later career is defined by transatlantic travel, spending his career's most productive years abroad. Leading opposing literary lives, Bentley and

Irving also receive inverse afterlives; while Bentley's fame quickly fades in the years following his 1819 death, resurrected by recent scholars merely, Irving's wide popularity will prove enduring and international, his works remaining freshly modern through endless imitations and adaptations into new media.[11]

Intersecting such contrasts across American generation and genre is a surprising commonality implied by the Osgoods' *Notes of Travel*; it is a shared interest in Islam that ironically bridges William Bentley and Washington Irving, synthesizing these discrete, yet distinctly American, figures. As Bentley before him, Irving's Islamic investments will be deep as well as domestic, extending not only to the literary, but also the linguistic; rather than reading generic Orientalism merely, Irving will foster first-hand engagement with targeted Muslim materials, privately writing and revising Islam's most sacred texts. As suggested by *Notes of Travel*, however, Irving's personal experiments with Islam will also lead to extensive publication, surpassing Bentley by garnering large audiences during Irving's own lifetime. Inspired by his initial sojourn through Spain, extending from 1826 to 1829, Irving's infatuation with Iberia's Islamic past will catalyze a unique period of creativity, giving rise to works such as *Chronicle of the Conquest of Granada* (1829) and *The Alhambra* (1832).[12] It will not be Moorish Romances merely, however, but a Muslim biography that is drafted during Irving's formative years of travel. Initiated in the midst of his three years in Spain, Irving will begin to sketch the life of Islam's own Prophet, finally published more than two decades later as the 1850 *Mahomet and his Successors*—an Islamic history that features Irving's own idiomatic renditions from the Qur'ān, including the translation of Chapter 81 quoted above, subsequently borrowed by the Osgood brothers, anonymously included in their *Notes of Travel* just four years later.[13]

Testifying to the influence of Irving's Islamic efforts, *Notes of Travel* ironically excises Irving himself, sustaining his words yet suppressing his identity. Recruiting Irving's "sublime" rendition to contextualize Muslim memorials that follow the "death of a relative," the Osgoods aptly situate Irving between family commemoration and casualty, their quotation of his Qur'ānic translation serving both to continue and to cut his own lineage of Islamic adaptation. The present chapter will account for the unlikelihood of uncovering such anonymous Qur'ānic quotations to be original to the "original Knickerbocker" himself. Prompting Irving's own "books" to "be laid open," I excavate fresh material evidence revealing the mechanics of Irving's personal experiments with Muslim sources. However, this chapter also suggests how the Osgoods' ambivalent memorial to Irving is entirely apt, reflecting the familial and the fatal contexts of his own Eastern efforts. Resurrected in the Osgoods' *Recollections*, yet bereaved of their authorial identity, Irving's Islamic adaptations are perpetually haunted by anxieties of attribution, arising from his own informal "notes" that are inscribed amid fraternal loss and forgotten legacies.[14] ☼

"You can read Arabic," said he, "suppose we go together to the tower and try the effect of the charm; if it fails we are no worse off than before, but if it succeeds we will share equally all the treasure we may discover."

"Legend of the Moor's Legacy," *The Alhambra* (1832)

This petition marks the crux of the "Legend of the Moor's Legacy"—a short story featured in the most successful product arising from Irving's travels through Muslim Spain: his 1832 *The Alhambra*.[15] Grappling with cultural dispossession and magical inheritance, Irving's "Legend" recounts a quest for lost "treasure" in Granada, left "hidden" by the city's former Muslim inhabitants, swept away by the *Reconquista*. As suggested by his protagonist's plea, however, Irving's tale is distinguished by a distinctly linguistic excavation, Granada's buried loot recoverable only through correctly pronouncing a "charm"—a charm written in "Arabic." Establishing Arabic literacy as key to its valuable "legacy," Irving sustains his tale's suspense with unexpected exchange and experiment, proposing a tentative partnership between Christian and "Moslem" as they seek to plunder their city's past riches. "You can read Arabic," the former says to the latter, suggesting that they "go together" to "try the effect of the charm," with hopes to "share equally all the treasure we may discover."[16]

This brief passage from the "Moor's Legacy," linking cultural literacy and collaborative discovery, mirrors the broader collection in which it is buried: Irving's 1832 *Alhambra*. A partial memoir of his 1829 residence at Granada's historic palace, Irving's *Alhambra* embodies its domestic namesake, negotiating opposing nations, religions, and languages. The sovereign seat of Muslim Spain, until falling to Ferdinand and Isabella in 1492, the Alhambra witnessed also the beginnings of American exploration, with Columbus securing support for his New World voyages at the palace.[17] The very name of both building and book represents an etymologic pivot from East to West; deriving originally from the Arabic term *al-ḥamra'* ("the red," the color of the palace's clay walls), the Alhambra acquires an inset "b" from later Spanish speakers.[18] This hybrid of Arabic origins and European additions implied in the very title of Irving's own textual *Alhambra* receives explicit treatment as he addresses the layered architecture of the "Alhambra" itself, his second chapter concluding its nostalgic meditation "Moslem Dominion in Spain" with this poignant inquiry:

Where are they [i.e., "the Morisco-Spaniards"]? Ask the shores of Barbary and its desert places. The exiled remnant of their once powerful empire disappeared among the barbarians of Africa, and ceased to be a nation. They have not even left a distinct name behind them, though for nearly eight centuries they were a distinct people. The home of their adoption, and of their occupation for ages refuses to acknowledge them except as invaders and usurpers. A few broken monuments are all that remain to bear witness to their power and dominion, as solitary rocks left far in the interior bear testimony to the extent of some vast inundation. Such is the Alhambra. A Moslem pile in the midst of a Christian land; an Oriental palace amidst the Gothic edifices of the West; an elegant memento of a brave, intelligent, and graceful people, who conquered, ruled, and passed away.[19]

Offering this "elegant" elegy on Muslim "exile," the Alhambra palace becomes for Irving a "broken" emblem to a "home[land]" irretrievably lost, and a cultural achievement with weak ascription. Refusing to "acknowledge them," the original Arabic authors of Andalucía fail "even" to leave "a distinct name behind," the Alhambra serving as a solitary "memento" of a "people" who "passed away." A "testimony" to a heritage "left far in the interior," the ruins of Moorish history are embodied by this derelict "Moslem pile," standing as a misplaced Eastern "monument," which is stranded "amidst the Gothic edifices of the West."

The national nostalgia, and anxieties of authorial attribution, suggested in this sketch of the Alhambra reflect equally Irving's own *Alhambra*—a text fashioned during Irving's long exile from American "shores," and published with his own authorial identity suppressed, its U.S. cover page dispensing with Irving's name, ambiguously claiming only "The Author of the Sketch Book" as its creator.[20] Hearkening back to his own layered career, recalling his prior embrace of ironic pseudonyms, such deferral of authorial identity also hints at the *Alhambra*'s own complex authorship, arising from collaboration and cultural embezzlement. Leaving a "testimony" to his compositional process in his personal diaries, the jottings "left far in the interior" of Irving's own journals suggest the extent to which his *Alhambra* relies on stories related to him by the Alhambra's actual inhabitants. Arriving in Granada on March 9, 1828, and receiving his first glimpse of the palace, Irving also meets a palace resident—"Matteo Ximenes"—whose vivid storytelling is hurriedly transcribed by Irving in the following diary entry:

> Matteo Ximenes Says that there was much treasure buried by the Moors. Thinking that they would return & not having much time to carry off their things (doubtless at time of banishment)—one Moor made <an enchanted> ↑a↓ cave put all his treasure there and left an enchanted Moor to guard it—An hundred years passed away—The inhabitants of the house began to see apparitions—hear clinking of chains—Consult <friend> a Moor turned christian—He has a book in arabic characters—tells the way to recover enchanted treasure—they must read prayers ↑at midnight↓[21]

Drawing a dizzying spiral of transmission, this entry in Irving's diary finds him excavating raw material for his *Alhambra*'s "Legend of the Moor's Legacy" from the Alhambra itself, uncovering this fictional "treasure" within the walls of the factual building. Centered on "a book in arabic characters," Irving will himself "carry off" this specific "enchanted" tale, polishing its extemporaneous and elliptical expressions, working it into his own "book" entitled with "arabic characters"—his *Alhambra*. Mirroring the Moorish tale received from his new "friend," Irving receives this textual "treasure" through social exchange, even as he listens to hauntings from the Andalucían past, with the "clinking chains" of narrative transmission heard via one of the current "inhabitants of the house," Matteo Ximenes himself.[22]

A ghostly foreground to Irving's published "legend," merging Arabic literacy and collaborative legacies, this diary entry from the spring of 1828 also eerily anticipates a private moment that occurs later in the same season; after first glimpsing Granada in March, Irving returns to his temporary home in Seville, where he records the diary entry below on May 29, 1828, summarizing his day as follows:

> Correct Columb. At the Cathedral Library—Evg. at home Tertullia—Mr
> Hall arrives—moonlight walk to the Fabrica
> Mr John Nalder Hall.[23]

Abbreviated and fragmentary, Irving's entry unfolds from solitude to sociality, first writing his biography of "Columb[us]," before hosting a "Tertulia" party at "home." It is cozy companionship, however, that concludes Irving's day, taking a "moonlight walk" after the sudden "arrival" of "Mr Hall," a new acquaintance whose name Irving memorializes in full as the final words in his entry. This moonlit closeness of Irving's meeting with "Mr John Nalder Hall" also forecasts the relationship that rapidly develops between the two through the summer of 1828—a relationship marked by household companionship and haunting intimacy. A "consumptive young Englishman," Hall "arrives" in Spain to seek remedy from his pulmonary condition; meeting Irving in May, the two soon decide to share quarters, renting a "cottage in the vicinity of Seville" by the beginning of July, and then moving to the Port of Saint Mary in September, seeking the temperate climate offered by the Bay of Cádiz.[24] It is not therapy alone, but also philology, that Hall seeks in Spain, however, pursuing his aspirations to become "an Arabist" while rooming with Irving; as Stanley Williams notes, Hall will dedicate himself to "recondite Arabic and Persian studies" through the summer of 1828, devoting himself to Islamic literacy even while lodging as Irving's intimate companion.[25]

Almost as suddenly as Hall "arrives" in Irving's life, however, he departs, succumbing to his disease by December 1828. Reporting his recent bereavement to his boyhood friend, Henry Brevoort, Irving writes from Seville on December 20, memorializing Hall and recalling his recent death:

> We lived like hermits, but very pleasantly. He was intelligent, well bred
> and accomplished. His malady confined him almost entirely in the house.
> Some times he rode out a little and I accompanied him either on horse-
> back or afoot—but the most of our time was passed at home, I writing, he

drawing and studying Persian and Arabic. I left him at Port S'Mary's and came up here to provide a retreat for him for the winter but in the interval he died. Riding out one day his horse became restive and reared and fell with him. The shock brought on an access of his complaint and hurried him off in the course of a couple of days. I cannot tell you my dear Brevoort how mournful an event this has been to me. It is a long while since I have lived in such domestic intimacy with anyone but my brother.[26]

Accenting their cloistered "intimacy," it is alliterative terms such as "hermits," "house," and "home" that Irving invokes in describing his "domestic" closeness with Hall. Opening this memorial to his friend, Irving emphasizes their acts of mutual accompaniment, depicting their tandem efforts, which are analogous, yet inverse. While Hall "rode out a little," Irving escorted him "on horseback or afoot." And while Irving was "writing," Hall would also sit with him, "drawing and studying Persian and Arabic." Synthesizing American literature and Middle Eastern literacy in the same physical space, Irving's fraternal companion is a reader of foreign languages, spending his last months "studying" Islamic tongues. Even while he authors his "Moslem" histories, elegizing "a brave, intelligent, and graceful people" who "passed away" from Spain, Irving shares a table with his own "intelligent" friend, who studies Islamicate languages in the final days before he himself passes away.

More like a "brother" than any before him, Hall is memorialized by Irving in the emphatic past, his death representing an "event" that "has been to me" inexpressibly "mournful." However, Hall's presence will also echo imperfectly and posthumously into Irving's later life; for instance, in the weeks following Hall's death, Irving undertakes to settle his "Arabist" friend's accounts, writing to Hall's "cousin and heir," detailing not only "the particulars of his death," but also his "extremely private" funeral.[27] However, it was not as Hall's earthly executor, but as his spiritual communicant, that Irving's connection would continue most memorably with his friend; as recounted first by Irving's nephew, Pierre, Irving himself entered into an occult compact with Hall before his untimely death, recalling that

during a talk about ghosts, he [Hall] turned suddenly towards me [Irving], and asked me somewhat abruptly whether I would be willing to receive a visit from him after death, if he should go before me, as he was so likely to do? "Why, Hall," I replied, "you are such a good fellow, we have lived so amicably together, I don't know why I should fear to welcome your apparition, if you able to come." "Nay," said Hall, "I am serious, and I wish you to say you will consent, if the thing is practicable." "Well, then" said I, "I am serious too, and I will." "Then," said Hall, "it is a compact; and, Irving, if I can solve the mystery for you, I engage to do it."

Pierre concludes his report of his uncle's recollections, adding:

> After his death, the horse of Hall was brought to [Irving] at Seville, and one
> evening he rode him to their old retreat, at Casa Cera, near that city. Here,
> solemnized by the scene and its associations, and recalling their strange
> compact, [Irving] breathed an appeal for the promised presence of his de-
> parted friend. "But," said he, "he did not come, and though I have made
> similar invocations before and since, they were never answered;" adding
> half playfully, half mournfully: "the ghosts have never been kind to me."[28]

Characteristic of Irving's own romantic writings, his oral recollections are infused with endearing humor, his eternal "compact" with Hall made less weighty
by touches of irony. Perhaps most conspicuous, however, are the larger ironies of
Irving's contract with his "Arabist" friend, seeking to commune in Spain with this
deceased student of Islamicate languages. Situating Irving on the threshold between
life and death, this moment recalls Irving's own afterlife receptions in texts such as
the Osgoods' *Notes of Travel*—a travelogue that will rely on Irving even as it describes mourners who seek to "converse with their dead friends' spirits." More immediately, Irving's recollected attempt to speak with his "Arabist" friend beyond the
grave is closely contemporaneous with Irving's own authorship of "The Legend of
the Moor's Legacy"—a tale in which Arabic serves as the vehicle between the here
and the hereafter, with a Moorish charm holding the key for the dead to speak again.
Typical of Irving, however, is the inversions and interruptions of familial lineage
enacted here, with communications between Irving and Hall "compacted," yet ultimately cut. While the "Legend of the Moor's Legacy" owes its origins to "inhabitants of the house" who "see apparitions," Irving's own companion in his Moorish sojourn remains invisible after death, leaving the American entirely bereft, even after
repeated "invocations." And yet, despite such disappointments following the death
of his "Arabist" friend, Irving will nevertheless hold on tight to "a book in arabic
characters" as his own life unfolds, retaining a material "treasure" of Arabic study
that has long laid buried amid the "Gothic edifices" of his American fictions. ✿

Losing his former housemate in the winter of 1828, Irving gained a new home by
the spring of 1829; however, unlike the humble cottage shared with Hall in 1828,
it was Granada's historic fortress that accommodated Irving in 1829, residing "in
the fabled Alhambra palace for three brief months in 1829," from "May 12 through
the first days of August," as noted by Rolena Adorno.[29] Contrastive in size and significance, a consistency between Irving's diverse households emerges in their linguistic character; bereaved of his "domestic intimacy" with his "Arabist" friend,
Irving's next home helps him to retain close companionship with Arabic, discovering the very "walls of the Alhambra" to be "covered" with inscriptions, as described

in Chapter 3 of the *Alhambra* itself, in which Irving surveys the rooms of his new residence:

> On one side of the court, a portal, richly adorned, opens into a lofty hall, paved with white marble, and called the Hall of the Two Sisters. A cupola, or lantern, admits a tempered light from above, and a free circulation of air. The lower part of the walls is encrusted with beautiful Moorish tiles, on some of which are emblazoned the escutcheons of the Moorish monarchs: the upper part is faced with the fine stucco-work invented at Damascus, consisting of large plates, cast in moulds, and artfully joined, so as to have the appearance of having been laboriously sculptured by the hand into light relievos and fanciful arabesques, intermingled with text of the Koran, and poetical inscriptions in Arabian and Cufic characters.[30]

Mourning the winter death of John Nalder Hall, elegizing their days "passed at home" where Hall spent days "drawing and studying Persian and Arabic," Irving begins a new season housed in the Alhambra with its own "Hall of the Two Sisters"—a "Hall" overdrawn with Middle Eastern languages. No longer living with an "Arabist" like "my brother," Irving now resides amid Arabic sorority, the sibling walls of the "Two Sisters" inscribed with "Arabian and Cufic characters." Recalling his own *Alhambra*'s "Legend of the Moor's Legacy," Irving discovers the Alhambra's actual "legacies" to be encased in "fanciful arabesques," the palace's treasured past opened by the key of Middle Eastern literacy, fully accessible only if "You can read Arabic." Obliquely mirroring Irving's own writings, the actual Alhambra stands too as a literary pastiche, "intermingling" sources and styles, its artistry spanning individuals and eras; uncertain as to authorship, the Alhambra's inscriptions are themselves anonymous, passively described merely as "laboriously sculptured by the hand." Wondering at these walls of etched multiplicity and mystery, a single weighty name does come into relief among these "light relievos," however. Perceptible alongside "poetical inscriptions" is Muslim prophecy, Irving raising the "text of the Koran" from among these "fanciful arabesques."

Anonymously inscribed, Irving's discovery of Qur'ānic Arabic buried within the Alhambra's interior mirrors the sole material witness to Irving's own interior study of "Arabian" script. Among Irving's journals now housed at the New York Public Library is a single notebook that stands apart, distinguished not for its literary content, but for its linguistic "characters"—a notebook dedicated entirely to the "studying" of Arabic.[31] Filling dozens of pages with Middle Eastern inscriptions, Irving's "Arabic Notebook" parses the rudiments of alphabet and grammar, featuring Semitic script that is "laboriously sculptured by the hand." However, recalling the Alhambra's own Arabic miscellany, Irving's "Arabic Notebook" also lacks all clear attribution, offering no certain signature, confessing neither when nor where it was inscribed. An "elegant memento" to Irving's interests in Arabic, his notebook itself has "not even left a distinct name behind," embodying a philological legacy that evades precise memory. The problem of identifying this notebook's provenance has been exacerbated by years of critical neglect; although the sole "testimony" to Irving's Arabic study, his notebook has largely "disappeared" from contemporary scholarship, its foreign language inhibiting analysis by scholars of Irving's more familiar writings. However, like Bentley's own Middle Eastern studies, Irving's "Arabic Notebook" was first recognized by his earliest readers, who generally assumed this journal to represent Irving's handiwork. Pioneer of Irving biography George Hellman takes especial interest in the "Arabic Notebook" in his 1925 *Washington Irving, Esquire*, understanding the journal to evidence Irving's own practicing of Arabic script.[32] Later Irving scholarship would be less certain as to the notebook's authorship, however; writing in the 1970s, Layla al-Farsi suggested that this notebook possibly represents the work of Irving's brother, Peter.[33] Even earlier, E. N. Feltskog and Henry Pochmann, leading authorities on Irving's manuscripts, too voiced doubts; unable to say whether the journal was written by Irving or not, the "Historical Note" included as appendix to Feltskog and Pochmann's critical edition of *Mahomet* characterizes Irving's "Arabic Notebook" as "not certainly in his hand," concluding by speculating that this notebook was perhaps inherited from none other than Irving's friend, John Nalder Hall.[34] Again situating Arabic in Irving's life with touches of the fraternal and the fatal, the mystery of his notebook's complex attribution and compound authorship is also deepened by a fact largely overlooked by previous theorists: namely, Irving's "Arabic Notebook" represents not a single act of writing, but multiple writings and rewritings. Beneath its bold ink letters, the "Notebook" also features faint pencil emendations, parsing Arabic inscriptions both in English and in Spanish, with these distinct instruments and idioms "artfully joined" in this journal's "intermingled" pages.

The complex lineage and compromised legacies of Irving's "Arabic Notebook" are signaled from its outset, confronting readers on its very cover; offering the sole testimony to its provenance, the notebook's title, inscribed on its end-leaf, reads as follows:

Memoranda Book of
Washington Irving of
Sunnyside
given to me by Mrs Pierre M. Irving
January 1885

Offering no hint of the Arabic philology within, this English cover does trace conduits of an American family; indexing a series of bequests, the Notebook is "given" to an anonymous "me" by "Mrs Pierre Irving"—Helen Dodge Irving, the wife of Irving's executor and nephew.[35] Passing through multiple hands before arriving in the New York Public Library archives, this cover situates Irving not only in a familial lineage, but also in "domestic intimacy," identifying the author with his iconic home on the Hudson—"Sunnyside," the historic "Irving homestead."[36] Implied in a series of genitives, Irving's Arabic Notebook introduces itself as the "Memoranda Book *of* Washington Irving *of* Sunnyside," linking this journal of Middle Eastern literacy in a chain that stretches from remembrance to residence. While Irving memorializes the "time" he "passed at home" with Hall "studying Persian and Arabic," Irving's own Arabic studies are written in a book of "memoranda" that is equally domestic, with his Middle Eastern studies attributed to the author "of Sunnyside."

The familial contexts implied on the cover of the "Memoranda Book" find oblique complement in the opening text of Irving's notebook, which begins by situating Arabic in broader families of Semitic language. In adjacent columns, the alphabets of Arabic, Hebrew, and Syriac are compared in the notebooks' initial pages, the scripts of these three Middle Eastern siblings affiliated in parallel lines.[37] Recalling both Stiles and Bentley by appealing to biblical languages as an entrée to Arabic, Irving's "memoranda" soon turn from alphabets to "accents," shifting from mere script to Arabic sounds—a shift witnessed on the notebook's page 29 (Fig. 3.1).

Conspicuous first on page 29 is the messy practicality of Irving's "Memoranda Book," its scattered pages marked with smudges, featuring Arabic that is imperfectly inscribed, the language's fluid lines interrupted by hesitant spaces. Evidencing "broken monuments" to the notebook's rudimentary Arabic study, this page's tentative style nevertheless offers targeted specifics, parsing the minute details of syllabic length. However, even while emphasizing orality, it is an authorial interest that emerges in this treatment of "Accents," the center of this page occupied by examples of Arabic pronunciation that ironically imply the writing process:

| | | |
|---|---|---|
| كاتب | *kátibon* | (writing) |
| كتاب | *kitábon* | book |
| مكتوب | *mektúbon* | written |
| رحيم | *rahímon* | compassionate<br>misericordioso |

Derived from the same Arabic root—"كتب" (*k-t-b*) "to write"—this page's first "syllabic" samples aptly parallel Irving's own profession as a "writer," suggesting a concern with literary inscription itself, even while offering rules for intonation. It is the fourth and final word offered above, however, that is perhaps most reflective of Irving's Arabic interests; moving from human composition to divine clemency, this list concludes with "*rahīm*" ("رحيم")—a noun that means "mercy," but that also qualifies as the most common of Qur'ānic names for God, appearing for instance in the *basmala* itself, which appeals to *Allāh* as "*ar-rahīm*" ("The Merciful").[38]

Starting with three Arabic terms that suggest the "scripted," it is the Arabic scripture that seems implied in this list's last word. Distinguished for its divine flavor, "*rahīm*" is distinct too in its double definition, this single term meriting two

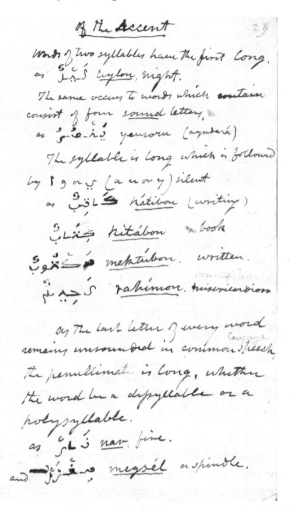

*Figure 3.1* Washington Irving, "Arabic Notebook," page 29, "Of the Accent." Image courtesy of the Manuscripts and Archives Division, The New York Public Library, Astor, Lenox and Tilden Foundations.

equivalents. Parsed in pen as the Spanish *"misericordioso," "raḥīm"* is also explained in English superscript, with "compassionate" written weakly in pencil. Recalling the Iberian origins of Irving's Middle Eastern interests, this synthesis of Arabic, Spanish, and English also testifies to his notebook's staggered authorship, its multilingualism in pencil and pen gesturing to multiple stages of inscription. This triangulation of religious subtexts and rendered superscripts is even more complexly drawn a few pages later, however, as suggested by Figure 3.2, which reproduces pages 34 and 35 of Irving's notebook.

Dedicated to describing the Arabic *"techdid"* (i.e., the *tashdīd*, a diacritic mark whose "office is to double" a letter's pronunciation), these dual pages themselves are double in inscription, featuring again composition in pen as well as penciled

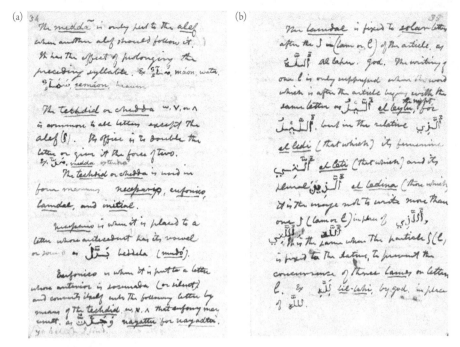

*Figure 3.2* Washington Irving, "Arabic Notebook," pages 34 and 35, on the Arabic "techdid," exemplified by "وجدت (*yo hallé*) I find" at the bottom of page 34 and "لله *lil-lahi*, by god" on page 35. Image courtesy of the Manuscripts and Archives Division, The New York Public Library, Astor, Lenox and Tilden Foundations.

corrections and qualifications.[39] Confronting together distinct voices and vernaculars, these facing pages align Arabic with English, but also again include significant Spanish interventions, engaging the very languages and lands that shape Irving's own Andalucían sojourn, and especially his encounter with the Alhambra. A microcosm of cultural accretion, Irving's notebook triangulates the same three traditions he finds implied in the Alhambra, reflecting not only its balance between Arabia and Europe, but also its launch of American exploration, serving as the historic site from which Columbus secures royal support in 1492. And it is "discovery" itself that receives accent at the very middle of this American notebook's discussion of the Arabic "*techdid.*" At the bottom of page 34, the last line of this left-hand page invokes the term "*wajattu*" as an example of the diacritic marker, the *techdid* doubling this term's "t." Inscribed as "وجدت," this Arabic word is then parsed underneath in tentative pencil, defined by a phrase in both Spanish and English that is barely visible as the final words of page 34, reading "(*yo hallé*) I find." Aptly refracting its own obscure place on the page, this first-person statement of spontaneous discovery unfolds from Arabic, to Spanish, and finally to English ("وجدت" to "*yo hallé*" to "I find" [or, "I found"]), recreating a cultural matrix that mirrors the

Alhambra's pivot from Middle East to far West, as well as Irving's own personal American approach to Andalucía's complex history and heritage.

A verb defined in its person, but lacking a definitive object, the "finding" at the bottom of page 34 contrasts with the less ephemeral, and more eternal, content enshrined at the top of page 35. It is not subjective discovery, but the divine subject that emerges in the notebook's next examples, however, with "*Allāh*" Himself invoked from the top to the bottom of the right-hand page. The very last words of this page recognize that the common Arabic preposition "*l*"—"ﻝ," signifying "of," "to," "for"—becomes absorbed into "*Allāh*" when prefixing this divine name, asserting that if the "letter *l*" is added, God's name does not appear as

ﻟﻠﻪ

[i.e., *lilallāhi*]

but rather reads as

"ﻟﻠﻪ *lil-lahi*, by god"

Studying this minor idiom involving a single Arabic letter, it is the Almighty that is ironically invoked, the ultimate Arabic name for God illustrating an irregular item of orthography. Linking spelling conventions with Islam's supreme name, this uncanny example also gestures, however, to an issue essential to the entirety of Irving's notebook, approaching "*Allāh*" through a preposition that implies attribution and ascription. Concluding these confronting pages with "ﻟﻠﻪ *lil-lahi*"— "to God," or "of God"—Irving's notebook muses on *Allāh's* multivalent "possession," even as the provenance of this American notebook itself remains uncertain. Lacking human autograph, yet accenting divine attribution, Irving's notebook begins on its cover with genitives anonymously inscribed—"The Memoranda Book *of* Washington Irving *of* Sunnyside"—but includes within its pages an integral testament to God's possession, highlighting a genitive particle that itself melts into the deity's Arabic name.[40] ☼

> *Ashaed la Allahe ill Allah! Ashaed la Allahe ill Allah! Ashaed Mohammed rasul Allah!*[41]
>
> [I testify that there is no god but Allāh! I testify that there is no god but Allāh! I testify that Muḥammad is the messenger of Allāh!]

While Irving's "Arabic Notebook" is housed at the Manuscripts and Archives Division of the New York Public Library, it is the library's Berg Collection that holds the bulk of Irving's personal papers, including handwritten notes for his most celebrated works, such as *The Sketch Book of Geoffrey Crayon, Gent.* Marking the private origins of his prominent publications, such seminal Irving manuscripts also share shelves with a diminutive notebook that is also inscribed in his hand, but that has never before appeared in print. A humble holograph, five inches high with red binding, it is this Berg Collection notebook that features on its sixty-seventh page the words quoted above—an attempted transliteration of the Arabic *shahāda*, Islam's core confession of faith.[42]

Transcribed from the third edition of Joseph Pitts' *A Faithful Account of the Religion and Manners of the Mahometans* (1731), Irving copies this version of the Arabic creed as vocalized in Latin characters, recording an earlier Western transliteration of this essential Muslim testimony. Although apprehending Arabic through its sounds, not its script, Irving here recalls his "Arabic Notebook" as he again turns attention to *Allāh*; however, rather than grammatical niceties, it is the grounds for belief that now concerns Irving's copied Arabic, invoking "Allah" theologically rather than philologically.[43] It is not this quotation's beginning, however, but its end that reflects the unfolding of Irving's interests, shifting from "Allah" to "the messenger of Allah." Culminating with the Prophet "Mohammad," these unpublished lines of imperfect Arabic forecast a primary interest of Irving's evolving career, his own literary life nearing culmination with a prophetic biography that spans two volumes and more than eight hundred pages: *Mahomet and his Successors*, published in 1850.[44]

One of the final major works published by America's "first major writer," *Mahomet* occupies a unique place among Irving's most mature writings, this Islamic biography appearing even as Irving enters his last decade of life.[45] However, as befits its prophetic subject, *Mahomet* was long foretold in Irving's own biography, its late publication hiding a protracted revisionary process that reaches back to Irving's earliest literary efforts in Andalucía. The final term of his copied *shahāda*, and one of the final texts in Irving's career, "Mohammad" holds a surprising precedent in Irving's writings, anticipating all of his historical works inspired by Moorish Spain. Years before publishing his 1829 *Chronicle of the Conquest of Granada* and his 1832 *Alhambra*, Irving had begun to pen his life of the Prophet, already "writing at Mahomet" by the middle of November 1827, as Irving records in his diary.[46] Originally entitled *The Legendary Life of Mahomet*, Irving would complete nearly half of *Mahomet's* projected seventy chapters by 1831, sending them to his editor, John Murray, who ultimately declined to move forward with publication, much to Irving's frustration.[47] Deferred in 1831, Irving's drafted *Mahomet* survives through the next twenty years, this suspended project crossing not only multiple decades, but also multiple continents; conceived in Spain in the late 1820s, and pursued in England in the early 1830s, Irving will bring his *Mahomet* manuscript to America when he finally arrives home in 1832. However, it is not until Irving returns to Spain a decade later, becoming America's "Envoy Extraordinary and Minister Plenipotentiary" in 1842, that he would begin "revising the manuscript" once again, as he himself notes.[48] Enveloping these circular movements that span the Atlantic, returning to mind even as Irving returns to Spain, the Muslim Prophet surfaces not only in Irving's publication plans, however, but also in his personal letters, aptly invoked as

Irving writes home from Spain regarding an act of moving house in America. Writing to his niece, Sarah Storrow, from Madrid on March 12, 1845, Irving acknowledges her news that "the family" has relinquished its "old residence" in New York, quipping:

> I thank you for the extract from the pleasant little letter from dear little Abby. The removal of the family from the old residence in Chamber Street will be equal to the flight of Mahomet from Mecca. I think your aunt ought thence forward to date every thing, as the Mahometans do, such and such a year of the *Hegira*.[49]

A domestic mirror reflecting across cultures and continents, Irving appeals to Islamic history while marking this intimate moment, invoking the "flight of Mahomet" from Arabian antiquity to contextualize an American family's contemporary "removal." Ironically elevating the slight to the sacred, Irving ludicrously "equates" personal history with the prophetic, aligning the relinquishing of an "old residence in Chamber Street" with Muḥammad's escape from his enemies. Hidden behind Irving's humor, however, is the ironically self-reflective nature of his analogy, hinting at his own cycles of Islamic "removals." Himself a perpetual exile, Irving speaks westward from Spain to America even while reaching to the "Orient" for a precedent; pivoting East and West from the Iberian Peninsula, Irving mediates between America and Arabia, speaking from his temporary home in Madrid, which stands as a medial space between lost homes in Manhattan and Mecca. Gesturing to the impermanence of place—experienced by both himself and by the Prophet—it is not space, however, but time that concludes Irving's quote, proposing a new calendar anchored in homes abandoned. Facetiously suggesting that the extended family follow the precedent of "Mahometans" by adopting a personal system of "*Hegira*" dating, Irving aptly invokes "Mahomet" to reframe American time, even as he belatedly re-begins his own *Mahomet*—a work whose incremental revision through more than two decades resists any simple ascription to "such and such a year."

Reflecting on American "removal" from Madrid in 1845, Irving anticipates his own American return, arriving home to Sunnyside from Spain in the fall of 1846, where he continues to revise *Mahomet*. Renovating his old manuscript through the following year, Irving also begins to renovate his mansion in 1847, adding "an Oriental-style tower" to Sunnyside, seeking to scaffold his interests in Eastern texts onto his house's actual architecture.[50] This parallel between revisions and remodeling receives material expression in an intriguing letter—previously highlighted by Feltskog and Pochmann—sent by Irving to his nephew in 1847. Addressing Pierre's concern at the increasing costs of Sunnyside's additions, Irving writes:

> That you may not be frightened at my extravagance, and cut off supplies, I must tell you that I have lately been working up some old stuff which

had lain for years lumbering like rubbish in one of my trunks, and which,
I trust, will more than pay the expense of my new building.[51]

Recovering "old stuff" to cover "the expense of my new building," Irving speaks in
a self-deprecatory voice, likening his lost manuscripts to "rubbish" that has "lain
for years lumbering." Although silent as to titles, it is *Mahomet* that Irving has recently rescued and that he is currently "working up," this Islamic history projected
to support Irving's domestic "extravagance." Driven from his own home, forced in
his "flight [. . .] from Mecca," the Prophet's story now aids the rebuilding of Irving's
own house, the Muslim "*Hegira*" allowing for an American home on the Hudson.
Although long buried as waste in "one of my trunks," the Prophet's *Life* rises from
American interiors to bolster American exteriors, rescued to fashion a new façade
for Sunnyside.

When finally published a few years later, the stages of deferral and domestic
structures that surround Irving's *Mahomet* receive oblique expression in its opening words. In a brief preface to his prophetic biography, Irving first explains its long
foreground in his own life. Composed first "during a residence in Madrid" in the
late 1820s, as Irving recalls, *Mahomet* was intended to appear as part of the British
"Family Library" series "of Mr. John Murray"; "prevented" from "publication" in
1831, the manuscript was "thrown aside for years," revived only during Irving's "last
residence in Spain" (1845–46).[52] Irving concludes his preface, however, by bringing
his American reader both back home and up to the present day:

> Such is the origin of the work now given to the public; on which the author
> lays no claim to novelty of fact, nor profundity of research. It still bears the
> type of a work intended for a Family Library; in constructing which the
> whole aim of the writer has been to digest into an easy, perspicuous and
> flowing narrative, the admitted facts concerning Mahomet, together with
> such legends and traditions as have been wrought into the whole system
> of oriental literature; and at the same time to give such a summary of his
> faith as might be sufficient for the more general reader. Under such cir-
> cumstances, he has not thought it worth while to encumber his pages with
> a scaffolding of references and citations, nor depart from the old English
> nomenclature of oriental names.
>
> W.I.
> Sunnyside. 1849.[53]

Describing *Mahomet* as a mere "digest"—a "summary" that "might be" generally "sufficient"—Irving apologizes for his biography's "easy" abbreviations,
even while he abbreviates his own identity, autographing with his initials merely.
Closing his introduction by admitting his failure to provide full versions of "oriental names," preferring instead to retain "old English nomenclature," Irving

withholds too his own full name, casually signing off as "W.I./Sunnyside. 1849."
Reflecting the domestic character of *Mahomet*, Irving ends his introduction to
this "work intended for a Family Library" by situating himself within his newly
renovated home—"Sunnyside"—even while highlighting his "narrative" renovations. Although "constructing" *Mahomet* from "admitted" materials, Irving is
nevertheless able to dispense with all "scaffolding," leaving his "pages" free of all
scholarly "encumbrance."

Intersecting literary composition and literal construction, Irving ends his preface before beginning *Mahomet* with his domestic place, as well as the present date
("1849")—a last gesture to the American moment before his Arabian history
begins with the following first words of *Mahomet's* Chapter 1:

> During a long succession of ages, extending from the earliest period of re-
> corded history down to the seventh century of the Christian era, that great
> chersonese or peninsula formed by the Red Sea, the Euphrates, the Gulf of
> Persia, and the Indian Ocean, and known by the name of Arabia, remained
> unchanged and almost unaffected by the events which convulsed the rest
> of Asia, and shook Europe and Africa to their centre. While kingdoms
> and empires rose and fell; while ancient dynasties passed away; while
> the boundaries and names of countries were changed, and their inhabit-
> ants were exterminated or carried into captivity, Arabia, though its fron-
> tier provinces experienced some vicissitudes, preserved in the depths of
> its deserts its primitive character and independence, nor had its nomadic
> tribes ever bent their haughty necks to servitude.[54]

Promised a "perspicuous" account of the Prophet's life, readers may be surprised
to find "Mahomet" entirely absent from the opening of his own biography; instead,
the lineage of the Arabian Prophet begins expansively with the land of "Arabia"
itself. Retreating to chronologic limits, tracing Arabia's "preservation" in antiquity,
Irving also commences with concerns that seem self-reflective; akin to the land that
grounds this opening vignette, Irving's *Mahomet* too has endured "a long succession
of ages," surviving the vagaries and "vicissitudes" of Irving's own biography, transcending any single moment within the "recorded history" of his life. Mirroring his
complex process of authoring *Mahomet*, with this prophetic biography "preserved"
despite its own "nomadic" progress, Irving seems too to offer an ambivalent reflection on his own nation in 1850, refracting America in this "frontier" land skirted
about by "ocean[s]," whose immunity from continental "convulsions" allow for
"independence," even while surrounded by specters of "servitude," "captivity" and
"exterminat[ion]."

Mapping a general locality before the specifics of a single life, Irving will defer
the entrance of the Prophet in *Mahomet* until its Chapter 2. When arriving finally
at the birth of Muḥammad, however, it is again Irving's own concerns that echo

into his account; emphasizing not only the familial, but also the philological, the Prophet's presentation to his people is recounted by Irving as follows:

> His grandfather, Abd al-Motalleb, gave a feast to the principal Koreishites, the seventh day after his birth, at which he presented this child, as the dawning glory of their race, and gave him the name of Mahomet (or Muhamed), indicative of his future renown.[55]

This genesis moment in *Mahomet*'s Chapter 2 involves a twofold lineage for "Mahomet," complexly situating the Prophet within a patriarchal line that extends in dual directions, implying foregoing generations, embodied by "His grandfather," while also pointing forward to his "future renown." These dual directions find complement in the double name that Irving ascribes to the Prophet, using not only a standard English transliteration, but also a transliteration that better matches original Arabic, labeling his central subject as "Mahomet (or Muhamed)." Contradicting his own prefatory edict—promising that his biography would not "depart from the old English nomenclature of oriental names"—Irving elects in this special instance to offer a more accurate impression of Arabic "nomenclature," supplementing English's imprecise "Mahomet" with the much improved "Muhamed." Gesturing to more accurate orthography, Irving also implies his interest in etymologic origins, suggesting that the Prophet's "renown" is foretold by his original name: "Muhamad"—a term that indeed implies "praised."[56] Subtly reflecting his own Arabic engagements even while identifying "Mahomet" for the very first time, Irving too mirrors the textual history of his own *Mahomet*, suggesting the overlapping languages and literary stages that "intermingle" to produce this prophetic biography. Revealing to readers the inaccuracy of his own standard "nomenclature," Irving's appeal to authentic Arabic ironically implies that the name otherwise used throughout his 1850 text is itself a pseudonym, the English "Mahomet" merely a nominal pretense, a false surface under which hides the actual Arabic "Muhamad." Parenthetically granted a twofold name, the Muslim founder seems to mirror America's own master of the pseudonym, the "dawning glory" of Islam reflecting Sunnyside's aged author, with "W.I." gesturing to the Arabic foregrounds of his American biography by balancing between "Mahomet" and "Muhamad." ✿

Intended primarily as "an easy, perspicuous and flowing narrative," Irving also promises in his preface that *Mahomet* will supply "a summary" of the Prophet's "faith." It is this latter pledge that is finally fulfilled in Irving's Chapter 8, entitled "Outlines of the Mahometan Faith." Excusing his abrupt break from biography, Irving opens this chapter by noting, "Though it is not intended in this place to go fully into the doctrines promulgated by Mahomet, yet it is important to the right appreciation of his character and conduct, and of the events and circumstances set forth in the following narrative, to give their main features."[57] Claiming spiritual "doctrines" as essential for understanding his subject's "character," Irving anticipates Chapter 8's personal "appreciation" of the Prophet's religion, situating Islam within intimate lines of Abrahamic influence. The familial foundations of "the Mahometan Faith" are particularly emphasized in Chapter 8's description of the Qur'ān, which is understood by Irving as a pastiche of previous revelations, arising from a complex textual pedigree:

> Much of the Koran may be traced to the Bible, the Mishnu and the Talmud of the Jews, especially its wild though often beautiful traditions concerning the angels, the prophets, the patriarchs, and the good and evil genii. [Mahomet] had at an early age imbibed a reverence for the Jewish faith, his mother, it is suggested, having been of that religion. [ . . . ]
>
> [ . . . ] Most of the benignant precepts of our Saviour were incorporated in the Koran. Frequent alms-giving was enjoined as an imperative duty, and the immutable law of right and wrong, "Do unto another, as thou wouldst he should do unto thee," was given for the moral conduct of the faithful.[58]

These two discrete passages from Chapter 8 portray "the Koran" as emerging from two testaments, "incorporating" material from both the "Old" and the "New." Heir of the Hebrew "patriarchs," Irving finds the Qur'ān shaped too by a Judaic matriarch, the Muslim scripture informed by the "mother" of the Prophet and her "Jewish faith." Although "wild" in content, Irving claims domestic contexts for the Qur'ān, this scripture "traced" not only to antique textual influence, but also to a tender "imbibing" that takes place during the Prophet's "early age."[59]

A hint of self-reflection seems again implied in Irving's textual criticism, with the complex genealogies ascribed to the Muslim scripture refracting *Mahomet*'s own intricate and intimate composition. Indeed, Irving's understanding of "the Koran" as a revisionary source seems especially apt in light of his own revisionary approach to the scripture. Interspersed liberally throughout his *Life* of the Prophet, Irving includes dozens of Qur'ānic quotations; however, these quotations themselves arise through Irving's own innovative acts of "incorporation," making it difficult to discern where "[m]uch of the Koran may be traced to" in Irving's *Mahomet*. Indeed, it is only by retreating back to Irving's "earlier age," opening the unpublished manuscripts that precede his published *Mahomet*, that the source for his Qur'ānic revisions are revealed. In reading Irving's notebooks housed at the New York Public Library's Berg Collection, dozens of discrete pages are found to be dedicated to Qur'ān quotations, transcribed from foregoing English translations. For instance, in the same notebook that features Irving's *shahāda* quoted above—"*Ashaed la Allahe ill Allah!* [ . . . ]"—he also copies out copious English extracts from Du Ryer's *The Alcoran of Mahomet* (trans. Alexander Ross, 1649), choosing selections that span the entire Muslim scripture, from its opening Chapter 1 to its final Chapter 114.[60] Irving's verbatim Qur'ān quotations spill over into other notebooks and into other translations as well; a second manuscript journal held at the Berg Collection, for in-stance, reserves over twenty pages to transcriptions from George Sale's 1734 *Koran*, not only quoting from this classic English rendition, but also recording Sale's con-textual notes, preserving in Irving's own hand Qur'ānic texts as well as paratexts.[61]

Copying multiple translations through multiple notebooks, the Qur'ān's cover-age in Irving's private manuscripts anticipates his published *Mahomet*, whose chap-ters are regularly punctuated with scriptural quotations, as frequently recognized by the notes to Feltskog and Pochmann's critical edition.[62] However, what Irving ne-glects to reveal, and what his editors have failed to recognize, is that *Mahomet*'s quo-tations frequently deviate from previous Qur'ān renditions, matching neither Du Ryer's *Alcoran* nor Sale's *Koran*. Such uniqueness is witnessed in *Mahomet*'s most extended quotation from the Qur'ān, supplied aptly at the very close of Irving's "Outlines of the Mahometan Faith." Although Chapter 8 had opened by admitting its inability "to go fully into the doctrines promulgated by Mahomet," the very close of the chapter offers a fulsome quotation from the Qur'ān, ending apocalyptically with the following final words:

> Nevertheless, the description of the last day, as contained in the eighty-first chapter of the Koran, and which must have been given by Mahomet at the outset of his mission at Mecca, as one of the first of his revelations, partakes of sublimity:
>
> "In the name of the all merciful God! a day shall come when the sun will be shrouded, and the stars will fall from the heavens.
>
> "When the camels about to foal will be neglected, and wild beasts will herd together through fear.
>
> "When the waves of the ocean will boil, and the souls of the dead again united to the bodies.
>
> "When the female infant that has been buried alive will demand, for what crime was I sacrificed? And the eternal books shall be laid open.
>
> "When the heavens will pass away like a scroll, and hell will burn fiercely; and the joys of paradise will be made manifest.
>
> "On that day shall every soul make known that which it hath performed.
>
> "Verily, I swear to you by the stars which move swiftly and are lost in the brightness of the sun, and by the darkness of the night, and by the dawning of the day, these are not the words of an evil spirit, but of an angel of dignity and power, who possesses the confidence of Allah, and is revered by the angels under his command. Neither is your companion, Mahomet, distracted. He beheld the celestial messenger in the light of the clear horizon, and the words revealed to him are intended as an admonition unto all creatures."[63]

Shifting from commentary to quotation, Irving's Chapter 8 concludes with the "eighty-first chapter of the Koran," reserving its last lines for this "description of the last day." Introduced "as one of the first of his revelations," received by "Mahomet at the outset of his mission at Mecca," this Qur'ānic quotation points back to our own beginnings as well, echoing the very "outset" of the present chapter. Portrayed by Irving as "partak[ing] of sublimity" in his 1850 *Mahomet*, these words are the very same cited by the Osgoods, precisely matching "the sublime description of the Koran" offered in the 1854 pages of their *Notes of Travel*.

If recognizable to us, Irving's quotation was entirely new to his readers in 1850, this translation from "the eighty-first chapter of the Koran" appearing for the very first time in his *Mahomet*, matching no previous English rendition. Although intimately familiar with translations produced by Du Ryer/Ross (1649) and Sale (1734), as testified by his notebook transcriptions, Irving often elects to rewrite rather than reproduce previous renditions, voicing the Qur'ān anew in his own *Mahomet*. This revisionary process is uniquely witnessed in Irving's manuscripts, again housed at the Berg Collection; filed in a miscellaneous folder of Irving's "Memoranda extracts" are the undated pages reproduced as Figure 3.3, featuring the refashioned Qur'ānic quotation of Irving's *Mahomet* in its early stages.

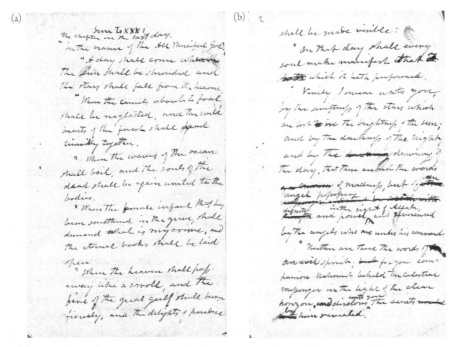

*Figure 3.3* Washington Irving, "Sura LXXXI," manuscript pages from his "[Mahomet and his successors] Memoranda extracts, etc. for the Chronicle of the Caliphs, from the death of the prophet to the invasion of Spain by the Saracens. n.d. 72 p." Image courtesy of the Henry W. and Albert A. Berg Collection of English and American Literature, The New York Public Library, Astor, Lenox and Tilden Foundations.

Loose sheets scribbled over with Irving's scrawl, these pages are more miscellaneous, yet more meaningful, than his notebook's transcriptions from the Qur'ān, witnessing Irving as he actively reconstructs, rather than passively copies, Muslim scripture. Although building from the base of previous renditions, such as Sale's *Koran*, Irving also seeks to edit and amend, expressing Islamic verses in his own American accent. And more than merely confirm his ownership of this Qur'ānic rendition, Irving's manuscript pages make clear the kind of interventions he is eager to undertake. Headed "Sura LXXXI/The chapter on the last day," Irving's left-hand page is cleanly inscribed; however, on the right-hand page, revisions to both the Qur'ān's substance and style emerge. For instance, in the middle of his right-hand page, Irving strikes out a series of phrases, proposing substitutes in superscript:

> [. . .] that these are not the words ~~of a madman~~ of madness, but of ~~a true messenger endued by Allah with strength~~ an angel possessing dignity and power in the sight of Allah and reverenced by the angels who are under his command.[64]

Amending a passage that itself concerns "the words" of prophecy, and the "messenger" who conveys them, Irving elects to communicate this passage anew, delivering its content through fresh verbal conduits. Replacing the claim "that these are not the words of a madman," Irving prefers to assert "that these are not the words of madness"; striking out "a true messenger," Irving opts instead for "an angel possessing dignity and power," to which he adds the anthropomorphic supplement "in the sight of Allah." Unsteadily rewriting Islam's most sacred text, these manuscript revisions are themselves further revised in Irving's final published version, which reads, as quoted above:

> [. . .] these are not the words of an evil spirit, but of an angel of dignity and power, who possesses the confidence of Allah, and is revered by the angels under his command.

Removing "madness" altogether from this passage, Irving introduces an "evil spirit" into his definitive version, this devilish identity complementing the "angel" that had entered his draft revisions. Surviving into publication, Irving's "angel" is also slightly altered, however, no longer defined as "possessing dignity and power in the sight of Allah," but described instead as "an angel of dignity and power, who possesses the confidence of Allah." Aptly shifting the place of the verb "to possess" in this passage, even as it progressively becomes his own possession, Irving's published version of this passage also removes divine "sight," preferring to conclude by boldly appealing to "the confidence of Allah" instead.

Revealing the detailed mechanics of his "Koran" renditions, Irving's multistage revisions are materially witnessed on the right-hand page of his manuscript, with

phrases from this "eighty-first chapter" still in flux, susceptible to further amend-
ment. It is his manuscript's left-hand page, however, that features the most original, and audacious, of Irving's edits, revising lines that envision the apocalypse.
Although describing the day when all "will be made manifest," Irving covertly contours the Qur'ān itself, ironically adapting its account of when the "books shall be
laid open" in the private pages of his own manuscript. Subtly adjusting this chapter's
most "sublime" verses, the meaning of Irving's revised line largely matches George
Sale's own *Koran*, but crucially deviates in style, as can be seen by comparing Sale's
standard version of these verses with the same passage in Irving's unpublished manuscript, as well as his published *Mahomet*:

Sale (*Koran*, 1734):

when the seas shall boil; and when the souls shall be joined again to their
bodies; and when the girl who hath been buried alive shall be asked for
what crime she was put to death; and when the books shall be laid open;

Irving ("Sura LXXXI"; Fig. 3.3):

when the waves of the ocean shall boil, and the souls of the dead shall be
again united to the bodies; when the female infant that has been smoth-
ered in the grave shall demand what is my crime, and the eternal books
shall be laid open;

Irving (*Life of Mahomet*, 1850):

when the waves of the ocean will boil and the souls of the dead be again united
to the bodies; when the female infant that has been buried alive will demand,
for what crime was I sacrificed?—and the eternal books be laid open;[65]

Reviving these vivid Islamic lines in his own words, Irving fleshes out specific
images through minor additions, newly embodying the content of Qur'ān's resurrection, while also refiguring its form. Instead of "the seas" in Sale's translation,
for instance, Irving supplies "the waves of the ocean"; rather than "girl" merely,
Irving offers "female infant." It is not the descriptive imagery, but a dramatic interrogative, that Irving includes that marks his most decisive innovation. Reversing
prior renditions, including Sale's *Koran*, the slain "girl" in Irving's account is not
questioned at the resurrection, but becomes the questioner; rather than being
"asked for what crime she was put to death," Irving first asserts in manuscript that
this "female infant" will "demand what is my crime," and, more dramatically, in his
published version, she will "demand for what crime was I sacrificed?"[66] Revising
passive victim as active accuser, Irving grants speech to this silenced "girl," infusing
Islam's ancient scripture with a fresh petition from a child so unjustly "put to death."
Framed maternally, with its traditions "imbibed" from the Prophet's own "mother,"

the Qur'ān is also revised by Irving to include a daughter's poignant "demand," the Muslim scripture enveloped by both "female" influence and interrogative across familial generations. Recovered from its own burial beneath his unpublished writings, Irving's personal manuscript witnesses the precise site where a child "buried alive" initially verbalizes her plight in the first person, Irving rewriting the "Koran" in his own hand, even while his translated text ensures that a nameless "female infant" newly takes "possession" of her own voice. ☼

DIARY
MONDAY, SEPTEMBER 4, 1854.
I Left home to-day to pay a long promised visit to my son at Jerusalem.[67]

These words open the first chapter of *A Diary of a Journey to the East,* a two-volume travelogue penned by British solicitor William Beamont Sr. Advertised as his personal journal, Beamont's published *Diary* begins as a paternal "journey," launching with his 1854 departure from Lancaster, voyaging to visit his "son" and namesake, William Beamont Jr.—Anglican priest and amateur linguist, future author of *A Concise Grammar of the Arabic Language* (1861).[68] Recording several stops on his staggered way to "Jerusalem," where his son serves as principal of the city's fledgling English College, Beamont Sr. sojourns three days in Egypt, touring Muslim sites and musing on Muslim history—a layover that leads him also to meditate on the Muslim Prophet, recording the following reflections under the date September 22, 1854:

> It is as easy to see that Mahomet derived his knowledge of the being and attributes of God from the Old Testament, as it is to trace in the sublime language and sublimer morality of the new, his description of the last day,—"In the name of the all-merciful God! a day shall come when the sun will be shrouded and the stars will fall from the Heavens . . .. When the Heavens will pass away like a scroll, and Hell will burn fiercely, and the joys of Paradise will be made manifest," and some also of his best precepts "do unto another as thou wouldst he should do unto thee," and "deal not unjustly."[69]

Although highly abridged, it is "easy to see" that the quotation included in Beamont Sr.'s 1854 *Diary*—beginning with its *basmala* "In the name of the all-merciful God"—is the very same one that is published in the Osgoods' 1854 *Notes of Travel,* these two travelogues of the contemporary "East" sharing a common Western source for the Qur'ān: Washington Irving. Citing this "description of the last day," while suggesting the Qur'ān's "sublime language" to be borrowed from the Bible, Beamont quietly copies Irving's own "manifest" quotation, this British *Diary* deriving its material from the American *Mahomet,* even as it ironically accuses "Mahomet" of being "deriv[ative]."

Testifying to the wider transatlantic circles influenced by Irving's Islamic interests, William Beamont's *Diary* also reaffirms the intimate contexts that surround the American's Qur'ānic renditions. Invoked even as Beamont travels to see his own son, Irving's *Mahomet* intersects yet another family alliance, infusing not only the Osgoods' fraternal partnership in 1854, but also this fatherly pilgrimage to the Holy Land. And, echoing the Osgoods' *Notes of Travel*, it is diary recollections that again appeal to Irving, the American's own privately fashioned Islamic renditions finding once more an informal and intimate home in Beamont's memoir of foreign travel. Perhaps most familiar in this resurrection of Irving in the pages of yet another travelogue is simply the American's persistent anonymity, his own authorial identity hidden behind his Islamic iterations. Supporting Beamont as he pontificates on Islam and the Prophet's "attributes of God," Irving's own attribution is entirely missing, his authorial identity remaining "shrouded" underneath the Qur'ān's apocalyptic account.[70]

Advancing while also obstructing the legacy of Irving's Islamic interests, Beamont publishes his paternal memoir just five years before Irving himself passes away without issue, dying "childless" in 1859 at his grand "homestead" on the Hudson.[71] Bequeathing his literary and landed estates primarily to both his brother and his nephew, Irving's Sunnyside will remain in the family well into the twentieth century. Marking the centenary of his most celebrated work—the 1819–20 *Sketch Book of Geoffrey Crayon, Gent.*—Charles Anson Ingraham penned a memorial profile of Washington Irving for a 1920 issue of *Americana*, recalling his recent visit to Sunnyside, which is still owned by a "Mr. Irving":

> Mr. Irving is a great-great-nephew of Washington Irving, and his sons are the fifth generation of the family who have lived in the home. Sunnyside is sought out by many visitors, and it no doubt will continue for many generations to be the Mecca of admirers of the father of American Literature.[72]

A complex portrait of both paternal lineage and literary legacy, Irving is pictured as the childless "father of American Literature," whose family obliquely unfolds through five "generations," extending to his "great-great-nephew." At the center of these familial lines is "Sunnyside" itself, which with unconscious irony Ingham equates with "Mecca"—the sacred site of Islamic pilgrimage, and the hometown of Islam's Prophet. Although surely unrecognized by readers of *Americana*, Ingham's memorializing of Irving's complex paternity, leading ultimately to the "Mecca" of "Sunnyside," hides in plain sight the lost Islamic legacies of this "father of American Literature," his own domestic renditions of Muslim scripture and history now obscured from view, despite the "many generations" of "admirers" that have made the pilgrimage to Irving's ancestral "home."

The text that inspired Ingraham's centenary account is the same that continues to attract generations of visitors to Irving's Sunnyside, his 1819–20 *Sketch Book*. One of

Irving's earliest works, penned several years before his first sojourn in Moorish Spain, the *Sketch Book* nevertheless also anticipates the conflicting legacies of Irving's later Islamic interests. Published precisely forty years before his own death in 1859, Irving includes in his *Sketch Book* a meditation on literary afterlives—"The Mutability of Literature"—a vignette that vividly describes the faded futures of an author's "fame":

> He finds the language in which he has embarked his fame gradually alter-
> ing, and subject to the dilapidations of time and the caprice of fashion. He
> looks back and beholds the early authors of his country, once the favorites
> of their day, supplanted by modern writers. A few short ages have covered
> them with obscurity, and their merits can only be relished by the quaint
> taste of the bookworm. And such, he anticipates, will be the fate of his own
> work, which, however it may be admired in its day, and held up as a model
> of purity, will in the course of years grow antiquated and obsolete; until
> it shall become almost as unintelligible in its native land as an Egyptian
> obelisk, or one of those Runic inscriptions said to exist in the deserts of
> Tartary.[73]

A prophecy of legacies lost, with literary "language" itself "subject to the dilapida-tions of time and the caprice of fashion," Irving has largely evaded the exhaustions that his sketch here "anticipates"; qualifying as an American "favorite of [his] day," Irving's own "fame" has endured nationally, preventing his being "supplanted by modern writers." However, it is the Eastern tendencies of this passage's conclusion that covertly gesture to facets of Irving's literary life that have indeed been "cov-ered [ . . . ] with obscurity." Although dedicating much of his domestic energies to Islam, offering Qur'ānic translations for his contemporaries to copy anonymously, Irving's efforts with Arabic and Islamic studies have assumed the status of "Runic inscriptions," growing both "antiquated and obsolete" as if they were penned "in the deserts of Tartary," rather than in the vicinity of Tarrytown. However, despite their forgotten anonymity, Irving's Muslim renditions have also left material traces, his published *Mahomet* and unpublished manuscripts offering "broken monuments" erected in plain sight, which, like "an Egyptian obelisk," demand recovery from "unintelligible" neglect in their "native land."

# "To look at the Koran through his spectacles"

## The Muslim Progress of Lydia Maria Child

*Job Ben Solomon*, was the son of the Mohammedan king of Bunda, on the Gambia. He was taken in 1730, and sold in Maryland. By a train of singular adventures he was conveyed to England, where his intelligence and dignified manners gained him many friends; among whom was Sir Hans Sloane, for whom he translated several Arabic manuscripts. After being received with distinction at the Court of St James, the African Company became interested in his fate, and carried him back to Bunda, in the year 1734. His uncle embracing him, said, "During sixty years, you are the first slave I have ever seen return from the American isles." At his father's death, Solomon became king, and was much beloved in his states.[1]

Simple in style, this brief biography of "Job Ben Solomon" is coastally complex, triangulating seaports that span the Atlantic world. A Gambian Muslim enslaved in colonial Maryland, Ben Solomon's story circulates from Africa, to America, to England, before returning home again, concluding with Job "carried [. . .] back to Bunda." Transferred transatlantically between disparate lands, it is linguistic transfers that intersect this vignette, with Ben Solomon rendering "Arabic manuscripts" in England even as he passes between an African East and an American West. An international "adventure," Ben Solomon's sketch is also an intimate homecoming, his continental circulations enclosed by an avuncular "embrace" at their end. Enveloped by the patriarchal, this paragraph begins not only by naming Job with his Arabic patronymic—Job *Ben* Solomon, Job *the son* of Solomon—but also concludes with his father's death, leading to Job's own filial succession as his nation's new "king." A story of circumnavigation as well as succession, Ben Solomon's biography also interrupts a six-decade sequence, breaking cyclical chains of enslavement. Arriving back in "Bunda" and receiving his uncle's hug, Job learns that he is unprecedented, being "the first slave" to have "return[ed] from the American isles" in "sixty years."

A tale of social inversion and religious encounter, witnessing an American slave elevated as a "Mohammedan king," the exceptional content of Job's story is mirrored by its published context, appearing in the pioneering antislavery work

*An Appeal in Favor of That Class of Americans Called Africans.* "One of the first book-length arguments in favor of abolition published in the United States," the 1833 *Appeal* invokes Ben Solomon as exceptional, but also as exemplary, his biography cited to demonstrate the "Intellect of Negroes"—the title of the *Appeal*'s Chapter 6, which includes the account of Job quoted above.[2] Offered as evidence of African "intelligence," it is Ben Solomon's Arabic facility and his Muslim identity that are useful for the *Appeal*'s antislavery polemic; subverting U.S. racial stereotypes and inverting expected hierarchies, this African servant is revealed as an Arabic teacher, rising pedagogically to instruct even the political elite, educating "Sir Hans Sloane" himself.[3] An apt venue for Ben Solomon's vignette, the 1833 *Appeal* may seem an ironic home for this patriarchal tale, however, as the *Appeal* itself claims distinctly maternal origins, authored by early America's leading female writer, named on this work's front cover in all capitals as

MRS. CHILD,
AUTHOR OF THE MOTHER'S BOOK, THE GIRL'S OWN BOOK,
THE FRUGAL HOUSEWIFE, ETC.[4]

Recounting Ben Solomon's transatlantic enslavement and paternal succession, the *Appeal* yet opens with feminine domesticity, its "author" defined as a writer of manuals that target the American "mother," "girl," and "housewife." Mirroring Job's own patronymic, however, the *Appeal*'s author is also introduced by the name of her nearest male relative: not her father, but her husband. Labeled merely by her married name—"Mrs. Child"—the title page of the *Appeal* confesses, yet covers, the original identity of its author, Lydia Maria Francis: antebellum America's most celebrated woman writer, an "author" who was also "much beloved in [her] states." Of the three "books" credited to "MRS. CHILD" on the *Appeal*'s cover, it is the last, *The Frugal Housewife*, that merits most attention; published in 1829, this guide to household economy proved an "enduring best-seller" in America, garnering "more than thirty printings during Child's lifetime."[5] It is the abbreviation that follows *The Frugal Housewife*, however, that best expresses Child's diverse authorial career. A literary life of "ETC.," Child's writings are as capacious as they are various, spanning advice books and children's tales, journal articles and historical fiction. Already a "household name in America" by 1833, the *Appeal*'s frontispiece aptly associates Child with homespun wisdom, even while heralding her progress beyond the merely private, shifting from domestic polity to political polemic. Known previously for her "parenting and household management," representing "one of the chief publicists for the cult of domesticity," the *Appeal* signals Child's pivot from gentle advice to vocal activism, her fame increasingly founded on her advocacy for social justice, earning praise from abolitionist leaders such as William Lloyd Garrison, who famously pronounced Child to be "the first woman in the republic."[6] Echoing its sketch of Ben Solomon, it is Child's own *Appeal* that conveys her from intimate households to international politics, supporting Child as her interests advance from family environs to global enslavement.

If aspects of Child's own identity seem refracted in her sketch of "Job Ben Solomon," his profile more obviously offers a polar opposite, contrasting Child not only in gender and race, but also in religion. And yet, rather than posing a conflict for Child, it is the "Mohammedan" creed of Ben Solomon that offers yet another continuity, reflecting an interest in Islam fostered by Child since her youth. Publishing much shorter pieces with subtler antislavery motives in the years before her *Appeal*, Child regularly chose Muslim settings and subjects; in 1831, for instance, Child's "Jumbo and Zairee" was inspired by the life of Muslim American slave Ibrāhīm 'Abd ar-Raḥmān.[7] It is in the decades following Child's *Appeal*, however, that her investment in Islam deepens, culminating in her 1855 *The Progress of Religious Ideas*—a pioneering three-volume compendium of comparative religion, which dedicates its final body chapter, spanning nearly seventy pages, to "MOHAMMEDANISM."[8] Intersecting these published expressions, however, Child also cultivates a domestic Islamicism that rivals male contemporaries, with Muslim traditions echoing from her earliest memoirs to her last literary moments, surfacing to occupy the final words of the last book she publishes before her 1880 death.[9] As Job Ben Solomon, Child's progressive life is enveloped by Islam, with her own personal and political liberation in the "American isles" advanced even as she appeals to "Mohammedan" precedents, facilitated by her own "translation" of "Arabic manuscripts."

A fleeting vignette in her 1833 *Appeal*, the story of "Job Ben Solomon" yet hints at primary concerns that punctuate Child's career, from racial equality to religious otherness. However, hidden underneath this story's social and spiritual content is a literary strategy that will also prove essential to Child. Tracing a complex family lineage, spanning the seizure of Job from his native land to his ultimate succession as king, this passage itself arises from a complex lineage, implicated in a process of textual seizure and succession. Although unacknowledged in her own *Appeal*, Child adapts her account of Ben Solomon from a version authored by "Abbé Grégoire"— Father Henri Grégoire, Catholic priest and antislavery activist (d. 1831). Published in 1808, Grégoire's *De la Littérature des Nègres* offered an "immediate rallying point for the nascent abolitionist cause in America" when translated into English by David Baillie Warden, appearing as *An Enquiry Concerning the Intellectual and Moral Faculties, and Literature of Negroes* in 1810.[10] Celebrated especially for its "examples of African-American achievement," Child liberally refashions Grégoire's liberating story of Job, as made evident by comparing her *Appeal*'s own account with the corresponding paragraph in the 1810 *Enquiry*:

Grégoire (*Enquiry* 1810)

Stedman knew a negro, who could repeat from memory the Alcoran. The same thing is told of Job Ben Solomon, son of the Mahometan king of

Bunda, of the Gambia. Solomon taken in 1730, was brought to America, and sold in Maryland. A train of extraordinary adventures, which may be read in the *More-lak*, brought him to England, where his dignified air, amenity of character and talents, gained him friends, and among others, Hans Sloane, baronet, for whom he translated several Arabic manuscripts. After being received with distinction at the court of St. James, the African company, interested in his fate, in 1734, reconducted him to Bunda. One of the uncles of Solomon embracing him, said, during sixty years thou art the first slave that I have seen return from the American isles. He wrote letters to all his friends in Europe, and in the new world, which were translated and perused with interest. At his father's death he became his successor, and was beloved in his states.

### Child (*Appeal* 1833)

Job Ben Solomon, was the son of the Mohammedan king of Bunda, on the Gambia. He was taken in 1730, and sold in Maryland. By a train of singular adventures he was conveyed to England, where his intelligence and dignified manners gained him many friends; among whom was Sir Hans Sloane, for whom he translated several Arabic manuscripts. After being received with distinction at the Court of St James, the African Company became interested in his fate, and carried him back to Bunda, in the year 1734. His uncle embracing him, said, "During sixty years, you are the first slave I have ever seen return from the American isles." At his father's death, Solomon became king, and was much beloved in his states.[11]

Vacillating between verbatim quotation and creative revision, Child's adaptation subtly amplifies the sentimental and the sympathetic, isolating adjectives that support her chapter's advocacy of the "Intellect of Negroes," adding even the word "intelligence" itself. Editing the European *Enquiry* to produce her American *Appeal*, Child condenses Grégoire's sentences, but also covers over his sources; although the *Enquiry* acknowledges its own foregoing authority—a French book entitled "*More-lak*"—this reference is excluded from Child's account. Cutting textual precedents, Child clears textual peripheries as well; while Grégoire is reminded of Ben Solomon's story due to this slave's Qur'ānic memorization, this extraordinary scriptural retention is itself forgotten by Child, her American adaptation dispensing with her original's emphasis on "repeat[ing] from memory the Alcoran."[12]

Adapting this story of Muslim slavery from a French "Father," America's "author of *The Mother's Book*" also covertly cuts ties between her own 1833 *Appeal* and its parent text in 1810—a familial interruption that ironically also helps link Child to a new national lineage, implicating her within a broader U.S. tradition of Islamic adaptation. Distilling European scholarship to manufacture her own account of this "Mohammadan" identity, Child's revisionary act seems especially reminiscent of Washington Irving, this specific moment hinting at broader parallels between their lives of Islamic investment. Recalling Irving's own intimate interest in Islam's Prophet and prophecy, culminating in the late 1840s, Child will also fashion renditions of the Qur'ān at precisely the same time, inventing new iterations of the Muslim scripture for her 1855 *Progress* during the very years that Irving revives his *Mahomet* for 1850 publication.[13] This coincidence in time and technique between the "father of American Literature" and "the first woman in the republic" also reveals a striking asymmetry between the two, embodied not in their shared approach to Islamic sources, but in their agendas. Quietly cribbing from European predecessors, Child appeals to Islam not to maintain her lifestyle, nor magnify her literary style, but rather to advance her social activism. Aiming not for Irving's "easy and the perspicuous," Child's concern is not eloquence primarily, but emancipation, striving for social equality, not aesthetic "sublimity." A leader of the next New England generation, known for its idealism and reform, Child cuts literary chains of transmission while also seeking to cut literal chains, releasing America's "cruelly oppressed race" through her revisionary appeal to Islamic sources.[14] As the present chapter will suggest, the *Appeal*'s sketch of "Job Ben Solomon"—a vignette straddling the domestic and the political, surfacing in public pages but reflecting private adaptation—forms an emblematic link in a lineal chain of Islamic indebtedness, stretching from Child's early life to her last published words, culminating in the shining polish of Child's crowning effort, her 1878 *Aspirations of the World: A Chain of Opals.* ☼

> The evening star was sailing along its peaceful course, and seemed, amid the stainless sanctity of the heavens, like a bright diadem on the brow of some celestial spirit. "Fair planet," thought Mary, "how various are the scenes thou passest over in thy shining course. The solitary nun, in the recesses of her cloister, looks on thee as I do now; mayhap too, the courtly circle of king Charles are watching the motion of thy silver chariot. The standard of war is fluttering in thy beams, and the busy merchantman breaks thy radiance on the ocean. Thou hast kissed the cross-crowned turrets of the Catholic, and the proud spires of the Episcopalian. Thou hast smiled on distant mosques and temples, and now thou art shedding the same light on the sacrifice heap of the Indian, and the rude dwellings of the Calvinist. And can it be, as my father says, that of all the multitude of people who view thy cheering rays, so small a remnant only are pleasing in the sight of God? Oh, no. It cannot be thus. Would that my vision, like thine, could extend through the universe, that I might look down unmoved on the birth and decay of human passions, hopes, and prejudices."[15]

Glimpsing the interior life of Child's most famous heroine, this reflective moment from *Hobomok: A Tale of Early Times* finds Mary Conant charting global religions through the cynosure of a single star, a celestial light that itself involves a more plural corona, seeming "a bright diadem on the brow of some celestial spirit." Consistent with an autobiographic reading of *Hobomok* adopted regularly in Child scholarship, Mary seems to map the broad ecumenical horizons embraced by Child herself from her own "early times," discovering in this lone star a symbol of spiritual diversity, as well as a critique of religious chauvinism.[16] A celestial light that illumines both West and East, Mary straddles cultural divides as her mind reaches from "Calvinists" and "Indians" at home, to regions and religions farther afield. Not satisfied merely with understanding her deity's perspective, however, Mary aspires for universal sight herself; "Would that my vision, like thine, could extend through the universe," Mary's prayer concludes, "that I might look down unmoved on the birth and decay of human passions, hopes, and prejudices." Perhaps the most audacious moment in her appeal, however, is the very middle of Mary's prayer; invoking the Divine, Child's young heroine testifies that "Thou hast smiled on distant mosques and temples," envisioning God's grin as enfolding not only the East in general, but Islam specifically.[17]

Appealing to "distant mosques" from the Massachusetts frontier, Child's 1824 *Hobomok* supports a transnational "vision"; however, the novel also defines itself nationally, Child publishing this first work of fiction without her personal name, signing the novel simply as "an American."[18] Set in seventeenth-century New England, it is the country's own conflicted past that seems dramatized in Child's *Tale of Early Times*, critiquing in particular the "prejudice" of the Puritan Fathers, vividly resisted in Mary's rejection of what her own "father says." Rebelling against aged patriarchy, national and familial, *Hobomok* would be published, however, even as Child turns her attention in another generational direction, not pursuing a critique of American elders, but appealing to the American youth, speaking to the nation's children in their own "early times." Appearing in the months following *Hobomok*, 1824 witnesses the publication of Child's first book for children, her *Evenings in New England: Intended for Juvenile Amusement and Instruction*, which leads soon to the launch of her periodical, *The Juvenile Miscellany, Or, Friend of Youth*—a series whose run will enjoy a full eight years, from 1826 to 1834.[19] Reflecting the captious "ETC." that ends Child's credits on the cover of her *Appeal*, her bimonthly *Miscellany* embraces a plethora of genres, its pages featuring poetry, stories, sketches, and reviews. Amid this variety would be a unity of purpose, *The Juvenile Miscellany* aiming to become not only an external educator, but an intimate companion, gaining the confidence of its "youthful" readership. Qualifying as the "country's first successful children's magazine,"[20] the *Juvenile Miscellany*'s nurturing approach would have national consequences, gaining readers destined to become America's most prominent women writers—including Louisa May Alcott—while also spawning successors, including a journal edited by Child's close friend, Eliza Lee Cabot Follen, begun in 1843 and aptly entitled *The Child's Friend*.[21]

The *Miscellany*'s eight-year run would overlap Child's own *Appeal*, with one of the periodical's last issues published in the fall of 1833, even as the *Appeal* appeared on Boston bookshelves. Coinciding in time, these discrete projects also surprisingly coincide in theme, with Child's Islamic interests meriting mention in her *Miscellany* during the same months that her sketch of the "Mahommedan" Ben Solomon appears in the *Appeal*. Published in the fall of 1833, Child anonymously contributes an article to the *Miscellany* that opens with the following:

### A FEW WORDS ABOUT TURKEY

FOR one nation to be perfectly kind and candid toward other nations, is as important as it is for an individual to be perfectly just and fair-minded toward his neighbor. The Americans are accused of being vain of their country. There is a great deal of truth in this charge; and it is likewise true that this tendency makes them willing to speak disparagingly of other nations, compared with their own. This is a wrong feeling. We ought to respect what is good, wherever we find it, and rather seek to imitate the virtues of others, than to excuse faults of our own. We ought to love our country, as the child loves its mother; and we should feel deeply grateful to our Heavenly Father for the great prosperity with which He has blessed our land; but in respecting ourselves, never let us forget to respect others.

A highly interesting book has lately been published in New York, called Sketches of Turkey, in 1831 and '32, by an American. We are apt to say "*as wicked as a Turk,*" "*as cruel as a Turk,*" &c.; but the author of this book resided in Turkey nearly a year, and he gives an account of the habits and manners of that country, which in many respects may well make us blush for our own.[22]

Framing international relations through intimate relationships, Child's first paragraph begins by equating nations with neighbors and ends by emphasizing "respect" between "ourselves" and "others." Establishing links between the political and the familial, Child frames patriotism as filial "love," insisting that America should be embraced "as the child loves its mother." Shifting parental metaphors as her paragraph closes, Child reaches up from human mother to patriarchal God; celebrating "our Heavenly Father" and "the great prosperity with which He has blessed our land," Child rounds out a complex family portrait, offering her youthful reader both a maternal nation and a divine father. Targeting her *Juvenile* audience, Child's familiar tone and familial topics seem sensible, but also surprising, considering her Islamic subject. Announcing in all capitals her casual aim to speak "A FEW WORDS ABOUT TURKEY," Child opens with domestic and divine metaphors even as she turns attention to the "world's leading Muslim power," reviewing a "highly interesting book" entitled *Sketches of Turkey*.[23] Authored by James Ellsworth De Kay, Child names her author merely as "an American," while also accenting the national identity and idioms of her young readers.[24] Invoking a collective "we," Child notes that "our" colloquial usages—"'cruel as a Turk,' &c."—contrast sharply with the actual experience of the American "author [who] resided in Turkey nearly a year," whose "account of the habits and manners of that country [. . .] may well make us blush for our own." Initially celebrating love of home country, it is contrastive shame that ends Child's introduction, the mirror of Muslim examples revealing U.S. inadequacies, prompting "us" to offer an intimate sign of modesty—the "blush"—as a signal of "our" national shortcomings.

Published in the same year, Child's "A Few Words About Turkey" shares her *Appeal*'s interest in refracting U.S. social ills through Islamic identities. This common aim, however, is also expressed through a common approach; while seeming to quote De Kay's *Sketches of Turkey* in her review, Child elects instead to ameliorate her source, adapting De Kay for her youthful reader. Emendations emerge especially as Child presents Islamic practices, distilling positive impressions from material that is more ambivalent; for example, lauding hygiene in Turkey, Child celebrates Islamic "ablutions," quoting ostensibly from De Kay:

> Of the cleanliness of the Turks their constant and frequent ablutions are a proof. This custom was enjoined upon them by their prophet, and no person enters a place of worship without having first purified themselves in the bath. "These continued ablutions are not taken in a literal sense alone, but are applied to cleansing the heart from all injustice, wickedness, and vicious inclinations."[25]

Lauding the Muslim "prophet" while addressing America's youth, Child credits Muḥammad with "the cleanliness of the Turks," concluding with a supporting citation from De Kay; although seemingly precise, however, Child subtly adapts her actual source, whose content and context are more nuanced, De Kay's treatment of "Ablutions" in his *Sketches of Turkey* instead beginning:

> *Ablutions.* These are to be daily practised before every prayer, and likewise upon extraordinary occasions, and they are in fact most scrupulously observed. "Water," observes the worthy *Agapida*, "is more necessary to these infidels than bread, making use of it in repeated daily ablutions enjoined by their damnable religion, employing it in baths, and in a thousand other idle and extravagant modes of which we Spaniards and Christians make little account." These continual ablutions are not taken in a literal sense alone, but are applied to cleansing the members of the body from all wickedness and unjust actions, and the heart from all secret vicious inclinations.[26]

Rearranging De Kay's original, which asserts that Islamic ablutions are "applied to cleansing the members of the body from all wickedness and unjust actions, and the heart from all secret vicious inclinations," Child quotes him as suggesting that "ablutions" are instead "applied to cleansing the heart from all injustice, wickedness, and vicious inclinations." Condensing and "cleansing" De Kay, Child covertly expunges the "body" from her own body text, removing in "secret" all mention of physical "members" and "unjust actions." It is through decapitating this passage from De Kay, however, that Child "purifies" its most "vicious inclinations," cutting the material that stands at the head of the "Ablutions" section in his *Sketches of Turkey*: a lengthy quotation from "the worthy Agapida," who attributes the "daily ablutions" of Muslims to their "damnable religion." Child's excision of this caustic critique is, however, ironically comic; the "Agapida" quoted by De Kay is a fictional identity, who serves as the intolerant and unreliable pseudonym behind *A Chronicle of the Conquest of Granada: From the Mss. of Fray Antonio Agapida*, the first Moorish romance authored by none other than Washington Irving.[27] Haunting the margins of her Muslim interests, Irving's sarcasm oddly emerges in De Kay's historical *Sketch*, appearing immediately adjacent to precisely the passage that subsequently inspires Child's own revisionary citation in her 1833 review. Emblematic of their parallel yet inverse projects of Islamic adaption, Child begins her quotation from De Kay exactly where his own quotation of Irving ends, seeking to correct American prejudice not through "extravagant" and adult satire, but rather through editing a new "literal sense" for her youthful reader.

A minor author mediating between major American figures, De Kay will nevertheless continue to influence Child's career, his "highly interesting book" echoing into her next work of social progress. Resisting racial oppression in her 1833 *Appeal*, Child advances to gender equality in 1835, publishing her two-volume *The History of the Condition of Women in Various Ages and Nations*. Credited by the leading Child critic, Carolyn Karcher, with laying "the groundwork for later feminist theory," the broad scope of chronology and culture in Child's *History* includes a significant Middle Eastern emphasis, not only "variously" critiquing misogyny in Muslim "nations," but also praising Islamic practices to highlight American inequalities.[28] Dedicating an entire chapter of her *History* to Turkish women, Child relies on De Kay once more, truncating treatments such as the following from his *Sketches'* Chapter 27, entitled "Considerations upon the Condition of Females in Turkey—Their Souls":

> It is gravely stated, and repeated by every traveller in this country, that the Turks firmly believe their females to have no souls. [. . .] Nothing indeed can be more explicit than the language used in their religious code in reference to the souls of women. In the third chapter of the Koran it is said, "The Lord sayeth, I will not suffer the work of him among you who worketh good to be lost, whether he be male or female; the one of you is from the other." In chapter 13 we have, "The reward of these shall be paradise, whether he be male or female we shall surely raise him to a happy life." In chapter 16, "Whoso worketh good, whether male or female, and is a true believer, they shall enter paradise."[29]

Distilled from De Kay's account of Muslim doctrine, Child more succinctly suggests in her own chapter on "Turkish Women" in her 1835 *History of the Condition of Women* that:

> The common idea that Mohammedans believe women have no souls, is not founded upon any thing contained in the Koran. Mohammed expressly says: "Whoso worketh good, male or female, shall enter paradise;" and the pilgrimage to Mecca, for the salvation of their souls, is enjoined upon women as well as men, with the proviso that they must be accompanied by their husbands, or near male relations.[30]

Echoing De Kay's efforts to debunk the "common idea" that Muslims "firmly believe their females to have no souls," Child also references "their religious code," even while significantly condensing her source's Qur'ānic proofs. Reduced to a single example that appears without citation, Child's lone quotation clearly recalls, yet quietly revises, De Kay. Rather than his "Whoso worketh good, whether male or female, and is a true believer, they shall enter paradise," Child instead offers "Whoso worketh good, male or female, shall enter paradise." Easing entrance requirements for "paradise," Child isolates "good" works while omitting "belief," opening heaven to any benevolent "male" or "female." Reflecting her own preference for active compassion over religious creed, this passage finds Child again personally adapting her source to fit her own polemic. However, unlike her prior revisions, it is not just a Western author, but Islam's ultimate authority, that is adjusted by Child, altering a verse of the "Koran" itself. Seeking to "worketh good" by authoring her own *History*, Child herself "enters" into sacred Islamic spaces, covertly revising the Qur'ān to promote her progressive politics—an audacious act that increasingly becomes habitual practice as Child's career unfolds.[31] ☼

> September 23, 1841.
>
> I lately visited the Jewish Synagogue in Crosby-street, to witness the Festival of the New Year, which was observed for two days, by religious exercises and a general suspension of worldly business. The Jewish year, you are aware, begins in September; and they commemorate it in obedience to the following text of Scripture: "In the first day of the seventh month ye shall have a Sabbath, a memorial of blowing of trumpets, a holy convocation. Ye shall do no servile work therein."
>
> It was the first time I ever entered any place of worship where Christ was not professedly believed in. Strange vicissitudes of circumstance, over which I had no control, have brought me into intimate relation with almost every form of Christian faith, and thereby given me the power of looking candidly at religious opinions from almost any point of view. But beyond

the pale of the great sect of Christianity I had never gone; though far back in my early years, I remember an intense desire to be enough acquainted with some intelligent and sincere Mohammedan, to enable me to look at the Koran through *his* spectacles.[32]

On September 17, 1841, Child celebrated Rosh Hashanah with America's oldest Jewish congregation, Shearith Yisrael, visiting this community's "Synagogue in Crosby Street" as it commemorated this new year's "Festival."[33] Ushering in a fresh "Jewish year," Child's epistolary account of her visit ironically echoes themes long established in her literary life. Emphasizing the variety and "strange vicissitudes" of her spiritual experience, Child offers a typically miscellaneous report of this interreligious moment. Triangulating the three Abrahamic traditions, Child's "entrance" into this Jewish "space" highlights the exclusively Christian color of her previous life experience, while also triggering memories of her earliest Islamic interests. Ecumenically progressive, Child's synagogue visit regresses autobiographically, prompted by this foreign exterior to reflect back on interior spaces most familiar. Conveying her reader through a series of "before[s]," Child sits in "suspended" silence even while she retreats from the very recent past ("lately") to arrive "far back in my early years." Poised between passivity and "power," Child credits "circumstance[s] over which [she] had no control" for introducing her to diverse Christian expressions, from which she gains "the power of looking candidly at religious opinions from almost any point of view." This perspectival fluency itself ultimately leads back to Child's earliest recollection, finding roots in a surprisingly urgent and intimate "desire": "an intense desire to look at the Koran."

Echoing the ecumenism of Ezra Stiles seven decades before, whose own Islamic studies were punctuated by attending Rosh Hashanah services in 1769, this moment in Child's life again situates her within a broader national lineage.[34] It is, however, more individual and "intimate relations" that are Child's own concern, amplified in the epistolary contours of her passage. Expressing her synagogue experience as a letter, published first in the *National Anti-Slavery Standard* and later re-collected in her *Letters from New-York* (1843), Child opens with "I" but soon reaches out directly to her reader ("you are aware," she exclaims in her second sentence), establishing an "intimate relationship" that pervades her *Letters*, as noted previously by Stephanie A. Tingley.[35] If reflected in its form, it is the final focus of Child's letter that is most "intimate"; traveling back to biographic origins, Child rehearses her desire not only to read Muslim scripture but to share Muslim "spectacles," ending this inward account by wishing to examine "the Koran" from an insider's perspective. Ultimately, it is "some intelligent and sincere Mohammedan" that Child yearns for in youth, seeking not religious speculation but rather interreligious "spectacles." Blurring together spiritual traditions, Child also bridges genders, wishing to wear the eyeglasses of a male "Mahommedan," even emphasizing in italics the "*his*" pronoun of her imagined Muslim interlocutor.[36] A moment of merging perspectives, Child's memory also seems to merge fiction and fact, recalling the spiritual soliloquy spoken in her *Hobomok* from the perspective of Mary Conant. Paralleling Mary's youthful petition—"Would that my vision, like thine, could extend through the universe"—Child's remembered adolescence finds her too pining for an inter-religious "thou." However, unlike her autobiographic romance, this first-person recollection has Child aspiring not for a divine and universal prospect, but for a viewpoint both human and specific, desiring not God's own "vision" but rather a new lens for Qur'ānic interpretation.

In situating the "Koran" as a site for social exchange and visual focus, Child's recollection of her "early years" also forms a forecast of her maturing career. Remembering this "intense desire" in the fall of 1841, Child unconsciously predicts the decade to come, with the Muslim scripture increasingly magnified for Child through the 1840s. And while Child will never realize her childhood hopes, failing to find a "Mohammadan" to assist her hermeneutics, she does closely "look at the Koran" on her own, recording her "sincere and intelligent" efforts in a single, unpublished notebook.[37] Now housed at the Boston Public Library, this holograph notebook (cataloged as Ms.A.5.1) features Child's own handwritten notes on the Muslim scripture, supplying an invaluable lens for understanding her interests and approach, offering an opportunity "to look at the Koran through *her* spectacles." Untitled and undated by Child herself, this Boston Public Library notebook has been labelled as "Notes on George Sale's commentary and translation of the Koran"—an extended title that emphasizes a familiar source: the 1734 rendition of George Sale. The same British translation examined by her American predecessors, Child's review of Sale's *Koran* in the 1840s reaches back again to Ezra Stiles, returning a full half-century to his own Qur'ānic "read$^g$" in the 1790s. More immediately, however, it is Irving that Child parallels, not only by benefitting from Sale's "translation" and "commentary," but also by leaving behind a material record of her *Koran* reading, transcribing selections from Sale's edition into her surviving notebook. As Irving, Child privately constructs a "commonplace book" of Qur'ānic quotation, copying out passages that span dozens of scrawled pages—including pages 53 and 54 of her notebook, which read respectively:

> [*top of page 53*] for their sins, and persevere not in what they have done knowingly. Their reward shall be pardon from their Lord, and gardens wherein rivers flow, they shall remain therein for ever."
>
> [3:145] "No soul can die unless by the permission of God, according to what is written in the book containing the determination of things."
>
> [4:1] "O men, fear your Lord, who hath created you out of one man, and out of him created his wife, and from them two hath multiplied many men, and women: and fear God by whom ye beseech one another; and

respect women who have borne you, for God is watching over you. [4:2] And give the orphans when they come to age their substance; and render them not in exchange bad for good: and devour not their substance, by adding it to your own substance; for this is [*top of page 54*] a great sin. [4:3] And if ye fear that ye shall not act with equity towards orphans of the female sex, take in marriage of such other women as please you, two, or three, or four, and not more. But if ye fear that ye cannot act equitably towards so many, marry one only, or the slaves which ye shall have acquired. This will be easier, that ye swerve not from righteousness.

[4:7] "Men ought to have a part of what their parents and kindred leave behind them when they die: and women also ought to have a part of what their parents and kindred leave whether it be little, or whether it be much; a determinate part is due to them."

(The pagan Arabs did not suffer women and children to inherit any part of a husband's or father's property; saying only those ought to inherit who went to war.)[38]

Progressing chronologically through the Qur'ān, pages 53 and 54 of Child's notebook find her transcribing select verses from the scripture's earliest chapters, picking out passages spread over many pages in Sale's edition. For instance, at the very top of her page 53, Child quotes from the Qur'ān 3:135–36 ("for their sins, and persevere not in what they have done knowingly") before jumping next to 3:145 ("No soul can die unless by the permission of God, according to what is written in the book containing the determination of things"); by the bottom half of this same page, Child has moved on to 3:194 ("O Lord, give us the reward which thou hast promised by thy apostles"). Plucked from their Qur'ānic context, and transcribed haphazardly without headings, these selections reflect acts of Child's idiomatic reading, expressing her own interest in individual verses. By the bottom of page 53, however, Child has reached the fourth chapter of the Qur'ān—simply entitled "Women"—a chapter that unsurprisingly attracts her close attention. Child's transcriptions suddenly become more dense here, not leaping wildly between distant portions, but rather copying successively, verse after verse. Rather than skipping selectively, it is a single locus that Child transcribes, quoting three verses in succession (Chapter 4:1–3) before taking a small step forward, copying 4:7 ("Men ought to have a part of what their parents and kindred leave behind them [...]"). It is the content of this transcription cluster, however, that makes it significant; although addressed to men—"O Men, fear your lord"; or "Men ought to have"—it is "women" who aptly anchor these verses from Chapter 4. Mirroring Child's own concerns, it is the Qur'ān's grappling "with equity towards orphans of the female sex" that she chooses to record, noting too restrictions on polygamy, the scripture warning that "if ye cannot act equitably towards so many, marry one only." Perhaps most poignant, it is the rights of women to inherit their own property that Child seems especially eager to inscribe in her own hand, copying the Qur'ān's injunction that "and women also ought to have a part of what their parents and kindred leave, whether it be little, or whether it be much"—a scriptural verse that is also contextualized, Child paraphrasing in parentheses Sale's observation that "The pagan Arabs did not suffer women and children to inherit any part of a husband's or father's property; saying only those ought to inherit who went to war." Reflecting the extended title of her notebook, Child copies not only the "Koran" but also "Sale's commentary," his paratext clarifying the social advances heralded by Islam's sacred text, with regressive Arabian antiquity indexing the progressive character of the Qur'ān.[39] In an act of prophetic self-reflection, Child emphasizes material rights accorded to women in the Muslim scripture, even while she takes material possession of these Qur'ānic texts, scribbling Islamic verses in the very notebook that Child herself will "leave" behind as "property" for later inheritance. ☼

The progressive content of Child's "Koran" notebook reflects its original purpose, serving as the private foreground for her own published *Progress*—Child's *The Progress of Religious Ideas, Through Successive Ages*, which appeared in 1855. A "landmark in comparative religion," Child's *Progress* supplies an expansive genealogy of world spirituality, its more than 450 pages spanning East and West, ancient and modern.[40] Characteristic of Child is this work's diverse topics and ambitious scope, the three bulky volumes of her *Progress* unfolding a global chronology. Beginning with Oriental "Antiquity"—treating traditions original to "Hindostan," "Egypt," and "China"—Child's *Progress* proceeds up through Judaism and Christianity before concluding with a final body chapter dedicated to "Mohammedanism," reserving its culminating treatment for Islamic revelation and religion. Unprecedented in its "successive" sweep through human history, *The Progress of Religious Ideas* has been justly labeled Child's *"magnum opus"*; however, it is not only its historical coverage, but the biographical time it consumed, that qualifies Child's *Progress* as her "grand work."[41] Occupying "eight years to write," as Carolyn Karcher has detailed, the *Progress* was long in development due in part to Child's distance from essential sources for her research; living in rural New York and Massachusetts, Child's infrequent visits library visits were spent hurriedly transcribing substantive selections before returning home, staying "very busy in making extracts" as Child herself notes in 1848.[42]

Child's protracted process of research for her *Progress* is best exemplified and materially embodied by her Qur'ānic "Notes," a manuscript of Child's hurried "extracts" which is now barely legible, its current utility complicated by its original use. As seen in Figure 4.1, Child's quotations from Sale's *Koran* are often struck through with pencil, with entire pages crossed out by vertical lines—lines that signify not Child's disregard, but rather signal material marked for inclusion in her *Progress*.[43] Indexing the stages of her authorial process, Child's notebook finds her not only

*Figure 4.1* Lydia Maria Child, Ms.A.5.1 "Mahometans." From the Koran, translated from the original Arabic, by George Sale. pages 25–26. n.d. Image courtesy of the Trustees of the Boston Public Library/Rare Books.

making "extracts," but also editorial choices, scoring out the specific passages she elects to use, fashioning informal notebook transcripts into formal writing for publication. A precedent for her *Progress*, Child's "Koran" notebook also recalls precedents in her own career, however, evidencing not simple reliance on Muslim sources, but also Child's own revisions to style and substance. A medial step between mere copying and her mature composition, Child's notebook forms a layered palimpsest, serving as a revisionary space where Sale's "translation and commentary" is transformed into Child's "Mohammedanism." Domesticating the *Koran* in a double sense, Child's notebook acts not only as the literal vessel that conveys her "extracts" home from distant sites of research, but also as the literary site that transports these "extracts" into home idioms, expressing Qur'ānic text and paratexts in Child's own words.

This complex evolution from verbatim quotation to various composition is evidenced by the set of successive pages in Child's notebook pictured in Figure 4.1. Differing from her pages 53 and 54, which copy the *Koran* proper, pages 25 and 26 of Child's notebook transcribe not Sale's translation but his "Preliminary Discourse," the lengthy preface introducing his *Koran*.[44] Shifting place, these pages of Child's notebook shift practice as well, finding her no longer passively transcribing, but actively transforming, her source. The top of page 26, for instance, is loosely based on a passage from Sale's preface that addresses Qur'ānic interpretation—a passage that Child herself reinterprets, not replicating but rewriting Sale's original, adapting his British passage for inclusion in her American *Progress*. This unfolding process of paraphrase is charted below, paralleling its three stages: (1) Sale's original passage; (2) the version copied by Child in her notebook (pictured in Fig. 4.1); and (3) the passage ultimately published in her 1855 *Progress*:[45]

### Sale, *Koran* (1734)

The opinion of al Jahedh, chief of a sect bearing his name, touching the Korân, is too remarkable to be omitted: he used to say it was a body, which might sometimes be turned into a man, and sometimes into a beast; which seems to agree with the notion of those who assert the Korân to have two faces, one of a man, the other of beast; thereby, as I conceive, intimating the double interpretation it will admit of, according to the letter or the spirit. [. . .]

The Korân being the Mohammedans' rule of faith and practice, it is no wonder its expositors and commentators are so very numerous. And it may not be amiss to take notice of the rules they observe in expounding it.

One of the most learned commentators distinguishes the contents of the Korân into allegorical and literal. The former comprehends the more obscure, parabolical, and ænigmatical passages, and such as are repealed or abrogated; the latter those which are plain, perspicuous, liable to no doubt, and in full force.

To explain these severally in a right manner, it is necessary from tradition and study to know the time when each passage was revealed, its circumstances, state, and history, and the reasons or particular emergencies for the sake of which it was revealed. Or more explicitly, whether the passage was revealed at Mecca, or at Medina; whether it be abrogated, or does itself abrogate any other passage; whether it be anticipated in order of time, or postponed; whether it be distinct from the context, or depends thereon; whether it be particular or general; and lastly whether it be implicit by intention, or explicit in words.

### Child, "Notes" (c. 1850; Fig. 4.1)

One sect asserted that the Koran was sometimes a man sometimes a beast; probably meaning that it had a double interpretation, one according to the letter the other according to the spirit.

The expounding of the Koran is considered to require much learning. To distinguish between the parts which are literal and the parts allegorical, to determine the time when any place where ^of which each passage was revealed, and the particular ~~purpose for which it was revealed~~ circumstances attending it  emergencies which called for it. Whether any particular passage was afterward abrogated, or whether itself abrogates some other passage; whether it be distinct from the context or depends thereon &c. Immense number of commentators and controversies.

↓

### Child, *Progress* (1855)

Having been in existence over twelve hundred years, it of course fails to meet all the wants of modern times, even where society is so very slightly progressive as in Asia. But they stretch its capacities by resorting to the same process that Hindoos did with the Vedas, and Jews with the Pentateuch; they give ingenious interpretations, and resort to allegorical significance where the literal meaning is unsatisfactory. An immense number of commentaries have been written upon it. It is supposed to require much learning to distinguish rightly between what was intended to be allegorical and what literal; to determine for what emergencies particular passages were written, and whether they were abrogated by succeeding passages.

Cascading from top left to top right and finally to bottom right, the fluid process of Child's revisions show her success in submerging her original source, even while saving a few of its idiomatic details; for instance, Sale's distinctive "half man and half beast" characterization of the Qur'ān survives, conveyed from Sale's *Koran* through Child's notebook, finally to arrive in the pages of her *Progress*. However, exemplifying Child's adaptive process, this analogy is significantly condensed, its context especially cut. While Sale introduces this idea by asserting that "The opinion of al Jahedh, chief of a sect bearing his name, touching the Korân, is too remarkable to be omitted," this historical frame is itself "omitted" by Child; denuding this passage of its detail, Child first mentions merely that "One sect asserted that the Koran was sometimes a man sometimes a beast" in her notebook, leading to further distillation in publication, this idea appearing merely in her *Progress* as "One class resorted to allegorical interpretation of the Koran; styling it half man and half beast." Editing Sale, Child also adds elements, not only narrowing her source but broadening its significance. Recruited for her ecumenical *Progress*, this passage on Qur'ānic interpretation acquires new interreligious potential, Child asserting that attempts by Muslims to read their sacred book allegorically recall "the same process that Hindoos did with the Vedas, and Jews with the Pentateuch."[46]

Uniquely revealed in Child's private manuscript is the derivative kinship of seemingly discrete passages from Sale's *Koran* and her *Progress*, divorced in their published form by a process of distillation and digression undertaken in Child's Qur'ānic "Notes." Perhaps most striking, however, is the self-reflective irony of Child's notebook revisions, her amendments to Sale's passage performing ideas essential to this passage itself. Interpretively flexible and fluid, the material manipulated by Child ironically concerns the Qur'ān's own pliability; the sentences that Child transcribes from Sale at the top of her page 26, for instance, represent a commentary that not only addresses, but also embodies, the scripture's reformulation:

> The expounding of the Koran is considered to require much learning. To distinguish between the parts which are literal and the parts allegorical, to determine the time when any place where ^of which each passage was^ revealed, and the particular ~~purpose for which it was revealed~~ ^circumstances attending it^ emergencies which called for it. Whether any particular passage was afterward abrogated, or whether itself abrogates some other passage; whether it be distinct from the context or depends thereon &c. Immense number of commentators and controversies.[47]

Outlining the Qur'ān's interior process of "abrogation," Child herself externally abrogates Sale's *Koran* through copying selectively from its preface, "expounding" her source with editorial control, allowing a "particular passage" to supersede "some other passage." In the very sentence that highlights the original "emergencies" that occasioned Qur'ānic revelations, Child draws a literal line through the "purpose" of her original transcript, adding a fresh "when" and "where" in superscript. Recognizing that traditional readers of the Qur'ān adjudicated whether a certain verse "be distinct from the context or depends thereon," Child herself develops her own Qur'ānic account by cutting "context" from Sale's original, ironically becoming one of the *Koran*'s "immense number of commentators" by assuming modern authority "to distinguish rightly between what was intended."

It is the frame that Child's passage assumes in print that offers an oblique apology for the manuscript revisions she silently undertakes, arguing that future human growth is rooted in the reinterpretation of antique revelation; as she opens the published passage above, Child asserts that "Having been in existence over twelve hundred years, [the Qur'ān] of course fails to meet all the wants of modern times, even where society is so very slightly progressive as in Asia." Reporting on "progressive" efforts to renovate the Qur'ān for "modern times," Child obeys this very imperative in her *Progress*, adapting subtly her own versions of the Muslim scripture. In her notebook's page 26, Child reinterprets Sale's overview of Qur'ānic interpretation; immediately prior, however, on her notebook's page 25, Child's revisions lead her to retreat further back, arriving at Islam's scriptural source itself. Paraphrasing another section from Sale's "Preliminary Discourse," the middle of Child's page 25, pictured in Figure 4.1, intervenes again between his 1734 *Koran* and her own 1855 *Progress*, as charted in the passages paralleled below:[48]

**Sale, *Koran* (1734)**

By what has been said the reader may easily believe this book is in the greatest reverence and esteem among the Mohammedans. They dare not so much as touch it without being first washed or legally purified[2] which lest they should do by inadvertence, they write these words on the cover or label, "Let none touch it, but they who are clean." They read it with great care and respect, never holding it below their girdles. They swear by it, consult it in their weighty occasions[3], carry it with them to war, write sentences of it on their banners, adorn it with gold and precious stones, and knowingly suffer it not to be in the possession of any of a different persuasion.

[2] The Jews have the same veneration for their law; not daring to touch it with unwashed hands, nor then neither without a cover. Vide Millium, de Mohammedismo ante Moh. p. 366

[3] This they do by dipping into it, and taking an omen from the words which they first light on: which practice they also learned of the Jews, who do the same with the scriptures. Vide Millium, ubi sup.

**Child, "Notes" (c. 1850; Fig. 4.1)**

By Mahometans of all sects it is held in the greatest reverence. Like the Jews, they never touch it without first washing their hands. Lest they should do so by inadvertence, they place a label on the cover "Let none touch this but those who —→ are clean." They never hold it below their girdles; and on weighty occasions open it reverently to seek an omen or guide from the first words the eye rests on. They carry it to war, inscribe sentences of it on their banners, adorn its copies with gold and precious stones, and never knowingly allow an unbeliever to have possession of a copy.

↓

**Child, *Progress* (1855)**

All sects hold it in the greatest possible reverence. Like the Hindoos and the Jews, they never touch the Sacred Book without first washing their hands. Lest it should be done inadvertently, they place a label on the cover: "Let no one touch this, but those who are clean." They never hold it below their girdles; and never knowingly allow an unbeliever to possess a copy. On important occasions, they consult it as an oracle, taking the first verse they open upon as an inspired guide. They swear by it, carry it with them to war, inscribe sentences of it on their banners, and believe it will finally be established in every kingdom of the earth. The wealthy have copies of it enclosed in golden covers set with precious stones.

Erasing borders between text below and text above in Sale's source, Child again mirrors the Qur'ānic concerns of the very passage she copies—a passage that itself highlights a moment of textual migration, with the scripture's exterior adorned by a slice of its interior. On the outside "cover" of the Qur'ān, Sale notes that a single verse from inside the Qur'ān is regularly "written," warning believers that "Let none touch it, but they who are clean" (Qur'ān 56:79). Enjoining "cleanliness" as readers approach the Qur'ān, demanding the book be persevered pure, this scriptural selection is itself cleansed in Child's own account, preserved yet also purified through another progressive revision. Initially copying into her notebook, Child provides new pronouns, substituting Sale's "Let none touch *it*, but *they* who are clean," with her own "Let none touch *this* but *those* who are clean" (emphasis added); finally, in preparing her *Progress* for publication, Child elects to break apart Sale's "none" into an emphatic "no one," resulting in her own iteration of this Qur'ānic verse in print, appearing in her *Progress* as "Let no one touch this, but those who are clean." Offering merely minor revisions to Sale, Child retains the meaning of her sacred source yet also resists its own imperative, covertly touching and retouching "the Koran" before it reaches the hands of her American readers. From private interiors to published exteriors, Child's subtle revisions unfold outward from her "Koran" notebook to her *Progress*, revising a verse already extracted from the Qur'ān's own interior, selected from within to be inscribed on its "cover or label" without. Gilding a new iteration of the Qur'ān, Child freshly adorns sacred words that are "enclosed in golden covers," forging her own individual version even as her passage concludes by forecasting the Qur'ān's universal future, alluding to the climactic "belief" that the Qur'ān will "finally be established in every kingdom of the earth." Personally revising this scripture of global aspiration, adorning anew this "book" that is "set with precious stones," the revisions that begin in Child's Qur'ānic "Notes" reach forward not only to her *Progress* but prevision the climax of her own authorial life, anticipating her concluding work, her 1878 *Aspirations of the World: A Chain of Opals*. ✦

"When the inevitable day of judgment shall come, it will abase some, and exalt others. Those on the left hand shall dwell amid burning winds, and scalding water, and in the shadow of black smoke. Those on the right hand shall approach near unto God. They shall dwell in gardens of delight, reposing on couches adorned with gold and precious stones. Youths, blooming with immortal beauty, shall wait upon them with whatsoever birds or fruits they may desire, and with goblets of wine, the drinking of which shall not disturb their reason, or cause their heads to ache. As a reward for that which they have wrought they shall have for companions fair damsels, resembling pearls hidden in their shells, and having large black eyes. They shall not hear any charge of sin, nor any vain discourse; but only the salutation, Peace! Peace!"

Child, *Progress* (1855), III: 385

Appearing in the midst of her "Mohammedanism" chapter, the above is one of the "extracts" from the Qur'ān that Child publishes in her *Progress* to exemplify the scripture's "character."[49] Spiritual in content instead of societal in concern, this quotation seems unconnected with Child's progressive interests; rather than advocate for women's liberation through marital equality or material inheritance, it is "fair damsels" who are here envisioned, bequeathed as "companions" to believers in paradise. If seemingly extraneous to Child's politics, this Qur'ānic "extract" does covertly reflect Child's revisionary practices. Presented as a continuous and coherent translation, this selection is instead a highly edited version of the Qur'ān's Chapter 56, arising from Child's own restructuring of Sale's *Koran*. Inverting verse order while omitting vivid images, Child's original source had instead begun with paradise, not punishment, first describing "Those on the right hand" before its lengthy treatment of "Those on the left hand." Electing to lead instead with the blamed, and not the blessed, Child also cuts all but one sentence from Sale's translation that describes Hell, reserving nearly her entire "extract" for heavenly delights.[50] Polishing the Qur'ān's lusters while covering over its darker colors, Child's adaptations produce a passage itself "adorned with gold and precious stones," its lines "resembling pearls" largely evading the shadows of "black smoke." Another instance of her editorial dexterity, Child's specific privileging of "right hand" over "left" in the Qur'ān's Chapter 56 will, however, proceed beyond the pages of her *Progress*, appearing in print again more than two decades later. This chapter on the afterlife, emphasizing "pearls" and priceless "stones," will be resurrected again in the most explicitly "precious" of Child's works, appearing in the introduction to her 1878 *Aspirations of the World: A Chain of Opals*.

Youthful in its yearning title, Child's *Aspirations* nevertheless marks a fitting close to her career, representing the most miscellaneous of her works. A composite anthology rather than an authored composition, *Aspirations* filters hundreds of quotations from diverse global religions, combining these fragments to produce what Child herself would call her "Eclectic Bible."[51] And while the religious genealogy traced in Child's *Progress* was grounded in extensive research, copying "extracts" from distant libraries, her 1878 *Aspirations* offers these extracts themselves, presenting readers with a commonplace book of spiritual epigrams that recalls Child's own private notebooks. Featuring quotations arranged under headings that frequently reflect Child's social commitments (e.g., "Family and Friends," "Benevolence," "Fraternity of Religions," "Natural Law of Justice," and even "Childlike Character"), the philanthropic content of *Aspirations* is reflected too in its target audience; "I aim directly at the *common people*," Child confesses in an 1878 letter, characterizing her motives in publishing *Aspirations* by adding, "I have altered nothing, but I have put Oriental and Grecian ideas into a plain English dress."[52]

Assembled in the years following the fractious Civil War, severing chains of slavery but also national bonds in the United States, *Aspirations* is a work of "Reconstruction" in a double sense, not only published at the height of this American period, but also seeking to reconstruct a worldwide *Chain* of religious wisdom, stringing together *Opals* of spiritual insight. If global in scope and miscellaneous in method, *Aspirations* is, however, also consistent with Child's career in its Islamic concentrations, integrating copious quotations from the Qur'ān while also citing the Prophet as well as Sufi mystics, invoking Persian poets such as Saʿdī and Ḥāfiẓ.[53] Considering its appeal to "precious stones," it is perhaps not surprising to find that *Aspirations* quotes the Qur'ān 56 in particular, citing the same version reproduced above, which Child had adapted for publication in her 1855 *Progress*. Offering an overview of her anthology and the traditions it embraces, Child's introduction to her *Aspirations* includes a discussion of the discrete afterlives envisioned by different religions, including Islam:

> Mohammed gave glowing pictures of the joys that awaited true believers, "if they have forsaken their sins, and prayed to God to pardon them, and have given alms freely, and bridled their anger, and forgiven men." He declared that he saw "gardens, where rivers flow; and angels were building palaces with blocks of gold and silver and rubies, cemented with the soil of Paradise, which is pure musk. In those gardens of delight the faithful shall repose on couches adorned with gold and precious stones. Youths blooming with immortal beauty shall wait upon them with whatsoever birds or fruits they may desire, and with goblets of wine, the drinking of which shall not disturb the reason, or cause their heads to ache. They shall have for companions fair damsels, resembling pearls hidden in their shells, and having large dark eyes. They shall not hear any charge of sin, nor any vain discourse; but only the salutation. Peace! Peace!"[54]

The bulk of the above selection is familiar, its final lines virtually identical to the version of the Qur'ān 56 previously published in Child's *Progress*. However, despite Child's claim to "have altered nothing," it is clear that the opening of this Qur'ānic quotation is new. Reframing its attribution, ascribing this quotation to "Mohammed," Child also alters its opening words, removing all sinister material, making no mention of the "day of judgment," as well as the damned who are relegated to "the left hand." Replacing infernal images of "burning winds," "scalding water," and "black smoke," Child adds new paradisal features, painting a scene in which "angels were building palaces with blocks of gold and silver and rubies, cemented with the soil of Paradise, which is pure musk." Entirely unconnected with the Qur'ān's Chapter 56, these vivid phrases derive instead from a separate source, borrowed from a book that had engaged Child's interest since its publication in 1850: *The Life and Religion of Mohammed*, rendered by James Lyman Merrick, a book that indeed features an account of the celestial realm, envisioning "angels [who] were building palaces of gold and silver bricks," asserting too that "the soil of paradise is musk."[55] Stringing together discrete fragments, Child seamlessly threads a new chain of transmission, the opening of her *Opals* merging diverse Muslim sources, fused in their shared possession of "rubies," "pearls," and "precious stones."

Mirroring the titular trope of her *Chain of Opals*, this doubly adapted quotation erected in the introduction to her *Aspirations* aptly gestures not only to adornment, but also to architecture, this newly "cemented" quotation in Child's writing itself concerned with "building palaces" on "the soil of Paradise." Recounting "angels" as they stack precious "blocks," this quotation is itself assembled from anterior materials, its building blocks quietly sourced from diverse sites. However, due to arising from textual deconstruction and reconstruction, Child's citation inevitably contains fissures, with a noticeable fracture between the metaphors it seeks to fuse. Amalgamating two sources, Child's resulting quotation abruptly shifts from the palatial to the pastoral, its heavenly towers sourced from Merrick's *Life and Religion of Mohammed* uneasily adjacent to the low-lying gardens and reclining couches sourced from Sale's *Koran*. The lofty opening installed at the beginning of Child's passage also helps overshadow a more minor chink hidden near the very end of the passage. Although the last half of her *Aspirations'* quotation matches its appearance in Child's *Progress* verbatim, there is one slight variation in its concluding words. While in 1855 Child had described celestial virgins as "having large black eyes," in her 1878 anthology these same virgins are depicted instead as "having large dark eyes." A miniscule revision—intended perhaps to avoid the connotation in English of a "black eye"—Child's substitution of "dark eyes" lends a seductive appeal to her passage, yet seems possibly a mere error; could this incidental change have arisen accidently, simply a slip in copying this passage for republication? It is the actual manuscript of her *Aspirations*, produced and preserved by Child, that resolves this speculative question. Housed at Cornell University's Carl A. Kroch Library, Division of Rare and Manuscript Collections, Child's draft of her final book demonstrates that this ocular change was performed manually, with Child's correction to eye color visible near the bottom of her manuscript's page 45 (Fig. 4.2).[56]

In black ink, near the bottom of this page, Child strikes out the "black" of the virgins' eyes, adding "dark" in her own superscript hand. Revising this single phrase from her original source in Sale's *Koran*, Child offers a new impression of the feminine eye, ameliorating her fair copy text to ensure that it reads more fair. Reviewing her own prior adaptations of Sale's *Koran*, Child adjusts again her British male source, taking fresh possession of the feminine eye in her American "Eclectic Bible." Although Child had reported a youthful yearning to "look at the Koran" through Muslim "spectacles," it is her final *Aspirations* that allows her to innovate such speculative changes. Still refocusing the Muslim scriptures in her own manual draft, Child's last book's manuscript witnesses her willingness to adjust her own vision of this Qur'ānic verse, even as she adjusts the very color of eyes in the Qur'ān.[57]

If the bottom of page 54 pictured in Figure 4.2 features a color change in its written text, perhaps more conspicuous is the color change at page top, with a piece of yellow paper pasted over the pale original. Mirroring her pastiche of sources, this manuscript page is itself a pastiche of discrete substances, its head material regarding "Mohammad"

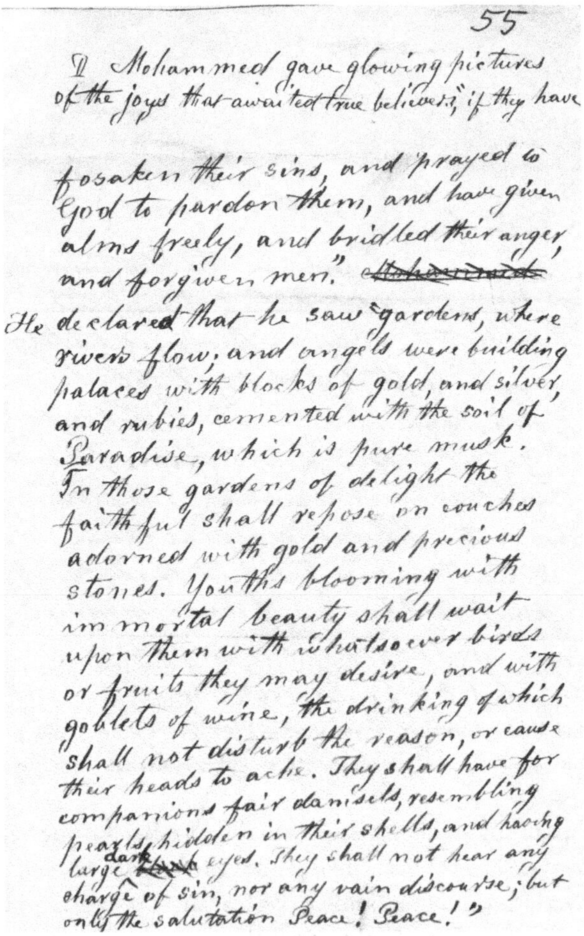
55

I Mohammed gave glowing pictures
of the joys that awaited true believers," if they have
forsaken their sins, and prayed to
God to pardon them, and have given
alms freely, and bridled their anger,
and forgiven men."
He declared that he saw "gardens, where
rivers flow; and angels were building
palaces with blocks of gold, and silver,
and rubies, cemented with the soil of
Paradise, which is pure musk.
In those gardens of delight the
faithful shall repose on couches
adorned with gold and precious
stones. Youths blooming with
immortal beauty shall wait
upon them with whatsoever birds
or fruits they may desire, and with
goblets of wine, the drinking of which
shall not disturb the reason, or cause
their heads to ache. They shall have for
companions fair damsels, resembling
pearls, hidden in their shells, and having
large dark eyes. They shall not hear any
charge of sin, nor any vain discourse; but
only the salutation Peace! Peace!"

*Figure 4.2* Lydia Maria Child, *Aspirations of the World*, manuscript draft, page 55. Image courtesy of the Division of Rare and Manuscript Collections, Cornell University Library.

added by Child's affixing a physical strip of paper. Amassing her *Aspirations* through a process of literal and literary layering, this page offers a tangible symbol to Child's textual reconstruction; however, it is not Child's pasting over material on the front of her pages, but the material that is overshadowed on the back of these pages, that is most intriguing. Rather than blank spaces, the reverse of Child's pages from her *Aspirations* manuscript are themselves inscribed with a variety of family correspondences, comprising letters and notes received by the Child family during the 1870s. Instead of writing her miscellaneous compilation of global religions on fresh paper, Child elects instead to assemble *Aspirations* on the back of domestic messages, these two sides of her book synthesizing a *World* of spirituality with a household miscellany.[58] In this juxtaposition between the private and the published, eerie echoes also emerge between the *Aspiration*'s foreign religions and the familial writings upon which they are

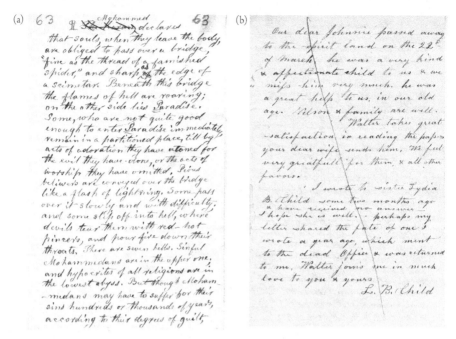

*Figure 4.3* Lydia Maria Child, *Aspirations of the World*, manuscript draft, page 63, recto and verso, the former featuring Child's treatment of Muslim eschatology, the latter representing a letter from "L.B. Child," reporting the recent death of "a very kind & affectionate child." Image courtesy of the Division of Rare and Manuscript Collections, Cornell University Library.

inscribed. Perhaps the most potent example of this reverberation occurs on page 63 of Child's draft, the two sides of which are reproduced as Figure 4.3.

Paired on inverted sides of this same loose leaf are two seemingly unrelated literary acts, merging a page from Child's draft *Aspirations*, concerning Muḥammad's view of heaven and hell, and the last page of a letter autographed "L.B. Child" (Levi Bigelow Child, the brother of Lydia's husband, David Lee Child).[59] Composing on the back of her brother-in-law's letter, Child repurposes this piece of family correspondence as the physical basis for her spiritual writings, inscribing her Islamic interests literally onto this folio of intimate exchange. However, this page not only serves as a striking symbol of the mirroring between Child's daily routines and her Islamic researches, but offers instead a moment where these spheres seem to bleed through a single page, sympathetically blending Child's professional and personal interests. The draft page of Child's *Aspirations* (Fig. 4.3), eventually published as her work's pages 39 to 40, reads as follows:

> Mohammed declares that souls, when they leave the body, are obliged to pass over a bridge, "fine as the thread of a famished spider," and sharp as the edge of a scimitar. Beneath this bridge the flames of hell are roaring; on the other side lies Paradise. Some, who are not quite good enough to

enter Paradise immediately, remain in a partitioned place, till by acts of adoration they have atoned for the evil they have done, or for the acts of worship they have omitted. Pious believers are conveyed over the bridge like a flash of lightning. Some pass over it slowly and with difficulty; and some slip off into hell, where devils tear them with red-hot pincers, and pour fire down their throats. There are seven hells. Sinful Mohammedans are in the upper one; and hypocrites of all religions are in the lowest abyss. But though Mohammedans may have to suffer for their sins hundreds or thousands of years, according to their degrees of guilt [. . .][60]

Reflecting Child's concern with Islam's eschatology, this material recalls her previous accounts of the Muslim afterlife; however, distinct from Child's prior reflections on "Paradise," this page emphasizes also the perilous in eternity, describing the precarious bridge all must posthumously cross. A testament to Child's Islamic interests, this page's significance is amplified, however, if its verso and recto are compared, the two sides of this same leaf manifesting a strange symmetry. Turning this page over to read the letter received from "L.B. Child," all mention of "Mohammed" is absent, of course; however, an interest in the afterlife endures, with the first lines of his letter's final page reading:

Our dear Johnnie passed away to the spirit land on the 22[d] of March, he was a very kind & affectionate child to us & we miss him very much. he was a great help to us in our old age

In the midst of a newsy note exchanged between family members, it is an intimate account of bereavement that emerges, L. B. Child reporting the recent "pass[ing] away" of "Johnnie"—an "affectionate child" whose flight to "the spirit land" has left him and his wife in mourning.[61] Heightening the significance of her decision to inscribe *Aspirations* on the reverse of family letters, Child's page 63 finds her repurposing the most personal and profound of letters from her brother-in-law to serve as the basis upon which she inscribes her Islamic reflections, with this passing of an "affectionate child" to the afterlife situated as poignant complement to the material written on this page's reverse. Enveloped by ghosts—merging a memorial of an earthly death and the promises of eternal life—this single page becomes a double portal between the here and hereafter, pairing an ineffably personal event in an American family with Islam's message proclaimed for all mankind. Mapping the "spirit land" on both its front and back, the barrier of this sole sheet of paper is itself crossed by a common concern, with both sides occupied with our crossing over to the beyond. Selecting an intimate family note to render her own impressions of the Muslim unseen, the morbid mirroring between this manuscript's front and back also becomes a basis for a textual resurrection, the tragic death of a young member of the extended Child family transformed into a vehicle for advancing

"Mohammedan" prophecy in Child's *Aspirations*, this American fatality forming the physical grounds for Child's exploration of Islam's envisioned afterlife. ☼

> MADOURA (running forward). Oh! do not cause my death! He has been ever kind to me! I will not part from him! Oh! be merciful, good Caliph!
> CALIPH. Yes, Madoura, I will be merciful! I will allow Codabad to be bettered by your influence. Retire beyond the walls of Bagdat. Make a pilgrimage to Mecca. The prophet has said, "Whoso worketh good, male or female, shall enter paradise."
> MADOURA. Women may have souls! I'll think on this.
> CALIPH. Here, Madoura, take this as a mark of my approbation. (The CALIPH gives her a chain from his own neck.) The wisest of men has said, "Seest thou a virtuous woman; her price is above rubies." (CODABAD and MADOURA make profound bows and retire on one side.)[62]

This dramatic dialogue between the "good Caliph" and "Madoura" regarding the fate of her beloved, "Codabad," marks the climactic moments of "The Olive Merchants of Bagdat," an anonymous comedy in a single act, first published in 1850. Appearing initially in London, as the fourth play in a collection entitled *Pleasant Pastime; or, Drawing-Room Dramas, for Private Representation by the Young*, "The Olive Merchants of Bagdat" was re-collected in America, published again in 1859 as part of *Home Dramas for Young People*, an anthology printed in Boston, compiled by Child's own close friend, Eliza Lee Cabot Follen.[63] It is not Follen's role in publishing this play, however, that seems its primary connection to Child. Triangulated between Islamic subject, adolescent audience, and a concern for women's rights, "The Olive Merchants of Bagdat" not only reflects Child's own interests broadly, but features direct discussion of the female "soul"—a discussion that distinctly recalls Child's own treatment in her 1835 *The History of the Condition of Women in Various Ages and Nations*. Overlapping in topics and tropes, it is the translation that intersects this passage that especially links this *Home Drama* to Child's own *History*. At the crux of the above exchange between the Caliph and Madoura is a Qur'ānic quotation that sounds distinctly familiar. Ascribed to Muḥammad himself, the Caliph insists that "the prophet has said, 'Whoso worketh good, male or female, shall enter paradise' "—an English rendition of the Qur'ān 16:97, which, in fact, is original to Lydia Maria Child, first published as part of her 1835 chapter on "Turkish Women," as traced above.[64]

Printed initially in 1850 and republished in 1859—the very years of Irving's *Mahomet* and his death respectively—"The Olive Merchants of Bagdat" signals an afterlife for Child's Muslim receptions that parallels Irving's own Islamic endurance; as with Irving, Child's Qur'ānic adaptations will be subject to additional adaptation, borrowed from Child's works and integrated silently into new productions. However, while Irving's Qur'ānic renditions will appear in subsequent narratives of foreign adventure, Child's iterations of the Qur'ān here appear in more domestic contexts, punctuating a play designed for "private" performances. Reflecting Child's own familial approach to Islamic sources, her engagement with Islam enjoys an afterlife in "the drawing-room," reaching for new readers among women and children. Unconsciously matching Child's favorite tropes, her Qur'ānic rendition is even invoked as the Caliph names Madoura "a virtuous woman [whose] price is above rubies," offering too a "mark of [his] approbation," namely "a chain from his own neck." A link conveying Child's Islamic interests to future audiences, her translation of the Qur'ān appears in this *Drama* together with a donation of precious links, her rendition from the Muslim scripture untied from her authorship, even as another valuable chain is transmitted from this drama's Muslim sovereign to his female subject.

Aligned yet inverted, it is not only the audience, but the attitude and agenda, that differentiates the Islamic afterlives of Irving and Child. An extension of their own intentions, Irving's Qur'ānic renditions will be largely appropriated for entertainment, while Child's are picked up with political purpose, adapted not to enliven accounts of travel, but to instill ideals of social justice. Extending her own revision and reuse of Muslim materials, fellow female authors especially will borrow Child's Islamic borrowings; her *History of Women*, for example, informs the Islamicism of works such *Claims of the Country on American Females*, published by Margaret Coxe in 1842.[65] Influencing present-day contemporaries, Child's Qur'ānic interests also persist posthumously, echoing into the decades that follow her 1880 death, informing authors such as Jenkin Lloyd Jones, Unitarian minister and Chicago spiritualist.[66] Authored in 1906, Jones' essay "The Rosary of a Holy Life" not only recalls the central symbol of Child's *Chain of Opals*, but reports his experience reading Child's work, aptly invoking her *Aspirations* even as Jones meditates on the "thread of life":

> Jesus cautioned his disciples against the use of vain repetitions in their prayers. It was this danger that the Persian poet saw, perhaps, when he broke out in the words of my text,
>> He needs no other rosary whose thread of life is strung with beads of love and thought.
> A loving deed is the best call to prayer, and a high thought brings God near. Our St. Lydia in finding this text found many others teaching the same lesson. Her beautiful little book, *Aspirations of the Soul*, is open before me at the page where we found our text. On the same page I read:
>> One came to Mohammed, saying, "My mother has died; What shall I do for the good of her soul?" and the prophet replied, "Dig a well, that the thirsty may have water to drink."
> On the opposite page I read a text from the Koran which says:
>> One hour of justice is worth seventy years of prayer.[67]

Adapting Child's own title, Jones relabels her "beautiful little book" as *Aspirations of the Soul* rather than the *World*, inadvertently internalizing Child's global survey of religions. However, perhaps most striking is the way in which Jones' "Rosary" adds authentic links to Child's own life of Islamic adaptation, selecting these specific passages while memorializing Child's own life as "strung with beads of love and thought." Citing two discrete passages from her *Aspirations*—the first a prophetic *ḥadīth*, spoken by "Mohammed," the second original not to the Muslim scripture but to al-Ghazālī—Jones not only encourages the endurance of Child's Islamic interests by importing her work into a new context and century, but also consecrates Child herself as he appeals to her ostensible quotation from "the Koran."[68] Canonized now as "St. Lydia," Child is positioned by Jones between her Muslim sources and the maternal sacred, recognized in this complex elegy as both a saintly matriarch who has departed and the author who has passed along an Islamic injunction to promote healing in the wake of the "death" of the "mother."

Child's own 1880 death followed only two years after "[h]er beautiful little book" appeared; however, as her final substantive work, the 1878 *Aspirations* also features a final valediction from Child that is intimately tied to the Islamic, its closing pages again dedicated to "Mohammedanism." As the last links in her own *Chain of Opals*, Child strings together a brief section which offers an overview of the world's "Sacred Books," her voice emerging at the very end of her miscellaneous anthology. Closing her survey of "Sacred Books," the concluding pages of Child's *Aspirations*—pages 275 and 276 as printed in its 1878 publication—read as follows:

## MOHAMMEDAN

In former ages, the Arabian Tribes were universally addicted to the worship of images. Their countryman Mohammed believed he was divinely commissioned to abolish idolatry, and inculcate the doctrine of One Invisible God. He lived about a thousand years before the invention of printing, when a knowledge even of written characters was very rare; and he had never practised the art. But the thoughts that were seething in his mind were recorded, from time to time, by one of his friends. In the dearth of better materials, some of them are said to have been originally written on shoulder-blades of mutton. Thus began, about 609 years after the Christian era, the Sacred Book afterward widely known as Al Koran, which in Arabic means The Reading.

Mohammed was a travelling-agent in his youth, and became intimately acquainted with Jews, Sabaeans, and Christians; the traces of whose influence appear in the writings he dictated. He inculcated reverence for the prophets of all religions, and represented himself as one of many prophets.

After his death, traditions of his sayings and doings were published in a volume called The Mishkat.

All the Sacred Books of the world were written in ancient times; some of them are extremely ancient. [*page 276*] They all contain internal evidence of having been written when knowledge was in its infancy, and when the world, being in its childhood, manifested a child-like tendency to accept the miraculous. All over the world, we see human beings, with one or another of these lamps in their hands, wandering through labyrinths of theory and fogs of superstition. Everywhere we hear voices of supplication; everywhere we see hands stretched toward the Infinite, "seeking after God, if haply they may find him." Let us recognize them all as fellow-pilgrims on the same mysterious journey; and let us give each other cheerful assurance that through devious paths we are all being guided homeward by the UNIVERSAL FATHER.[69]

At the end of both her *Aspirations* and her authorial career, Child's final pages form an epilogue that moves from a summary of "Mohammedan" scripture, to a more "universal" overview of "Sacred Books." Situating Islam as its final faith, *Aspirations* follows a global chronology predicted in Child's *Progress*, again positioning Muslim traditions as penultimate, before providing a broader conclusion, with the Prophet's teachings emerging as the last religion particularized in Child's career publishing books. Aptly, however, it is not Islam in general, but rather the problematic transmission of Islamic texts, which assumes center stage in Child's concluding treatment. Obliquely echoing her own career of adaptations, Child accents the vagaries of passing down sacred verses during a time "when a knowledge even of written characters was very rare." According to Child, the endurance of Islamic traditions "before the invention of printing" was ensured through social circles, the Prophet's companions conveying his words forward; "the thoughts that were seething in his mind were recorded, from time to time, by one of his friends," Child insists, emphasizing not only the familiar, but the fragmentary nature of Islam's textual genealogy, with selections written even on the "shoulder-blades of mutton," the Muslim scripture surviving in literal corporeal slices.

Itself exemplifying the enduring "influence" enjoyed by "the writings [the Prophet] dictated," Child's *Aspirations* pivots finally from a "Mohammedan" summary to her own last words—last words which also span a familial spectrum, stretching from human "infancy" to divine paternity. Dedicating her last section aptly to our collective "childhood," Child transitions from Islam on page 275 to broader religious contexts on page 276, asserting that Muslim scripture, along with sibling spiritual writings, "manifested a child-like tendency"—a richly ironic observation, considering the degree to which Islamic revelation was literally rendered "Child-like" through her long career of Qurʾānic revisions. Amidst the domesticating impulses of Child's final pages, perhaps most clear is an urgent nostalgia, projecting an ideal homecoming as her *Aspirations* reaches an end. Prefaced by her final passage on Islamic antiquity, Child lastly envisions a universal future, which stretches not only forward, but upward and backward, yearning for celestial parentage. Recalling Child's early interest in "Job Ben Solomon," who ultimately returned to a familial embrace after an extended journey of literal and literary rendition, the final steps of Child's own "devious paths" too find her offering the most basic translation of the "Koran," supplying a rendition of the very name of this "sacred book," invoking "Al Koran, which in Arabic means The Reading." And while Job had returned to succeed his "Mohammadan" elders, claiming his throne at his father's death, Child here progresses beyond "Mohammadan" precedents as she aspires for an eternal paternity; concluding her "mysterious journey" with a penultimate Muslim step, this "American" author of the *"Mother's Book"* lastly performs her own "childhood" on the very page that follows her concluding Islamic allusions, reaching up in her final words to embrace the "UNIVERSAL FATHER."

# 5

# "He knows the Koran by heart"

## The Sufi Circulations of Ralph Waldo Emerson

The weeks leading up to William Bentley's sudden death in the final days of 1819 marked the midpoint of Ralph Waldo Emerson's undergraduate career. Returning to Harvard to begin his junior year in the fall of 1819, Emerson also returns again to writing his "College Theme Book," a diary indexing his diverse interests, from the intimate to the academic. Announcing the autumn term's October opening, Emerson inaugurates his third year at Harvard with the following words:

> *Digressive Continuity*
> First Junior Term.     Oct 1819.
> "In aforetime I created *Jan* from out of a scorching fire."
> Alcoran
> "Coming events cast their shadows before."
> Campbell
> Our imaginations of all our mental powers are those to whose impulses we are most alive—to whose pleasures we cling most closely. It is with difficulty & reluctance that man brings himself to exercise the reasoning faculties, & the more so when the subject of thought is intricate <&> or doubtful. True, by long & frequent habit of disciplining his reasoning powers a man may learn to feel pleasure & satisfaction in these exercises, but [it] is only by long & frequent habits of ratiocination that the pleasure is gained.[1]

Anticipating his coming semester at college, Emerson anticipates too the "coming events" of his postgraduate career, dedicating the bulk of this bold tirade to concerns that will ultimately lead Emerson to become "America's first Romantic philosopher."[2] Weighing human feelings and faculties, privileging the personal and the "pleasurable," this entry not only is prophetic of Emerson's future fame, but itself opens with prophetic quotations; lending a sense of occasion and urgency to his juvenilia, Emerson cites Thomas "Campbell," borrowing a line from "Lochiel's Warning" that ominously promises that "Coming events cast their shadows before."[3]

It is, however, the quotation that is "cast before" Campbell's own prediction that perhaps seems most audacious, this verse of English poetry preceded by a verse of Islamic prophecy. Heading Emerson's October 1819 entry, which announces his "First Junior Term," is a quotation from the Qur'ān, the Muslim scripture inhabiting the very heart of the American's Harvard education.

Curious as it is to find the "Alcoran" initiating this formative transition in Emerson's intellectual life, it is perhaps equally curious to find this specific selection chosen: "In aforetime I created *Jan* from out of a scorching fire." A translation of the Qur'ān 15:27, Emerson introduces his undergraduate musings with the introduction of the *"Jan"*—unseen and mythic beings, also known as the *"Jinn"* (the "hidden" ones), the Arabic term that is the origin of "genie" in English.[4] Inscribed at the genesis of Emerson's term is the *Jan*'s own genesis, their "scorching" creation serving as cosmic analog for the American's newly kindled life as a Harvard junior. Writing from the crucible of his own college career, Emerson records a spiritual rise from physical fire, offering a distant "shadow" of his own "coming" intellectual commitments. Elemental and invisible, this act of Qur'ānic creation is cited by the same American author who will pioneer Transcendentalism—a New England Idealist tradition that ties together the elemental and the invisible, synthesizing natural and spiritual worlds.[5] Associated with cerebral sparks and unseen inspiration, Emerson is himself identified with tropes such as the "Mind on Fire" and the "Transparent Eyeball," the former serving as title to Emerson's definitive biography, authored by Robert D. Richardson (1995), and the latter qualifying as Emerson's own most "iconic" image, forged in his classic manifesto, *Nature* (1836).[6]

Aligning a stage of his own personal history with this precedent from sacred prehistory, Emerson's undergraduate appeal to the "Alcoran" not only broadly foreshadows his future interests and identity, but also hints at the specific impact, pivotal and private, that Islam will have on the American's literary life. Aptly paired with Campbell's predictive verse, Muslim traditions stand "before" Emerson's authorship, the "imaginative" meditations of his 1819 entry inscribed immediately after his Islamic appeal. Mirroring the invisible creation implied in his Qur'ānic citation, Islam will not only offer fiery inspiration for Emerson's subsequent creativity, but will also elude the eyes of his later critical readers. Invoking a Qur'ānic origin at the opening of his American career, this Muslim moment in Emerson's own "aforetime" forecasts the persistent hiddenness that attends his Islamic interests. Unlike his New England precursors—including Stiles and Bentley—Emerson's literary engagements with Islam have not been neglected entirely, attracting attention especially in recent years; however, his Islamic interests have nevertheless remained "shadowy" due to persistent underestimation and misattribution.[7] And it is again Emerson's 1819 appeal to the "Alcoran" that sets an instructive precedent, his citation of the *Jan*'s creation evading scholarly efforts to find from where it was quoted. Appearing in print for the first time in 1960, Emerson's 1819 entry was published in the initial volume of the *Journals and Miscellaneous Notebooks of Ralph Waldo Emerson*;

this volume neglected, however, to account for the origins of Emerson's "Alcoran" quotation, his editors remaining silent as to the source of Emerson's citation. More recently, in her influential 2006 study *Through Other Continents: American Literature Across Deep Time*, Wai Chee Dimock invokes this same "journal entry from October 1819" as an example of Emerson's early Islamic interests, but without identifying accurately from where he acquired this quotation.[8] And, in 2009, when I myself first mentioned Emerson's Qur'ānic citation in print, I too failed to account for its origins, confessing that "I have been unable to identify the translation source for Emerson's verse."[9]

We may well wonder if anything is truly at stake in such omissions and errors. Do such slips in source attribution—which all critics naturally make—have a meaningful impact on our understanding of Emerson and his Islamic engagements? This question is partially answered by the very process required to unearth this quotation's authentic origins, prompting a review of the actual sources Emerson was reading during his undergraduate years—sources that include *The Asiatick Miscellany*.[10] A Calcutta periodical, first published in 1785, the initial issue of *The Asiatick Miscellany* included translated selections from *Khulāṣat al-Akhbār*, a medieval Persian account of the world's beginnings, reaching up to the advent of mankind. Rendered into English as *An Account of the Preadamites*, this mythic historiography in the 1785 *Asiatick Miscellany* features a section entitled "*Of the* GENII," whose introduction as printed on page 62 of the journal reads as follows with an attendant footnote included below:[11]

ACCORDING to this verse of the Koran, "In aforetime I created Jan [2] from out of a scorching fire," the Eternal, before the formation of Adam, had created a race from fire, and whom he ordered to worship him.

As long as this race of Jan (or Genii) were obedient to the divine commandments, they passed their lives in a state of utmost delight [. . .]

------------------------------------------------------------------------------

جان [2]

Offering a genealogy "*Of the* GENII," this section launches with a familiar Qur'ānic quotation—"In aforetime I created *Jan* from out of a scorching fire"— suggesting that it is this page from *The Asiatick Miscellany* that served as Emerson's source, offering the quotation affixed to the very opening to his "Junior College Term." Rather than a standard English edition of Muslim scripture, for example George Sale's 1734 *Koran*, it is page 62 of this less visible source that sparked Emerson's idiomatic allusion—a source that nevertheless predicts the textual sites and strategies that will inform Emerson's future Islamic interests. Encountering the Qur'ān for the first time within layered environs, Emerson's 1819 quotation from the "Alcoran" is actually a quotation of a quotation, selected not from an integral source itself, but from the periodical pages of *The Asiatick Miscellany*. Rather than

Arabic scripture, it is a Persian intermediary which Emerson cites; by singling out a solitary line already highlighted in his "miscellaneous" source, the *Jan*'s genesis is twice removed by the time it enters Emerson's 1819 entry, borrowed from a translated Muslim chronicle before it is cited anew in private musings penned by a New England undergraduate.

Specifying the correct location of Emerson's *Asiatick* source also helps relocate Emerson himself within a domestic American tradition of Islamic engagement. Published in Calcutta by Francis Gladwin, a translator whose influence will return later in Emerson's life, *The Asiatick Miscellany* arose from a circle of British linguists in the Indian subcontinent whose celebrated center is William Jones, leading philologist of the eighteenth century.[12] Addressee of one of Ezra Stiles' last and longest letters, William Jones and his Calcutta coterie also had a concrete impact on William Bentley, aiding from afar his early attempts to learn Middle Eastern languages. As we saw in Chapter 2, Bentley filled the last pages of his own Harvard College notebook with quotations from Jones' *Asiatick Researches*, the sibling periodical to Gladwin's *Asiatick Miscellany* invoked by Emerson in his own Harvard notebook. Perhaps most intriguing, this page from *The Asiatick Miscellany* reveals that Emerson, like earlier American authors, initially encounters the Qur'ān enveloped by Arabic, gaining access as did Stiles and Bentley before him to splinters of this scripture's actual language. Equipped with paratexts at page bottom, *The Asiatick Miscellany* parses English transliterations with pieces of authentic Arabic; the very verse from page 62 that Emerson cites in 1819 is interrupted with a numeric marker—"[2]"—directing his attention down to a footnote that supplies the original text for this line's primary subject, the *Jann*—"جان."[13] Rather than read the English *Koran* of George Sale merely, Emerson's undergraduate encounter with the Qur'ān is instead accompanied by Arabic. However, this linguistic echo of Stiles and Bentley's Middle Eastern engagements implies dissonance as well: while access to Arabic was considered a precious commodity for his predecessors, Emerson evidences little interest. As a Harvard undergraduate, Bentley's notebook exhibits his eagerness to copy Semitic languages into his own hand; Emerson's Harvard notebook suggests no such sign, overlooking altogether the Arabic offered by his *Asiatick* source.[14] Leaning not toward linguistic precision but rather literary "pleasure," Emerson breaks from Bentley by gravitating to the "imagination" of English rendition rather than Arabic's "intricate" learning. In locating Emerson's Qur'ānic quotation in *The Asiatic Miscellany*, we discover the invitation to Arabic offered to him, but also declined, reflecting a new American appeal to Islam for philosophic innovation rather than antique philology.

The generational continuities and contrasts that surround Emerson's Qur'ānic quotation are symptomatic of his early career's broader ties to national predecessors. Citing the "Alcoran" at the midpoint of his undergraduate years, Emerson will briefly be employed after graduation as a schoolteacher before accepting ordination and assuming the ministry of a historic New England church—a path that closely resembles the youthful progress of both Stiles and Bentley.[15] These professional parallels have personal margins as well, with descendants of both Stiles and Bentley surrounding Emerson's early career. Seeking to establish a school in Boston after his Harvard graduation, Emerson finds himself in direct competition with Bentley's namesake and nephew, William Bentley Fowle; "Fowle runs afoul of me," Emerson quips in a May 1824 letter to his brother, lamenting his inability to attract students away from the "Boston Monitorial School," which was opened by William Bentley Fowle just a year before.[16] Evolving from didactic ambitions to divinity, Emerson's installation in 1829 as a Unitarian minister was also sustained by another namesake, Ezra Stiles Gannett; grandson of Ezra Stiles, and Emerson's Harvard classmate, Gannett was selected to deliver an address at Emerson's ordination on March 11, 1829.[17] It is not the echoes, but the evolution, of New England legacies implied by Emerson's early life that seems most urgent, however, embodied by relinquishing the religious commitments of his revolutionary and republican forebears. Rejecting the Calvinist roots clung to by Ezra Stiles through the Revolution, William Bentley in the early Republic instead pioneered an American Unitarianism—an Unitarianism from which Emerson himself departs, resigning his own ministry by the spring of 1832, founding instead a "New School" of thought: American Transcendentalism.[18]

Complexly paralleled with his New England past, the layered significance of Emerson's appeal to the "Alcoran" at the opening of his "First Junior Term" is amplified too by its inscription in 1819—a critical year of religious progress and passage in the early United States. In May 1819, the "clarion call" of America Unitarianism had been sounded by Emerson's own future tutor, William Ellery Channing.[19] Defining the tradition's emergent doctrines, Channing's springtime sermon, now known simply as "Unitarian Christianity," signaled a new stage in the religion's growth, opening a year that concluded with the loss of Unitarianism's formative pioneer, Bentley himself. However, the death of Bentley in December 1819 also offered a platform for the newest light of the next Unitarian generation, a figure whose early impact on Emerson would outstrip all others: Edward Everett—Emerson's "favorite teacher" and "first intellectual hero."[20] Harvard's most recent hire, starting to teach during the same academic year inaugurated by Emerson with his Qur'ānic quotation, Everett was chosen to officiate at Bentley's funeral in Salem, even as he assumed his new role in Cambridge as the college's professor of Greek.[21] Charged with Bentley's last eulogy, as well as young Emerson's education, Everett stands as another broad link between New England generations, but also as a specific conduit for Near Eastern interests. Returning home from Germany in 1819 after receiving his Ph.D. from the University of Göttingen, Everett's Harvard teaching reflected his study with one of Europe's leading scholars of Semitic languages: Johann Gottfried Eichhorn, founding biblical critic and Arabic translator.[22] Bidding Bentley goodbye at his East Church funeral on January 3, 1820, it would be Eastern concerns that occupied the "Introductory lecture" delivered by Everett to his Harvard students on April 4, 1820—a lecture summarized by Emerson again in his college journal, copying down a single direct quotation from Harvard's newly minted professor: "All tends to the mysterious east."[23]

It would not be ancient Eastern mysteries, however, but rather Everett's academic training in modern Germany that proved most pivotal to Emerson's intellectual formation and ultimately to his future Islamic interests. Returning to his alma mater inspired by German learning and literature, Everett was the first at Harvard to extoll the power of poets such as Johann Wolfgang Goethe, whose own career in 1819 had culminated with the publication of his *West-oestlicher Divan*, perhaps the most celebrated German poem to engage substantially with Islam.[24] Bridging languages and lands in its very title, Goethe's *West-oestlicher Divan*—his *West-Easterly Poetry Collection*—pairs Germany's most iconic author with Muslim identities and idioms, Goethe's *Divan* identifying him as a Western "twin" of the medieval Persian poet Muḥammad Shamsuddīn Ḥāfiẓ, even while proclaiming that "If Islam means submission to God/then we all live and die in Islam's dominion."[25] Published in the same months that feature young Emerson's first quotation from the "Alcoran," Goethe's 1819 *Divan* represents not only one of his last major works, but also one of the most important literary precedents for Emerson's own later translation and imitation of Islamic poetry. Awoken by Everett to "a new morning" of German literature in 1819, Emerson will subsequently study the language, eventually reading not only Goethe's *Divan* but also German translations of Persian poetry, and especially renditions produced by Joseph von Hammer-Purgstall.[26] Inspired by these German sources to fashion his own English versions of Muslim verse, Emerson launches in 1846 a campaign of Islamic translation that unfolds over three decades, amounting to more than two thousand lines—a translation campaign not only unprecedented in early America, but also still underestimated by modern Americanists.[27] Claiming complex origins in Emerson's autobiographic quotation of the Qur'ān, penned privately in the pivotal year of 1819, his later Islamic engagements aptly embody a "Digressive Continuity" obliquely echoing a genesis both "unseen" and intimate, initiating a genealogy that has remained largely misidentified, despite propagating abundant lines of poetry and multiple family lineages. ✿

> Mr. Emerson, through many years, occasionally diverted himself by writing the traits and adventures of the imaginary Osman, many of which—by no means all—were autobiography. In this instance Osman's experiences are humbler and more practical and he has a social gift, the absence of which in himself Mr. Emerson used sometimes to deplore, and yet often said, "Solitude is my doom, and my strength." But in many other cases Osman appears a sublimed self, a sort of ideal man.[28]

In 1909, Emerson's private journals began to appear in print, with the release of the initial installment of the ten-volume *The Journals of Ralph Waldo Emerson with Annotations* (1909–1914). Recalling Stiles and Bentley, Emerson's personal jottings merited public notice; however, far surpassing Stiles and Bentley, Emerson's diaries appeared more quickly and comprehensively. Published mere decades, rather than centuries, after Emerson's death in 1882, his journals have appeared too in multiple editions, attracting exhaustive editorial attention and scholarly "annotations."[29] It is his journals' first edition in 1909, however, that included the comment quoted above, Emerson's editors parsing one of the many diary pages he devotes to praising "Osman"—an identity invented by Emerson as "a sublimed self, a sort of ideal man." Privately invoked "through many years," "Osman" serves as a vehicle for Emerson's self-reflection, refracting his own complex "autobiography." Although a surrogate presence, "Osman" ironically reveals Emerson's "absence," his editors suggest, with Osman's "social gift" inverting Emerson's characteristic "solitude." Indeed, the very isolation revealed by Osman's imagined sociality leads Emerson's editors to remark on the dialectical quality of "Solitude" itself, described paradoxically by Emerson as "my doom" as well as "my strength." It is not personal and social ironies, but national and cultural tensions, that seem most obvious in Emerson's autobiographic appeal to "Osman"—a name with a Middle Eastern etymology and a distinctly Muslim resonance.[30] Electing to fashion a "sublimed self" in his personal journals, Emerson invents his own Islamic alias, mirroring himself in a Muslim persona.

The dialectical identity discovered by Emerson's editors in his invented "Osman" is complicated further by the identity of Emerson's editors themselves. Seeking to promote Emerson's literary posterity by publishing his private journals, this first edition in 1909 was prepared by Emerson's literal posterity, collaboratively authored by his son and his grandson: Edward Waldo Emerson (1844–1930) and Waldo Emerson Forbes (1879–1917). Deepening the intimacy implied by his Eastern alias, Emerson's "Osman" not only offers an Islamic pseudonym but also aids his sons as they exhume their father's identity, this fictitious persona offering posthumous access to their own familial predecessor.[31] However, in exposing "Osman" as Emerson's *alter ego*, Edward Emerson and Waldo Forbes recover a Muslim mirror not only for their father and grandfather, of course, but also for "the founding father of nearly everything we think of as American in the modern world," with Emerson's traditional status as "Mr. America" also raising the stakes for his private Islamic appeal.[32] Fashioning his "sublimed self" privately in his 1840s journals, "Osman" seems to subvert Emerson's public reputation as American "prophet of self-reliance" and the "quintessence of American individuality"—a reputation forged during precisely these years, solidified by the appearance of Emerson's famed essay "Self-Reliance" in 1841.[33] Perhaps most surprising, however, is the fertile power of "Osman" himself, this Islamic alias giving birth to another Muslim pseudonym for Emerson in the following years. By 1842, "Osman" is gradually supplanted in Emerson's journals, succeeded by another *alter ego* that is less "imaginary" although no less Islamic: Saadi. The actual name of a medieval Persian poet—indeed, the same Persian poet quoted by William Bentley in his 1814 sermon discussed in Chapter 2 (see Fig. 2.5)—"Saadi" replaces "Osman" as Emerson's "sublimed self" in the first years of the 1840s, this historical moniker serving as a new iteration of the American's "ideal man."[34] In supplanting "Osman," "Saadi" shifts not only the form of Emerson's "sublimed self," however, but also its function and format; rather than Osman's mere mention in scattered journal entries, "Saadi" will supply the very title for Emerson's personal journals. For instance, in a notebook once owned by his own father—William Emerson (1769–1811)—Emerson repeatedly inscribes the name "Saadi" on its flyleaves, tracing in stylized calligraphy this single identity.[35] Writing in pages passed down from the American deceased, Emerson births his new Islamic name, his "sublimed self" pivoting between discrete paternities, reaching back to rebrand a notebook owned by his own father even while offering private material for his son and grandson to recover, annotating for the twentieth-century public their famous father's evolving Islamic alias.

A historical poet, "Saadi" would also enjoy a historic impact on Emerson's own poetry, appearing as the very title to one of his first major poems in print. Published in the April 1842 issue of *The Dial*, Emerson's "Saadi" recruits a specifically Persian subject and setting to meditate on the vocation of "the poet" more broadly. Drafted privately in the same notebook originally owned by his father, Emerson's poem externalizes his Islamic alias, his "ideal self" reaching outward to enjoy a "public" existence, as Farida Hellal has previously suggested.[36] However, although now offered to a new audience outside, it is inward concerns that continue to sustain Emerson's interest in "Saadi," his poem dramatizing the same tensions between "solitude" and "sociality" that will be later accented by Emerson's filial editors; consider, for example, the second and third sections of "Saadi," quoted here respectively:

> God, who gave to him the lyre,
> Of all mortals the desire,
> For all breathing men's behoof,
> Straitly charged him, 'Sit aloof;'
> Annexed a warning, poets say,
> To the bright premium,—
> Ever when twain together play,
> The harp shall be dumb.
> Many may come,
> But one shall sing;
> Two touch the string,
> The harp is dumb.
> Though there come a million,
> Wise Saadi dwells alone.
>
> Yet Saadi loved the race of men,—
> No churl immured in cave or den,—
> In bower and hall

> He wants them all,
> Nor can dispense
> With Persia for his audience,
> They must give ear,
> Grow red with joy, and white with fear;
> Yet he has no companion,
> Come ten, or come a million,
> Good Saadi dwells alone.[37]

Offering alternate adjectives for "Saadi"—epistemic and ethical, "wise" and "good"—the refrains that conclude these two sections overlap in their shared emphasis on seclusion, equally insisting that "Saadi dwells alone." However, echoing Emerson's own ambivalent embrace of "solitude," confessed as both his "doom" and his "strength," these dialectical lines also point in opposing directions, warning the poet to "sit aloof," even while celebrating his "love" for "the race of men"; offering an "image of the poet as solitary," as Parvin Loloi has recently noted, the "Saadi" portrayed in Emerson's poem is yet unable to "dispense" with all of "Persia for his audience."[38] Balancing "solitary" quarantine and solicitous company, it is the conclusion to Emerson's published poem, however, that most poignantly reflects his private Persian persona; witnessing a phantom presence emerge from lonely "absence," the climactic last lines of "Saadi" record an admonition from the "Muse," who advises Saadi not to seek external influences:

> Nor scour the seas, nor sift mankind,
> A poet or a friend to find,
> Behold, he watches at the door,
> Behold his shadow on the floor.
> Open innumerable doors
> The heaven where unveiled Allah pours,
> The flood of truth, the flood of good,
> The Seraph's and the Cherub's food;
> Those doors are men; the Pariah hind
> Admits thee to the perfect Mind.[39]

Although "alone," separated from "sift[ing] mankind," Saadi is notified that he is invisibly accompanied, with a nameless "he" haunting Saadi's domestic spaces; indeed, this hidden companion not only "watches at the door," but has his "shadow on the floor." Mirroring Emerson's own private appeal to "Saadi," these lines dramatize an isolated artist who shares space with an unseen identity, a "sublimed self" who prompts this poem's own sublime climax. Transferred from his own "door" below to celestial "doors" above, Saadi is elevated finally from invisible companion to divine vision, gnostically ascending to the "truth" embodied by "the perfect

Mind." Involving elements essential to Emerson's Transcendentalism, this moment of transparent witnessing parallels American philosophy; but, like his own "*alter ego*" forged in his private journals, these published verses are annunciated through idioms that are inescapably Islamic. Initially expressing himself through a personal appeal to Muslim identities—first "Osman" and then "Saadi"—Emerson's public poem concludes by invoking Islam's own ultimate identity, culminating with a disclosure in "heaven," with Saadi directed to behold "unveiled Allah" Himself.

An imaginative climax to his Islamic alias, Emerson's lines of apocalyptic opening also recall his autobiographic origins, offering a faint "shadow" of the invisible Qur'ānic quotation affixed to his 1819 musings on "our imaginations" that had opened his "First Junior Term." However, in embracing the "love of men" while accenting the beneficence of "Allah," "Saadi" also points forward to Emerson's publications through the 1840s, which include an essay on "Love" itself—an essay that aptly features one of Emerson's most prominent Islamic appeals. Published first in his 1841 *Essays*, appearing alongside iconic pieces such as "Self-Reliance," Emerson's "Love" would be republished in 1847; the revised essay featured an epigram absent in 1841, accompanying its title with a couplet quotation, this essay's first words reading in 1847:[40]

LOVE

"I was as a gem concealed;
Me my burning ray revealed."

*Koran.*

Invoking the Muslim divine to contextualize human affection, Emerson selects the "*Koran*" as the most suitable introduction to his "Love," presenting this intimate yet universal ideal through language that is explicitly Islamic.[40] Of all possible textual precedents to quote, Emerson entitles his essay of personal passion by appealing to Muslim scripture—an act that recalls the Qur'ān's former and "fiery" intersections in Emerson's personal life. And yet, it is not merely Emerson's appeal to Islam that seems reminiscent in this citation but rather its specific symbols. Echoing his 1819 quotation of the "Alcoran," which witnesses the "scorching" emergence of the unseen "*Jan*," this epigram to "Love" again synthesizes the invisible and the incendiary; however, rather than the dubious and "devilish" genii, Emerson's Qur'ānic quotation now implies God Himself, whose "burning" radiation "reveals" His presence. Again appealing to Islam to illumine the "ideal self," Emerson's opening to "Love" emphasizes the disclosure of a divine subjectivity, a triplicate of first-person pronouns punctuating these two short lines, with Emerson's "I," "Me," and "my" deepening the "autobiographic" resonance of his Islamic interests.

Introducing his "Love" with an urgent epiphany, shifting from inward "concealed" to outward "revealed," Emerson's opening allusion is itself an ironic act of textual deception; although ostensibly sourced from the "*Koran*," Emerson's attribution for his quotation is entirely misleading. The epigraph that opens Emerson's revised "Love" in 1847 is not a simple citation, but is itself a revision, representing a loose paraphrase from lines spoken by the Muslim Prophet that Emerson discovered in *The Practical Philosophy of the Muhammadan People*—an 1839 translation of a fifteenth-century Persian treatise, the *Akhlāq-e Jalālī*, which Emerson had begun to read in advance of republishing his "Love."[41] Pursuing his strategy of selective quotation, Emerson no longer merely cites the "Alcoran" privately from a Persian source, as in 1819, but rather relies on a Persian source to publish a quotation mislabeled "*Koran*"—a convoluted act of reception that is entirely "concealed" from Emerson's own 1847 readers, and that has complicated again our later critical efforts to identify the correct source for his Qur'ānic "quotation."[42]

Endowed with pseudo-epigraphic authority, the "*Koran*" is ascribed verses that are instead adapted by Emerson himself, his "Love" entitled with the Muslim scripture yet reflecting his own first-person participation, the "I," "Me," and "my" of this Qur'ānic epigram gesturing obliquely back to the American himself. Rebranding his past essay for its second publication in 1847, Islamic identities also emerge, however, during this very same time to rebrand Emerson's educational past, invoked as he attends the April 30, 1846 ceremony at which Edward Everett is installed as president of Harvard.[43] Although a seeming cause for celebration, witnessing his former "favorite teacher" elevated to lead his alma mater, Emerson is instead disappointed by Everett's appointment; increasingly disillusioned by his professor's political ambitions, Emerson was disturbed in particular by Everett's 1825 decision to resign "his Harvard professorship for a seat in the U. S. House of Representatives," where Everett "strongly defended the legality and morality of slavery," as James W. Mathews has noted.[44] "It is in vain that Everett makes all these allusions to his public employments," Emerson summarizes in his diary, after returning home from Everett's 1846 installation, "he would fain deceive me and himself; he has never done anything therein, but has been with whatever praises and titles and votes, a mere dangler and ornamental person."[45] Emerson closes this harsh review of Everett's induction by commenting on the very conclusion to his former teacher's "Inaugural Discourse":

> The close of Everett's Inaugural Discourse was chilling and melancholy. With a coolness indicating absolute skepticism and despair, he deliberately gave himself over to the corpse-cold Unitarianism and Immortality of Brattle Street and Boston.
>
> Everett's genius is Persian. The poetry of his sermons in his youth, his delight in Destiny, the elements, the colours & forms of things; & the mixture he made of physical & metaphysical, strongly recalls the genius of Hafiz.[46]

This diary entry features Emerson's most oft-quoted critique of his earliest influences, Unitarianism and Edward Everett, condemning the two together as "frigid"; Emerson's native religion is dismissed as "corpse-cold," while his college "hero" is characterized as "chilling," Everett's words understood as infected with "coolness." A repudiation of inheritances, personal and religious, Emerson not only bemoans recent trends in these elder institutions, however, but also offers an elegy of glory long past. Although rarely quoted, Emerson's pithy critique concludes by retreating back to his undergraduate days, nostalgically recalling the youthful fire of "Everett's genius."[47] In shifting to remember this faded ideal, however, Emerson turns again to an Islamic identity, equating Everett with a "Persian" poet, his American rhetoric recalling Sufi verse. Straddling the spiritual and the sublime, Everett's "sermons" are understood as sources of "poetry," performances that merge "physical & metaphysical," invoking divine "Destiny" while also instilling "delight." Juxtaposing the "corpse-cold" Everett of today with the "genius" of "his youth," Emerson ironically also shifts to the present tense even as he recalls his yesteryears, insisting that Everett's brilliance "*is* Persian" (emphasis added). Oddly translating Everett's past into the present, even while projecting him eastward, Emerson aptly reorients the very teacher who had first introduced him to the "mysterious east"; however, in this cross-cultural equation, Emerson also rounds out his own Eastern autobiography, no longer innovating an Islamic alias for himself, but rebranding his former professor as a Muslim poet. Discovering his own education to be shaped by a Sufi "genius," Emerson rescues his intellectual past from current political timekeeping by revising Everett himself, recuperating this early American influence through identifying him with the same "Persian" poet whose impact Emerson had just begun to feel in 1846. Opening with the name of his first "hero"—Everett—Emerson closes the above quotation with a name that will increasingly represent an enduring ideal for Emerson, celebrated in his writings until the end of his days: "Hafiz." ✿

> Loose the knot of the heart, says Hafiz. At the Opera I think I see the fine gates open which are at all times closed, and that tomorrow I shall find free & varied expression. But tomorrow I am mute as yesterday. Expression is all we want: Not knowledge, but vent: we know enough; but have not leaves & lungs enough for a healthy perspiration & growth. Hafiz has: Hafiz's good things, like those of all good poets, are the cheap blessings of water, air, & fire. The observation, analogies, & felicities which arise so profusely in writing a letter to a friend.[48]

Written just one year after attending Everett's installation, and just months before his essay "Love" was republished with its Qur'ānic epigram, this 1847 entry in Emerson's journals echoes familiar themes, with imperative expression and revelatory rhetoric framed again by an Islamic identity. No longer "fiery" merely, Emerson's Muslim subject is linked with sibling "elements" such as "water" and "air," appealing to "Hafiz" as expansive embodiment of "the colours & forms of things." Complaining of the "mute[ness]" of contemporary U.S. culture, Emerson contrasts the linguistic lack of both himself and his generation—"I" and "we"—with the singular richness of Hafiz, whose "good things" include "the cheap blessings" now missing from America. Rather than the Muse of "Saadi," it is music that provokes this meditation on another Persian poet, with Hafiz reliably representing the "leaves & lungs" that Emerson glimpses fleetingly at "the Opera." Perhaps most reminiscent in this entry is the intimate and inward approach to an Islamic identity; enveloped by urgent self-disclosure, Emerson opens with a cardiac "loose[ning]" and closes with companionship, specifying Hafiz's poetry as infused with "felicities" that normally arise only in our "writing a letter to a friend."

Identifying Hafiz with the expressive "heart," Emerson gestures not only to the poet's "friend[ly]" intimacy but also offers a gentle pun on Hafiz's own name—a name that "signifies one gifted with so good a memory that he knows the Koran by heart," as Emerson himself records in his "Notebook Orientalist."[49] It is the epistolary frame of the above entry, however, that has not only a literary, but a literal, resonance in Emerson's own life, with Hafiz first invoked by the American through acts of "writing a letter to a friend." Purchasing Joseph von Hammer-Purgstall's two-volume German edition of Hafiz's *Divan* in early April 1846, just weeks before attending Edward Everett's inauguration, Emerson begins immediately to generate his own translations and imitations of Hafiz, launching a process of poetic rendition that unfolds across the succeeding three decades.[50] Reflecting on his very recent literary labors in a July 1846 letter, Emerson writes to his close friend and confidante, Elizabeth Hoar, concluding with the following lines:

> We should be no better than parsnips, if we could not still look over our shoulders at the Power that drives us, and escape from private insignificance into a faith in the transcendent significance of our doing & being which That charges itself with interpreting one day to all & to us. However, I wrote lately some verses called "Mithridates"; others called "Merlin"; others called "Alphonso of Castille"; which I shall be impatient to show you, I doubt not, on your return,—for which I am impatient. The verses were long to write now in the end of an afternoon; yet if I learn that you are to stay long away, I shall send them; specially some called "Bacchus" not however translated from Hafiz.
>
> > Your brother
> > Waldo.[51]

Anticipating his private journal entry in 1847, this personal letter to Elizabeth Hoar in 1846 again urgently calls for communal "expression." Looking back to the invisible "Power that drives us," Emerson also forecasts the shift "from private insignificance" to "transcendent significance," looking forward to an apocalyptic "interpreting" that will be available "one day to all & to us." This prophetic expectation of divine expression prefaces Emerson's own urge for artistic exchange, confessing himself "[i]mpatient to show" his most recent poetry to his friend Elizabeth. Culminating these discrete acts of expected disclosure is, again, an Islamic identity; Emerson's letter climaxes with an allusion to "Hafiz," who is invoked even as the American claims his poetry to be original, and "not however translated" from the Persian poet. And yet, even in denying Hafiz's authorship, Emerson's autograph is ironically inscribed immediately after "Hafiz"; ending with a fraternal farewell, Emerson's own signature is separated from the Persian's moniker merely by a familial phrase, the last words of his letter aptly reading "Hafiz./Your brother/Waldo." Perhaps most remarkable in Emerson's letter is the hesitancy of his poetic hopes, his "impatience" to share his verses haunted by anxieties regarding their attribution. Although advocating the artist's "escape from [the] private," Emerson insists on the "[un]translated" privacy of his own most recent poetry, and especially the piece "called 'Bacchus.'" This irony is compounded, of course, by Emerson's own previous appeal to Persian pseudonyms, authoring his earlier poem literally under the name "Saadi." In the spring of 1846, even as Emerson begins to translate Persian poetry into his own tongue, he feels the need to "sit aloof," seeking to gain some distance from his Muslim source. Acclaimed by Emerson privately as the ideal instrument for self-disclosure, Hafiz seems also to threaten Emerson's public self-expression, potentially winning acclaim for poems such as "Bacchus."

The anxiety implied by Emerson's valediction to Elizabeth Hoar in 1846 would, moreover, prove well justified in the coming months. Despite Emerson's personal denial, the publication of his "Bacchus" at the end of this same year immediately prompts his critics to recognize this poem's reliance on Hafiz—a recognition facilitated by this poem's publication as part of Emerson's first verse collection, which was explicitly indebted to Persian poetry. Unconventional in style and transcendental in content, Emerson's 1846 *Poems* not only embodied the "free & varied expression" associated with Hafiz, but would include pieces that bear titles such as "From the Persian of Hafiz" and "Ghaselle: From the Persian of Hafiz," the former a translation that spans more than 150 lines, introduced by Emerson as a "mystical and allegorical" poem, earning "for Hafiz the honorable title of 'Tongue of the Secret.'"[52] In addition to such renditions, Emerson included in *Poems* original pieces enlivened with Persian tropes; his 1842 "Saadi," for example, appears again in *Poems*, while other contributions, such as Emerson's "Merlin" and "Hermione," have long been identified as betraying a "Persian touch."[53] As anticipated by Emerson in his 1846 letter, however, it would be "Bacchus" that garnered immediate association with Hafiz, as made clear from one of *Poems'* initial reviews, authored anonymously and published in the August 1847 issue of the *American Review*; although receiving only a brief mention, "Bacchus" is characterized and quoted by Emerson's reviewer as follows:

Here, then, we have it, in this piece, entitled "Bacchus," an imitation of the
Persian mystic, Hafiz. [ . . .]
> ["]Wine which music is,––
> Music and wine are one,
> That I, drinking this,
> Shall hear far Chaos talk with me,
> Kings unb[orn] shall walk with me,
> And the poor grass shall plot and plan
> What it will do when it is man.
> Quickened so, will I unlock
> Every crypt of every rock."[54]

Realizing his fears first confessed to Elizabeth Hoar, Emerson's "Bacchus" is
quickly recapped in the *American Review* as an "imitation" of "Hafiz," this poem
dismissed as plagiarizing a "Persian mystic." Critiquing the poem's reach across
cultures and chronology, Emerson's reviewer offers selections from "Bacchus" that
themselves breach significant divisions, bridging life and death, while transcending
too geography and history. Recalling his vision at the "Opera" in which "the fine
gates open," the intoxicating "music" of these lines from Emerson's "Bacchus" leads
to the "unlock[ing]" of tombs, opening "[e]very crypt of every rock," rendering fatal
absence into living presence. Indeed, it is the "quickened" intimacy of Emerson's
Persian-inspired verses that perhaps seems most familiar; bringing close the distant
future as well as the "far" off, these first-person lines keep lively company across
spatial dimensions and temporal divides, predicting that "Kings unborn shall walk
with me," while adding that "[I] [s]hall hear far chaos talk with me."

Associated privately with "felicities which arise so profusely in writing a letter
to a friend" in 1846, Hafiz's own name is publically invoked in 1847, emerging
in *The American Review*'s quotation of communal verses selected from Emerson's
"Bacchus." Epistolary in character and "mystic" in meaning, Hafiz's influence also
receives expression in actual epistolary materials, his intimate communications
concretely reflected in the contexts Emerson chooses for his translations and "imitations" of Persian poetry. Performed primarily in his private journals, Emerson's
urgent engagement with Hafiz migrates into media more unexpected as well, his
verses rendered in whatever venue is closest to hand.

Among the Houghton Library's rich collection of Emerson manuscripts is the
small brown envelope reproduced as Figure 5.1—an envelope addressed to "Mr.
R.W. Emerson" and postmarked "Boston Mass" on "Jun 13." Reading closer, it
becomes clear that this simple small envelope is not only sent to Emerson, but
also inscribed with markings in Emerson's hand. Interrupting his own home address, Emerson scribbles "an order of dervishes" between "Concord" and "Mass,"
while adding near the top of the envelope "1301" and "1389," dates that approximate a traditional estimate for Hafiz's years of birth and death.[55] Calculating

*Figure 5.1* Ac85.Em345.Zy812h (recto), envelope addressed to "Mr. R.W. Emerson/ Concord/Mass." Image courtesy of the Ralph Waldo Emerson Memorial Association deposit, Houghton Library, Harvard University.

the medieval span of a poet's Persian life on contemporary correspondence from Boston, Emerson's jottings serve to "order" anew his own letter's reception, this envelope no longer testifying merely to a "Concord" delivery, but also to a community of "dervishes." These curious fragments on this envelope's façade are superseded, however, by its reverse, where Emerson and Hafiz explicitly emerge in expressive correspondence (Fig. 5.2).[56] Transforming the blank space on his envelope's back into a site for his rough rendition, Emerson generates an entire *ghazal* of "Hafiz," heading his translated lines by citing their original home in Hammer-Purgstall's German *Diwan* ("[volume] II [page] 339"):

*Hafiz II 339*

How happy is the Amber horse of the Ost East!
Early stands he up, full of desire for thee.
O beautiful feathered bird, show the way.
Mine eye melted out of longing after the dust of thy foot.
I swim in blood, & thinking of me,
~~Considers~~ The new moon looks on with affection.
Out of love of thy cheek will hereafter

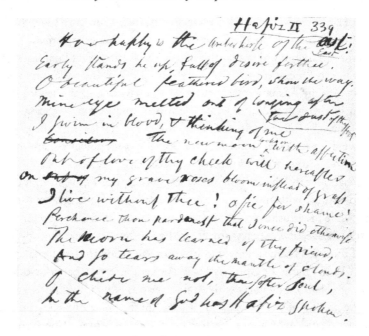

*Figure* 5.2   Ac85.Em345.Zy812h (verso), back of Emerson's envelope, featuring his translation that concludes "In the name of God has Hafiz spoken." Image courtesy of the Ralph Waldo Emerson Memorial Association deposit, Houghton Library, Harvard University.

> On ~~Out of~~ my grave roses bloom instead of grass
> I live without thee! O fie for shame!
> Perchance thou pardonest that I once did otherwise.
> The Morn has learned of thy friend,
> And so tears away the mantle of clouds.
> O chide me not, thou softer soul,
> In the name of God has Hafiz spoken.[57]

Mirroring the very material upon which it is rendered, this poem yearns for intimate communion across space, seeking the means to reach the beloved from afar. Invoking standard tropes of flight in its opening lines, Hafiz personifies his "desire for thee" both in the "East" wind and the "beautiful feathered bird," his life "without thee" alleviated only by agents of the air. Eerily evocative of Emerson's own "Bacchus," this rendition from Hafiz again dramatizes the overcoming of distances, transcending borders not only between lands apart, but also between life and death, with the poet's "love" expressed posthumously and organically, his ardor ensuring that "On my grave roses bloom instead of grass."

Rendering literal Emerson's literary appraisal of Hafiz, these translated Persian lines are inscribed on an envelope that originally enclosed "a letter to a friend," this piece of paper not only delivered to Emerson from afar, but also transformed into a vehicle for Hafiz's elegy on distance, featuring his own address to the beloved from beyond. Erotic verses of "love," this epistolary poem is perhaps most poignantly familiar in its ending illumination, the divine disclosure of its final lines recalling the beginning to Emerson's own "Love." As his 1847 essay, which opened by insisting that "Me my burning ray revealed," it is a dawning of disclosure that again emerges in Emerson's rendition, with "the Morn" pictured as "tear[ing] away the mantle of clouds," leading finally to "Hafiz" himself in the last line, the poet's name aptly scrawled across a crease in Emerson's envelope, graphically spanning a material fold on the bottom right of this repurposed page.[58] Again envisioning a heavenly light that "reveals" the esoteric, Emerson's inscriptions of Islamic "Love" share a common source, with his envelope translation again gesturing to the "*Koran.*" However, while the Muslim scripture was falsely accredited in the opening epitaph to Emerson's "Love," it is actual words from the Muslim scripture that surface in the last line of Emerson's translation; shifting from the erotic to the eternal, the poem ends with "In the name of God has Hafiz spoken," a verse that concludes with a Persian poet (Hafiz), but starts with Arabic scripture, its initial phrase borrowed from the beginning of the *basmala* itself (i.e., "*In the name of God*, [the Merciful, the Compassionate]").[59] Capping his transformation of prosaic American materials into sacred Islamic space, Emerson ends his envelope by scribbling the very start to the Muslim scripture, secreting this slice of Islamic revelation into an interior corner of this common New England letter. Reaching back to his diary entry in 1819, where he had copied the "Alcoran" while "shadowing" his own "coming events," Emerson now renders a Qur'ānic fragment on the shadowed reverse of his own correspondence, with Muslim scripture literally enveloping his domestic life. ☼

We add to these fragments of Hafiz a few specimens from other poets.

### CHODSCHU KERMANI.
### THE EXILE.

"In Farsistan the violet spreads
        Its leaves to the rival sky,—
I ask, How far is the Tigris flood,
        And the vine that grows thereby?

"Except the amber morning wind,
        Not one saluted me here;
There is no man in all Bagdad
        To offer the exile cheer.

"I know that thou, O morning wind,
        O'er Kerman's meadow blowest,
And thou, heart-warming nightingale,
        My father's orchard knowest.

"Oh, why did partial Fortune
    From that bright land banish me?
So long as I wait in Bagdad,
    The Tigris is all I see.

"The merchant hath stuffs of price,
    And gems from the sea–washed strand,
And princes offer me grace
    To stay in the Syrian land:

"But what is gold for but for gifts?
    And dark without love is the day;
And all that I see in Bagdad
    Is the Tigris to float me away."
                    Ralph Waldo Emerson,
            "Persian Poetry" (1858), p. 732.[60]

Published in *The Atlantic Monthly*, Emerson's April 1858 essay "Persian Poetry" marked the culmination of a dozen years spent in private translation. Filtering favorite renditions produced since his purchase of Hafiz's *Divan* in April 1846, Emerson's essay is dedicated primarily to this "prince of the Persian poets," copying and contextualizing a variety of verse translations from Hafiz.[61] At his essay's end, however, Emerson pivots to "other poets," opening with the above quotation from "Chodschu Kermani," one of Hafiz's Persian predecessors. Distinct in its source, Kermani's "The Exile" is also distinct in span, representing a lengthier "specimen," much longer than the lyrical "fragments of Hafiz" offered earlier in Emerson's essay. And yet, in this rendition from Kermani, echoes of Hafiz himself also seem audible. A nostalgic elegy for homelands lost, "The Exile" again articulates a yearning across "far" distances, seeking to relieve the "dark [of] day" through recalling to mind an absent "love." Most reminiscent is Kermani's intimate invocations of airy messengers, "The Exile" appealing not only to the "heart-warming nightingale," but also to the salutary "amber morning wind" that had opened the rendition of Hafiz on Emerson's envelope (see Fig. 5.2).[62]

If Kermani's "The Exile" echoes themes essential to Hafiz—whose poetry occupies the bulk of the 1858 "Persian Poetry"—this rendition also offers a fit conclusion to Emerson's essay by evoking its very opening, mirroring concerns with "far" spaces that first emerge in the introduction to "Persian Poetry," whose initial words read as follows:

To Baron von Hammer Purgstall, who died in Vienna in 1856, we owe our best knowledge of the Persians. He has translated into German, besides the "Divan" of Hafiz, specimens of two hundred poets who wrote during a period of five and a half centuries, from A.D. 1050 to 1600. The seven masters of the

Persian Parnassus—Firdusi, Enweri, Nisami, Jelaleddin, Saadi, Hafiz, and Jami—have ceased to be empty names; and others, like Ferideddin Attar and Omar Khayyam, promise to rise in Western estimation. That for which mainly books exist is communicated in these rich extracts. Many qualities go to make a good telescope,—as the largeness of the field, facility of sweeping the meridian, achromatic purity of lenses, and so forth; but the one eminent value is the space-penetrating power; and there are many virtues in books, but the essential value is the adding of knowledge to our stock by the record of new facts, and, better, by the record of intuitions which distribute facts, and are the formulas which supersede all histories.[63]

Opening with acute awareness of spaces in between, Emerson first transports American readers transatlantically, introducing them to the "Austrian" responsible for rendering Persian poetry for "Western estimation." Memorializing "Hammer Purgstall," who has recently crossed from life to death, Emerson confesses his own distance from medieval Muslim verse by emphasizing first this European intermediary, indexing especially the historical span of his "German" translations, which bridge "two hundred poets who wrote during a period of five and a half centuries."[64] Shifting from spaces transatlantic to interstellar, Emerson moves from linguistic conduit to spiritual connotation, adopting a surprisingly scientific metaphor to express the meaning of Sufi poetry. Recruiting the telescope as analogy for this tradition, Emerson aligns Persian verse with visual traversal, this poetry's "virtue" recalling a telescope's "space-penetrating power" that enables us to see the stars. Collapsing distance, Emerson's introduction then ends by translating spatial transcendence into temporal; celebrated for its "largeness of field" and "purity of lenses," the "intuitions" recorded in Persian poetry allow readers to pierce not spaces merely, but "all" times, offering us "the formulas which supersede all histories."

Extravagantly praising its "space-penetrating power," Emerson advertises not only Persian poetry in general, but his "Persian Poetry" specifically, preparing readers for an essay that will fuse a range of "rich extracts." Miscellaneously "sweeping the meridian" of his own diary translations, Emerson's 1858 essay is filled with selected "intuitions," quoted mostly from Hafiz, who himself is seen as transcending barriers, Emerson declaring in the very midst of his "Persian Poetry" that

[Hafiz'] complete intellectual emancipation he communicates to the reader. There is no example of such facility of allusion, such use of all materials. Nothing is too high, nothing too low, for his occasion. He fears nothing, he stops for nothing. Love is a leveller, and Allah becomes a groom, and heaven a closet, in his daring hymns to his mistress or to his cupbearer. This boundless charter is the right of genius.[65]

Recalling his 1847 "Love," Emerson finds Hafiz's own "Love" offering intimate access to "Allah," the Muslim divine pictured in Hafiz's "daring hymns" as a familiar "groom," encountered in the enclosure of "heaven," which is snug as "a closet." Telescopic in his reach to celestial heights, Hafiz is also microscopic in his reach downward, his poetry spanning "all materials." "Nothing is too high, nothing too low" for Hafiz, Emerson insists, expositing the "complete intellectual emancipation" that his poetry "communicates to the reader."

Echoing his essay's expansive introduction by celebrating Hafiz's "boundless charter," Emerson also offers covert apology for his own compositional strategy; although presented under the broad title "Persian Poetry," it is Hafiz's personal voice that pervades nearly all "all materials" in Emerson's essay, infiltrating areas ostensibly separated from his influence. Specifically reserved for "other poets," the appendix with which Emerson ends "Persian Poetry" opens with "THE EXILE" (as seen above), which is framed as a rendition from "Chodschu Kermani." This "specimen," however, represents not a simple translation from a single poet, but rather a collaborative pastiche, synthesizing discrete poetic voices, including Hafiz's own—a pastiche first recognized by the pioneering critic, John D. Yohannan. Pushing beyond the published façade of his "Persian Poetry," the private pages of Emerson's journals suggest the itinerant complexity of his "Exile," a translation that migrates through several stages across multiple notebooks.[66] Starting with core material rendered from a Kermani poem sourced from Hammer-Purgstall's German translation, Emerson gradually enlarges on his verbatim rendition, not only adding his own ideas to "The Exile," but also infusing this poem with translations from Hafiz. The hybrid anatomy of Emerson's resulting poem is schematized below, sketching the discrete original sources for each section of this composite "specimen":

Stanza 1 ("In Farsistan the violet spreads [. . .]"):
  Emerson's stylized translation of Hafiz, sourced from *ghazal* "Nun: IV" in Hammer-Purgstall's 1812–1813 *Diwan* (i.e., "*Die Rose Farsistans entblüht/Für mein Vergnügen nicht./Wie schön ist nicht des Tigris Fluth,/ Und durchgewürzter Wein*")

Stanza 2, first half ("Except the amber morning wind,/Not one saluted me here"):
  Emerson's paraphrase of Hafiz based on his translation of lines sourced from *ghazal* "Mim: LXXVI" in Hammer-Purgstall's *Diwan* (i.e., "*Außer dem Ost und außer dem West verstehet mich Niemand. O ich Seliger! der Keinem vertraut als dem Wind*")

Stanza 2, second half ("There is no man in all Bagdad/To offer the exile cheer."):
  Emerson's own composition, inspired by his Persian poetry translations

Stanzas 3 and 4 ("I know that thou, O morning wind [...]"):
    Emerson's stylized translation from Kermani, sourced from Hammer-
    Purgstall's 1818 *Geschichte der schönen Redekünste Persiens*
Stanzas 5 and 6 ("The merchant hath stuffs of price, [...]"):
    Primarily Emerson's own composition, although his final two lines
    appear to echo the conclusion of stanza 4 rendered from Kermani[67]

Featuring a first stanza loosely rendered from Hafiz, and a second stanza that
merges Hafizean paraphrase and Emersonian composition, only the third and
fourth stanzas of "The Exile" represent material derived from Kermani, with its
stanzas 5 and 6 again transitioning away from translation, representing instead
Emerson's own inspired invention. Of its two dozen lines, only eight lines of "The
Exile" are thus translated from its supposed author, with Kermani's verses keeping
covert company with material authored by both Emerson and Hafiz. Embodying
in poetic practice Emerson's abstract theory, the hybrid "Exile" finds Hafiz securing a secret ubiquity, his voice here "stop[ping] for nothing," claiming a "boundless
charter" by infiltrating lines attributed to a "rival" poet. As airy and invisible as the
"amber morning wind" regularly invoked in his poetry, Hafiz stays largely "unseen"
as he wafts through these lines attributed to Kermani, breathing fresh influence into
"The Exile" even while remaining an identity that "not one salutes."

Perhaps more startling than its Hafizean hybridity, however, is Emerson's own
contributions to this "Kermani" poem; lending lines to "The Exile," Emerson generates a poetic medium between translation and composition, with Persian verses
inflected with his own American voice. Effacing barriers and borders, Emerson's
lines penetrate Sufi spaces, his authorship subjectively occupying the very "extracts"
he purports to analyze objectively. Discretely synthesizing disparate sources into a
seamless whole, it would have been impossible for Emerson's 1858 readers to dis-
entangle the different speakers that harmonize in "The Exile," this poem's twenty-
four lines appearing thematically cohesive and metrically consistent. However, the
complexity of such Emersonian "translations" is also infrequently emphasized by his
contemporary readers, reflecting broader scholarly neglect of Emerson's modified
Muslim renditions. Although a precise editorial summary of "The Exile" was finally
offered by the editors of *The Poetry Notebooks of Ralph Waldo Emerson* (1986), subsequent scholarship has frequently avoided a detailed analysis of the adaptive mechanics that are typical of Emersonian "translation." The single study to explore significantly "The Exile" and its sources was authored by the sole scholar who has sought
to outline the size and scope of Emerson's translation campaign: John D. Yohannan.
In two articles published in 1943 issues of *American Literature*, Yohannan provided
an overview of Emerson's Persian renditions, concluding that he translated "seven
hundred lines"—an evaluation regularly repeated in twenty-first-century studies, despite the seven decades that have elapsed since it first appeared in print.[68]
Instructive and original, Yohannan's articles possess enduring value; his conclusions,

however, are unsurprisingly outdated, formulated with only limited access to the essential sites of Emerson's Islamic interests: his private journals. Although aware of some Emerson diaries, including the *Journals* edited by his son and grandson (1909–1914), Yohannan's studies in 1943 predated the published bulk of Emerson's personal papers, with the first volume of the more comprehensive *Journals and Miscellaneous Notebooks of Ralph Waldo Emerson* not appearing until 1960. The resulting slips in Yohannan's scholarship are exemplified by his own treatment of "The Exile" itself. Perceptively recognizing this poem to be "astonishing" in its adaptive rendition, incorporating lines that are "pure Emerson," Yohannan also insightfully suspects Hafiz's impact on "The Exile"; however, as he is unfamiliar with primary Emerson notebooks—such as "Notebook Orientalist"—Yohannan cannot pinpoint this impact precisely, not realizing that "The Exile" borrows lines translated from two discrete *ghazals* of Hafiz, as later articulated by the 1986 *Poetry Notebooks of Ralph Waldo Emerson*. Perhaps more surprising, when enumerating his "Check-List of Emerson's Persian Translations"—the "check-list" that led to the oft-quoted total of "seven hundred lines"—Yohannan elects to describe "The Exile" as a translation that comprises "20 lines from Kermani," shielding this poem's more complicated identity, merging translation and composition.[69]

Unaware of hundreds of lines rendered from Persian sources imbedded in the pages of Emerson's unpublished journals, Yohannan's "some 700 lines" understandably underestimates Emerson's translation campaign, which tops two thousand lines, as I clarify in an appendix attached to this chapter. More significant than the precise number, however, is the private spaces that must be traversed to enumerate Emerson's renditions; recalling his undergraduate appeal to the Qur'ān, Emerson's mature campaign of Muslim translation remains elusive due to its intimate identity and environs, his versions of Persian poetry not only fashioned in the pages of Emerson's personal journals, but also infused by his own personality, with Sufi lines increasingly reflecting the American's subjectivity through repeated rendition. Consider, for example, this couplet attributed to "Hafiz" that was published in Emerson's 1858 "Persian Poetry," printed just a few pages before "The Exile":

> Fit for the Pleiads' azure chord
> The songs I sung, the pearls I bored.
> "Persian Poetry" (1858), p. 729[70]

Couched in meter and rhyme, this formal couplet hides an informal process of creative translation that transpires initially in Emerson's "Notebook Orientalist," as witnessed in Figure 5.3, which reproduces the bottom half of this notebook's page 24.

> Songs ~~hast thou~~ he sung, pearls ~~hast thou~~ he bored,
> ~~Worthy~~ Fit to string against the Pleiads azure cord ~~of Heaven~~

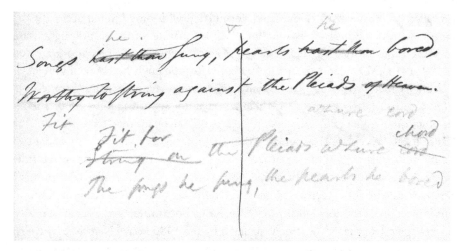

*Figure 5.3*  MS Am 1280 (115), Ralph Waldo Emerson, "Notebook Orientalist,"
page 24. Image courtesy of the Ralph Waldo Emerson Memorial Association deposit, Houghton
Library, Harvard University.

Fit for ~~Strung on~~ the Pleads azure ~~cord~~ chord
The songs he sung, the pearls he bored[71]

Starting with a simple translation of his source, Emerson pens first a rendition
that reads "Songs hast thou sung, pearls hast thou bored,/Worthy to string against
the Pleiads of Heaven"; however, returning to these lines in pencil, Emerson elects
to replace material in both lines, revising them to read instead "Songs he sung,
pearls he bored,/Fit to string against the Pleiads azure cord." Instead of intimately
addressing a "thou," Emerson's lines now objectively account for a "he," shifting
the subject of this Persian poem, advancing from second person to third person
with penciled adjustments. These initial revisions also signal Emerson's attempt
to superimpose poetry on his prose translation, effecting rhyme by exchanging
"of Heaven" for the idiomatic "azure cord," harmonizing with line 1's "bored." Not
satisfied with the resulting couplet, however, the very bottom of his Notebook's
page 24 finds Emerson further refining his rendition, polishing the imagery and
orthography of this poetic "pearl." First rewriting these lines, and then redact-
ing his own revision, Emerson ultimately produces two lines that read "Fit for
the Pleads azure chord/The songs he sung, the pearls he bored." Abandoning the
trope of "stringing" altogether, Emerson abbreviates "Worthy to string against,"
offering instead the more minimal "Fit for"—a condensation that also helps confirm a metrical scheme, with both lines now amounting to four feet in length.
Most striking in this last revision is not line size, however, but line sequence, with
Emerson inverting his original's verse order, leading to this couplet's final iteration published in "Persian Poetry":

Fit for the Pleiads' azure chord
The songs I sung, the pearls I bored.[72]

A poetic paraphrase rather than prosaic rendition, Emerson's concluding version has undergone yet another revision in voice, its person shifting once again, with third-person description now replaced by first-person testimony. Although commencing with a "thou," and then shifting through a "he," Emerson aptly concludes his pronominal substitutions with an "I," culminating this process of private revision with a personal identity. Ascribed in print to Hafiz, the proud individuality of Emerson's published lines is revealed in his journals as embracing more than a mere solitary "I." Boasting of the "songs I sung," this couplet's voice is complex and compound, its first-person singular identified publically with an original Persian poet, even while privately originating with its American translator. ✡

Offering access to alien cultures while giving voice to his own alienation and "Exile," the "space" traversed by Persian poetry points Emerson in diverse directions, external and internal. Telescopic in vertical vision, Emerson's Islamic engagements are horizontal too in transatlantic reach, prompting him to pass through European intermediaries to reach Middle Eastern sources. These spaces of literary transmission are complemented by literal travel, with Emerson's appeal to Islam punctuating his own exiles abroad, emerging in moments of transport and transition. In the months following publication of his *Poems*, and the republication of his "Love," Emerson would prepare to embark for England in the autumn of 1847, sending a farewell note to his brother William in the days before his departure. Rather than hopes for his time abroad, however, Emerson begins with domestic reflections, alluding to actual homes undergoing construction, his last letter before leaving for England reading in its entirety:

Boston 2 October 1847

Dear William,

I received yesterday at Concord your letter & the cheque inclosed, on the Massachusetts Bank for $139.38 (I believe) at all events I had the money & the account,—in every way satisfactory. It seems that you also have experience of the delays of carpenters. Well, the work will be the better done. "Haste" say the Mahometans "is of the devil; delay is from the All-giving."

My little fuss of preparation marches on, every day a little, meantime the sky clears at last & perhaps by Tuesday we shall have good wind I have made sort of settlement of all my home affairs, have got a good loan of the Concord Bank have spoken or written plentiful directions for the care of things in the coming months and am almost ready for the weighing of the anchor & the sailor's song. It is a very happy circumstance to us here little

Edward's returning health.—Yes I shall no doubt find some matter for letters to you as I go or stay, and always love.

Goodbye!

Waldo.[73]

Poised on the cusp of his transatlantic travels, Emerson anticipates his impend-
ing absence from America by seeking to settle "home affairs." Commiserating with
William, who is constructing a new house on Staten Island, Emerson notes his
own recent difficulties with "carpenters" in Concord—an oblique allusion to New
England's most celebrated homebuilder, Henry David Thoreau, who in 1847 had recently returned from his cabin on Walden pond, lending aid to Amos Bronson Alcott
in constructing a quixotic summerhouse for the Emersons, later simply dubbed "The
Ruins."[74] Straddling spaces, it is temporal climates that contour Emerson's valedictory
letter, incrementally preparing for his expected departure, making progress "every day
a little," even while warily eyeing the weather off the coast, as well as his child's welfare at home, noting especially the "returning health" of "little Edward"—Emerson's
son and future editor, Edward Waldo Emerson. Indexing the velocity of his various
concerns, from homebuilding to the "weighing of the anchor," Emerson's letter is
also intersected by a single quotation; cited to console both his brother and himself,
Emerson interrupts his letter with a sentiment that inverts temporal conventions, re-
interpreting rapid pace as a demonic curse, and postponement as God's gift. Called to
mind by his own mention of the "delays of carpenters," Emerson's ideas find echo in
a celebrated ḥadīth spoken first by the Muslim Prophet, recalling for his brother that
" 'Haste' say the Mahometans 'is of the devil; delay is from the All-giving.'"[75]

Vacillating between continents, a consistency emerges in the familial envelope
that surrounds Emerson's Islamic appeal; if "I go or stay" there is "always love,"
Emerson insists as he closes his letter, departing for Europe as he fraternally imparts
a slice of Muslim wisdom. Leaving half-built homes in his wake, while invoking the
Prophet before his transatlantic progress, Emerson offers distinct echoes of another
American author, Washington Irving, whose own travels had recently returned him
home from Spain, allowing him to continue reconstruction of both Sunnyside and
his biography of the Prophet through 1847 (see Chapter 3).[76] These inverse parallels are made more ironic by the very name of the vessel that conveys Emerson
abroad: he embarks three days after writing to William on a brig christened the
Washington Irving.[77] Quoting Muḥammad immediately before crossing the Atlantic,
it is the Irving that brings Emerson to Europe, leaving American shores even as
Irving himself had recently returned home to finish his house renovations and his
revisions of Mahomet. Intersecting continental travel and domestic construction,
Emerson's departure in 1847 reaches not only across to Irving, but also forward in
his own life, anticipating Emerson's next and last trip abroad, undertaken twenty-
five years later. However, rather than serene "delay" from the "All-giving," Emerson's
final transatlantic sojourn was precipitated by familial crisis and infernal loss: the

burning of "Bush," the beloved Concord home of the Emersons. "[A]wakened by the crackling sound of fire in the wall of his bedroom" on the morning of July 24, 1872, Emerson "ran downstairs and out into a pouring rain to his front gate in his nightgown, shouting as loudly as he could for help," with his neighbors "[a]lmost immediately [. . .] running to his aid," as Gay Wilson Allen recounts.[78] Reporting the aftermath of the fire to his friend, Caroline Tappan, on July 30, 1872, Emerson credits these same neighbors for rescuing his family's possessions, noting that "Our household stuff was almost all saved by crowd of benefactors—men & women,— with tenderest care, &, I think, all my books & MSS. though sadly dispersed. Much of the house still stands, & the carpenters have not yet decided how much or how little must be removed. So you shall hope the best for us."[79] Witnessing not only the destruction of his "house," but also the "dispers[al]" of his "books & MSS," Emerson finds himself again at the mercy of "carpenters" and their "decisions," and elects therefore to travel abroad with his daughter, Ellen, while his home is rebuilt, leaving America again in October 1872. And, while his delayed departure in October 1847 was marked by a letter of "Mahometan" citation, it would be a Muslim destination that Emerson selects as he hastily departs in 1872, not only visiting Europe during his last transatlantic trip, but also electing to take a six-week tour of Egypt.[80]

Framed through fire, the elderly Emerson's arrival in Muslim regions recalls his youthful appeal to Muslim scripture, these diverse events each arising "out of a scorching fire." Unlike his "imaginative" quotation of the "Alcoran" in cozy environs at Harvard College, however, Emerson's actual encounters in Arab lands would offer less "pleasure & satisfaction," inscribed instead with "difficulty & reluctance." Arriving in North Africa at the end of December, Emerson and Ellen disembarked at Cairo, where they lodged at the Old City's historic "Shepheard's Hotel," situated less than two miles from the *al-Azhar*, one of Islam's primary centers of religious learning.[81] Trekking south down the Nile, father and daughter arrived in Luxor by January 19 before returning back north to coastal Alexandria by February 15.[82] However, despite the sights and sounds he doubtlessly experienced during these weeks—from Mosque architecture to the Muslim *adhān*—Emerson's diaries provide scant details of his sojourn, his silence perhaps reflecting the linguistic frustration Emerson encountered in Egypt. While it was a Muslim poet who had helped remedy Emerson's own "muteness" in his 1847 journal entries, he reluctantly discovers himself again to be "mute" in traveling through Muslim lands two-and-a-half decades later, having no facility with Arabic. "All this journey is a perpetual humiliation, satirizing and whipping our ignorance," Emerson bitterly complains in the first weeks of 1873, adding that "The people despise us because we are helpless babies who cannot speak or understand a word they say."[83]

Distinguished from American predecessors such as Stiles and Bentley in his entire lack of Middle Eastern languages, Emerson finds this same lack also distancing him from Egyptian contemporaries; while William Bentley's Arabic facility had permitted him to gain personal friends from afar, Emerson's "ignorance" prevents in-person engagement with Arabs. However, Bentley's Eastern exchanges also form a surprising precedent for a more productive interaction enjoyed by Emerson during his Egyptian visit. Despite his "humiliation," Emerson's journals suggest that he was not wholly excluded from social interactions; on Sunday, January 19, for instance, Emerson records meeting "Mustapha Aga," the British consul stationed in Luxor.[84] A colorful character who merits mention in other contemporary travelogues, Mustapha's time with Emerson was not without benefit, as recorded by the latter in a brief diary entry, which reads simply:

eye-glass for Mustapha Aga, Eng.[lish] Consul Luxor.[85]

Recording his gift of an "eye-glass," Emerson's minor bequest to Mustapha unconsciously implies broader ironies, forming the cynosure of complex circulations, dilating beyond Emerson's own biography to touch the lives of his American predecessors. Verbally frustrated, Emerson yet lends visionary aid in Egypt, the author of the "Transparent Eyeball" materially supporting Mustapha's sight. And while it was a "good telescope" that had formed Emerson's literary metaphor for Muslim poetry, it is literal magnification that he now offers to the Muslim "Consul," passing on this instrument of "space-penetrating power." Oddly mirroring Bentley's own early gift to "Sheik Ahmet," Emerson offers his own interlocutor in the Middle East a "lens," not a "Dolland" with "the facility of sweeping the meridian," but rather a mere "eye-glass" to help distinguish details of everyday life.

The reticence of Emerson's diaries during his Egyptian visit reflects not only his linguistic frustration, but also a broader waning of his literary powers. Precipitated perhaps by the trauma of Bush's burning in 1872, Emerson's last decade witnesses his slow decline, with both memory and mental acuity weakening in advance of his 1882 death. Before the final collapse of his faculties, however, Emerson returned from his final trip abroad to complete his last major work, an essay collection entitled *Letters and Social Aims*—a work completed with the aid of his traveling companion, Ellen.[86] Aptly epistolary and intimate in its title, this family collaboration appeared in 1875 and would include Emerson's "Persian Poetry," republishing this 1858 piece that had first appeared in *The Atlantic Monthly*. Featuring this essay on Hafiz in his final collection, Emerson's *Letters and Social Aims* appeals to Hafiz in another essay as well, the Persian poet aptly insinuating himself into Emerson's initial offering, "Poetry and Imagination," which features the following brief passage near the essay's middle:

The world is an immense picture-book of every passage in human life. Every object he beholds is the mask of a man.
  "The privates of man's heart
  They speken and sound in his ear.
  As tho' they loud winds were";
for the universe is full of their echoes.

Every correspondence we observe in mind and matter suggests a substance older and deeper than either of these old nobilities. We see the law
gleaming through, like the sense of a half-translated ode of Hafiz. The
poet who plays with it with most boldness best justifies himself—is most
profound and most devout. Passion adds eyes,—is a magnifying-glass.
Sonnets of lovers are mad enough, but are valuable to the philosopher, as
are prayers of saints, for their potent symbolism.[87]

Recalling the Transcendentalism of his earlier years, Emerson expresses in old
age his continued faith in the "correspondence" between "mind and matter," reaching back to his own first principles, even while identifying the universe's primitive
origins. In restating his youthful idealism, Emerson's meditation on a "substance
older and deeper" implies tensions deeply rooted in his own oldest writings.
Discerning the "privates of man's heart" in the invisible "winds," Emerson's poetic
passage is yet communal and ocular in emphasis, accenting what "we see," including the "eyes" that emerge from "Passion." Perhaps most familiar, however, is this
paragraph's culmination, accenting revealed illumination centered on an Islamic
poet: "We see the law gleaming through," Emerson suggests provocatively, "like the
sense of a half-translated ode of Hafiz."

Discerning transcendence through dynamic translation, Emerson discovers the
"oldest" emerging in new creation, the exoteric form of a rendered "ode" allowing the esoteric "law" to "gleam" through. Rather than Hafiz himself, it is Hafizean
rendition that Emerson endows with revelatory import, perceiving the "law" between "mind and matter" as shining in Muslim translation. Offering a fit description
of his own hybrid practices, Emerson privileges acts of poetic "transition" rather
than settled poetic products—a privileging that recalls Harold Bloom's reading of
Emerson as an author who "always locates power in the place of crossing over."[88]
However, even as he emphasizes Sufi lines that are "half-translated," Emerson
himself abruptly transitions, asserting that "The poet who plays with it with most
boldness best justifies himself—is most profound and most devout." Juxtaposing
apparent opposites—poetic playfulness and philosophic profundity, assertive au-
dacity and devoted humility—Emerson seems to offer an implicit apology for his
own "half-translations," constructing a passage that covertly "justifies himself." It is
this passage's conclusion, however, that seems to reflect transitions most recently
featured in Emerson's lived experience. Shifting dizzily between the senses, spanning the visual and the verbal, Emerson ends his synesthetic confession by suddenly swinging from Hafizean "ode" to asserting that "Passion adds eyes,—is a
magnifying-glass." Recently returned from his own donation of an "eye-glass" in the
Muslim world, Emerson's passage follows its appeal to Muslim poetry not with telescopic "power" but with a "magnifying" metaphor, with the American's *Letters and
Social Aims* offering an oblique "picture-book" of a recent "passage in" Emerson's
own "human life." ☼

"The Exile" first found a home on page 100 of "Notebook Orientalist," where Emerson rendered the material from Kermani that ultimately formed the core of this hybrid poem published in his 1858 "Persian Poetry."[89] On the page that immediately precedes this initial iteration of "The Exile," however, Emerson scrawled a translation that never surfaced in print during his lifetime, but that perhaps best expresses his personal engagement with Persian poetry. On page 99 of his "Notebook Orientalist," Emerson tentatively translates "In Senahar my first born sleeps," a poem authored originally by Saadi:

> In Senahar my first born sleeps
> Stupid with grief still Saadi weeps
> No ↑Tho'↓ youth more fresh than Jussuf blooms
> The charnel worm his cheek consumes
> Where is the palm startopped earthfooted
> Which the ↑brute↓ storm has not uprooted
> I said <o Lord> ↑God↓ die for shame on high
> Since pure youth dies as greybeards die
> I staggered downward to his tomb
> And tore the sealed stone therefrom
> I groped into that narrow pit
> With rolling eyeballs void of wit
> When back from grief my reason came
> Methought my darling did exclaim
> If thy sense the darkness <r>fright
> Strive thou upwards to the light
> Must the <cavern> ↑black grave↓ blaze like noon
> Virtue works that wonder soon
> The crowd believes that harvests grow
> Where never man did barely sow.[90]

Returning to Saadi years after publishing his own "Saadi" in 1842, Emerson selects a poem that reflects familiar themes, straddling life and death, disclosure and illumination. Recalling the "unlocking" of "every crypt," or the "grave" on which "roses bloom," from earlier Persianate poems and renditions, Emerson's "In Senahar my first born sleeps" is grounded in a graveyard revelation, witnessing the dead revive and the tomb "blaze like noon," with Saadi himself tearing away the sepulcher's "sealed stone," receiving a directive from the deceased to "Strive thou upwards to the light." And yet, unlike the resurrections of Emerson's more "rosy" translations, this moment of disclosure seems neither abstract nor erotic, but arises from actual despair, describing Saadi's reaction to the death of his own "first born" son. Reflecting personal grief rather than poetic gratification, these lines lean toward biography rather than theology, recounting Saadi's life experience after his own "son" died "in the prime of youth."[91] Opening with hopeful Qur'ānic allusion to "Jussuf" (i.e., "Joseph," Jacob's lost son, who ultimately returns to his father), Saadi moves immediately to the morbid, imagining the "charnel worm" that "consumes" the "cheek" of his lost son. And although his dead beloved is endowed with speech after Saadi opens "his tomb," the posthumous words of his son are introduced ambiguously; "Methought my darling did exclaim," Saadi reports, hinting that this filial colloquy might perhaps merely be the imaginings of a father overwhelmed by grief and "void of wit."[92]

Performed on page 99 of "Notebook Orientalist," the significance of Emerson's decision to render privately this biographical Persian poem is made more profound by his own American biography. Bridging not only languages but lives, Saadi's "In Senahar my first born sleeps" reflects an experience shared by Emerson, who also had lost his "first born" son more than a decade earlier: i.e. "Waldo," who died of scarlet fever when he was five years old in January 1842, the same year Emerson published his poem "Saadi."[93] If broadly mirroring paternal bereavements, Persian and American, Saadi's "In Senahar my first born sleeps" also offers a more concrete and macabre parallel for Emerson, due to a singular act he committed in the summer of 1857. Very near to the time that he fashioned this translation of Saadi's poem, which recounts the opening of his son's crypt to encounter his corpse, Emerson himself travels to Waldo's "tomb" and "tore the sealed stone therefrom." In a diary entry penned on July 8, 1857, Emerson reports that

> Wednesday, 8 July, 1857. This morning I had the remains of my mother & of my son Waldo removed from the tomb of Mrs. Ripley to my lot in "Sleepy Hollow." The sun shone brightly on the coffins, of which Waldo's was well preserved—now fifteen years. I ventured to look into the coffin. I gave a few white-oak leaves to each coffin, after they were put into the new vault, & the vault was then covered with two slabs of granite.[94]

Oddly echoing the poetic "blaze like noon" that attended Saadi's opening the tomb of his "first born," Emerson himself records in prose that the "sun shone brightly on the coffins" before he "ventured to look in," viewing the body of his own beloved son, long after burial. Eerie and intimate, Emerson's encounter is not, however, unprecedented, enacting a type of unconscious translation, physically repeating in America an act poetically reported in Persia eight centuries earlier. Aptly for Emerson, however, this repetition is also a reversal, a "half-translation" instead of mere recurrence; rather than the revelatory words that culminate Saadi's "In Senahar my first born sleeps," Emerson's own diary entry ends in poignant and painful silence, refusing to disclose details of his experience, closing not with revitalized speech, but with a quiet "vault" conclusively "covered with slabs of granite."

Exhuming his "first born" not once but twice, Emerson recovers his son through surrogate Persian rendition and physical American "removal," with Waldo encountered again after "fifteen years" in translated lines from Emerson's private journal, as well as at his public "lot" in "Sleepy Hollow"—a cemetery whose name aptly recalls Washington Irving, whose own efforts to commune with the dead too were surrounded by Islamic interests.[95] The ironies of Emerson's posthumous encounter, however, are heightened by Saadi's role during precisely this time in fashioning Emerson's own afterlife; speaking to the dead through Saadi's poetry, Emerson is portrayed in these same months as speaking to Saadi as the "dead lyrist of Persia." Published a year before Emerson opened Waldo's tomb, William Rounseville Alger's 1856 *The Poetry of the East* offered American readers an early overview of Islamic and Indic verse, but not without including an oblique appeal to Emerson himself. In a stunning passage first recognized by John Yohannan, Alger's *The Poetry of the East* introduces Saadi with the following description:

> Saadi was asked what he, an idle poet, was good for. In turn he inquired what was the use of the rose; and on being told that it was good to be smelled, replied, "And I am good to smell it!" So our Concord Saadi sings, as if responding from to-day and America, over the ages and the sea, to the dead lyrist of Persia:—
>
>> "Tell them, dear, if eyes were made for seeing,
>> Beauty is its own excuse for being."[96]

Citing Saadi's apology for aesthetics, Alger immediately ranges across "ages" and the Atlantic to cite another "lyrist," tying together poets that span country and chronology. Saadi's smiling reply itself receives a response from the "America" of "to-day," Alger quoting a couplet whose rhyme links "seeing" and "being"—a couplet authored by Emerson himself, excerpted from his "The Rhodora," a poem published originally in 1839 and republished as part of his 1847 *Poems*.[97] Juxtaposing the present and the past, the living and the dead, Alger finds not only an echo but an answer in Emerson's lines, imagining him as "responding from to-day and America, over the ages and the sea, to the dead lyrist of Persia." Most audacious in Alger's account, however, is its deliberate anonymity; endowed again with the ability to dialog with the dead, Emerson appears without his own name, characterized merely as "our Concord Saadi"—an identity that recalls Emerson's own earliest strategies of Muslim pseudonym, now solely named as a New England echo of a Near Eastern original.

Claiming the "Concord" poet as "our" communal voice, Alger's equation of Emerson with "Saadi" would receive republication a decade later, his anthology appearing in a new edition under the revised title of *The Poetry of the Orient* in 1865—the same year that witnessed the initial American publication of Saadi's own *Gulistan*.[98] Translated by none other than Francis Gladwin, whose *Asiatic Miscellany* had offered Emerson his "Alcoran" quotation in 1819, the 1865 appearance of Saadi's *Gulistan* would aptly receive support from "our Concord Saadi," this edition coming equipped with a substantive "Preface" penned by Emerson himself.[99] Introducing his domestic readers to this foreign tradition, Emerson no longer appeals to Saadi to promote his own poetry, but instead promotes Saadi in America; rather than gracefully inscribe the name "Saadi" on the flyleaves of his private journals, Emerson's own name is printed on the front cover of Saadi's published poetry. And inverting the portrait of Saadi offered by Alger's *The Poetry of the East*, Emerson emphasizes the living potential of "the dead lyrist of Persia," asserting in his preface's concluding paragraph:

> The Persians have been called "the French of Asia"; and their superior intelligence, their esteem for men of learning, their welcome to Western travellers, and their tolerance of Christian sects in their territory, as contrasted with Turkish fanaticism, would seem to derive from the rich culture of this great choir of poets, perpetually reinforced through five hundred years, which again and again has enabled the Persians to refine and civilize their conquerors, and to preserve a national identity. To the expansion of this influence there is no limit; and we wish that the present republication may add to the genius of Saadi a new audience in America.
>
> R.W.E.<br>Concord, February, 1864.[100]

Nationally contextualized, Saadi's virtues are seen as reflective of his ethnic roots, Emerson opening this paragraph with a comparative portrait of "the Persians"; described as "The French of Asia," while distinguished from "Turkish fanaticism," Saadi's home culture is celebrated for hospitality, known for its "welcome to Western travellers." Amid this international appraisal, it is Emerson's own contemporary nation that unsurprisingly emerges as most essential, with "America" situated as his introduction's last word. Shifting from the foreign past, spanning "five hundred years," Emerson arrives at subjective futures, framing the communal prospects of Persian verse in America with a hopeful "we wish" in his final sentence. Contrasting this optimistic national outlook, however, is the national outcomes implied by the date that closes Emerson's introduction: "February, 1864"—a pivotal moment in American history, marking one of the final months of the Civil War, as well as the first intimations of one of the war's most infamous acts, General Sherman's bloody "March through Georgia."[101] Written at the dawn of the war's darkest days, Emerson's appeal to national unity while introducing Islamic poetry assumes a meaning with renewed urgency and irony; praising "the Persians" in their capacity "to refine and civilize their conquerors, and to preserve a national identity," Emerson mirrors his divided and dismembered country by invoking medieval Muslim lands. In this American self-reflection, Emerson appeals not only to the "national" present, however, but to a future without frontiers, donning the mantle of literary prophet by predicting that "To the expansion of this influence there is no limit." Rather than America's own broadening Western horizons, it is Eastern poetry's "Manifest Destiny" that Emerson celebrates, forecasting a limitless Persian "influence" even while writing from an embattled America—a prediction that ironically has proved most true in the nation's twenty-first century, where Persian Sufi poetry has gained surprising popularity during the very years that marked another American trauma: 9/11. Embodying an irenic view of Islam, Jalāl ad-Dīn Rūmī—a poetic successor of Saadi—has been heralded as a "best-selling" author in contemporary America, popularly portrayed as an ideal of Muslim "tolerance" that resists stereotypes of "fanaticism."[102]

If the date of Emerson's concluding line has national connotations, its place is perhaps most personally resonant, with "our Concord Saadi" aptly ending his introduction to Saadi with "Concord" itself. Aiming to bequeath a literary appreciation of Islamic verse to his American countrymen, it is to his actual neighbors that Emerson bequeaths his literal Islamic holdings, seeking to ensure their availability at the local library. Returning to Concord in 1873 from his trip to Europe and Egypt, Emerson would deliver a public address on October 1, 1873, dedicating the new building of the Concord Free Public Library.[103] However, during this same time, Emerson also privately drafts lists of books for the library's acquisition, scribbling haphazard catalogs such as the following in a journal known as "Books Large," another personal notebook once owned by his father, William Emerson:

> For Concord Library
> ———
>
> Luther's Table Talk.
> Grimm: Memoires
> Lord Hervey's History of England
> Hobbes's Works
> Chesterfield's Letters
> ↑Duc de↓ Saint Simon. 20 vols
> ———
>
> Wilkinson's Egypt 2 vols
> ———
>
> Social Essays from Saturday Review
> ———
>
> Koran[104]

In this late list of books designated "For Concord Library," grouped with expected mainstays of American interest, the Muslim scripture again surfaces, newly domesticated alongside epistolary "Letters" and lively "Table Talk," as well as more international offerings, including "Wilkinson's Egypt." Forming another envelope in Emerson's life, the "Koran" is no longer implicated in his individual interests merely but points beyond his own biography, reaching back to both former generations and future descendants. First quoted at the private beginnings to a new college term in 1819, the Qur'ān returns near the end of Emerson's life marked for a new public library, emerging in this notebook inherited from his father even as Emerson seeks to make available the Muslim scripture for the city's next sons and daughters.

It is not a copy of the "Koran," but Emerson's own prefaced *Gulistan*, that will embody the most intimate witness to his unfolding Islamic lineages now housed at the Concord Library. Dying on April 27, 1882, Emerson will be laid to rest in the "Sleepy Hollow" cemetery, buried beside his beloved son, Waldo. However, if frustrated in his hopes for his "first born," it would be Emerson's last surviving child— Edward—who helped advance his father's literary legacy, exhuming especially his Islamic interests. Still held at the Concord Free Public Library is the very edition of Saadi's *Gulistan* used by Edward Emerson as he annotated his father's *Journals* in preparation for their publication beginning in 1909—an edition of the *Gulistan* whose page vii is reproduced as Figure 5.4.[105]

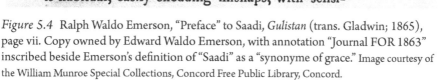

Saadi, though he has not the lyric flights of Hafiz, has wit, practical sense, and just moral sentiments.  He has the instinct to teach, and from every occurrence must draw the moral, like Franklin.  He is the poet of friendship, love, self-devotion, and serenity.  There is a uniform force in his page, and, conspicuously, a tone of cheerfulness, which has almost made his name a synonyme for this grace.  The word *Saadi* means *fortunate*.  In him the trait is no result of levity, much less of convivial habit, but first of a happy nature, to which victory is habitual, easily shedding mishaps, with sensi-

*Figure 5.4* Ralph Waldo Emerson, "Preface" to Saadi, *Gulistan* (trans. Gladwin; 1865), page vii. Copy owned by Edward Waldo Emerson, with annotation "Journal FOR 1863" inscribed beside Emerson's definition of "Saadi" as a "synonyme of grace." Image courtesy of the William Munroe Special Collections, Concord Free Public Library, Concord.

Marking another step in the *"Digressive Continuity"* of Emerson's Islamic engagements, Edward's brief note implies a dizzying set of circulations, spiraling across family generations and spilling from literary interiors to literal margins. Housed at Concord's library, these scribbles represent a son's personal marginalia on a page of his father's published work, pointing back to a passage in Emerson's own private "Journal"—"Journal FOR"—that Edward will also edit, appearing as part of his *Journals* (1909–1914).[106] At the genetic center of these gyrations is again a rendered Islamic identity, Edward gesturing to his father's explanation of the etymologic meaning of "*Saadi,*" translating this poet's Arabic name as "*fortunate.*"[107] In this final and felicitous rendition, a lineage seems to circle back to our study's initial bequest, this legacy from parent to child recalling Ezra Stiles' own circular donation to his son, Ezra Jr. However, while Stiles' efforts to pass forward his Arabic inscriptions to his namesake will be interrupted by the latter's early death, the untimely loss of Emerson's own namesake—Waldo—will be followed by other lines of literary descent, with his daughter Ellen and then later his son Edward advancing their father's Islamic engagements. Despite the myriad of tragic "mishaps," from the fiery "dispersal" of "books & MSS" to the death of the "first born," Edward's exhumed note marking "Saadi" as a "synonyme of grace" implies not only lineages cut but also legacies kept, embodying the material witnesses to Islamic interests that yet survive in familial American margins.

# APPENDIX

The aim of this appendix is to catalog every line of Persian poetry translated by Emerson from German sources. John D. Yohannan's 1943 "Check-List," although accounting for only a third of the material here presented, provided the essential starting point as well as an instructive precedent.[1] Cataloging efforts were also aided immensely by the footnotes to the *Topical Notebooks of Ralph Waldo Emerson* (1990–1994), as well as the scrupulous anatomies of Emerson's poems and translations supplied in *The Poetry Notebooks of Ralph Waldo Emerson* (1986); however, this appendix also aims to rectify several omissions I have spotted in these critical editions.[2] In seeking to assemble Emerson's German sources, Emerson himself also assisted, as he frequently labeled his translations with page numbers from Joseph Hammer-Purgstall's *Diwan* (1812–1813) and his *Geschichte* (1818). With hopes of establishing a conservative estimate of Emerson's translation campaign, I include in this appendix only rendered lines for which a German source may be ascertained with confidence.[3]

The appendix is divided into two sections, Category A and Category B.

Category A catalogs every line translated by Emerson from Muḥammad Shamsuddīn Ḥāfiẓ. The sequence of entries in this category follows the order of Hafiz's poems available to Emerson through Hammer-Purgstall's *Diwan* (1812–1813).

- The **first column** ("Location in Emerson's Texts") cites the page(s) in Emerson's journals where the *most complete* translation of the relevant source poem may be found (many of the poems listed in this appendix were translated by Emerson several times).[4] Citation of two or more sources in this column indicates that Emerson translated discrete sections from the same Hafiz poem in different locations.
- The **second column** ("Location in Hammer's *Diwan*") cites the book and number of the Hafiz poem as offered in Emerson's source, Hammer-Purgstall's

*Diwan.* For example, the entry for "Elif:VII" indicates the seventh *ghazal* of Book "Elif." The final seven entries of this column refer to other types of Hafizean poems found on page 478 and following in the second volume of Hammer-Purgstall's *Diwan* (e.g., "*Sakiname*").

- The **third column** ("Lines Translated") lists the number of lines Emerson translated from Hammer-Purgstall's *Diwan* as well as the specific lines rendered. The entry "**10**:(1-4/9-14)" in the twenty-fifth row of Category A, for example, indicates that Emerson translated **ten** lines from this source—specifically, lines **one through four** and lines **nine through fourteen**. If the lines translated have been underlined, this indicates that Emerson has rendered the *complete* Hafizean poem as offered by Hammer-Purgstall. The entry "**22**:(1-22)" in the fifth row of Category A, for example, indicates that Emerson translated all twenty-two lines of this *ghazal* as presented in Hammer-Purgstall's *Diwan*.

Category B catalogs every line Emerson translated from all Persian poets *besides* Hafiz from German sources. The sequence of the entries in this category follows the order of poems as given in Hammer-Purgstall's *Geschichte* (1818).

- The **first column** ("Location in Emerson's Texts"): same as Category A
- The **second column** ("Location, author & opening in Hammer's *Geschichte*") cites (1) the page number in the *Geschichte* where Emerson's source is found; (2) the Persian poet's name as provided by Hammer-Purgstall; and (3) either the title or the initial words of the poem from which Emerson translates.
- The **third column** ("Lines Translated") lists the number of lines Emerson translated from the source poem in Hammer-Purgstall's *Geschichte*.

The final two entries of Category B are descriptions of Emerson's translations from Persian poets other than Hafiz that he made from German sources other than Hammer-Purgstall's *Geschichte*.

At the conclusion of Category B, a tally of the lines enumerated in both categories is provided, adding Category A's total (1,492 lines) and Category B's total (553 lines), leading to a sum of 2,045 lines.

## Category A: Emerson's Translations from Hafiz

| # | Location in Emerson's Journals | Location in Hammer's *Diwan* | Lines Translated |
|---|---|---|---|
| 1 | "Orientalist," 57 | Elif:VII | **2**:(17-18) |
| 2 | "Orientalist," 24 & "EF," 97 | Elif:VIII | **4**:(1-2,17-18) |
| 3 | "EF," 109,114 | Elif:XIII | **3**:(6,15-16) |

*(continued)*

| # | Location in Emerson's Journals | Location in Hammer's *Diwan* | Lines Translated |
|---|---|---|---|
| 4 | "X,"171 | Ber:I | **4:**(9-12) |
| 5 | "EF,"105 | Ta:IX | **2:**(1-2) |
| 6 | "Orientalist,"158 | Ta:XIII | **22:**(1-22) |
| 7 | "X,"167-68 | Ta:XVII | **28:**(1-28) |
| 8 | "X,"172 | Ta:XXIV | **36:**(1-36) |
| 9 | "EF,"114 | Ta:XXX | **4:**(21-24) |
| 10 | "EF,"103 | Ta:XXXIX | **20:**(9-28) |
| 11 | "X,"174-76 | Ta:XL | **28:**(1-28) |
| 12 | "X,"176-77 | Ta:XLIII | **14:**(5-6,9-20) |
| 13 | "EF,"94 | Ta:XLV | **2:**(5-6) |
| 14 | "EF,"48(2) | Ta:L | **4:**(17-20) |
| 15 | "EF,"49 | Ta:LV | **18:**(1-18) |
| 16 | "EF,"98 | Ta:LXVII | **4:**(21-24) |
| 17 | "EF,"38 | Dal:VII | **3:**(34-36) |
| 18 | "EF,"97 | Dal:XLIII | **4:**(1-4) |
| 19 | "EF,"40 | Dal:XLVI | **4:**(13-16) |
| 20 | "EF,"89-90 | Dal:L | **32:**(1-32) |
| 21 | *JMN*,X,67-68 | Dal:LV | **24:**(1-24) |
| 22 | "EF,"113 | Dal:LXIV | **4:**(37-40) |
| 23 | *Topical*,III,349-50 | Dal:LXXII | **21:**(1-21) |
| 24 | "EF,"112 | Dal:LXXIV | **4:**(25-28) |
| 25 | "EF,"44 | Dal:LXXVI | **20:**(5-24) |
| 26 | "EF,"45(2) | Dal:LXXXII | **6:**(27-32) |
| 27 | "EF,"46-47 | Dal:LXXXIV | **14:**(1-14) |
| 28 | "EF,"47(2) | Dal:LXXXVII | **10:**(1-4/9-14) |
| 29 | "EF,"113 | Dal:XC | **4:**(49-52) |
| 30 | "Orientalist,"153-54 | Dal:CIX | **36:**(1-36) |
| 31 | "Orientalist,"232-34 | Dal:CX | **44:**(1-44) |
| 32 | "Orientalist,"235 | Dal:CXI | **4:**(33-36) |
| 33 | "EF,"114 | Dal:CXX | **4:**(9-12) |
| 34 | "Orientalist,"57 | Dal:CXXIX | **2:**(13-14) |
| 35 | "EF,"81-82 | Dal:CXXXII | **28:**(1-28) |
| 36 | "EF,"108 | Dal:CXXXVI | **2:**(5-6) |
| 37 | "EF,"109 | Dal:CXLV | **1:**(7) |
| 38 | "EF,"94 | Dal:CLI | **8:**(1-8) |
| 39 | "EF,"97 | Dal:CLVI | **4:**(13-16) |
| 40 | "EF,"96 | Dal:CLVII | **1:**(5) |
| 41 | "EF,"97 | Dal:CLXIV | **4:**(21-24) |

*(continued)*

| # | Location in Emerson's Journals | Location in Hammer's *Diwan* | Lines Translated |
|---|---|---|---|
| 42 | "EF,"109 | Dal:CLXV | **2:**(21-22) |
| 43 | "EF,"104,108 | Dal:CLXVII | **32:**(19-30/53-54/59-74/81-2) |
| 44 | "Orientalist,"7,151;"EF,"114 | Ra:I | **8:**(9-12/17-18/23-24) |
| 45 | "Orientalist,"168-71 | Ra:II | **28:**(9-36) |
| 46 | "Orientalist,"84-85 | Ra:IX | **24:**(1-24) |
| 47 | "EF,"80(1) | Ra:X | **4:**(25-28) |
| 48 | "X,"165 | Ra:XIII | **22:**(1-22) |
| 49 | "EF,"38 | Sin:VI | **2:**(15-16) |
| 50 | "EF,"80(1) | Schin:II | **2:**(19-20) |
| 51 | "EF,"80(1) | Schin:III | **4:**(17-20) |
| 52 | "Orientalist,"133 | Schin:VI | **18:**(1-18) |
| 53 | JMN,XIII,304-05 | Schin:X | **6:**(7-12) |
| 54 | "Orientalist,"150 | Schin:XI | **6:**(22-27) |
| 55 | "EF,"77 | Shin:XII | **8:**(25-32) |
| 56 | "Orientalist,"135 | Shin:XIX | **6:**(7-10/17-18) |
| 57 | "Orientalist,"135 | Shin:XXII | **2:**(27-28) |
| 58 | JMN,XIII,349-50 | Sad:I | **8:**(25-32) |
| 59 | "Orientalist,"137 | Sad:II | **14:**(1-14) |
| 60 | "Orientalist,"180 | Thy:I | **6:**(1-6) |
| 61 | "Orientalist,"138 | Ghain:I | **28:**(1-28) |
| 62 | "Orientalist,"176-77 | Kaf:I | **12:**(1-12) |
| 63 | "Orientalist,"177 | Kaf:II | **3:**(8-9/12) |
| 64 | "Orientalist,"177 | Kaf:III | **2:**(7/10) |
| 65 | "Orientalist,"177 | Kiaf:I | **4:**(21-24) |
| 66 | "Orientalist,"83; "X"184(2) | Kiaf:II | **28:**(1-28) |
| 67 | "Orientalist,"178-79 | Kiaf:III | **18:**(1-18) |
| 68 | "Orientalist,"181 | Lam:III | **4:**(21-24) |
| 69 | "EF,"114 | Lam:IV | **4:**(37-40) |
| 70 | "Orientalist,"182 | Lam:IX | **4:**(29-32) |
| 71 | "Orientalist,"182 | Lam:X | **4:**(25-28) |
| 72 | "Orientalist,"183 | Mim:I | **12:**(9-20) |
| 73 | JMN,IX,398-99 | Mim:V | **20:**(1-20) |
| 74 | "Orientalist,"184 | Mim:VI | **12:**(1-12) |
| 75 | "EF,"76 | Mim:IX | **2:**(21-22) |
| 76 | "EF,"76,77,109,114 | Mim:X | **14:**(5-8/13-14/29-32/37-40) |
| 77 | "Orientalist,"187 | Mim:XII | **2:**(13-14) |
| 78 | "EF,"80 | Mim:XIV | **2:**(9-10) |
| 79 | "EF,"98 | Mim:XXI | **3:**(7-9) |

*(continued)*

| # | Location in Emerson's Journals | Location in Hammer's *Diwan* | Lines Translated |
|---|---|---|---|
| 80 | "Orientalist,"9 | Mim:XXIII | **4**:(29-32) |
| 81 | *JMN*,XIV,152-53 | Mim:XXV | **4**:(9-12) |
| 82 | "Orientalist,"5 | Mim:XXVI | **4**:(5-8) |
| 83 | "EF,"48(1) | Mim:XXVII | **4**:(37-40) |
| 84 | "Rhymer,"139;" Orientalist,"60 | Mim:XXVIII | **8**:(13-20) |
| 85 | "EF,"50(1) | Mim:XXXII | **4**:(9-10/15-16) |
| 86 | "EF,"38 | Mim:XXXIV | **4**:(25-28) |
| 87 | "Orientalist,"188 | Mim:XLII | **4**:(29-32) |
| 88 | "Orientalist,"189 | Mim:XLIII | **13**:(3-6/8-16) |
| 89 | "Orientalist,"13 | Mim:LI | **12**:(33-44) |
| 90 | "EF,"55 | Mim:LXI | **4**:(13-16) |
| 91 | "Orientalist,"5 | Mim:LXIV | **8**:(17-24) |
| 92 | "Orientalist,"5 | Mim:LXVI | **4**:(13-16) |
| 93 | "Orientalist,"115 | Mim:LXXI | **12**:(25-36) |
| 94 | "Orientalist,"114 | Mim:LXXVI | **4**:(11-12/17-18) |
| 95 | "Orientalist,"112,113; "EF,"80(1) | Nun:II | **9**:(1-3/13-15/25-27) |
| 96 | "Orientalist,"116; *Topical*,II,378-79 | Nun:IV | **8**:(21-24/25-28) |
| 97 | "X,"254 | Nun:XII | **12**:(1-12) |
| 98 | "EF,"42 | Nun:XVI | **9**:(19-27) |
| 99 | "X,"196-97 | Nun:XXIV | **28**:(1-28) |
| 100 | "Rhymer,"140 | Waw:X | **2**:(9-10) |
| 101 | "X,"237 | He:I | **28**:(1-28) |
| 102 | *Topical*,II,400 | He:VI | **14**:(1-14) |
| 103 | "X,"178 | He:IX | **20**:(1-20) |
| 104 | "EF,"114 | Ja:II | **4**:(29-32) |
| 105 | "Orientalist,"7 | Ja:VII | **4**:(13-16) |
| 106 | "Orientalist,"51 | Ja:XV | **4**:(5-8) |
| 107 | "EF,"10(1)-11(1) | Ja:XVI | **40**:(1-40) |
| 108 | "EF,"109 | Ja:XIX | **2**:(1-2) |
| 109 | "EF,"93 | Ja:XX | **2**:(15-16) |
| 110 | "EF,"115 | Ja:XXVI | **4**:(37-40) |
| 111 | "EF,"54 | Ja:LII | **28**:(1-28) |
| 112 | "EF,"9 | Ja:LIV | **18**:(1-18) |
| 113 | "EF,"55 | Ja:LX | **4**:(9-12) |
| 114 | "EF,"109 | Ja:LXXVII | **2**:(21-22) |
| 115 | "X,"244-53 | Sakiname | **238**:(1-238) |
| 116 | "Orientalist,"237 | Kasside:I | **17**:(14-20/23-32) |

*(continued)*

| # | Location in Emerson's Journals | Location in Hammer's *Diwan* | Lines Translated |
|---|---|---|---|
| 117 | *Topical*,II,399 | Mokataat:III | **6**:(1-6) |
| 118 | "Orientalist,"198 | Mokataat:IX | **11**:(1-11) |
| 119 | "Orientalist,"190 | Mokataat:X | **8**:(1-8) |
| 120 | *Topical*,II,399-400 | Mokataat, XXI | **10**:(1-10) |
| 121 | "Orientalist,"110 | Mokataat, LXII | **4**:(1-4) |
| | | **Category A Total** | **1,492** |

# Category B: Emerson's Translations from All Persian Poets Besides Hafiz

| # | Location in Emerson's journals | Location, author & opening in Hammer's *Geschichte* | | # of Lines Translated |
|---|---|---|---|---|
| 1 | "Orientalist,"10 | p.41 | "Ammar" (*Könnt' ich...*) | 2 |
| 2 | "Orientalist,"11 | p.43 | "Pindar aus Rei" (*Umsonst...*) | 4 |
| 3 | *JMN*,XI,175 | p.44 | "Asdschedi" (*Es zieht...*) | 2 |
| 4 | "Orientalist,"12 | p.44 | "Asdschedi" (*Auf eine Melone*) | 4 |
| 5 | "Orientalist,"12 | p.44 | "Asdschedi" (*Man spricht...*) | 4 |
| 6 | "Orientalist,"29 | p.81 | "Omar Chiam" (*Du wünschest...*) | 16 |
| 7 | "Orientalist,"29 | p.82 | "Omar Chiam" (*Wo Tulpen...*) | 4 |
| 8 | "Orientalist,"30 | p.82 | "Omar Chiam" (*Ich trinke...*) | 4 |
| 9 | "Orientalist,"30 | p.82 | "Omar Chiam" (*In dem unendlichen...*) | 4 |
| 10 | "Orientalist,"16 | p.91 | "Enweri" (*An den Dichter...*) | 2 |
| 11 | "Orientalist,"36-37 | p.92 | "Enweri" (*Philosophische Lehre*) | 10 |
| 12 | "Orientalist,"33-35 | pp.92-3 | "Enweri" (*Schah Sandschar...*) | 62 |
| 13 | "Orientalist,"31 | p.94 | "Enweri" (*Die Sterne...*) | 2 |
| 14 | "Orientalist,"63 | p.96 | "Enweri" (*Im Garten...*) | 4 |
| 15 | "Orientalist,"27-28 | p.107 | "Nisami" (*Erzählung von...*) | 22 |
| 16 | "Orientalist,"64 | p.142 | "Attar" (*Der Tulip...*) | 1 |
| 17 | "Orientalist,"65 | p.153 | "Attar" (*Der Vögel Seele...*) | 60 |
| 18 | "Orientalist,"19 | p.197 | "Rumi" (*Ich bin der Falk...*) | 8 |
| 19 | "Orientalist,"18 | p.197 | "Rumi" (*Höre was für...*) | 4 |
| 21 | "Orientalist,"19 | p.198 | "Rumi" (*Im Osten...*) | 4 |
| 22 | "Orientalist,"222 | p.208 | "Saadi" (*Kein Land...*) | 15 |
| 23 | "Orientalist,"221 | p.209 | "Saadi" (*Wenn auf den...*) | 2 |
| 24 | *JMN*,XV,384 | p.212 | "Saadi" (*Dein Aug'...*) | 2 |
| 25 | *JMN*,XV,384 | p.212 | "Saadi" (*Keine Seele...*) | 4 |

*(continued)*

| #  | Location in Emerson's journals | Location, author & opening in Hammer's *Geschichte* | | # of Lines Translated |
|----|----|----|----|----|
| 26 | *JMN*,XV,384 | p.212 | "Saadi" (*Liebeschmerz...*) | 2 |
| 27 | *JMN*,XV,385 | p.212 | "Saadi" (*Wer mit Mondgesicht...*) | 8 |
| 28 | "Orientalist,"55 | p.213 | "Saadi" (*Wer seinen Freund...*) | 8 |
| 29 | *JMN*,XV,384 | p.215 | "Saadi" (*Jetzt ist...*) | 16 |
| 30 | "Orientalist,"76-77 | p.218 | "Saadi" (*Zu Sanaa...*) | 24 |
| 31 | "Orientalist,"41-50 | p.223 | "Nimetollah" (*So gestalt...*) | 34 |
| 32 | "Orientalist,"75 | p.225 | "Lutfallah" (*Mein Unstern...*) | 8 |
| 33 | "Orientalist,"72-74 | p.228 | "Seid Hosseini" (*Hör' dieß...*) | 46 |
| 34 | "Orientalist,"80-81 | p.233 | "Mewlana" (*Mahmud, mein Bruder...*) | 8 |
| 35 | "Orientalist,"90 | p.235 | "Ben Jemin" (*Du übertreibe...*) | 6 |
| 36 | "Orientalist,"90 | p.236 | "Ben Jemin" (*Ich sah...*) | 6 |
| 37 | "Orientalist,"91 | p.236 | "Ben Jemin" (*Ein Mühlrad...*) | 18 |
| 38 | "Orientalist,"94 | p.237 | "Ben Jemin" (*Welch eine Muhle...*) | 4 |
| 39 | "Orientalist,"92 | p.238 | "Ben Jemin" (*Bloß ob...*) | 8 |
| 40 | "Orientalist,"98 | p.239 | "Ben Jemin" (*Der freye...*) | 4 |
| 41 | "Orientalist,"144-47 | p.248 | "Chodschu Kermani" (*Willkommen...*) | 8 |
| 42 | "Orientalist,"104-07 | p.249 | "Mir Kermani" (*Ohne die Wangen...*) | 10 |
| 43 | "Orientalist,"118 | p.259 | "Dschelaleddin Adhad" (*Wie Blumenmärkte...*) | 13 |
| 44 | "Orientalist,"126 | p.337 | "Dschami" (*Ein Freund...*) | 4 |
| 45 | "Persian Poetry,"726 | p.360 | "Hatifi" (*Man kann das...*) | 2 |
| 46 | "Orientalist,"121 | p.364 | "Gilani" (*O trantes Herz...*) | 14 |
| 47 | "Orientalist,"122 | p.369 | "Hilali" (*Wenn du mich...*) | 2 |
| 48 | "Orientalist,"124 | p.401 | "Feisi" (*Ich bin's...*) | 6 |
| 49 | "Orientalist,"124 | p.401 | "Feisi" (*Der Trinker...*) | 4 |
| 50 | "Orientalist,"163-65 | | | 40 |

[A selection of Rūmī's *Mesnavi*, pp. 89–93 in August Tholuck's *Bluthensammlung aus der Morgenlandischen Mystik* (1825)]

| 51 | "Orientalist,"194 | | | 4 |

[A selection of Sa'dī's *Bostan*, p.152 of the first volume of K. H. Graf's *Moschlichedden Sadi's Lustgarten* (1850)]

|  | | **Category A Total** | 1,492 |
|--|--|----|----|
|  | | **Category B Total** | 553 |
|  | | **Appendix Sum Total** | 2,045 |

# NOTES

## Introduction

1. A concise overview of this recent tendency in American Studies is provided by Brian Edwards and Dilip Gaonkar in the "Introduction" to their co-edited *Globalizing American Studies* (Chicago: University of Chicago Press, 2010), 1–46, which also makes passing mention of Emerson's interest in Persian poetry, linking his nineteenth-century reading of Saʿdī with President Obama's quotation of this same Persian poet in 2009 (22–23).
2. Timothy Marr, *The Cultural Roots of American Islamicism* (Cambridge, UK: Cambridge UP, 2006), 5. For these recent studies of American literature in Middle Eastern contexts see respectively Brian Yothers, *The Romance of the Holy Land in American Travel Writing, 1790–1876* (Aldershot: Ashgate, 2007) and Jacob Rama Berman, *American Arabesque: Arabs, Islam and the 19th-Century Imaginary* (New York: New York UP, 2012).
3. Quoted from Mary Brooks' introduction to her edited volume *Textiles Revealed: Object Lessons in Historic Textile and Costume Research* (London: Archetype Publications, 2000), 2, where Brooks invokes Barbara Kirshenblatt-Gimblett in her phrase "material memories."
4. A recent comprehensive critique of "Orientalism" is offered by Daniel Martin Varisco's *Reading Orientalism: Said and the Unsaid* (Seattle: University of Washington Press, 2007); however, in American Literary Studies specifically, the recent departure from Said's "dominating versus the dominated" dichotomy is articulated by Wai Chee Dimock in her influential *Through Other Continents: American Literature Across Deep Time* (Princeton, NJ: Princeton UP, 2006), 28–29.
5. For instance, despite the numerous overlaps between the New England careers of Ezra Stiles, William Bentley, and Ralph Waldo Emerson, these figures have never received sustained consideration in a single study.
6. For Irving as "Father of American Literature," see Chapter 3, note 72.
7. These epithets for Lydia Maria Child are offered by Carolyn Karcher in the title and preface to her definitive biography, *The First Woman in the Republic: A Cultural Biography of Lydia Maria Child* (Durham, NC: Duke UP, 1994), xi. See also Chapter 4, note 6.
8. This characterization of Child is supplied by Margaret M. R. Kellow in her "The Divided Mind of Antislavery Feminism: Lydia Maria Child and the Construction of African American Womanhood" in *Discovering the Women in Slavery: Emancipating Perspectives on the American Past*, ed. Patricia Morton (Athens: University of Georgia Press, 1996), 107–26 (107).
9. For this superlative definition of Muḥammad Shamsuddīn Ḥāfiẓ, known to Emerson simply as "Hafiz"—the form of the poet's name used regularly in this book—see Ralph Waldo Emerson, "Persian Poetry," *Atlantic Monthly Magazine* 1 (1858): 724–34 (726).
10. Berman, *American Arabesque*, 10.

## Chapter 1

1. Ezra Stiles, *The Literary Diary of Ezra Stiles*, ed. Franklin Bowditch Dexter, 3 vols. (New York: C. Scribner's Sons, 1901), I, 457–59 (cited subsequently as "Stiles, *Diary*").

2. Reproduced courtesy of the Beinecke Rare Book and Manuscript Library, Yale University, Stiles' document, labeled *"Linguarum orientalium specimen quadrilinguale"* (MS Vault Stiles, Folder Theo 29) features several lines inscribed in Arabic, Latin, and Hebrew underneath his spherical diagram, which I address at the conclusion to this chapter.

3. For this "Journey to Connecticutt," see Stiles, *Diary*, I, 456.

4. In addition to quoting from the *Targum of Jonathan* (i.e., *Targum Yonatan*) in his "CHALD." circle, Stiles quotes from *Targum Onkelos* in his central circle, inscribing Deuteronomy 5:5 around its periphery. "DEUT. VI.4" is also cited in this central circle, included immediately below the Tetragrammatoxn, "יהוה."

5. Dedicating his right-hand circle to the Syriac of 1 John 5:5, Stiles also reproduces its text in Hebrew script, included immediately underneath his "SYRIACA" sphere.

6. The final phrase of Stiles' Arabic inscription—"وتبارك الله احسن الخالقين"—matches the final words of the Qur'ān 23:14, except that the latter begins with a "ف" rather than a "و" (i.e., reading "فتبارك الله احسن الخالقين"). My renditions of Qur'ānic quotations throughout this study, including the version of Qur'ān 23:14 provided here, are informed by A. J. Arberry, who offers "So blessed be God, the fairest of creators!" in his translation (see A. J. Arberry, trans., *The Koran Interpreted* [New York: George Allen & Unwin Ltd, 1955]). Arberry's "fairest" best articulates the superlative "احسن," hinting at not only this term's moral, but also aesthetic, connotation.

7. For early recognition of Stiles as "the most learned man of his time," see Amelia Leavitt Hill's "The New President of Yale College in 1778," *The Connecticut Magazine: An Illustrated Monthly* 5 (1899): 420. For Stiles as "one of the most learned men in America," see Edmund Morgan, *The Gentle Puritan: A Life of Ezra Stiles, 1727–1795* (New Haven and London: Yale UP, 1962), 134.

8. Stiles' 1765 Edinburgh doctorate—an honor that Franklin himself helped to procure—and his 1794 letter to William Jones are treated by Morgan, *The Gentle Puritan*, 159 and 443. For representative correspondence between Stiles and Jefferson, and their book exchange in particular, see Stiles' May 8, 1786, letter to Jefferson, *Thomas Jefferson Papers*, Library of Congress, reproduced at http://jeffersonswest.unl.edu/archive/view_doc.php?id=jef.00018. For Jefferson's visit to Stiles in 1784, see Kevin Hayes, *The Road to Monticello: The Life and Mind of Thomas Jefferson* (Oxford: Oxford UP, 2008), 271.

9. See, for instance, Edward Andrew's *Native Apostles: Black and Indian Missionaries in the British Atlantic World*, which regularly references Stiles, characterizing him as "an early modern embodiment of the global citizen" (Cambridge: Harvard UP, 2013), 210. Stiles is also featured in Linford D. Fisher's recent *The Indian Great Awakening: Religion and the Shaping of Native Cultures in Early America* (Oxford: Oxford UP, 2012), 100, 116, 126.

10. Stiles' association with Carigal has most recently been treated by Michael Hoberman, who dedicates the fifth chapter of his *New Israel/New England: Jews and Puritans in Early America* to their relationship (Amherst: University of Massachusetts Press, 2011); emphasizing the ecumenical outcomes of Stiles' encounter with Carigal, Hoberman recognizes Newport in particular as "a font of religious pluralism with no equivalent anywhere else in New England" (162).

11. For Abiel Holmes' treatment of Stiles' Arabic studies, see his *The Life of Ezra Stiles* (Boston: Thomas & Andrews, 1798), 133.

12. Despite prominent and regular mention of Arabic in Stiles' own *Diary*, Morgan's *The Gentle Puritan* largely overlooks the language, making only a couple cursory gestures to Arabic, in his Chapter 9 (142), and in the book's appendix (465).

13. See Shalom Goldman, *God's Sacred Tongue: Hebrew and the American Imagination* (Chapel Hill: UNC Press, 2003), 61. Goldman's claim that Stiles' "reading of Arabic" was "a secular pursuit" seems solely based on Stiles' reserving Sundays for his study of scripture.

14. Stiles' distinctive "conversion" from "Christian philosophe to evangelical Puritan"—contra broader eighteenth-century trends toward religious liberalism—has been well recognized since Morgan (1962), and most recently treated by Christopher Grasso, *A Speaking Aristocracy: Transforming Public Discourse in Eighteenth-Century Connecticut* (Chapel Hill: UNC Press, 1999), 233.

15. Princeton's *sammelband* binds together *Alphabetum Arabicum* (Rome: In Typographia Medicea, 1592) and *Syriacae linguae prima elementa* (Antwerp: Christophori Plantini, 1572). I am indebted to Stephen Ferguson, Curator of Rare Books, Princeton University Library, for bringing this *sammelband* and its autograph to my attention, and for signaling its likely attribution to Isaak Chauncy (1632–1712). Although later New England figures named "Isaac Chauncy" are possible candidates for this *sammelband*'s signature, its Semitic language focus, as well as its early dates (1592/1572), seem to suggest its autograph is Isaak Chauncy's, son of seventeenth-century Harvard president, and Semitic language scholar, Charles Chauncy. For a brief overview of Isaak's own career, including his return to England, ultimately becoming "one of the most respected Congregational divines in the capital," see Francis Bremer, *Congregational Communion: Clerical Friendship in the Anglo-American Puritan Community, 1610–1692* (Boston: Northeastern UP, 1994), 183. Despite widespread New England interest in Arabic before the Revolution, there exists no major study of this tradition; Arabic's prominence during this same era in England has been treated expertly by G. J. Toomer, including in his *Eastern Wisedome and Learning: The Study of Arabic in Seventeenth-Century England* (Oxford: Oxford UP, 1996).

16. For the teaching of Arabic at Harvard "during the presidency of Charles Chauncy," see Ernest McCarus, "History of Arabic Study in the United States" in *The Arabic Language in America*, ed. Aleya Rouchdy (Detroit: Wayne State UP, 1992), 207–50 (207). See also Samuel Eliot Morison's *Founding of Harvard College* (Cambridge: Harvard UP, 1935) for the rise of Arabic at Cambridge University "in Chauncy's time," leading to the establishment of a "chair of Arabic [. . .] at Cambridge in 1632" (75–76); this same period is treated by Toomer—without, however, mention of Chauncy—in his *Eastern Wisedome and Learning*, 85–93.

17. "A Letter of President Dunster to Professor Ravis," *Collections of the Massachusetts Historical Society* 4:1 (1852): 251–54 (254).

18. McCarus, "History of Arabic Study in the United States," 207.

19. Jonathan Edwards, *The Blank Bible*, ed. Stephen Stein, 2 vols. (New Haven: Yale UP, 2006), I, 145. Stein reproduces Edwards' Arabic phrase as the doubtful "خشب جمر," rather than "شمشار," as I provide; however, it is this latter term that seems to be intended by Edwards, as his entire passage is a direct quotation from Arthur Bedford's *The Scripture Chronology* (London, 1730), 21, which features "شمشار."

20. Edwards, *The Blank Bible*, I, 280. Edwards' passage continues on to again cite "Bedford," and his "*Scripture Chronology*, pp. 326 and 353."

21. Isaac Stiles' complex relationship with the Edwards family—both Timothy and Jonathan—is treated by Morgan, *The Gentle Puritan*, 35–41.

22. For Stiles' Calvinist "infidelity," see Chapter 4 of Morgan, *The Gentle Puritan*, 58–77. Stiles himself notes his student "neglect" of Hebrew in his 1768 "Memoir concerning my learning Hebrew," authored just a year after Stiles recommenced his study of the language in May 1767; see also Holmes, *Life of Ezra Stiles*, 128–29, and Morgan, *The Gentle Puritan*, 142.

23. This quotation largely matches the printed edition of Stiles' *Diary*, edited by Dexter (*Diary* [I, 3]); however, I supply Stiles' entry for January 7 from the first page of the initial volume of his manuscript *Diary* as Dexter does not include this entry in his published edition. Stiles' manuscript *Diary* is held as part of the Beinecke's MS Vault Stiles, and my transcripts are made courtesy of the Beinecke Rare Book and Manuscript Library, Yale University. Dexter's practice of editing and suppressing material from Stiles' *Diary* is addressed further in notes 70 and 71 below.

24. Samuel King's oil on canvas portrait of Stiles—that is, "Ezra Stiles (1727–1795), B.A. 1746, M.A. 1749"—is housed at, and appears courtesy of, the Yale University Art Gallery. This

portrait is regularly reproduced in studies that mention Stiles (see, e.g., Grasso, *A Speaking Aristocracy*, 232). For Stiles' lengthy *Diary* entry that minutely details the "Picture" which "M$^r$ King [just] finished," including the "two Shelves of Books" which appear "Behind & on [Stiles'] left side," see Stiles, *Diary*, I, 131–33.

25. In his *Diary*, I, 131, Stiles himself notes his portrait's inclusion of "Maimonides." The Arabic title inscribed on this volume—"موره نبوكيم"—seems to be Stiles' own transliteration of Maimonides' Hebrew title ("מורה נבוכים," i.e. *Guide for the Perplexed*).

26. Stiles, *Diary*, II, 339. This passage is excerpted from a protracted entry, recorded by Stiles on May 24, 1779, dedicated to "Presidents of Colleges with whom I have been personally acquainted" (see Stiles, *Diary*, II, 335). The "M$^r$ Thatcher" labeled by Stiles as Chauncy's "Disciple" is Thomas Thatcher (1620–1678; often spelled "Thacher"), physician and minister, whose knowledge of Arabic is regularly mentioned in biographical summaries (e.g., Howard Kelly, *A Cyclopedia of American Medical Biography*, 2 vols. [Philadelphia and London: W. B. Saunders Company, 1912], II, 438).

27. Printed by Samuel Hall in Newport, the 1765 *Laws of the Redwood-Library Company* features a preface by Stiles (3–7), with the library's "Catalogue" immediately following. For the Redwood's aim of "diffusing Light and Truth to Places far and wide," see *Laws of the Redwood-Library Company*, 3.

28. The pagination of the *Laws of the Redwood-Library Company* recommences after Stiles' preface (i.e. at the beginning of the "Catalogue" proper); this list of "Quarto Volumes" derives from p. 7 of the "Catalogue."

29. Milton defined "Mr. Selden" as "the chief of learned men reputed in this land" in his celebrated *Areopagitica* (1644); see John Milton, *The Complete Poetry and Essential Prose of John Milton*, ed. William Kerrigan, John Rumrich, and Stephen Fallon (New York: Modern Library, 2007), 938.

30. The Redwood's edition of Selden's *Opera Omnia, tam edita quam inedita*, ed. David Wilkins (London, 1726) is three volumes in six, and is designated as the library's "Original Volume 91." I am grateful to Lisa Long, then Ezra C. Stiles Librarian, for her assistance during my 2010 research visit to the Redwood Library and Athenaeum.

31. Stephen Sewall (b. 1734) had himself trained at Harvard in Hebrew under Judah Monis, and succeeded Monis as Harvard's instructor in Hebrew before his elevation as the first "Hancock Professor of Hebrew and Other Oriental Languages." No major study on Sewall has yet appeared; however, he increasingly features in histories of the Revolution and early Republic. See, for example, Frank Manuel and Fritzie Manuel, *James Bowdoin and the Patriot Philosophers* (Philadelphia: American Philosophical Society, 2003), 128. Sewall is also treated further in Chapter 2 below.

32. Quoted and reproduced courtesy of the Beinecke Rare Book and Manuscript Library, Yale University, this unpublished letter and its accompanying four-page pamphlet (which Stiles designates as Sewall's "Specimen of an Arabic Grammar") is held as part of the Beinecke's MS Vault Stiles, Correspondence Box, Folder 833 ("29 July 1768 Stephen Sewall to ES"). The letters exchanged between Stiles and Sewall are essential witnesses to Oriental studies in early America but have not received previous treatment. I was first alerted to their exchange of letters, however, by a brief mention in Jonathan Helmreich's *Eternal Hope: The Life of Timothy Alden, Jr.* (Cranbury, NJ: Cornwall Books, 2001), 28.

33. This paratext, parsing the letter "*Sad*" ("ص"), is included at the bottom of the columns on the first page of Sewall's pamphlet, reading "the power of ʃ as in pleasure, measure &c."

34. Quoted courtesy of the Beinecke Rare Book and Manuscript Library, Yale University, this unpublished letter is held as part of the Beinecke's MS Vault Stiles, Correspondence Box, Folder 519.

35. Quoted courtesy of the Beinecke Rare Book and Manuscript Library, Yale University, this unpublished letter is held as part of the Beinecke's MS Vault Stiles, Correspondence Box, Folder 576, and opens with Stiles noting to Sewall that he is now "return[ing] your Arabic & Syriac grammar, with my Thanks."

36. "Eutychius"—Greek name for Saʿīd ibn Baṭrīq (877–940)—was Melkite Patriarch of Alexandria (935–940), and the first Christian historiographer writing in Arabic; Eutychius' primary work, "نظم الجو هر" (*String of Pearls*), is often referred to as his *Annals*, and spans Creation to 938 CE. Selden's *Opera* includes only a targeted Arabic excerpt from the *Annals*' ecclesiastic portions, published on pp. 419–26 of *Opera Omnia*'s third volume under the Latin title "*Eutychii Origines Ecclesiæ Alexandrinæ.*" As Toomer notes, Selden "had a long borne affection" for Eutychius, valuing his *Annals* as a tool to "bear down Episcopacy"—a value that Stiles too sees in Eutychius (*Eastern Wisedome and Learning*, 164). However, also see Toomer for a critique of Selden's Arabic proficiency, including his suggestion that Selden's "translation [of Eutychius] contains several blunders" (*Eastern Wisedome and Learning*, 67–68).

37. Quoted courtesy of the Redwood Library and Athenaeum, Stiles' marginalia at the opening to Eutychius is found in the Redwood's copy of Selden, *Opera Omnia*, III, 419–20.

38. See, for instance, Stiles' marginalia at the conclusion to Eutychius' text, where he records his completed reading of this Arabic chronicle on "Nov 9. 1768" and "March 2 1769" (inscribed in the Redwood's copy of Selden, *Opera Omnia*, III, 426; quoted courtesy of the Redwood Library and Athenaeum).

39. Stiles, *Diary*, I, 21.

40. Figure 1.4, comprising the initial page of Stiles' translation of Eutychius' Arabic, rendered from Selden's *Opera Omnia*, is reproduced courtesy of the Beinecke Rare Book and Manuscript Library, Yale University. This document is held as part of the Beinecke's MS Vault Stiles, Box MP, Folder 539, and features a full heading on its first page, reading "The Antiquities of the Church of Alexandria, written by the Patriarch Eutytius or Eutichius, who flourished A.D. 900. Translated from the Original Arabic 1769 By Ezra Stiles."

41. Stiles, *Diary*, I, 25–26.

42. Before beginning his diary on New Year's day, 1769, Stiles kept "Itineraries" (the first extant dating from 1760), as well as a "Thermometrical Register," now held by the Beinecke Rare Book and Manuscript Library, Yale University. For Stiles as an "indefatigable measurer," see Morgan, *The Gentle Puritan*, 132; and as "among the most compulsive measurers," Chris Beneke, *Beyond Toleration: The Religious Origins of American Pluralism* (Oxford: Oxford UP, 2006), 126.

43. This quotation appears on p. 2 of Stiles' 1759 copy of the *New York Pocket-Almanack* housed as part of the Beinecke's MS Vault Stiles, and quoted courtesy of the Beinecke Rare Book and Manuscript Library, Yale University.

44. Despite its "al" prefix, the Arabic etymology of "almanac" is debated; however, see Garland Cannon and Alan Kaye, *The Arabic Contributions to the English Language: An Historical Dictionary* (Wiesbaden: Harrassowitz Verlag, 1994), 131, which includes the term.

45. Stiles' copy of his 1768 almanac—*Mein and Fleeming's Register for New-England and Nova Scotia* (Boston, 1767)—is held as part of the Beinecke's MS Vault Stiles, and quoted courtesy of the Beinecke Rare Book and Manuscript Library, Yale University; these Arabic inscriptions appear on p. 24 of this edition, together with additional citations in Latin and Greek, some of which are difficult to decipher.

46. For Stiles' characterization of Benjamin West as "a man of genius," and seeking to procure for him an honorary "Degree" in 1770, see Ezra Stiles, *Extracts from the Itineraries and Other Miscellanies of Ezra Stiles*, ed. Franklin B. Dexter (New Haven: Yale UP, 1916), 561.

47. Reproduced courtesy of the Beinecke Rare Book and Manuscript Library, Yale University, this almanac is held in Box MP, Folder 539, in Beinecke's MS Vault Stiles ("Benjamin West/ *The New-England Almanack*/ 1770").

48. Stiles' marginal date is found in the Redwood's copy of Selden, *Opera Omnia*, III, xiv, inscribed in the "*Prologomena*" to Selden's "*De Successionibus in Bona Defunctorum*"; this page's image, reproduced above as Figure 1.6, appears courtesy of the Redwood Library and Athenaeum.

49. Selden's Arabic quotation is from the Qurʾān 2:53, and is cited in the course of his discussion of the Qurʾānic term "الفرقان" (*al-furqān*), which Selden defines as "*distinctionum volume.*"

I follow M. A. Abdel Haleem's rendition of "الفرقان" as "the means to distinguish," as this best reflects Selden's presentation of the term (Arberry translates "الفرقان" as "the Salvation"); see M. A. Abdel Haleem, trans., *The Qur'ān* (Oxford: Oxford UP, 2004).

50. For a recent treatment of the Latin etymology of "translation" as signifying "crossing over," see Peter De Bolla, *Harold Bloom: Towards Historical Rhetorics* (Oxon: Routledge, 2014), 132.

51. Stiles, *Diary*, I, 74; an ellipsis concludes this entry in Dexter's 1901 edition of the *Diary*.

52. The volume "examined" by Stiles and Sewall together is Richard Pococke's *A Description of the East and Some Other Countries*, vol. 1 (London, 1743), which does indeed reproduce "*Inscriptiones Sinaicæ*" following its p. 148. Returning to New Haven to take up Yale's presidency later in the decade, Stiles would also "lodge" with Stephen Sewall while passing through Boston (Morgan, *The Gentle Puritan*, 310).

53. Isaac Touro—for whose family the Newport synagogue is now named—is treated by Cora E. Lutz, "Ezra Stiles and the Learned Jews at Newport," *The Yale University Library Gazette* 70:3/4 (1996), 161–69 (162–63).

54. For Haim Isaac Carigal, and his visits to "a succession of Jewish communities throughout the Middle East and North Africa" before arriving to the New World, see Hoberman, *New Israel/New England*, 178.

55. Stiles, *Diary*, I, 357–58.

56. Mamluk ruler of Egypt from 1760 to his death, 'Alī Bey was killed just shortly after this March meeting between Stiles and Carigal, in May 1773; see Michael Winter, *Egyptian Society Under Ottoman Rule, 1517–1798* (London: Routledge, 2003), 26.

57. For these nonconsecutive entries, see Stiles, *Diary*, I, 385–88.

58. The "travels of Chevalier D'Arvieux into Arabia" mentioned by Stiles on June 12 appears to be Larent D'Arvieux's *The Chevalier D'Arvieux Travels into Arabia the Desert; Written by Himself* (London, 1718), an edition that also featured an appendix comprising an English translation of Abū al-Fidā's "General Description of Arabia."

59. This unpublished letter is classed as "Hebrew Copy Four" of "19 Jul 1773 ES to Raphael Isaac Haim Carigal," and is housed as part of the Beinecke's MS Vault Stiles, Correspondence Box, Folder 1096; this letter is reproduced and quoted courtesy of the Beinecke Rare Book and Manuscript Library, Yale University. The English translation of this Hebrew letter here offered is Stiles' own—a translation in his own hand and included within this same folder (i.e., "Hebrew Copy Four"). Denominated simply as "English Copy," this document was presumably drafted by Stiles as the basis for his Hebrew letter.

60. In fashioning his Arabic autograph, Stiles' transliteration of his first name—"عزرا" ("*'Izrā*")—corresponds closely to the Hebrew "עזרא" ("*'Ezrā*"), rather than matching, for instance, the Qur'ān's Arabic name for "Ezra" (i.e., "عزير"; see Qur'ān 9:30).

61. Stiles, *Diary*, I, 500. This boast of linguistic "Competency" is offered even as Stiles notes that "I have spent my Life from my Earliest youth among Books"; however, Stiles' broader intention in this diary entry is to recall that "the most valuable Knowledge I have been acquainted with is" not scientific, linguistic, historical, or political knowledge, but rather the "Knowledge of JESUS CHRIST & the Redemption of the Cross" (Stiles, *Diary*, I, 500).

62. This characterization is offered in *American Writers Before 1800: A Biographical and Critical Dictionary Vol. 3, Q–Z*, ed. James Levernier and Douglas Wilmes (Westport, CT: Greenwood Press, 1984), 1382.

63. Stiles, *Diary*, I, 20; for a "memorandum" authored by Stiles on the "Sons of Liberty" and "Tree of Liberty," see Stiles, *Diary*, I, 7.

64. Stiles, *Diary*, I, 20; on August 21, Stiles reports "Copying Rev. Jno. Lothrop's MS. Records of the beginning of the chhs. of Scituate and Barnstable [. . .]," while on August 23, he notes "Finished reading a second time all the Arabic in Seldeni Opera, v. 3. Fol." No entry, however, is provided by the *Diary*'s published edition for August 22.

65. This quotation from Ezra Stiles' manuscript *Diary*, held as part of the Beinecke's MS Vault Stiles, is transcribed courtesy of the Beinecke Rare Book and Manuscript Library, Yale University. This entry is found at the bottom of p. 23 of the first volume of Stiles' manuscript *Diary*.

66. For Qur'ānic characterization of Jesus as "the Messenger of God, and His Word that He committed to Mary, and a Spirit from Him," as translated by A. J. Arberry, see the Qur'ān 4:171.

67. See Selden's *Opera Omnia* (III, 815–16) for the original Arabic in this entry, as well as its Latin translation; as Selden provides no transliteration, Stiles' interlinear Hebrew appears to be his own.

68. See Robert Allison, *The Boston Massacre* (Beverly, MA: Commonwealth Editions, 2006), 27, for the "Massacre" as offering "the most famous image of the American Revolution."

69. Stiles, *Diary*, I, 41. This entry concludes with Stiles' ominous pronouncement: "This day ends the prediction of Mr. Edwards of Philadᵃ."

70. This quotation, from p. 51 of the first volume of Ezra Stiles' manuscript *Diary*, which is held as part of the Beinecke's MS Vault Stiles, is transcribed courtesy of the Beinecke Rare Book and Manuscript Library, Yale University. A few of Stiles' entries—including this March 9 entry, featuring "Heb. Arab."—were previously published without Dexter's editorial suppressions by the *Cyclopædia of American Literature*, ed. Evert Augustus Duyckinck and George Long Duyckinck, 2 vols. (New York: Charles Scribner, 1856), I, 160–61.

71. Dexter himself gestures to this practice of editorial suppression, mentioning his "omissions" of "Daily or otherwise frequently recurring statements of the authors and subjects of [Stiles'] current reading and meditation" (Stiles, *Diary*, I, 2). For the victims of the Boston Massacre regarded as "martyrs," see Allison, *The Boston Massacre*, 23.

72. Stiles, "The United States Elevated to Glory and Honor" (New Haven, CT: Thomas & Samuel Green, 1783), 72.

73. Ibid., 65.

74. Ibid., 51.

75. For recent recognition of the importance of what Stiles designates as the "arabic of the *koreish*" to Islamic origins, see *The Qur'an: An Encyclopedia*, ed. Oliver Leaman (New York: Routledge, 2006), 367: "The majority of Muslims also hold that the Qur'an was revealed in the language of the Prophet's tribe, Quraysh, and that this was in itself an eclectic synthesis of 'all that was best' in the various tribal dialects." Stiles' 1783 sermon also features fleeting allusions to Islam itself, ambivalently associating it with "billigerent powers" (comparing the struggle between "*Tangrolipix*" and "*Mahomet*" with a host of other historic contests that lead to "tyranny," including that between "*Augustus*" and "*Antony*"), but also classing "the *mahometan*" together with "the *jewish*" and "the *christian*," viewing Islam, Judaism and Christianity as all belonging to "the unidolatrous religious," distinguished from both "the idolatrous religious" and "*Deism*" (see Stiles, "The United States Elevated to Glory and Honor," 16 and 76 respectively).

76. Stiles, *Diary*, II, 583. Public commencements at Yale were not held from 1774 until 1781, with diplomas instead received by "graduating seniors" in "a simple private ceremony" (Morgan, *The Gentle Puritan*, 361). Stiles' notes for his commencement address, delivered in 1781, are held as part of the Beinecke's MS Vault Stiles, Box MP, Folder 803; these notes suggest that Stiles had composed his address in 1778. See also Stiles, *Diary*, II, 243 and 244, where Stiles records his "Writing a Hebrew Sermon" in January 1778.

77. Stiles, *Diary*, II, 584.

78. As suggested by his concluding citation ("*Seldeni Opera* v.2. p.1701"), Stiles quotes these Arabic lines from Selden's *Opera Omnia*, II (although from pp. 1699–1700, rather than p. 1701). This Arabic material is quoted by Selden from Avicenna, although Selden also notes the Muslim ethos and specifically Qur'ānic origins of these lines; describing the *basmala* that prefaces this Arabic quotation, for instance, Selden recognizes that "*Quod & capiti cuique Alcorani praefigitur*" (1699). Despite the Latin translation that Selden provides to parse these Arabic lines (again, on p. 1699), Stiles intriguingly does not follow Selden's Latin entirely, choosing instead to assemble his own interlinear rendition, with his own errors. Most difficult to decipher in Stiles' Arabic is the second word following the *basmala*, which reads "سِ," and which Stiles incorrectly renders as "*ergo*." Stiles' error in rendering "احسن الخالقين" as "*pracellentissimus*

*omnium entium*" could be attributed to his mistaking "الخالقين" for two separate words, as suggested by the Hebrew transliteration that he includes below the "ARABICA" circle, expressing this single Arabic term as "אלכל אבין."

79. Although inscribed as a gift to his son—Ezra Jr.—Stiles' circular document is held as a part of his own manuscript collection (i.e., the MS Vault Stiles at the Beinecke Rare Book and Manuscript Library, Yale University, as mentioned above), likely suggesting this document to be a copy that Stiles himself made. However, this document's preservation as part of Stiles' own papers could also reflect the untimely death of its intended recipient—Ezra Jr.—who died in 1784, more than a decade before Ezra Stiles himself (see Chapter 2, note 5 below).

## *Chapter 2*

1. Stiles, *Diary*, III, 518.
2. Abiel Holmes had married Stiles' daughter Mary (called in this entry by her nickname, "Polly") in 1790. Obliquely implying her illness, Stiles notes that Mary is "stationary" for now; however, Mary would die soon after Stiles himself, passing away on August 29, 1795, followed later this same year by Elizabeth Stiles (i.e., "Betsy"), who died in Cambridge on November 16, 1795. Stiles recognizes both his daughters' illnesses in his *Diary* just a few weeks before his own death, noting that he "Rec[d] Lett. from Cambridge—Betsy & Polly very ill—dangerous" (Stiles, *Diary*, III, 553). For the death dates of his wife (Mary) and sister-in-law (Elizabeth), see Abiel Holmes's *Life of Ezra Stiles*, 375.
3. The achievements of Hannah Adams are treated by Gary Schmidt, *A Passionate Usefulness: The Life and Literary Labors of Hannah Adams* (Charlottesville: University of Virginia Press, 2004). See Schmidt's Chapter 3 (31 ff.) for Adams' *An Alphabetical Compendium of the Various Sects Which Have Appeared from the Beginning of the Christian Era to the Present Day*—a work that includes brief treatment of "Mahometans," as well as citations from the same *Koran* translation (i.e., Sale's) that Stiles is "read[g]" in 1795; see, for example, Hannah Adams, *A View of Religions in Two Parts*, 2 vols. (Boston: Manning & Loring, 1801), I, 316–27.
4. Published in 1734, George Sale's *Koran* was the most prominent English translation of the Muslim scripture during the time period covered in the present study; the edition cited subsequently is *The Koran: Commonly Called the Alcoran of Mohammed*, trans. George Sale, 2 vols. (London: T. Tegg, 1825).
5. For Ezra Stiles Jr.'s 1784 death in North Carolina's "Chowan C[ounty]" as recorded by his father, see Stiles, *Diary*, I, 139.
6. This is Louise Chipley's characterization of Bentley, included in the title to her article "William Bentley, Journalist of the Early Republic," *Essex Institute Historical Collections* 123 (1987): 331–47.
7. Bentley is described as "the famous William Bentley of the East Church, reputed to be the most learned man in America" by Henry Steele Commager in his "The Nature of History" in *The Vital Past: Writings on the Use of History*, ed. Stephen Vaughn (Athens: University of Georgia, 1985), 120–29 (126).
8. Malcolm Young, *The Spiritual Journal of Henry David Thoreau* (Macon: Mercer UP, 2009), 82, notes that Bentley "kept an astonishingly detailed diary of about 2,400 printed pages"; however, the printed edition of Bentley's *Diary* represents only a fraction of his personal writings, which are now primarily held at the American Antiquarian Society (AAS), Tufts University's Digital Collections and Archives, and the Phillips Library, Peabody Essex Museum. The *Diary*'s printed edition is William Bentley, *The Diary of William Bentley*, 4 vols. (Salem, 1905–14), and will be cited subsequently as "Bentley, *Diary*."
9. Lesley Doig, for instance, asserts that "the Bentley diaries are an invaluable source for life in Salem" in her "To Have and to Hold? Marital Connections and Family Relationships in Salem, Massachusetts, 1755–1810" in *Commerce and Culture: Nineteenth-Century Business Elites*, ed. W. Robert Lee (Farnham: Ashgate Publishing, 2011), 255–84 (278).

10. Bentley, *Diary*, II, 88.

11. The "Peguan language" mentioned by Bentley is the Mon language. For Gibaut as Bentley's friend and former student, see Albert Gallatin's letter to Thomas Jefferson in *The Papers of Thomas Jefferson, Volume 38*, ed. Barbara Oberg (Princeton UP, 2012), 178–79, in which Bentley recommends Gibaut to Gallatin for a "blank commission" at the "Secretary of State's office."

12. Although Richard Brown mentions Bentley's Middle Eastern interests in passing—including the Arabic and Persian letters received from Gibaut (*Knowledge Is Power: The Diffusion of Information in Early America, 1700–1865* [New York: Oxford UP, 1989], 204)—no previous study has indexed Bentley's Islamic engagements, nor recovered his actual Arabic letters (which I located at the Boston Athenaeum, Special Collections) and his Muslim manuscripts (at the Phillips Library, Peabody Essex Museum), as treated further below.

13. Brown asserts that "Indeed Jefferson, seeking the best scholars to guide the University of Virginia, invited Bentley to become its founding president" (*Knowledge Is Power*, 197). The origins for Brown's claim may have been Joseph G. Waters' "biographical sketch," prefixed to the printed edition of Bentley's *Diary*, which indeed asserts that "when Mr. Jefferson was maturing his plans for establishing the University of Virginia, which was incorporated in 1819, he consulted [Bentley] about it and tendered to him the honor of its Presidency" (Bentley, *Diary*, I, xx). However, in my own review of Bentley's manuscript papers—including his correspondence at the AAS, and the Phillips Library, Peabody Essex Museum—I have been unable to secure material evidence of Jefferson's "tender[ing]" this "honor." I also note that J. Rixey Ruffin in his illuminating *A Paradise of Reason: William Bentley and Enlightenment Christianity in the Early Republic* (New York: Oxford UP, 2009) makes no mention of such an invitation from Jefferson, although Ruffin's primary concern is Bentley's life up until 1805.

14. For the use of "post-Puritan" to characterize New England Unitarianism see George Kelly, *Politics and Religious Consciousness in America* (New Brunswick, NJ: Transaction Books, 1984), 73.

15. This quotation derives from Sewall, Stephen. Papers of Stephen Sewall, 1764–1797. Series: II. Lectures, 1765–1797. HUG 1782; Vol. 3, p. 71, courtesy of the Harvard University Archives. Sewall's unpublished 1765–1797 lectures, bound in four manuscript volumes, are entitled *Professor Sewall's Lectures on the Hebrew and Oriental Languages*; the selection above is transcribed from Lecture XXXIX. At the top of this first page of his lecture, Sewall notes the dates on which it was delivered, namely "Read 20th Feb^y. 1769/14th Sep^r. 1772./25th Nov^r. 1776./13 Nov^r. 1780."

16. This previous lecture (i.e., Lecture XXXVIII) begins on p. 59 of the third volume of the Harvard University Archives' four-volume *Professor Sewall's Lectures on the Hebrew and Oriental Languages*.

17. Bentley's Harvard studies are treated most recently by Ruffin in his *A Paradise of Reason*, 22ff.

18. For this quotation, see Sewall, Stephen. Papers of Stephen Sewall, 1764–1797. Series: II. Lectures, 1765-1797. HUG 1782; Vol. 3, pp. 71–72, courtesy of the Harvard University Archives.

19. See Chapter 1, footnote 18, for this quotation.

20. This unpublished and untitled notebook—cited here as Bentley's "Middle Eastern Languages Notebook" for clarity—is held as part of the William Bentley papers, 1783–1819, Tufts University, Digital Collections and Archives; this image is reproduced courtesy of Tufts University, Digital Collections and Archives. I am grateful to Dr. Susanne Belovari and Timothy Walsh for their guidance during my 2013 research at Tufts. Bentley's "Middle Eastern Languages Notebook" has never before been analyzed; however, it received brief mention in Ruffin, *A Paradise of Reason*, 23—a mention that aided my location of this invaluable source for Bentley's Middle Eastern language learning.

21. Quoted courtesy of Tufts University, Digital Collections and Archives, from the cover page of Bentley's "Middle Eastern Languages Notebook."

22. The original manuscripts for these works (i.e., Stephen Sewall's *A Chaldee Grammar, A Lexicon of the Chaldee Language,* and *A Compendious Syriac Grammar*) are housed as part of the Papers of Stephen Sewall, 1764–1797. Series: IV. Lexicons, 1772–1791. HUG 1782 at the Harvard University Archives.

23. Quoted courtesy of Tufts University, Digital Collections and Archives, this material derives from p. 33 of Bentley's "Middle Eastern Languages Notebook."

24. Quoted courtesy of Tufts University, Digital Collections and Archives, this material derives from p. 41 of Bentley's "Middle Eastern Languages Notebook."

25. See Ruffin, *A Paradise of Reason,* 23, for previous recognition of Bentley's copying from Sewall's private notes through the "winter vacation."

26. Reproduced courtesy of Tufts University, Digital Collections and Archives, this image derives from p. 33 of Bentley's "Middle Eastern Languages Notebook."

27. Bentley's Arabic transcription from Sewall may be traced to Edmund Castell's entry for the Arabic term "دخن", which he includes in the first volume of his *Lexicon Heptaglotton: Hebraicum, Chaldaicum, Syriacum, Samaritanum, Aethiopicum, Arabicum, Conjunctim, Et Persicum, Separatim,* 2 vols. (London: Thomas Roycroft, 1669).

28. Ruffin, *A Paradise of Reason,* 24.

29. For this description of Sewall's dismissal, see Conrad Wright, *Revolutionary Generation* (Amherst: University of Massachusetts Press, 2005), 151.

30. Bentley, *Diary,* I, 28.

31. Bentley's abbreviated title for the Hancock professorship perhaps reflects his own anxiety regarding its future; after Sewall's removal, the professorship will be redefined, with less emphasis on Eastern languages, expanded instead "to include instruction in English grammar" (see Robert Rothschild, *Two Brides for Apollo* [New York: iUniverse, 2009], 246).

32. For early abbreviation of Salem's Second Church simply as "the East," see James Flint, *Two Discourses* (Salem: Observer Office, 1846), 22. The most comprehensive overview of this Salem parish in anticipation of Bentley's 1783 arrival is provided by Ruffin, *A Paradise of Reason,* 47ff.

33. See John Lathrop, "A sermon, preached at the ordination of William Bentley, A.M. colleague with the Rev. James Diman, to the pastoral care of the Second Church in Salem, September 24, 1783" (Salem: Samuel Hall, 1783), 1–34 (22).

34. The last page in this notebook that Bentley inscribed as an "under-graduate" seems to be p. 41 of his "Middle Eastern Languages Notebook," quoted courtesy of Tufts University, Digital Collections and Archives. The pages immediately following in Bentley's notebook first address "Syriac Characters" on p. 42, and, by p. 45, quote the "Samaritan grammar" of "[Georg] Otho."

35. Quoted courtesy of Tufts University, Digital Collections and Archives, see pp. 45 and 51; 68 and 74; and 78 ff. of Bentley's "Middle Eastern Languages Notebook" respectively for his citation of Georg Otho, John Borthwick Gilchrist, and William Jones. On pp. 88ff., Bentley also cites the periodical most associated with William Jones (i.e., *Asiatick Researches*), which surfaces again in Chapter 5 of this volume.

36. These pages—70 and 83—from Bentley's "Middle Eastern Languages Notebook" are reproduced courtesy of Tufts University, Digital Collections and Archives.

37. For Salem's seal, adopted in 1839 three years after the city's incorporation, including its Latin text and this English translation, see "The Municipal Seal of Salem," *Historical Collections of the Essex Institute* 8.1 (1868): 3–9 (7).

38. Robert Doherty, *Society and Power: Five New England Towns, 1800–1860* (Amherst: University of Massachusetts Press, 1977), 13.

39. Bentley's Octavo Notebooks form part of the William Bentley Papers, AAS, and are classed according to their method and subject (e.g., "Commonplace Books," "Notes on Reading," and "Commentaries on the Scriptures"). Bentley himself numbered his Octavo Notebooks, but this differs from the AAS numbering; the former is used for citation in the body of my Chapter 2. I am deeply grateful for the research support I have received from the AAS

during my repeated visits beginning in 2012; I thank, in particular, Tom Knowles, the Marcus A. McCorison Librarian at the AAS, whose profound knowledge of Bentley is an invaluable resource for all researchers working with the Bentley papers.

40. James Fraser, *The History of Nadir Shah, Formerly Called Thomas Kuli Khan, the Present Emperor of Persia*, 2nd ed. (London: W. Strahan, 1742).

41. Quoted courtesy of the AAS, these lines derive from p. 146 of Bentley, Octavo Notebook 18 (AAS numbering: Octavo Notebook 19); Bentley quotes this passage featuring the *shahāda* from Fraser, *The History of Nadir Shah*, 124.

42. In consulting the *shahāda* as transcribed by Fraser, it is clear that the error is Bentley's own. See Fraser, *The History of Nadir Shah*, 124, for the *shahāda* reproduced in full, which reads:

"لا اله الا الله محمد رسول الله وعلي ولي الله."

43. Ruffin, *A Paradise of Reason*, 94, notes that "in the fall [of 1784], in a sermon he called 'Unity of God,' [Bentley] argued that the worship of Jesus was in fact idolatrous because God alone deserves the praise."

44. Niebuhr's German original is *Beschreibung von Arabien: Aus Eigenen Beobachtungen und im Lande Selbst Gesammelten Nachrichten* (Copenhagen: Möller, 1772). The first French translation was published as *Description de L'Arabie: d'après les Observations et Recherches Faites Dans le Pays Même* (Copenhagen: Nicolas Möller, 1773), which is the edition cited below.

45. Reproduced courtesy of the AAS, this is p. 40 of Bentley, Octavo Notebook 27 (AAS numbering: Octavo Notebook 21). Bentley himself notes inside the front cover of Octavo Notebook 27 that it was "Received 28 July 1794. used Nov. 1797."

46. Bentley's map and description—including his Arabic "جبل موسى"—is based on Niebuhr, *Description de l'Arabie*, 346–53. For the accuracy and impact of Niebuhr's *Description* overall, see Lawrence Baack, *Undying Curiosity: Carsten Niebuhr and the Royal Danish Expedition to Arabia* (Stuttgart: Franz Steiner Verlag, 2014).

47. William Bentley Papers, MH 36, Phillips Library, Peabody Essex Museum, Salem, Mass. Quoted courtesy of the Phillips Library, Peabody Essex Museum, this letter from William Bentley to Henry Elkins is dated February 4, 1804, and is held as part of the Subseries A: Correspondence section of the library's William Bentley Papers. The letter is entirely legible except a single word or phrase that interposes between "Sir" and "our request" in its first line; I supply here "as per" as my best approximation of the intended meaning in the context of this sentence. I am deeply grateful to Tamara Gaydos, who provided immense help during my 2014 research at the Phillips Library.

48. William Bentley Papers, MH 36, Phillips Library, Peabody Essex Museum, Salem, Mass. Quoted courtesy of the Peabody Essex Museum, Phillips Library, this two-page "memoranda" begins on the verso of Bentley's letter to Elkins, cited immediately above. The second half of the second page features additional sources from which Bentley derives his knowledge of the East, listing books under the heading "Among the Books relating to Asia [. . .]."

49. The material from Niebuhr rendered in Bentley's letter is based on Niebuhr, *Description de L'Arabie*, 164–65.

50. The *Nafā'is al-'Arā'is* requested by Bentley was authored by Abū Isḥāq Aḥmad ibn Muḥammad ath-Tha'labī and is more frequently known under the title *Qiṣaṣ al-Anbiyā'* (*Stories of the Prophets*); however, yet another title for this same work is *'Arā'is al-Majālis* (*Brides of the Sessions*), which is closer to the title cited by Bentley. For ath-Tha'labī and his *Qiṣaṣ al-Anbiyā'* see Marianna Klar, "Human–Divine Communication as a Paradigm for Power: Al-Tha'labī's Presentation of Q. 38:24 and Q. 38:34" in *Sacred Tropes: Tanakh, New Testament, and Qur'an as Literature and Culture*, ed. Roberta Sabbath (Leiden: Brill, 2009) 159–72 (160–61).

51. For the Arabic language materials requested by Bentley, and for Niebuhr's companion "Mr Forskål," see Niebuhr, *Description de L'Arabie*, 164–65. Niebuhr here cites *"Durr el mantur,"* without transcribing this title in Arabic script. Bentley's transcription of this title in Arabic seems therefore to be his own, and is missing its "ث" (*"th"*)—a slip that is characteristic more broadly of his memoranda's frequently defective transcripts, often featuring muddled or

inaccurate readings of Arabic titles (also, more common than Niebuhr's suggested "*Durr el mantur*" [i.e., "دّر المنثور"], the title of this work by as-Suyūṭī is often cited as *ad-Durr al-Manthūr* [i.e., "الدر المنثور"]).

52. Niebuhr, *Beschreibung von Arabien*, 102–103, offers a comparative chart of differing Arabo-Persian scripts, including "*Nessich*" and "*Talik*" (i.e., *Naskh* and *Nastaʿlīq*); for these different scripts juxtaposed in sources contemporary with Bentley, see Robert Heron, *A Collection of Late Voyages and Travels* (Edinburgh: Watson and Co., 1797), 85.

53. For the first glimpse afforded of the Pacific Ocean to the Lewis and Clark expedition on November 7, 1805, see William Foley, *Wilderness Journey: The Life of William Clark* (Columbia: University of Missouri Press, 2004), 125.

54. These quotations derive from Elizabeth Chew's 2009 entry on www.lewis-clark.org, namely "Unpacking Jefferson's Indian Hall" (http://www.lewis-clark.org/article/3086).

55. For this startling sum of imported coffee, see Winthrop Marvin, *The American Merchant Marine* (New York: Scribner, 1902), 202, and Luther Luedtke, *Nathaniel Hawthorne and the Romance of the Orient* (Bloomington, Indiana UP, 1989), 24. For Bancroft's *Commerce* as the seventh ship to arrive from Mocha in 1805, see Duane Hamilton Hurd, *History of Essex County, Massachusetts*, 2 vols. (Philadelphia: J.W. Lewis, 1888), I, 83.

56. Reproduced courtesy of the Boston Athenaeum, Special Collections; I discovered this unpublished letter in the Athenaeum's "Mss. L452," a manuscript box entitled "Collection of Arabic and Oriental manuscripts, ca. 1799-ca. 1830." I am profoundly grateful for support received from the Boston Athenaeum, particularly during my tenure as the Mary Catherine Mooney Fellow (2013–2014), from Mary Warnement (Head of Reader Services), and Stanley Cushing (Anne C. and David J. Bromer Curator of Rare Books and Manuscripts).

57. The first of this Arabic letter's Qurʾānic quotations—from the Qurʾān 5:82—is selectively edited from the scripture, whose original verse instead begins with material relating to "the Jews," before beginning to speak of "the Christians," its second half opening with "اقربهم" ("the closest of them") rather than merely "اقرب" ("closest") as above. In translating the Qurʾānic quotations in Bentley's Arabic letter, I have again consulted A. J. Arberry's *The Koran Interpreted*; however, the rendition I provide here departs from Arberry's own, aiming to offer a more literal impression of these quoted verses. I express my thanks to Mustafa Shah, who reviewed the majority of my translations and transcriptions from Bentley's Arabic letter featured in this chapter, and offered illuminating corrections and suggestions. Any remaining errors are entirely my own.

58. William B. Sprague, *Annals of the American Unitarian Pulpit* (New York: R. Carter & Brothers, 1865), 156. While Joseph E. Sprague provides this memorial of Bentley's learning, it seems that Bentley did not similarly regard Sprague, describing him in 1811 as "a lawyer without talents" (see Bentley, *Diary*, IV, 69).

59. George Cooke, *Unitarianism in America: A History of Its Origin and Development* (Boston: American Unitarian Association, 1902), 72.

60. As noted above Ruffin makes mention of Bentley's Middle Eastern interests and his copying of Sewall's manuscripts (*A Paradise of Reason*, 23); Ruffin does not, however, treat Bentley's later engagements with Arabic and Persian.

61. The Boston Athenaeum's "Collection of Arabic and Oriental manuscripts, ca. 1799-ca. 1830" (Mss. L452) contains at least four Arabic letters addressed specifically to Bentley, in addition to an undated manuscript leaf in Bentley's hand, evidencing his study of Arabic verb conjugations.

62. This entry is published in Bentley, *Diary*, III, 194, but features an error in its transcription, naming Bentley's correspondent as "Said Aimed" rather than "Said Ahmed." This October 2 entry concludes with Bentley adding that "He mentioned the wish of a Jew to write to me in that country from whom I may expect to hear by Capt. Elkins"—a detail corroborated near the conclusion to Bentley's Arabic letter reproduced as Figure 2.4, courtesy of the Boston Athenaeum, Special Collections.

63. For this definition of "*sayyid*," see David Harris, *The Crisis: The President, the Prophet, and the Shah 1979 and the Coming of Militant Islam* (New York: Little, Brown and Co, 2004), 29.

64. I translate here lines 3 through 6 of the Arabic letter reproduced as Figure 2.4, courtesy of the Boston Athenaeum, Special Collections. The term I render as "minister" is in Arabic "الفادري" (*al-fādirī*)—a curious usage, which I suspect is an approximate transliteration of the term "*padre*" (literally "father," but signifying "pastor," "clergyman").

65. For this characterization of the Saqqāf family, see W. G. Clarence-Smith, "The Rise and Fall of Hadhrami Shipping in the Indian Ocean, 1750–1940," in *Ships and the Development of Maritime Technology on the Indian Ocean*, eds. Ruth Barnes and David Parkin (London: RoutledgeCurzon, 2002), 227–58 (235).

66. The terms rendered here as "priest" and "monk" ("القس" and "الراهب") represent the singular forms of the plural nouns that appear in Aḥmad's Qur'ānic quotation at his letter's opening (i.e., "قسيسين ورهبانا").

67. I translate here lines 8 through 13 of the Arabic letter reproduced as Figure 2.4, courtesy of the Boston Athenaeum, Special Collections. I am especially grateful to Mustafa Shah in his review of my translation for clarifying Aḥmad's usage of "شفنا" ("we have seen") and "استجبنا" ("we have responded").

68. In his description of Bentley, Aḥmad here repeats his selective quotation from the Qur'ān 5:82, isolating this verse's final words, namely "منهم قسيسين ورهبانا وانهم لا يستكبرون" ("among them are priests and monks and they are not arrogant").

69. This mention of "نفايس العر ايس" ("*Nafā'is al-'Arā'is*") stretches across the seventh last and sixth last lines of Aḥmad's letter. For ath-Tha'labī see footnote 50.

70. Bentley's collection of Muslim manuscripts is now held at the Peabody Essex Museum, Phillips Library, as detailed further below.

71. This specific Muslim salutation is a customary greeting offered to correspondents in the Christian West; see, for instance, its usage in early "letters sent from Moroccan rulers to England" as noted by Nabil I. Matar, *Europe Through Arab Eyes, 1578–1727* (New York: Columbia UP, 2009), 254. Although somewhat difficult to decipher, it is clear that Aḥmad concludes his letter by offering a dual date, inscribing the time of his authorship in terms of both Christian and Muslim calendars, dating his letter to August and Jumādā al-Awwal (i.e., in A.D. 1805 and A.H. 1220, respectively).

72. For the comet "C/1807 R1," and its nearing earth at the end of September 1807, see Gary Kronk and Maik Meyer, *Cometography: A Catalogue of Comets*, 5 vols. (Cambridge: Cambridge UP, 1999–2010), II, 10.

73. Bentley, *Diary*, III, 321.

74. Bentley, *Diary*, III, 122. Bentley's election is recorded in the 1804 *Journal of the House of Representatives*, which notes that on Wednesday, November 7, 1804, "The House then proceeded, by ballot, to the appointment of a Chaplain to Congress, on the part of this House; and, upon examining the ballots, a majority of the votes of the whole House was found in favor of the Reverend William Bentley"; *Journal of the House of Representatives of the United States, Volume 5* (Washington: Gales & Seaton, 1826), 7.

75. Bentley, *Diary*, III, 122.

76. This characterization by Joseph G. Waters derives from the "biographical sketch" prefixed to the published edition of Bentley's *Diary*, and is offered by Waters as the reason why Bentley did not accept the "Presidency" of the "University of Virginia" (Bentley, *Diary*, I, xxi).

77. A single, short letter from Aḥmad in Arabic, which also features an unknown English hand, is held as part of the AAS's William Bentley Papers (Ms. Box 3, Correspondence, 1803–1810), asserting that this Arabic book has been sent, specified in English as "a copy of *Bedou-al Kalch*" and in Aḥmad's Arabic as "بدوي الخلق و الحقايق"; quotations courtesy of the AAS.

78. For Pringle's contribution to Bentley's collection of Muslim manuscripts, see an unpublished letter held as part of the AAS's William Bentley Papers (Ms. Box 3, Correspondence, 1803–1810), sent to Bentley from Mocha, and dated August 13, 1804, in which Pringle pledges to

"continue my endeavors to procure the Books" mentioned in Bentley's February 1804 "memoranda" to Elkins, and notes that "I trust however you will find the Koran such as you wished for" (quoted courtesy of the AAS). Bentley records receiving this letter, and quotes this positive forecast for his acquiring the "Koran" in particular, in his own *Diary* (see Bentley, *Diary*, III, 132).

79. Quoted courtesy of the AAS, this entry derives from Bentley's "Account of Book" as contained in Folio Volume 4 of the William Bentley Papers, on the page that records acquisitions in 1808, stretching from "Oct. 8" to "Nov. 9" (unpaginated). Bentley's "ثلثون" is missing the expected *alif* after its *lam*, and its second *thā'* is written as a *tā'*.

80. For Salem's Wellman family (spelled "Welman" by Bentley), including Adam and Timothy, see Joshua Wellman, George Chamberlain, and Arthur Wellman, *Descendants of Thomas Wellman of Lynn, Massachusetts* (Boston: A.H. Wellman, 1918), 168ff.

81. The Qur'ān is traditionally divided into thirty parts (*ajza'*, singular *juz'*), with its "Thirtieth Part" comprising chapters 78 through 114.

82. The most recent and conspicuous publication to take its cue from Jefferson's copy of Sale's *Koran* is Denise Spellberg's *Thomas Jefferson's Qur'an: Islam and the Founders* (New York: Alfred A. Knopf, 2013), which makes no mention of Bentley or Stiles. See also Kevin Hayes, "How Thomas Jefferson Read the Qur'an," *Early American Literature* 39:2 (2004): 247–61.

83. The two volumes of "Commentaries on the Scriptures" are held as part of the William Bentley Papers, AAS, classed as Octavo Notebooks 21 and 49 (according to Bentley's numbering) or Octavo Notebooks 37 and 38 (according to AAS's numbering).

84. Quoted courtesy of the AAS, this entry derives from p. 224 of Bentley's first volume of scriptural commentary (i.e., Octavo Notebook 21 [or 37 according to AAS's numbering]) held as part of the AAS's William Bentley Papers. Bentley's allusion to the Qur'ān opens with his noting that "I was pleased with Michaelis['] illustration of Hagar from the Koran [. . .]."

85. The original text of this Qur'ānic verse (numbered 2:60 rather than Bentley's "2:57") does indeed feature the Arabic word traced by Bentley (i.e., "الحجر" ["rock"]), recording God's imperative to Moses: "اضرب بعصاك الحجر" ("strike the rock with thy staff").

86. Ruffin, *A Paradise of Reason*, 5. The primary cache of Bentley's sermons is held as part of the William Bentley papers, 1783–1819, Tufts University, Digital Collections and Archives; however, the AAS's William Bentley Papers also include unpaginated volumes of Bentley's late sermons, featuring dozens of Arabic inscriptions.

87. Quoted courtesy of the AAS, this sermon on Psalm 122:2 is numbered as sermon 1308 in Bentley's Octavo Notebook 25 (or Notebook 32 according to AAS's numbering) held as part of the AAS's William Bentley Papers.

88. Quoted courtesy of the Tufts University, Digital Collections and Archives from sermon 3215, which is featured in the single bound volume of Bentley sermons held as part of Tufts' William Bentley papers, 1783–1819. Although this volume of sermons does not bear a number, Bentley himself inscribes inside the front cover: "Continued from number xxx. January 1814/ ended September 1815./from n° 3202, to n° 3406."

89. Quoted and reproduced courtesy of the AAS from Bentley's sermon 3042 featured in his Octavo Notebook 35 (or 29 according to AAS's numbering) held as part of the AAS's William Bentley Papers.

90. For the use of "دانه" ("seed") in Saʿdī's *Gulistan*, and the epigram that likely served as the basis for Bentley's reference, see the eighteenth section of Book I in Saʿdī, *The Gulistan, Rose Garden of Saʿdi: Bilingual English and Persian Edition with Vocabulary*, trans. W. M. Thackston (Bethesda, MD: Ibex Publishers, 2008), 30.

91. William Bentley Papers, MH 36, Phillips Library, Peabody Essex Museum, Salem, Mass. Quoted courtesy of the Phillips Library, Peabody Essex Museum, this letter from William Bentley Fowle to Timothy Alden is dated January 6, 1820, and is held as part of the Subseries A: Correspondence section of the library's William Bentley Papers.

92. For Bentley's bequest to Alden's Allegheny College, and their friendship, see Helmreich, *Eternal Hope: The Life of Timothy Alden, Jr.*, 112–13. Helmreich accounts for Bentley's decision not to bequeath his materials to his alma mater, noting that Bentley "had become disaffected regarding Harvard" (112).

93. This quotation is sourced from the article "Will of Dr. Bentley," as it appears on the first page of the *New-England Palladium* (50:3), 11 January, 1820. The head of this article notes that it derives "From the Salem Register."

94. Edward Elbridge Salisbury, "Valuable Arabic Manuscripts, at Worcester, Mass," *Journal of the American Oriental Society* 2 (1851): 337–39.

95. In searching for Bentley's Muslim manuscripts, I received invaluable assistance from several archivists at both the AAS and the Peabody Essex Museum, Phillips Library. Subsequent to my onsite research at the Phillips Library in the spring of 2014, I generated the first detailed catalog of all of Bentley's Muslim manuscripts now extant—a catalog that informs the present chapter's findings. I am grateful to the Phillips Library, Peabody Essex Museum, for permission to describe Bentley's collection in this chapter.

96. These three items—authored by (1) al-Wardī, (2) al-Anṣārī, and (3) al-Bayḍāwī—are classed by Bentley according to his own library's numbering as (1) numbers 13 and 16 (two copies of al-Wardī's *Kitāb kharīdat al-'ajā'ib wa-farīdat al-gharā'ib*); (2) number 14 (one copy of al-Anṣārī's *Fatḥ al-Jalīl bi-Bayān Anwār at-Tanzīl*); and (3) number 26 (one copy of al-Bayḍāwī's *Anwār at- Tanzīl wa Asrār at-Ta'wīl*).

97. In addition to Bentley's copy of the *30th Portion* [*of the Qur'ān*] (i.e., *al-Juz' ath-Thālathūn*), volumes included as part of Bentley's collection of Middle Eastern manuscripts at the Peabody Essex Museum, Phillips Library, are al-Hamadānī's *Kitāb as-Sab'iyāt fī Mawā'iẓ al-Barīyāt* (*Book of the Sevenfold, respecting the Admonition of Creatures*); Qāḍī 'Iyāḍ's *Kitāb ash-Shifā bi-Ta'rīf Ḥuqūq al-Muṣṭafā'* (*The Book of Healing, by the Recognition of the Rights of the Chosen One*); al-Ḥarīrī's *al-Maqāmāt* (*The Assemblies*); as well as two volumes of al-Bukhārī's classic *ḥadīth* collection, *Saḥīḥ al-Bukhārī*.

98. Reproduced courtesy of the AAS, this image derives from p. 141 of Bentley's Octavo Notebook 55 (or Octavo Notebook 14 according to AAS's numbering) held as part of the AAS's William Bentley Papers. For Samuel Briggs, who was about to join the "East India Marine Society in November 1819," see Walter Whitehill, *Portraits of Shipmasters and Merchants in the Peabody Museum of Salem* (Salem: Peabody Museum, 1939), vii.

## Chapter 3

1. For Bentley and "Eastern Tongues," see Ernest Smith, *Allegheny—a Century of Education: 1815–1915* (Meadville: Allegheny College History Co., 1916), 31, as well as Robert Booth, *Death of an Empire: The Rise and Murderous Fall of Salem, America's Richest City* (New York: Thomas Dunne Books, 2011), xii.

2. *Notes of Travel: Or, Recollections of Majunga, Zanzibar, Muscat, Aden, Mocha, and Other Eastern Ports* (Salem: George Creamer, 1854). The title page of *Notes of Travel* features no author name; however, its edition notice registers the work as being "Entered according to Act of Congress, in the year 1854, by Joseph B.F. Osgood."

3. For the brothers Joseph Barlow Felt Osgood and John Felt Osgood see *The Felt Genealogy: A Record of the Descendants of George Felt of Casco Bay*, ed. John Morris (Hartford: Press of the Case, Lockwood & Brainard Co., 1893), 294–95. Although named in the edition notice for *Notes of Travel*, Joseph Barlow Felt Osgood was not, like his brother John, a mariner. After "receiv[ing] his early education in the English high and Latin grammar schools of his native city," Joseph entered "Harvard University, from which he was graduated in 1846"; soon after, he "was chosen a representative to the general assembly of the state, his first session being that of 1850" and was finally "elected on the Republican ticket, mayor of the city for the year 1865." See *Genealogical and Personal Memoirs Relating to the Families of Boston*

and Eastern Massachusetts, ed. William Richard Cutter, 4 vols. (New York: Lewis Historical Publishing Company, 1908), III, 1359. See also the Houghton Library's copy of *Notes of Travel* (*AC85.Os247.854n. Houghton Library, Harvard University), which features manuscript annotations authored by John Felt Osgood clearly suggesting that the experiences reported in *Notes of Travel* are his own.

4. *Notes of Travel*, 223–24.

5. I provide here the translations from *Notes of Travel* itself (i.e., "The Well of Life" and "God lives always") to parse its imperfect Arabic transliterations (*"Bere al Warma* and *"Yalla hi l' Allah"*).

6. This rendition's ultimate source is the eighty-first chapter of the Qur'ān; however, the English version provided in *Notes of Travel* is highly stylized and edited, for reasons that will be made clear below.

7. Although Irving is the source for the Osgoods' quotation, he is not mentioned in these pages from *Notes of Travel* (223–24), nor in Chapter 32 as a whole. However, Irving is referenced by name once in *Notes of Travel*, invoked at the opening of the very next chapter, with Chapter 33 noting near its beginning that "One must read that 'stupendous monument of solitary legislation,' as Irving calls the Koran, and the history and life of Mahomet, to learn how the dependent orphan of Mecca, from early age, so astutely employed his mental and physical attributes as to win a wealthy alliance [. . .]" (*Notes of Travel*, 225). Irving's contribution, both covert and overt, to *Notes of Travel* is particularly interesting as the Osgoods' chronicle is increasingly attracting attention from modern historians of nineteenth-century Arabia. For recent citations of *Notes of Travel* see, for instance, John Peterson, *Historical Muscat: An Illustrated Guide and Gazetteer* (Leiden/Boston: Brill, 2007), 77, 78, 87, 90, 95; Dionisius Agius, *Seafaring in the Arabian Gulf and Oman: People of the Dhow* (London: Kegan Paul, 2005), 186; and Christiane Bird, *The Sultan's Shadow: One Family's Rule at the Crossroads of East and West* (New York: Random House, 2010), 362.

8. Brian Jay Jones, *Washington Irving: An American Original* (New York: Arcade, 2008), ix.

9. For Irving's literary strategy of employing pseudonyms, including his first ("Jonathan Oldstyle"), see Jones, *Washington Irving*, 19.

10. The Romantic dichotomies of "fact and fiction" and "the history and the fairy tale" are invoked by Irving in his chapter dedicated to "Westminster Abbey" in his 1819–20 *Sketch Book*; see Washington Irving, *The Sketch Book of Geoffrey Crayon, Gent.* 2 vols. (London: J. Murray, 1820), II, 11.

11. Irving's afterlife in film has proved particularly expansive; his "Rip Van Winkle" alone has "been a favorite on screen with over twenty film adaptations," as Thomas Hischak notes in his *American Literature on Stage and Screen: 525 Works and Their Adaptations* (Jefferson, NC: McFarland, 2012), 198.

12. Irving sojourned twice in Spain, initially between 1826 and 1829, a span that received early treatment from George Sidney Hellman in his *Washington Irving, Esquire, Ambassador at Large from the New World to the Old* (London: Jonathan Cape, 1924), 149ff., and more recently by Jones, *Washington Irving*, 233ff.

13. Published as the two-volume *Mahomet and his Successors* in 1850 (New York: George Putnam), it is the first volume of Irving's Islamic history that is dedicated to the Prophet's life; however, this first volume was also published concurrently as a separate entity under the title *Life of Mahomet* (London: H.G. Bohn, 1850). The entire two-volume work was also published in 1850 as *Lives of Mahomet and his Successors* (London: G. Routledge & Co). In the current chapter, for the sake of clarity, I will use the latter title—*Life of Mahomet*—when referring to Irving's biography of the Prophet (i.e., to the material contained originally in the first volume of his two-volume *Mahomet and his Successors*). The complex compositional process that gave rise to Irving's *Mahomet* has been most comprehensively treated in the substantive "Historical Note" included as appendix to E. N. Feltskog and Henry Pochmann's critical edition, Washington Irving, *Mahomet and his Successors* (Madison: University of Wisconsin Press, 1970), cited subsequently as "Irving, *Mahomet* (1970)." Although this edition's "Historical

Note" was the "responsibility" of Feltskog, it also "required a true collaboration," as did this edition's "textual commentary," which was primarily authored by Pochmann (see Irving, *Mahomet* [1970], 512). I have also treated Irving's *Mahomet* and its composition in my "The Early American Qur'an: Islamic Scripture and US Canon," *Journal of Qur'anic Studies* 11:2 (2009): 1–19 (3–6), and my *Islam and Romanticism: Muslim Currents from Goethe to Emerson* (London: Oneworld, 2014), 166–76. However, the detailed mechanics of Irving's Qur'ānic renditions have not received treatment in previous scholarship, due partly to the unpublished status of select personal papers featuring his Islamic adaptations, explored for the first time later in this chapter.

14. The "Original Knickerbocker" is derived from the title of Andrew Burstein's biography *The Original Knickerbocker: The Life of Washington Irving* (New York: Basic Books, 2007).

15. Irving's *The Alhambra: A Series of Tales and Sketches of the Moors and Spaniards*, 2 vols. (Philadelphia: Carey and Lea, 1832), II, 28. For David Wilkie's claim that the *Alhambra* had proved "so popular that Irving was now considered 'the founder of a school,'" as well as Burstein's more nuanced assessment that the *Alhambra* has proved instead "resilient," see Burstein, *The Original Knickerbocker*, 230–31.

16. The Moor to whom Irving's Christian protagonist ("Peregil") is speaking is named explicitly as a "Moslem" in the passage that follows the one quoted above; see Irving's *The Alhambra*, II, 28.

17. For Columbus' journals recording his witnessing the transition of the Alhambra from Muslim to Christian sovereignty in January 1492, see John Thacher and Samuel Morison, *Christopher Columbus: His Life, His Work, His Remains as Revealed by Original Printed and Manuscript Records* (New York and London: G.P. Putnam's Sons, 1903), 435–36.

18. For the etymology of "Alhambra," see Ana Ruiz, *Vibrant Andalusia: The Spice of Life in Southern Spain* (New York: Algora Publishing, 2007), 146.

19. Irving, *The Alhambra*, I, 73–74.

20. As Burstein notes, the original American edition of *The Alhambra* is attributed to "The Author of the Sketch Book" (which presumably could suggest either Irving himself, or his pseudonym, Geoffrey Crayon); however, the London edition of *The Alhambra*, also published in 1832, names "Geoffrey Crayon" as its author (*The Original Knickerbocker*, 230).

21. Washington Irving, *Journals and Notebooks, Volume IV: 1826–1829*, ed. Wayne Kime and Andrew Myers (Boston: Twayne, 1984), 179–80. Matteo Ximenes remained a resident at the Alhambra long after Irving's departure, and was later encountered there by Edward Curr; see Samuel Furphy, *Edward M. Curr and the Tide of History* (Canberra: ANUE Press, 2013), 78–79. For Matteo Ximenes as a covert contributor to *The Alhambra*'s authorship, see Pere Gifra-Adroher, *Between History and Romance: Travel Writing on Spain in the Early Nineteenth-Century United States* (Madison, NJ: Fairleigh Dickinson UP, 2000), 144.

22. Washington Irving, *Journals and Notebooks, Volume IV*, 203.

23. Jones, *Washington Irving*, 252.

24. For this quotation, and for Irving's living with Hall in July (near Seville) and September (in the Port of Saint Mary), see Pierre M. Irving, *The Life and Letters of Washington Irving*, II, 265 and 278.

25. Stanley T. Williams, *The Life of Washington Irving*, 2 vols. (New York: Oxford UP, 1935), I, 339.

26. Washington Irving, *The Letters of Washington Irving to Henry Brevoort*, ed. George S. Hellman, 2 vols. (New York: Putnam, 1915), II, 208–09.

27. Pierre M. Irving, *The Life and Letters of Washington Irving*, 4 vols. (New York: George P. Putnam, 1862–64), II, 291–93.

28. Ibid., II, 293–94. It is for this frustrated séance that John Nalder Hall is typically mentioned in Irving studies; see, for example, Burstein, *Original Knickerbocker*, 212; Hellman, *Washington Irving, Esquire*, 178; Edward Wagenknecht, *Washington Irving: Moderation Displayed* (New York: Oxford UP, 1962), 92, 162; and Williams, *The Life of Washington Irving*, I, 487, and II, 233, 239. Although John Nalder Hall is not mentioned, Wai Chee Dimock's 2009

article "Hemispheric Islam: Continents and Centuries for American Literature" also treats the rich intersections between Irving, Islam, and the ghostly; in particular, Irving is invoked by Dimock as she "map[s]" American literature "against the coordinates of hemispheric Islam, looking East and West as well as North and South, and finding, at every turn, the ghosts of the world" (*American Literary History* 21:1 [2009]: 28–52 [47–48]).

29. See Rolena Adorno, "Washington Irving's Romantic Hispanism and its Columbian Legacies" in *Spain in America: The Origins of Hispanism in the United States*, ed. Richard Kagan (Urbana: University of Illinois Press, 2002), 49–105 (54).

30. This passage first appeared in the 1832 Philadelphia edition of Irving's *The Alhambra* (I, 54–55); however, in this edition, the passage includes an error, featuring "Celtic" instead of "Cufic" (see the corrected passage in Washington Irving, *The Works of Washington Irving* [Philadelphia: Lea and Blanchard, 1840], II, 408).

31. Irving's "Arabic Notebook" is housed at, and these pages are reproduced courtesy of, the Manuscripts and Archives Division, The New York Public Library, Astor, Lenox and Tilden Foundations. Although it remains mostly unpublished and wholly unedited, a photocopy of this notebook is featured as an Appendix to Layla al-Farsy's unpublished Ph.D. dissertation, "Washington Irving's *Mahomet*: A Study of the Sources" (University of Wisconsin-Milwaukee, 1983), 143ff. I previously published other pages from Irving's notebook in my 2009 "The Early American Qur'an," 6.

32. See Hellman, *Washington Irving, Esquire*, 206, which asserts that "The first four months of 1829 went by uneventfully enough. [ . . . ] He added to his previous studies of German, French and Italian, the study of Arabic, thus, although he was never proficient in any of these tongues, acquiring a smattering of more foreign languages than was then usual among American men of letters. [ . . . ] His Arabic note-book is a rather fascinating thing to the eye, and that his study of Arabic was of use may be inferred from the fact that in the library of the Escurial alone there were two thousand Arabian manuscripts among its thirty thousand volumes."

33. See al-Farsy, "Washington Irving's *Mahomet*: A Study of the Sources," 36–37, which notes that while "[s]ome believe this notebook could have been Hall's [ . . . ] I observed that the hand-writing was similar to Peter Irving's" (36).

34. Irving, *Mahomet* (1970), 548.

35. Quoted courtesy of the Manuscripts and Archives Division, The New York Public Library, Astor, Lenox and Tilden Foundations, this provenance marker is inscribed on the unpaginated cover of Irving's "Arabic Notebook." The formula—"Memoranda Book/[ . . . ] given to me by Mrs Pierre M. Irving/January 1885"—is not unique to Irving's "Arabic Notebook," however, but also prefaces at least one other "Autograph Manuscript Notebook"; see Luther Livingston, *American Book Prices Current* (New York: Robert H. Dodd, 1914), 715.

36. See Pierre M. Irving, *The Life and Letters of Washington Irving*, IV, 303, for Irving's will, where he stipulates "I thus bequeath my estate [ . . . ] to some meritorious members of the family bearing the family name, so that Sunnyside may continue to be, as long as possible, an *Irving homestead*."

37. One of these "Alphabet" pages, indexing the alphabet of the "western Arabs," is reproduced in my "The Early American Qur'an," 6. Figure 3.1, comprising p. 29 of Irving's "Arabic Notebook," is reproduced courtesy of the Manuscripts and Archives Division, The New York Public Library, Astor, Lenox and Tilden Foundations.

38. For the *basmala*, and Bentley's own inscription of "الرحيم," see Chapter 2, Figure 2.6. The first Arabic term transcribed in this quoted example from Figure 3.1—i.e. "كاتب" (*kātib*)—is a participle signifying "writer" or "scribe."

39. Figure 3.2, comprising pp. 34 and 35 of Irving's "Arabic Notebook," is reproduced courtesy of the Manuscripts and Archives Division, The New York Public Library, Astor, Lenox and Tilden Foundations.

40. For "ل" (*lām*) as a "flexible" particle, see Adrian Gully, *Grammar and Semantics in Medieval Arabic: A Study of Ibn-Hisham's "Mughni l-Labib"* (Richmond, UK: Curzon Press, 1995), 194.

41. Quoted courtesy of the Henry W. and Albert A. Berg Collection of English and American Literature, The New York Public Library, Astor, Lenox and Tilden Foundations, these lines translated from Arabic are inscribed in Irving's hand on p. 67 of volume 3 of his unpublished holograph notebooks classified as "Mahomet [and his successors]. Three holograph notebooks, chiefly memoranda concerning the Arabs, written about 1830." Surrounding his copied transliteration of the Arabic *shahāda*, Irving also transcribes additional material derived from his source—that is, Joseph Pitts (see note 43 below) (e.g., "*Allah waik barik* [ . . . ]"). I provide the English equivalent that follows, which does not appear in Irving's notebook.
42. The 167 items that make up the "Washington Irving collection of papers" at the Berg Collection include not only Irving's "Holograph notes ca. 1817–1818" for his *Sketch Book*, but also drafts and notes for his *Mahomet*, including an undated seventy-two-page folder containing "Memoranda extracts, etc. for the Chronicle of the Caliphs, from the death of the prophet to the invasion of Spain by the Saracens," further treated below in note 63.
43. Irving himself cites Joseph Pitts on p. 63 of volume 3 of his manuscript notebooks "Mahomet [and his successors]. Three holograph notebooks, chiefly memoranda concerning the Arabs, written about 1830," recording that his quotations are derived from the 1731 "*A Faithful Account of the Religion and Manners of the Mahometans*," which is "by Joseph Pitts of Exon"; this notebook is quoted courtesy of the Henry W. and Albert A. Berg Collection of English and American Literature, The New York Public Library, Astor, Lenox and Tilden Foundations. For a recent critical edition of Pitts' *Faithful Account*, see Paul Auchterlonie, *Encountering Islam: Joseph Pitts: An English Slave in 17th-Century Algiers and Mecca* (London: Arabian Publishing, 2012).
44. I cite these page sums from Irving's first American edition (*Mahomet and his Successors*, 2 vols. [New York: George Putnam, 1850]), the first volume of which reaches 373 pages, and the second that ends on p. 500.
45. For Irving as America's "first major writer" see Paul Varner, *Historical Dictionary of Romanticism in Literature* (Lanham, MD: Rowman & Littlefield, 2014), 193.
46. This original moment of composing *Mahomet*—including Irving's "writing at Mahomet" by mid-November 1827—was first recognized by the "Historical Note" to Feltskog and Pochmann's critical edition (Irving, *Mahomet* [1970], 522).
47. For John Murray II's rejection of *Mahomet*, see the "Historical Note" to Feltskog and Pochmann's critical edition (Irving, *Mahomet* [1970], 525ff.), which also emphasizes that *Mahomet*'s originally projected title was *The Legendary Life of Mahomet* (533). I have previously summarized these publication challenges in my "Washington Irving in Muslim Translation: Revising the American *Mahomet*," *Translation and Literature* 18.1 (2009): 43ff.
48. For Irving's service as "Envoy Extraordinary and Minister Plenipotentiary" see Adorno, "Washington Irving's Romantic Hispanism and its Columbian Legacies," 54. It is Irving himself who notes that authorship of *Mahomet* was resumed during his second stay in Spain, noting in his "Preface" that "During his last residence in Spain, the author beguiled the tediousness of a lingering indisposition by revising the manuscript" (Irving, *Mahomet* [1970], 3).
49. Washington Irving, *Letters, Volume III: 1839–1845*, ed. Ralph Aderman, Herbert Kleinfeld, and Jenifer Banks (Boston: Twayne, 1982), 916.
50. Joanne Michaels, *Hudson River Towns: Highlights from the Capital Region to Sleepy Hollow Country* (Albany: SUNY Press, 2011), 155.
51. Pierre M. Irving, *The Life and Letters of Washington Irving*, III, 332. This letter on Sunnyside's remodeling was quoted and first linked to Irving's revision of *Mahomet* in the "Historical Note" to Feltskog and Pochmann's critical edition; see Irving, *Mahomet* (1970), 517.
52. Irving, *Mahomet* (1970), 3.
53. Ibid., 3–4.
54. Ibid., 5.
55. Ibid., 16.

56. The name "Muḥammad" is a passive participle originating from an Arabic verbal root that signifies "to praise" (i.e., حمد/Ḥ-M-D).
57. Irving, *Mahomet* (1970), 39.
58. For these two discrete passages, see ibid., 40 and 41 respectively.
59. I have quoted and discussed these specific characterizations of "the Koran" previously. See, for example, my "The Early American Qur'an," 4, as well as my *Nineteenth-Century U.S. Literature in Middle Eastern Languages* (Edinburgh: Edinburgh University Press, 2013), 58 and 59, which treats these passages as they have been subsequently translated into Arabic.
60. Quoted courtesy of the Henry W. and Albert A. Berg Collection of English and American Literature, The New York Public Library, Astor, Lenox and Tilden Foundations, volume 3 of Irving's "Mahomet [and his successors]. Three holograph notebooks, chiefly memoranda concerning the Arabs, written about 1830" opens with "extracts" from Alexander Ross' "The Alcoran of Mahomet translated out of Arabique into French, by the Sieur des Ryer," spanning p. 5 and 20. On p. 5, for instance, Irving transcribes Chapter 1 of the Qur'ān; on p. 20, he copies the Qur'ān's last chapters (i.e., 113 and 114).
61. Quoted courtesy of the Henry W. and Albert A. Berg Collection of English and American Literature, The New York Public Library, Astor, Lenox and Tilden Foundations, volume 1 of Irving's "Mahomet [and his successors]. Three holograph notebooks, chiefly memoranda concerning the Arabs, written about 1830" is dedicated to his reading of Sale's *Koran*, quoting, for instance, material relating to Solomon (pp. 7ff.), while inscribing on pp. 48–54 not only Qur'ānic extracts, but also transcriptions from Sale's own annotations.
62. For editorial recognition of Irving quoting from Sale's *Koran*, see, for example, the notes to Pochmann and Feltskog's critical edition, Irving, *Mahomet* (1970), 622. However, this edition's notes also overlook that many of Irving's Qur'ānic quotations represent not verbatim transcripts from Sale or Du Ryer, but rather his own adapted renditions, as explained further below.
63. Irving, *Mahomet* (1970), 43. While I have previously addressed Irving's "sublime" quotation from the Qur'ān's Chapter 81 at the conclusion to his *Mahomet's* Chapter 8—see, for instance, my "The Early American Qur'an," 5—the manuscript bifolium featured in the present chapter, revealing the mechanics of Irving's adaptations, has never before appeared or been analyzed in print.
64. Reproduced courtesy of the Henry W. and Albert A. Berg Collection of English and American Literature, The New York Public Library, Astor, Lenox and Tilden Foundations, Figure 3.3 represents pages from a bifolium contained in "Memoranda extracts, etc. for the Chronicle of the Caliphs, from the death of the prophet to the invasion of Spain by the Saracens," a collection held as part of the Berg Collection's "Washington Irving collection of papers." At the Berg Collection, I am indebted to Anne Garner for guiding my research during my visit to the New York Public Library in 2009; I also thank Isaac Gewirtz, Curator of the Berg Collection, for aiding my efforts to secure the reproductions pictured in Figure 3.3.
65. The passage visible under Irving's revisions faintly recalls Sale's own rendition of this passage. In his treatment of this particular verse, Sale offers "an honourable messenger, endued with strength, of established dignity," while Irving's prerevised version reads as "a true messenger endued by Allah with strength and power." See Sale, trans., *The Koran*, II, 477–78.
66. Unsurprisingly, it is Sale's rendition, rather than Irving's revised adaptation, that is closer to the Qur'ān's original Arabic verse (81:8), which does indeed suggest that the "female infant" is "asked" ("سئلت") for "what sin she was killed."
67. William Beamont, *A Diary of a Journey to the East, in the Autumn of 1854*, 2 vols. (London: Longman & Co, 1856), I, 1.
68. See William J. Beamont, *A Concise Grammar of the Arabic Language* (Cambridge: Deighton, Bell & Co, 1861). For Rev. William J. Beamont's short stint as president of Jerusalem's English College, see James Finn, *Stirring Times: Or, Records from Jerusalem Consular Chronicles of 1853*

*to 1856* (London: C. Kegan Paul, 1878), II, 104–05, which also notes that Beamont Jr. had traveled to Jerusalem to "prosecute his Hebrew and Arabic studies" (104).

69. Beamont, *A Diary of a Journey to the East*, I, 116.

70. Despite quoting Irving's Qur'ānic versions, Irving's own name is not mentioned in either of the two volumes of Beaumont's 1856 *A Diary of a Journey to the East*.

71. In his introduction to Irving's biography of George Washington, Charles Neider notes that Irving was "a bachelor [and] himself childless," suggesting that this may account for Irving's emphasis on Washington's "paternalism"; see Washington Irving, *George Washington: A Biography*, ed. Charles Neider (New York: Da Capo Press, 1994), xiv.

72. Charles Anson Ingraham, "Personal Characteristics of Washington Irving," *Americana* 14 (1920): 355–68 (365).

73. Irving, *The Sketch Book of Geoffrey Crayon, Gent.*, II, 264–65.

## Chapter 4

1. Lydia Maria Child, *An Appeal in Favor of That Class of Americans Called Africans* (Boston: Allen and Ticknor, 1833), 165–66.

2. John Shook, *The Dictionary of Early American Philosophers* (New York: Continuum, 2012), 223. Entitled "Intellect of Negroes," Child's chapter is dedicated to refuting "The intellectual inferiority of the negroes [which] is a common, though most absurd apology, for personal prejudice, and the oppressive inequality of the laws" (Child, *An Appeal*, 155). For Child's *Appeal* as "converting more men and women to abolitionism than any other publication" see Megan Marshall, *The Peabody Sisters: Three Women Who Ignited American Romanticism* (Boston: Houghton Mifflin, 2005), 526.

3. For "Sir Hans Sloane" and the rendition of his Arabic manuscripts by Job ben Solomon see Keith A. Sandiford, *Measuring the Moment: Strategies of Protest in Eighteenth-Century Afro-English Writing* (Selinsgrove, PA: Susquehanna UP, 1988), 40.

4. This description of Child is reproduced from the title page of the 1833 edition of her *Appeal*, printed immediately above a quotation from S. T. Coleridge's poem "Fears in Solitude."

5. For *The Frugal Housewife* as an "enduring best-seller," and its "going through more than thirty printings during Child's lifetime," see the *Encyclopedia of the Romantic Era, 1760–1850*, ed. Christopher J. Murray (New York: Fitzroy Dearborn, 2004), 176. These attributes of Child and her work were previously listed in my own "'Minding the Koran' in Civil War America: Islamic Revelation, US Reflections," *Journal of Qur'anic Studies* 16:3 (2014): 84–103 (94–95)—an article that includes a section that addresses Child's Islamic interests and that is expanded upon in present chapter.

6. As mentioned above, the most prolific scholar of Child studies, Carolyn Karcher, entitles her biography of Child with this quotation from William Lloyd Garrison; see Karcher's *The First Woman in the Republic*, xi, where Karcher also suggests that Child was "a household name in America." For Child as "one of the chief publicists for the cult of domesticity," see Glenna Matthews, *Just a Housewife: The Rise and Fall of Domesticity in America* (New York: Oxford UP, 1987), 23.

7. It is Karcher who recognizes that Child "radically revises the story of Abduhl Rahahman," in authoring "Jumbo and Zairee" (*The First Woman in the Republic*, 162–63). "Jumbo and Zairee" also anticipates other short pieces with Islamic interests authored by Child for young readers, such as her "Lariboo. Sketches of Life in the Desert" (1854), which alludes, for instance, to "a large caravan of Arabs"; see Lydia Maria Child, *Flowers for Children* (Boston: C.S. Francis & Co., J. H. Francis, 1854), 158.

8. The chapter that Child dedicates to "Mohammedanism" spans pp. 349 and 417 in the third volume of her *The Progress of Religious Ideas, Through Successive Ages*, 3 vols. (New York: Charles S. Francis, 1855). "Mohammedanism" is the final body chapter of Child's study, but is also followed by her *Progress'* "Concluding Chapter" (III, 418–61).

9. Published as Child's *Aspirations of the World: A Chain of Opals* (Boston: Roberts Brothers, 1878), this work has been identified as "her last book" by Lori Kenschaft, *Lydia Maria Child: The Quest for Racial Justice* (Oxford: Oxford UP, 2002), 110.

10. Abbé Henri Grégoire's study—*De La Littérature Des Nègres, Ou, Recherches Sur Leurs Facultés Intellectuelles, Leurs Qualités Morales Et Leur Littératur* (Paris: Maradan, 1808)—was translated into English as *An Enquiry Concerning the Intellectual and Moral Faculties, and Literature of Negroes* by David Warden (Brooklyn: Thomas Kirk, 1810). For Grégoire's *Enquiry* as the "immediate rallying point for the nascent abolitionist cause in America" and its "examples of African-American achievement," see the University of South Carolina website dedicated to Grégoire's *Enquiry* (http://library.sc.edu/digital/collections/gregoire.html).

11. See *Enquiry*, trans. David Warden, 160–61; the original French for this passage is found in Grégoire, *De La Littératur Des Nègres*, 182–83.

12. In Warden's translation, the "*More-lak*" is followed by an asterisk gesturing to a footnote that reads "Le More-lack, par le Cointe-Marsillac. 8VO. Paris. 1789, 6. XV."

13. For Child commencing the research for her *Progress* in 1848 see Karcher, *The First Woman in the Republic*, xxiii.

14. The phrase "cruelly oppressed race" is Child's own, sourced from her "A Tribute to Col. Robert G. Shaw," in Lydia Maria Child, *A Lydia Maria Child Reader*, ed. Carolyn Karcher (Durham, NC: Duke UP, 1997), 267.

15. Lydia Maria Child, *Hobomok: A Tale of Early Times* (Boston: Cummings, Hilliard, 1824), 61–62.

16. For *Hobomok*'s autobiographical resonance, see Karcher, *The First Woman in the Republic*, 8–9, 16–17.

17. A parallel Islamic allusion is included a few pages earlier in *Hobomok*, where Child ascribes to the Puritan governor Endicott a bigoted comment that invokes the Muslim Prophet: "'It is marvellous in my eyes that the Lord fighteth on our side, while we march under such a badge of Antichrist,' said Governor Endicott. 'It as much beseemeth a christian to carry the half-moon of Mahomet, as such an emblem of popish victory. However, the pleasure of the king be obeyed'" (Child, *Hobomok*, 55).

18. *Hobomok* announces on its cover that it is authored "By An American"; however, the novel also "opens" with a "Preface" that comprises "an autobiographical vignette," as Karcher notes (*The First Woman in the Republic*, 16).

19. It is Karcher who suggests that Child's *Evenings in New England. Intended for Juvenile Amusement and Instruction* (1824) "furnished the model for" her *The Juvenile Miscellany, Or, Friend of Youth* (*The First Woman in the Republic*, 157).

20. Kenschaft, *Lydia Maria Child*, 25.

21. Eliza Lee Cabot Follen was also invited to contribute to *The Juvenile Miscellany, Or, Friend of Youth*, as noted by Karcher, *The First Woman in the Republic*, 205. In reviewing Follen's *The Child's Friend*, Margaret Fuller frames this work as a successor to Child's own *The Juvenile Miscellany*; see Margaret Fuller, *Margaret Fuller, Critic: Writings from the New-York Tribune, 1844–1846*, ed. Judith Bean and Joel Myerson (New York: Columbia UP, 2000), 69.

22. Lydia Maria Child, "A Few Words about Turkey," *Juvenile Miscellany* 3rd ser. 5 (1833): 310–22 (310–11). This short piece is cited in Karcher, *The First Woman in the Republic*, 652, but with an error in pagination (i.e., as "310–11").

23. The book reviewed by Child is James Ellsworth De Kay's *Sketches of Turkey in 1831 and 1832* (New York: J. & J. Harper, 1833). The characterization of the Ottoman Empire as the "world's leading Muslim power" is offered by John Coatsworth, Juan Cole, and Michael Hanagan, *Global Connections. Politics, Exchange, and Social Life in World History. Volume 2: Since 1500* (Cambridge: Cambridge UP, 2015), 347.

24. The cover of De Kay's *Sketches of Turkey* announces that it is authored "By an American," ironically matching the same credit line Child offers for her own 1824 *Hobomok*.

25. Child, "A Few Words about Turkey," 320.

26. De Kay, *Sketches of Turkey*, 359.
27. Washington Irving, *A Chronicle of the Conquest of Granada: From the Mss. of Fray Antonio Agapida*, 2 vols. (Paris: Baudry at the Foreign Library, 1829), II, 210. De Kay, *Sketches of Turkey*, 359, imprecisely cites "Chronicles of Grenada" in his footnote referring to "*Agapida*." Irving characterizes his fictional "Fray Antonio Agapida" as "a personification of the monk-ish zealots who hovered about the sovereigns in their campaigns, marring the chivalry of the camp by the bigotry of the cloister, and chronicling in rapturous strains every act of intoler-ance towards the Moors" (see Stanley Lane-Poole and Arthur Gilman, *The Moors in Spain* [New York: G.P. Putnam's, 1911], 235).
28. See Carolyn Karcher, "Rape, Murder, and Revenge in 'Slavery's Pleasant Homes': Lydia Maria Child's Antislavery Fiction and the Limits of Genre" in *The Culture of Sentiment: Race, Gender, and Sentimentality in Nineteenth-Century America*, ed. Shirley Samuels (New York: Oxford UP, 1992), 58–72 (59).
29. De Kay, *Sketches of Turkey*, 263.
30. Lydia Maria Child, *The History of the Condition of Women, in Various Ages and Nations*. 2 vols. (Boston: J. Allen, 1835), I, 68.
31. It seems that De Kay's own source for his "Whoso worketh good, whether male or female, and is a true believer" is the Qur'ān 16:97—a verse rendered by A. J. Arberry in his *The Koran Interpreted* as "And whosoever does a righteous deed, be it male or female, believing, We shall assuredly give him to live a goodly life; and We shall recompense them their wage, according to the best of what they did."
32. Lydia Maria Child, *Letters from New-York* (New York: C.S. Francis, 1843), 25.
33. See Louis Harap, *The Image of the Jew in American Literature: From Early Republic to Mass Immigration* (Syracuse: Syracuse UP, 2003), 139, who treats Child's visit to Shearith Yisrael—a Jewish congregation which he characterizes as "the oldest [...] in the United States." See also Karla Goldman, *Beyond the Synagogue Gallery: Finding a Place for Women in American Judaism* (Cambridge: Harvard UP, 2001), 110–11.
34. See Chapter 1, note 41.
35. In her "'Thumping against the Glittering Wall of Limitations': Lydia Maria Child's 'Letters from New York,'" in *In Her Own Voice: Nineteenth-Century American Women Essayists*, ed. Sherry Linkon (New York: Garland Publishing, 1997), 41–60, Stephanie Tingley notes that "Child sets up an intimate relationship between 'I' and 'you' in her 'Letters from New York'" (p. 54). Chapter 13 of Karcher's *The First Woman in the Republic* also highlights the intimacy of Child's *Letters* (see 295ff.).
36. Child's "his" is italicized in her *Letters from New-York* (New York: C.S. Francis, 1843), 25; how-ever, this same pronoun in the *Letters'* 1843 London edition is not italicized (see Lydia Maria Child, *Letters from New-York* [London: Richard Bentley], 1843), 28.
37. Although untitled by Child, her notebook is cataloged by the Boston Public Library as Ms.A.5.1 "Mahometans." From the Koran, translated from the original Arabic, by George Sale. This notebook has not been edited, published, or addressed in prior scholarship; however, the Boston Public Library has previously made the manuscript notebook available via the website archive.org, where it is designated "Notes on George Sale's commentary and translation of the Koran." At the very conclusion to her *Progress*, Child includes "Sale's Translation of the Koran" within her "List of Books Used in the Preparation of these Volumes," although without speci-fying the edition (Child, *Progress of Religious Ideas*, III, 463–64).
38. Quoted courtesy of the Trustees of the Boston Public Library/Rare Books, pp. 53 and 54 of Child's Ms.A.5.1 do not feature verse numbers, which I here supply (beginning with "[3:145]"). Also, immediately after Child's parenthetical note near the bottom of p. 54—"(the pagan Arabs [. . .])"—she begins to quote Sale's translation of 4:17, which continues on to her notebook's p. 55. For Child's source in Sale's translation, see Sale, trans., *The Koran*, I, 84–86. In her transcription of Sale, Child neglects to indicate that many words in Sale's translation are italicized, suggesting words not original to the Qur'ān, but instead inserted by Sale himself.

For instance, concluding verse 4:1 as copied by Child above (i.e., "[. . .] beseech one another; and respect women who have borne you, for God is watching over you"), Sale's rendition instead reads "[. . .] beseech one another; and *respect* women *who have borne you*, for God is watching over you" (Sale, trans., *The Koran*, I, 84).

39. Sale's original paratext to this passage reads "This law was given to abolish a custom of the Pagan Arabs, who suffered not women or children to have any part of the husband's or father's inheritance, on pretence that they only should inherit who were able to go to war" (Sale, trans., *The Koran*, I, 86).

40. A similar characterization of Child's *Progress* previously appeared in my "'Minding the Koran' in Civil War America," 95. It is Arthur Versluis who labels Child's *Progress* as "a landmark in comparative religion" in his *American Transcendentalism and Asian Religions* (Oxford: Oxford UP, 1993), 237.

41. For *Progress* as "Child's magnum opus," and a "pioneering work," see Karcher, *The First Woman in the Republic*, 374. Child's *Progress* merits a brief section in Versluis' *American Transcendentalism and Asian Religions*, 236–42; Versluis does not, however, recognize the complex revisionary processes that give rise to Child's treatment of "Mohammedanism," as discussed in the present chapter.

42. Karcher, *The First Woman in the Republic*, 360, notes that Child's *Progress* "would in fact take Child eight years to write," and quotes Child's April 1848 letter to Marianne Silsbee, where Child notes that she has been "very busy in making extracts, and reading innumerable books."

43. For instance, the material from pp. 53 and 54 of Ms.A.5.1 transcribed above is struck through by Child with vertical penciled lines, signaling its integration into her *Progress of Religious Ideas*, published on p. 386 of its third volume.

44. For Sale's "Preliminary Discourse," see Sale, trans., *The Koran*, I, 1–255. Figure 4.1— comprising pp. 25 and 26 of Lydia Maria Child, Ms.A.5.1—is reproduced courtesy of the Trustees of the Boston Public Library/Rare Books; I thank, in particular, Kimberly Reynolds, Curator of Manuscripts at the Boston Public Library, for her assistance in securing images from Child's "Notes."

45. For Sale's original, see Sale, trans., *The Koran*, I, 93–95. Although Child's "Notes" are undated, I offer "c. 1850" as an approximate date, as Child's research for her 1855 *Progress* began in 1848 (see note 13). For these passages in Child's *Progress*, see III, 395 and 407.

46. In transcribing Sale's passage, Child also neglects many of the footnotes supplied in his *Koran* to contextualize this passage; however, see below for Child's integration of such footnotes into her manuscript "Notes."

47. Quoted courtesy of the Trustees of the Boston Public Library/Rare Books, I transcribe this passage from lines 5 through 15 on p. 26 of Child's Ms.A.5.1 (reproduced as part of Fig. 4.1).

48. For these three paralleled passages, see respectively Sale, trans., *The Koran*, I, 95; Child, Ms.A.5.1, 25; and Child, *Progress of Religious Ideas*, III, 394.

49. "The following extracts will serve to give some idea of its character" is Child's introduction to her section furnishing quotations from the Qur'ān (*The Progress of Religious Ideas*, III, 382); Child's Qur'ānic "extracts," including many that were first inscribed in her Boston Public Library manuscript "Notes," unfold over seven pages, ending finally on *The Progress of Religious Ideas*, III, 388.

50. For Child's source, see Sale, trans., *The Koran*, II, 410, which begins: "When the inevitable *day of judgment* shall suddenly come, no *soul* shall charge *the prediction of* its coming with falsehood: it will abase *some*, and exalt *others*. When the earth shall be shaken with a violent shock; and the mountains shall be dashed in pieces, and shall become *as* dust scattered abroad; and ye shall be *separated into* three *distinct* classes."

51. This phrase is Child's own, characterizing her approach to composing *Aspirations* in a letter as "I wanted to make an Eclectic Bible"; see Lydia Maria Child, *Lydia Maria Child, Selected Letters, 1817–1880*, eds. Milton Meltzer, Patricia Holland, and Francine Krasno (Amherst: University of Massachusetts Press, 1982), 545.

52. Child, *Selected Letters*, 545. For these titles forming part of Child's "List of Subjects" see Child, *Aspirations of the World*, v–vi.

53. Child frequently neglects to differentiate between the Muslim Prophet and Muslim prophecy, attributing quotations in her *Aspirations* to "*Mohammed, Arabian; Koran*, 609 A.C."; for examples of Qur'ānic quotations cited in this way, see Child, *Aspirations*, 64, 71, 86. The celebrated Persian poet Ḥāfiẓ is quoted on p. 217 of Child's *Aspirations*; for quotations from Sa'dī, see Child, *Aspirations*, 145, 167, 174, 190, 205–06.

54. Child, *Aspirations*, 34–35.

55. Child's source is James L. Merrick, trans., *The Life and Religion of Mohammed: As Contained in the Sheeāh Traditions of the Hyât-ul-Kuloob* (Boston: Phillips, Sampson, and Co., 1850), which comprises an English rendition of Muḥammad Bāqir ibn Muḥammad Taqī Majlisī's *Ḥayāt al-Qulūb*. See pp. 207 and 197 respectively of Merrick's *The Life and Religion of Mohammed* for the two quotations offered by Child above. Although "rubies" seems to have been inserted by Child in the phrase "and angels were building palaces with blocks of gold and silver and rubies," this term may have been suggested to her by neighboring passages in *The Life and Religion of Mohammed*; consider, for instance, "a carpet of paradise which was woven of pearls and rubies," which occurs on p. 188 of Merrick, trans., *The Life and Religion of Mohammed*.

56. Reproduced courtesy of the Division of Rare and Manuscript Collections, Cornell University Library. Child's draft of her *Aspirations* is held as part of the Lydia Maria Child papers in the library's May Anti-Slavery manuscript collection, 1749–1933.

57. The original verse in the Qur'ān is 56:22, reading simply "*wa ḥūr 'īn*," rendered by Arberry in his *The Koran Interpreted* as "wide-eyed houris."

58. Child's manuscript draft of her *Aspirations*, held at Cornell's Carl A. Kroch Library, is written on the back of a variety of items, including her draft's p. 27, which is inscribed on the verso of a letter addressed to Child dated "Sept. 28 1873" sent from the "The Office of the Women's Journal"; p. 35, which is inscribed on the verso of the "Extracts From the Constitution [of the Free Religion Association]"; and p. 51, which is inscribed on the verso of what seems to be a receipt for Child's donation to the "The Massachusetts Society for the Prevention of Cruelty to Animals" (quotations courtesy of the Division of Rare and Manuscript Collections, Cornell University Library).

59. For Levi Bigelow Child (b. 1796) as brother of David Lee Child (b. 1794) see *Genealogical and Personal Memoirs Relating to the Families of Boston and Eastern Massachusetts*, II, 1048. In this letter, Levi Bigelow Child makes reference to "sister Lydia B. Child" as well as "Walter," two of the other Child siblings (b. 1791 and 1789 respectively). Quoted courtesy of the Division of Rare and Manuscript Collections, Cornell University Library.

60. The conclusion to this paragraph in Child's published *Aspirations* reads "they will all attain to Paradise at last, because they believed the true faith, and because Mohammed continually intercedes with God for them" (see Child, *Aspirations*, 39–40).

61. I have been unable to ascertain with certainty the identity of the "dear Johnnie" eulogized by Levi Bigelow Child.

62. *Home Dramas for Young People*, ed. Eliza Lee Cabot Follen (Boston: J. Munroe, 1859), 53–54.

63. "The Olive Merchants of Bagdat" begins on p. 99 of *Pleasant Pastime; or, Drawing-Room Dramas, for Private Representation by the Young* (London: Arthur Hall, Virtue & Co., 1850). Contemporary notices of the 1850 *Pleasant Pastime* attribute this edition merely to "A Lady"; see *Publishers' Circular and Booksellers' Record, Volume 13* (London, 1850), 166.

64. For Child's rendition—"Whoso worketh good, male or female, shall enter paradise"—see note 31.

65. See, for example, Margaret Coxe, *Claims of the Country on American Females* (Columbus, OH: Isaac N. Whiting, 1842), I, 201, which borrows without attribution Child's own revised Qur'ānic verse, i.e. "whoso worketh good, male or female, shall enter paradise."

66. See Jenkin Jones' "The Rosary of a Holy Life" in *Love and Loyalty* (Chicago: University of Chicago Press, 1907), 417–33.

67. Jenkin Jones, "The Rosary of a Holy Life," 430–31.

68. "One hour of justice is worth seventy years of prayer" is not Qur'ānic, but rather a quotation from al-Ghazālī; see Colin Mitchell, *The Practice of Politics in Safavid Iran: Power, Religion and Rhetoric* (London: Tauris Academic Studies, 2009), 251. This misattribution is not Jenkins' own, however, but originates with Child, who ascribes this sentiment to "*Mohammed, Arabian; Koran,* 609 A.C." (Child, *Aspirations,* 116).

69. These pages represent Child, *Aspirations,* 275–76, and form the final words of the body text of her "last book"; following this conclusion, however, Child also adds a page that lists an "Approximate Census of Religions."

## Chapter 5

1. Ralph Waldo Emerson, *The Journals and Miscellaneous Notebooks of Ralph Waldo Emerson: 1832–1834,* eds. William Gilmann, Alfred Ferguson, Harrison Hayford, Ralph Orth, J. E. Parsons, and A. W. Plumstead, 16 vols. (Cambridge, MA: Belknap Press of Harvard UP, 1975), I, 171 (subsequently cited as *JMN*). The words *"Digressive Continuity,"* which head this entry, are provided by the *JMN* editors in a footnote to this page.

2. Russell Goodman, *American Philosophy and the Romantic Tradition* (Cambridge, UK: Cambridge UP, 1990), 35.

3. For an edition of Campbell's poetry that was contemporary to Emerson, see Thomas Campbell, *Gertrude of Wyoming and Other Poems* (London, 1814), which includes "Lochiel's Warning" on pp. 133ff. The verses quoted by Emerson appear on p. 139. In addressing Emerson's Qur'ānic interests, Chapter 5 expands on my article "The Early American Qur'an: Islamic Scripture and US Canon," *Journal of Qur'anic Studies* 11:2 (2009): 1–19; my prior treatment of Emerson's 1819 quotation appears on pp. 2–3 of this article.

4. "*Jan*" is a collective plural of the singular "*jinn*"—a term derived from the Arabic verbal root "*j-n-n*" signifying "to cover," "to hide." For the Arabic etymology of the English "genie," see Cannon and Kaye, *Arabic Contributions,* 220.

5. Emerson himself would equate "Transcendentalism" with "Idealism," defining it as "Idealism as it appears in 1842"; Ralph Waldo Emerson, *The Collected Works of Ralph Waldo Emerson,* ed. Alfred Ferguson et al., 8 vols. (Cambridge, MA: Belknap Press of Harvard UP, 1971–2010), I, 201.

6. See Robert Richardson, *Emerson: The Mind on Fire* (Berkeley: University of California Press, 1995). For Emerson's "Transparent Eyeball" as "iconic," promoted in particular by Christopher Pearse Cranch's satiric sketch, see David Dowling, *Emerson's Protégés: Mentoring and Marketing Transcendentalism's Future* (New Haven, CT: Yale UP, 2014), 104.

7. As discussed below, Emerson's Persian poetry translations were first cataloged by John D. Yohannan, whose 1943 articles are still cited in current scholarship, despite their understandably outdated conclusions. This chapter, including its appendix, publishes findings, and extends research, that first appeared as part of my "Ralph Waldo Emerson, Persian Poetry and the German Critical Tradition" (unpublished Ph.D. dissertation, University of Cambridge, 2005). Since my doctoral work, Emerson's Islamic interests have increasingly attracted attention, inspiring, for example, Paul Kane, "Emerson and Hafiz: The Figure of the Religious Poet," *Religion and Literature* 36.1 (2009): 111–139, as well as *Sufism and American Literary Masters,* ed. Mehdi Razavi (Albany: SUNY Press, 2014). In one of this collection's primary contributions on Emerson, Farhang Jahanpour relies on Yohannan's estimation that "Emerson translated about 700 lines of Persian poetry" ("Emerson on Hafiz and Sa'di: The Narrative of Love and Wine" in *Sufism and American Literary Masters,* 117–152 [128]). See also note 68.

8. See Dimock, *Through Other Continents,* 34, which highlights Emerson's Qur'ānic quotation in his "journal entry from October 1819," characterizing it as a "quotation from George Sale's translation: 'In aforetime I created Jan from out of a scorching fire.'" Emerson's quotation does not derive from Sale's *Koran;* Sale renders this verse as "and we had before created the devil,

of subtile fire" (see Sale, trans., *Koran*, I, 90). Emerson's quotation was also cited by Wai Chee Dimock in her "Hemispheric Islam: Continents and Centuries for American Literature," *American Literary History* 21:1 (2009): 28–52, where it was again attributed to "George Sale's translation of the Quran" (34–35).

9. See my "The Early American Qur'an," 16.

10. For Emerson's reading of *The Asiatick Miscellany*, see Steven Adisasmito-Smith, "Transcendental Brahmin: Emerson's 'Hindu' Sentiments" in *Emerson for the Twenty-First Century: Global Perspectives on an American Icon*, ed. Barry Tharaud (Newark: University of Delaware Press, 2010), 131–164 (135). Jahanpour has more recently highlighted Emerson's reading of *The Asiatick Miscellany* but without noting his Qur'ānic quotation from this source ("Emerson on Hafiz and Sa'di," 118).

11. Entitled "An ACCOUNT of the PREADAMITES, and the HISTORY of the WORLD to the Death of ADAM," this rendition of *Khulāṣat al-Akhbār* appears in *The Asiatick Miscellany*, ed. Francis Gladwin (Calcutta: Printed by Daniel Stuart, 1785), I, 60–70. This English quotation from the section "*Of the* GENII" derives from near the top of p. 62, while the footnote—"جان [2]"—appears at the bottom, alongside footnotes 1, 3, 4, and 5, which also feature single terms written in Arabic or Persian script.

12. Background for *The Asiatick Miscellany* is provided by Nair Thankappan, *A History of the Calcutta Press, the Beginnings* (Calcutta: Firma KLM, 1987), 116 and ff.

13. "جان" ("*Jānn*") is indeed the first noun in the Qur'an 15:27, although it appears in the scripture with the definite article prefixed (as "الجان"; "*al-Jānn*").

14. Emerson does not copy *The Asiatick Miscellany*'s Middle Eastern diction in his 1819 entry (*JMN*, I, 171); he also, however, does not transcribe the Arabic and Persian offered to him later in his career, ignoring for instance such vocabulary encountered in Joseph Hammer-Purgstall's translations of Persian poets (see note 64).

15. For Stiles' postgraduate career as a Yale tutor, see Holmes, *The Life of Ezra Stiles*, 18; for Bentley's stint as Harvard tutor, see Ruffin, *A Paradise of Reason*, 24.

16. Ralph Waldo Emerson, *The Letters of Ralph Waldo Emerson*, ed. Ralph Rusk and Eleanor Tilton, 10 vols. (New York: Columbia UP, 1939–1994), I, 144; this page includes a footnote that suggests it is William Bentley Fowle and his "monitorial school" that is Emerson's intended target.

17. See Guy Litton, "Gannett's Address at Emerson's Ordination," *Emerson Society Papers* 9.2 (1998): 1, 8–9.

18. Emerson's complex motivations for resigning the Unitarian ministry receive partial expression in his valedictory "The Lord's Supper" sermon, treated most recently in my "Emerson's Exegesis: Transcending Symbols" in *Symbol and Intuition: Comparative Studies in Kantian and Romantic-Period Aesthetics*, eds. Helmut Hühn and James Vigus (Oxford: Legenda, 2013), 158–71 (159–60).

19. Delivered as an "Ordination discourse" in Baltimore on May 5, 1819, Channing's "Unitarian Christianity" has been characterized as a "clarion call" by Glenna Matthews, *The Golden State in the Civil War: Thomas Starr King, the Republican Party, and the Birth of Modern California* (New York: Cambridge UP, 2012), 44. For Channing's tutelage of Emerson as he prepared to enter Harvard Divinity School, see Richardson, *Emerson*, 58.

20. Richardson, *Emerson*, 13, asserts that Everett "was more than Emerson's first intellectual hero; he was, for a time, his personal idol"; for Everett as Emerson's "favorite teacher" see John Irwin, *American Hieroglyphics: The Symbol of the Egyptian Hieroglyphics in the American Renaissance* (New Haven: Yale UP, 1980), 8.

21. Paul Varg notes Bentley as one of Everett's early influences, helping to "encourage" his development (*Edward Everett: The Intellectual in the Turmoil of Politics* [Selinsgrove, PA: Susquehanna UP, 1992], 17). On January 3, 1820, Everett delivered the "Funeral Sermon for Dr. William Bentley"; see Ronald Reid, *Edward Everett: Unionist Orator* (New York: Greenwood Press, 1990), 199.

22. For Everett as "enchanted" with Eichhorn, see Varg, *Edward Everett*, 22. Eichhorn as a "versatile expert in Hebrew and Arabic" is noted by Katharina Mommsen, *Goethe and the Poets of Arabia*, trans. Michael Metzger (Rochester, NY: Camden House, 2014), 11.

23. *JMN*, I, 12.

24. For Everett's 1816 meeting with Goethe in Weimar, see Anna Ticknor and George Ticknor, *Two Boston Brahmins in Goethe's Germany: The Travel Journals of Anna and George Ticknor*, eds. Thomas Adam and Gisela Mettele (Lanham, MD: Lexington Books, 2009), 61–62.

25. For this quote from Goethe's *Divan*, and for Hafiz as Goethe's "twin," see Mommsen, *Goethe and the Poets of Arabia*, 133 and 125 respectively.

26. Everett's "waking" Emerson up to "a new morning" of German learning is treated by Frederick Wahr, *Emerson and Goethe* (Ann Arbor, MI: George Wahr, 1915), 65, who also traces Emerson's German learning (74ff.). In tracing the origins of Emerson's interest in Hafiz, Kane's 2009 "Emerson and Hafiz" has previously noted the "curious parallel" between "Goethe's and Emerson's initial response to Hafiz" (113). Goethe's *Divan* is, however, often neglected in overviews of Emerson's Orientalism; for instance, see Mansur Ekhtiyar's otherwise comprehensive "The Chronological Development of Emerson's Interest in Persian Mysticism," recently published in the 2014 *Sufism and American Literary Masters* (pp. 55–73), which overlooks Goethe altogether.

27. See below, especially note 68 and the appendix to this chapter.

28. Ralph Waldo Emerson, *Journals of Ralph Waldo Emerson with Annotations*, eds. Edward Waldo Emerson and Waldo Emerson Forbes, 10 vols. (Boston: Houghton, Mifflin and Company, 1909–1914), V, 431.

29. Following Harold Bloom, Lawrence Rosenwald finds "that Emerson's journals are his authentic work, his greatest formal achievement, his true and adequate genre" (*Emerson and the Art of the Diary* [New York: Oxford UP, 1988], xii). In Ralph Waldo Emerson, *Emerson in His Journals*, ed. Joel Porte (Cambridge, MA: Belknap Press of Harvard UP, 1982), vii, Porte traces the early publication history of Emerson's journals, noting that a "large portion of Emerson's journals was first made available by his son and grandson."

30. It is not certain from where Emerson initially derived the name "Osman"; Farida Hellal suggests that it was in his reading of Beaumont and Fletcher (Farida Hellal, "Emerson's Knowledge and Use of Islamic Literature" [unpublished Ph.D. dissertation, University of Houston, 1971], 298).

31. Introducing their *Journals*, Emerson's son and grandson invoke "Osman" as they discuss their editorial approach, confessing that in their edition "The passages in which 'Osman' appears are not to be taken as exact autobiography, though they come near being so. 'Osman' represents, not Emerson himself, but an ideal man whose problems and experiences are like his own" (see Emerson, *Journals of Ralph Waldo Emerson*, I, xviii).

32. For "Osman" as Emerson's "*alter ego*" and the American afterlife of this identity, see Paul Jackson, "Henry Miller, Emerson, and the Divided Self" in *On Emerson*, eds. Edwin Cady and Louis Budd (Durham, NC: Duke UP, 1988), 160–71 (166). Denis Donoghue identified Emerson as "the founding father of nearly everything we think of as American in the modern world" (*Reading America: Essays on American Literature* [New York: Knopf, 1987], 37). This remark has been regularly requoted; see, for example, Gustaaf Van Cromphout, *Emerson's Modernity and the Example of Goethe* (Columbia: University of Missouri Press, 1990), 11. "Mr. America" derives from the title of a 1984 *New York Review of Books* article by Harold Bloom, as emphasized by Rosenwald, *Emerson and the Art of the Diary*, xi. It is, of course, precisely Emerson's nationalist repute that has been the target of transnational criticism; for recent "question[ing of] Emerson's representation as successful liberator and founding father of a genuine American literature" see Jan Stievermann, "Emerson's Vision of an American World Literature" in *Emerson for the Twenty-First Century*, 165–215 (204).

33. For Emerson as "prophet of self-reliance" and the "quintessence of American individuality" see respectively Harold Bloom, *Where Shall Wisdom Be Found?* (New York: Riverhead Books,

2004), 203, and T. S. McMillin, *Our Preposterous Use of Literature: Emerson and the Nature of Reading* (Urbana: University of Illinois Press, 2000), 115.

34. For early mentions of "Saadi" and Emerson's poetic employment of his name around 1842, see "Saadi loved the new & old," a quatrain included in Ralph Waldo Emerson, *The Poetry Notebooks of Ralph Waldo Emerson*, ed. Ralph Orth et al. (Columbia: University of Missouri Press, 1986), 88. An early discussion of Emerson's autobiographical appeal to "Saadi" appears in F. O. Matthiessen's classic *American Renaissance; Art and Expression in the Age of Emerson and Whitman* in a brief section entitled "Self-Portrait of Saadi" (London: Oxford UP, 1954), 71–75.

35. See *JMN*, VIII, 517, for Emerson's calligraphy of "Saadi," penned at the back of his journal "Dialling." On p. 102 of "Dialling," for instance, Emerson "wrote 'Saadi' in pencil in an ornate hand three times on the page." See also *JMN*, XI, 184ff., and Ralph Waldo Emerson, *The Topical Notebooks of Ralph Waldo Emerson*, ed. Ralph H. Orth et al., 3 vols. (Columbia: University of Missouri Press, 1990–1994), III, 28ff., for entire notebooks adopting the title of Saadi's classic, his *Gulistan*.

36. Hellal, "Emerson's Knowledge and Use of Islamic Literature," 302; for Emerson's "Saadi," see *The Dial* (October 1842): 265–69.

37. Emerson, "Saadi," 265–66.

38. Parvin Loloi, "Emerson and Aspects of Sa'di's Reception in Nineteenth-Century America," *Sufism and American Literary Masters*, 91–116 (104). For my own recent discussion of "Saadi," see *Islam and Romanticism* (2014), which briefly treats the poem, emphasizing its political implications (191–95).

39. Emerson, "Saadi," 268–69.

40. Emerson, *Collected Works*, II, 97. This discussion of Emerson's epigram to his 1847 "Love" expands my previous treatment featured in "The Early American Qur'an," 10.

41. For the *ḥadīth* source of Emerson's epigram, see W. F. Thompson, *The Practical Philosophy of the Muhammadan People* (London: The Oriental Translation Fund of Great Britain and Ireland, 1839), 145 and 416. For Jalāl al-Dīn al-Dawwānī's *Akhlāq-e Jalālī*, more properly titled *Lawāmiʿ al-Ishrāq fī Makārim al-Akhlāq* (*Flashes of Illumination on Praiseworthy Ethics*), see Chad Lingwood, *Politics, Poetry, and Sufism in Medieval Iran: New Perspectives on Jāmī's Salāmān va Absāl* (Leiden: Brill, 2013), 18.

42. See Emerson, *Collected Works*, II, 243, where Emerson's editors trace his 1847 epigram to *The Practical Philosophy of the Muhammadan People* but do not recognize that his source itself represents a *ḥadīth* of the Prophet.

43. An account of Everett's instillation ceremony is published as *Addresses at the Inauguration of the Hon. Edward Everett* (Boston: C.C. Little and J. Brown, 1846), esp. 4ff.

44. Treatment of Emerson's disillusionment with Everett, including this specific quotation, is offered by James Mathews, "Fallen Angel: Emerson and the Apostasy of Edward Everett," in *Studies in the American Renaissance, 1990*, ed. Joel Myerson (Charlottesville: University of Virginia Press, 1990), 23–32 (25).

45. *JMN*, IX, 381.

46. Ibid.

47. The phrase "corpse-cold Unitarianism" is regularly quoted without recognition that Emerson's critique of his New England roots is followed by an embrace of Persian poetry. See, for example, Mary Cayton, *Emerson's Emergence: Self and Society in the Transformation of New England, 1800–1845* (Chapel Hill: University of North Carolina Press, 1992), 178, and E. B. Holifield, *Theology in America* (New Haven, CT: Yale UP, 2003), 439.

48. *JMN*, X, 68–69. This striking entry has not received significant attention, including from scholars interested in Emerson's relationship with Persian poetry. Richardson does, however, cite this entry, noting that it finds Emerson "compar[ing] himself and his contemporaries to the great Persian poets" (*First We Read, Then We Write: Emerson on the Creative Process* [Iowa City: University of Iowa Press, 2009], 42–43).

49. Emerson derives this characterization of Hafiz from Hammer-Purgstall's *Diwan* (1812–1813); see Emerson, *Topical Notebooks*, II, 153.

50. Elizabeth Palmer Peabody's West Street bookshop was where Emerson bought his edition of Hafiz, namely *Der Diwan von Mohammed Schemsed-din Hafis*, trans. Joseph Hammer-Purgstall, 2 vols. (Stuttgart und Tubingen, 1812–1813); see Emerson's manuscript account book for 1845–1849, entry of April 9, as reproduced in Emerson, *Letters*, VIII, 249.

51. Emerson, *Letters*, III, 341. This 1846 letter to Elizabeth Hoar receives brief prior notice in Kane's 2009 "Emerson and Hafiz" (135). Noting the clear Hafizean influence on Emerson's "Bacchus," Kane also quotes some of the same lines highlighted below ("Shall hear far Chaos talk with me;/Kings unborn shall walk with me"), suggesting that "Bacchus" gestures to a "place prior or before time" (135).

52. For these two translations, see Ralph Waldo Emerson, *Poems* (Boston: James Munroe and Co., 1847), 209ff. and 217ff., with Emerson's characterization of Hafiz as quoted above appearing on p. 209.

53. For early attempts to trace a Persian influence in "Merlin" and "Hermione" see respectively Joel Benton, *Emerson as a Poet* (New York: Holbrook, 1883), 26, and John Yohannan, "The Influence of Persian Poetry upon Emerson's Work," *American Literature* 15.1 (1943): 25–41 (32); the phrase "Persian touch" is Benton's, used to characterize Emerson's "Merlin" (26).

54. See the anonymous "Emerson's Poems" in *The American Review: A Whig Journal of Politics, Literature, Art, and Science* 6 (1847): 197–207 (203). After introducing "Bacchus" as "an imitation of the Persian mystic, Hafiz," this review quotes from the first two lines of Emerson's poem, before offering the lines beginning "Wine which music is." The review also erroneously prints "unborn" as "unbron."

55. Ac85.Em345.Zy812h, reproduced courtesy of the Ralph Waldo Emerson Memorial Association deposit, Houghton Library, Harvard University. Emerson's envelope has been transcribed previously as part of Appendix I in Emerson, *Topical Notebooks*, II, 400. However, the second of Emerson's dates at the top of his envelope is recorded by his editors as "138<2>1"; I offer instead "1389," as it seems Emerson seeks to reformulate his "2" into a "9," producing the death date for Hafiz offered by Hammer-Purgstall in his *Der Diwan* (ix). For Hafiz's lifespan as "1301–1389," see Frederick Vanderburgh, "Oriental Literature," in *The Student's Course in Literature*, ed. Gerhard Lomer (New York: Warner Library Co., 1917), 1–28 (23). However, Hafiz's dates are more often and more accurately determined as "about 1315 [to . . .] 1389"; see Peter Avery, "Foreword: Ḥāfiẓ of Shīrāz" in *Hafiz and the Religion of Love in Classical Persian Poetry*, ed. Leonard Lewisohn (London: I.B. Tauris, 2010), ix–xviii (ix).

56. This verso of Ac85.Em345.Zy812h is reproduced courtesy of the Ralph Waldo Emerson Memorial Association deposit, Houghton Library, Harvard University.

57. See Emerson, *Topical Notebooks*, II, 400, for a prior transcript of this translation; my own transcript above differs slightly by representing Emerson's revisions graphically rather than through editorial markers (offering, for instance, "~~Considers~~ The new moon looks on with affection," rather than "<Considers> The new moon ↑looks on↓ with affection," as supplied by Emerson, *The Topical Notebooks of Ralph Waldo Emerson*, 400).

58. These final lines represent the *takhalluṣ* of Hafiz's *ghazal* (i.e., his concluding verses that feature an act of "self-naming"); see Emerson's treatment of this literary convention in his "Persian Poetry," 729, where he additionally defines the *takhalluṣ* as an "opportunity" for "playful self-assertion."

59. Rendered by Hammer-Purgstall as "*Im Namen Gottes*" (*Der Diwan*, II, 339), the final words of Hafiz's original Persian *ghazal* do indeed represent the first words of the Arabic *basmala*, namely "بسم الله" ("In the name of *Allāh*"; for this *ghazal* in Persian, see Ḥāfiẓ, *Dīvān-e Ḥāfiẓ*, ed. Parvīz N. Khānlarī [Tehran: Intisharāt-i Khvārazmī, 1983], 832).

60. Emerson, "Persian Poetry," 732.

61. Ibid., 726.

62. See below for the complex hybridity of "The Exile," which has been previously recognized by John D. Yohannan, "Emerson's Translations of Persian Poetry from German Sources," *American Literature* 14.4 (1943): 407–20 (413–14).

63. Emerson, "Persian Poetry," 724. For this "memorializing" of Hammer-Purgstall in the first words to "Persian Poetry," see my *Islam and Romanticism* which briefly treats Emerson's eulogy (pp. 205–206).

64. Emerson gestures here to Hammer-Purgstall's anthology of Persian verse translation— *Geschichte der Schönen Redekünste Persiens* (Wien: Heubner und Volke, 1818), cited subsequently as *Geschichte*—which traces an evolution of Persian poetry through the works of two hundred poets, the first being Rūdagī (*Geschichte*, 39) and the two-hundredth being Fayḍī (*Geschichte*, 400).

65. Emerson, "Persian Poetry," 728.

66. As previously recognized by the editors of Emerson, *Poetry Notebooks*, 785, material for Emerson's "The Exile" is rendered on pp. 114 and 116 of his "Notebook Orientalist" (Emerson, *Topical Notebooks*, II, 85–86), as well as on pp. 123 and 124 of his "Rhymer" 123–24 (see Emerson, *Poetry Notebooks*, 460–61).

67. This anatomy of Emerson's "Exile" has previously been traced meticulously by Emerson, *Poetry Notebooks*, 785. However, I differ from the *Poetry Notebooks* editors in specifying that the lines "Except the amber morning wind,/Not one saluted me here" are based on Emerson's rendition of *ghazal* "Mim: LXXVI" in Hammer-Purgstall's *Diwan* (also see number 94 of Category A of the Appendix).

68. Following his estimation of Emerson's campaign of translation at "seven hundred lines of Persian poetry"—first offered in his 1943 "Emerson's Translations of Persian Poetry," 407— Yohannan published his *Persian Poetry in England and America: a 200-Year History* (Delmar, NY: Caravan Books) in 1977, qualifying slightly his claim by asserting that "Altogether, Emerson translated some 700 lines of Persian verse, excluding prose paraphrases which are to be found scattered throughout the *Journals* and the *Works*." The endurance of Yohannan's findings is suggested by the single book-length study dedicated to Emerson's interest in "Persia": Mansur Ikhtiyar, *Emerson & Persia: Emerson's Developing Interest in Persian Mysticism* (Tehran: Tehran UP, 1976), which reprints a condensed version of Yohannan's "check-list" (141–42). However, Ikhtiyar's study also asserts in passing that Emerson "translated several thousand lines from German sources from the eminent mystical poets including Hafiz" without providing specific references to justify this much larger projection (71). For more recent repetition of Yohannan's "700 lines" claim, see Dimock, *Through Other Continents*, 45, as well as Jahanpour's "Emerson on Hafiz and Saʿdi," cited in note 7.

69. For Yohannan's treatment of "The Exile" and his "Check-list" see "Emerson's Translations of Persian Poetry," 413–14 and 417–19 respectively.

70. Emerson, "Persian Poetry," 729.

71. MS Am 1280 (115) is reproduced courtesy of the Ralph Waldo Emerson Memorial Association deposit, Houghton Library, Harvard University. Figure 5.3 shows the bottom half of p. 24 of MS Am 1280 (115) (Emerson's "Notebook Orientalist"). This transcript of Emerson's rendered lines from Hafiz reflects the manuscript as pictured; however, a previous transcript of these lines, expressed through editorial markers (e.g., "<String on> ↑Fit for↓ the Pleiads azure <cord> ↑chord↓"), appears in Emerson, *Topical Notebooks*, II, 51.

72. This final published version of these lines, which appears in "Persian Poetry" (1858), is anticipated by one additional iteration on p. 25 of "Notebook Orientalist," which features Emerson's initial use of the first-person voice to render these verses: "Fit for the Pleiads' azure chord,/The <pearls> songs I sung, the pearls I bored" (see Emerson, *Topical Notebooks*, II, 51).

73. Emerson, *Letters*, III, 419.

74. For "The Ruins" see John Matteson, *Eden's Outcasts: The Story of Louisa May Alcott and Her Father* (New York: W.W. Norton, 2007), 180–81.

75. This *ḥadīth* derives again from Emerson's reading of the *Akhlāq-e Jalālī*; see *Practical Philosophy of the Muhammadan People*, 75, and the editorial note to Emerson, *Letters*, III, 419.
76. For Irving's return from Spain, settling again at Sunnyside by the fall of 1846, see Jones, *Washington Irving*, 379.
77. For Emerson recording the name of this ship, the *Washington Irving*, see Emerson, *Letters*, III, 415.
78. Gay Allen, *Waldo Emerson: A Biography* (New York: Viking Press, 1981), 655.
79. *JMN*, X, 83.
80. Albert Von Frank's *An Emerson Chronology* (New York: G. K. Hall, 1994), 490–91, notes that Emerson and Ellen departed from Europe (Naples) on December 21, 1872, for Egypt, and departed Egypt finally on February 19, 1873.
81. Emerson notes his stay at "Shepard's Hotel" (*JMN*, XVI, 446). For the historic "Shepheard's Hotel," see Trevor Mostyn, *Egypt's Belle Epoque: Cairo and the Age of the Hedonists* (New York: Tauris Parke Paperbacks, 2006), 150.
82. For these dates and arrivals, see *JMN*, XVI, 446–48, which suggests that the Emersons were in Cairo until January 7, in Luxor by January 19, and by February 15 "At Alexandria." See also Von Frank, *An Emerson Chronology*, 490–91.
83. See *JMN*, XVI, 285. Richardson, *Emerson*, 568, has previously emphasized that "Emerson found it humiliating not to know the language" during his sojourn in Egypt.
84. For such parallel accounts see, for instance, Kristin Hoganson, *Consumers' Imperium: The Global Production of American Domesticity, 1865–1920* (Chapel Hill: University of North Carolina Press, 2007), 132. Although aptly contextualizing "Mustapha Aga" in terms of "American Domesticity," Hoganson does not mention Emerson's visit.
85. *JMN*, XVI, 447. Emerson also records "Mustapha Aga's eyeglasses" in 1873 "Pocket Diary 24"—a diary devoted to "recording Emerson's memoranda of his travels in Egypt and Europe during early 1873" while including also "miscellaneous financial transactions" (see *JMN*, XVI, 445 and 456).
86. For Emerson's decline, see Richardson, *Emerson*, 569–71, who notes that Emerson's "memory was getting worse" even while in "England" during his last trip abroad. For *Letters and Social Aims* as assembled with the assistance of Ellen, as well as James Elliot Cabot, see Emerson, *Collected Works of Ralph Waldo Emerson*, VIII, vi.
87. Emerson, *Collected Works of Ralph Waldo Emerson*, VIII, 4–5.
88. See Harold Bloom, "Introduction" in *Ralph Waldo Emerson, Updated Edition*, ed. Harold Bloom (New York: Chelsea House, 2007), 1–13 (4). Emerson's self-reflective reference to "a half-translated ode of Hafiz" has also received previous treatment from Kane's 2009 "Emerson and Hafiz," 131–32, which quotes this passage in discussing the "polyvalent" character of "Emerson's translations of Hafiz."
89. See Emerson, *Topical Notebooks*, II, 79.
90. Ibid.
91. For this account of Saadi's bereavement, see Saadi, *Selections from the Bostan, or the Pleasure-Garden* (Calcutta: C.B. Lewis, 1868), viii.
92. The Qur'ānic story of "Jussuf" is featured in the scripture's twelfth chapter—*sūra Yūsuf*—with Joseph's poignant return to his father recounted in Qur'ān 12:93ff.
93. For Waldo's death and its impact on the Emerson family, see, in particular, Emerson, *Letters*, III, 6–7. In his 2009 "Emerson and Hafiz," Kane briefly mentions Waldo's death (134) but does not link this trauma to Emerson's rendition of Saadi's "In Senahar my first born sleeps."
94. The source of this passage is *JMN*, XIV, 154; in the original, a "the" is crossed out before "Mrs. Ripley" and a "bo" before "each."
95. This opening of Waldo's coffin in 1857 is anticipated by Emerson's earlier opening of the coffin of his first wife, Ellen, in 1832—a striking moment that Richardson vividly invokes in the introductory pages to his *Emerson* (3).
96. William Rounseville Alger, *The Poetry of the East* (Boston: Whittemore, Niles, and Hall, 1856), 77. Alger's appeal to Emerson's verses was first recognized by Yohannan; see his *Persian Poetry*

*in England and America*, 142. In his recent "The Chronological Development of Emerson's Interest in Persian Mysticisim," Mansur Ekhtiyar also highlights Alger's early interest in Persian influences on Emerson (63–64).

97. For the publication history of "The Rhodora," see Emerson, *Poetry Notebooks*, 902.

98. See Sa'dī, *The Gulistan, or the Rose Garden, of Shaikh Sadi of Shiraz*, trans. Francis Gladwin (Boston: Ticknor and Fields, 1865), a translation first published as *The Gûlistân of Sâdy: With an English Translation* (Calcutta: Hindoostanee Press, 1806). For Emerson's "The Rhodora" as quoted in Alger's second edition, see his *The Poetry of the Orient* (Boston: Roberts Brothers, 1865), 77.

99. See Ralph Waldo Emerson, "Preface" in *The Gulistan, or the Rose Garden, of Shaikh Sadi of Shiraz*, trans. Francis Gladwin (Boston: Ticknor and Fields, 1865), iii–xv.

100. Emerson, "Preface," xiv–xv. Emerson's *Gulistan* "Preface" rarely receives critical attention; Loloi, in her recent "Emerson and Aspects of Sa'di's Reception in Nineteenth-Century America," quotes selections, including the above conclusion to the "Preface" (99). See also my *Islam and Romanticism* (2014), which quotes this "Preface" and places it within its Civil War context (201–03).

101. For Sherman's destruction of Meridian, Mississippi, see Stephen Davis, *Atlanta Will Fall: Sherman, Joe Johnston, and the Yankee Heavy Battalions* (Wilmington, DE: Scholarly Resources, 2001), who notes that "Sherman's campaign across Mississippi, from Vicksburg to Meridian in February 1864, presaged his later March to the Sea" (19).

102. As early as 1999, Jalāl ad-Dīn Rūmī was identified as an American "top-selling poet"; this assertion has been evaluated by Franklin Lewis, *Rumi: Past and Present, East and West: the Life, Teachings and Poetry of Jalal al-Din Rumi* (London: Oneworld Publications, 2007), 527. For this claim's recent reemergence, see Jane Ciabattari, "Why is Rumi the best-selling poet in the US?" *BBC Culture* 14 April 2014 <http://www.bbc.com/culture/story/20140414-americas-best-selling-poet>.

103. See Ralph Waldo Emerson, *Dedication of the New Building for the Free Public Library of Concord, Massachusetts* (Boston: Tolman & White, 1873).

104. I have previously addressed Emerson's inclusion of the "Koran" under his list "For *Concord Library*" in my "The Early American Qur'an," 14–15. This entry is published in *JMN*, XVI, 327–28; for "Books Large" as "an old prayer copybook kept by Emerson's father Rev. William Emerson," see *JMN*, XVI, 325.

105. Reproduced courtesy of the William Munroe Special Collections, Concord Free Public Library, Concord, Figure 5.4 represents p. vii of Edward Waldo Emerson's copy of *The Gulistan, or the Rose Garden, of Shaikh Sadi of Shiraz*, trans. Francis Gladwin (Boston: Ticknor and Fields, 1865), housed at the Concord Free Public Library.

106. Edward's marginalia refers to Emerson's "Journal *FOR*, 1863"—a manuscript journal that Emerson authored between April 1863 and January 1864, and that is published in *JMN*, XV, 313ff. "Journal *FOR*" does indeed contain material that serves as the source for Emerson's passage in his published "Preface" (see, for instance, *JMN*, XV, 396, where Emerson writes "But the trait which most characterises Saadi [. . .] is cheerfulness. His name means *Fortunate*").

107. The name "Saadi" ("سعدی," "*sa'dī*") implies "felicity," as James Ross emphasizes in his introductory essay to the same edition of the *Gulistan* to which Emerson contributes his "Preface" (see *The Gulistan*, trans. Francis Gladwin [1865], 24)

## Appendix

1. For Yohannan's "Check-list," see Chapter 5, note 69. An earlier version of this appendix originally appeared as part of my 2005 University of Cambridge unpublished Ph.D. dissertation "Ralph Waldo Emerson, Persian Poetry and the German Critical Tradition," 267–89.

2. For German sources of Emersonian translations not previously identified by editors of his *Poetry Notebooks* and *Topical Notebooks*, see Category A, entries 4, 12, 44, 47, 77, and 96,

which indicate sources in Hammer-Purgstall's *Diwan* previously designated as "unlocated" in Emerson, *Poetry Notebooks*, 970, 852, 837, 832, and Emerson, *Topical Notebooks*, II, 114, 379, respectively.

3. Emerson's translations also merit attention from Parvin Loloi in her *Hafiz, Master of Persian Poetry: A Critical Bibliography* (London: I.B. Tauris, 2004); offering a catalog of English translations of Hafiz, Loloi only includes Emersonian renditions of full Hafizean *ghazals* previously catalogued by Yohannan.

4. In listing locations in Emerson's personal papers, for the sake of specificity I cite his own page numbers provided in his manuscript journals. For the published editions of the relevant notebooks, see (1) "Notebook Orientalist" in Emerson, *Topical Notebooks*, II, 37–141; (2) "Notebook EF" in Emerson, *Poetry Notebooks*, 264–322; (3) "Notebook X" in Emerson, *Poetry Notebooks*, 109–263; and (4) "Notebook Rhymer" in Emerson, *Poetry Notebooks*, 424–67.

# BIBLIOGRAPHY

Adams, Hannah. *A View of Religions in Two Parts.* 2 vols. Boston: Manning & Loring, 1801.

*Addresses at the Inauguration of the Hon. Edward Everett, LL. D., As President of the University at Cambridge, Thursday, April 30, 1846.* Boston: C.C. Little and J. Brown, 1846.

Adisasmito-Smith, Steven. "Transcendental Brahmin: Emerson's 'Hindu' Sentiments." In *Emerson for the Twenty-First Century: Global Perspectives on an American Icon,* ed. Barry Tharaud. Newark: University of Delaware Press, 2010: 131–64.

Adorno, Rolena. "Washington Irving's Romantic Hispanism and its Columbian Legacies." In *Spain in America: The Origins of Hispanism in the United States,* ed. Richard L. Kagan. Urbana: University of Illinois Press, 2002: 49–105.

Agius, Dionisius A. *Seafaring in the Arabian Gulf and Oman: People of the Dhow.* London: Kegan Paul, 2005.

Alger, William Rounseville. *The Poetry of the East.* Boston: Whittemore, Niles, and Hall, 1856.

Alger, William Rounseville. *The Poetry of the Orient.* Boston: Roberts Brothers, 1865.

Allen, Gay W. *Waldo Emerson: A Biography.* New York: Viking Press, 1981.

Allison, Robert J. *The Boston Massacre.* Beverly, MA: Commonwealth Editions, 2006.

*American Writers Before 1800: A Biographical and Critical Dictionary Vol. 3, Q–Z,* eds. James A. Levernier and Douglas R. Wilmes. Westport, CT: Greenwood Press, 1984.

Andrew, Edward E. *Native Apostles: Black and Indian Missionaries in the British Atlantic World.* Cambridge, MA: Harvard UP, 2013.

Arberry, A. J., trans. *The Koran Interpreted.* London: Allen & Unwin, 1955.

Auchterlonie, Paul. *Encountering Islam: Joseph Pitts: An English Slave in 17th-Century Algiers and Mecca: A Critical Edition, with Biographical Introduction and Notes, of Joseph Pitts of Exeter's A Faithful Account of the Religion and Manners of the Mahometans, 1731.* London: Arabian Publishing, 2012.

Avery, Peter. "Foreword: Ḥāfiẓ of Shīrāz." In *Hafiz and the Religion of Love in Classical Persian Poetry,* ed. Leonard Lewisohn. London: I.B. Tauris, 2010: ix–xviii.

Baack, Lawrence J. *Undying Curiosity: Carsten Niebuhr and the Royal Danish Expedition to Arabia (1761–1767).* Stuttgart: Franz Steiner Verlag, 2014.

Beamont, William. *A Diary of a Journey to the East, in the Autumn of 1854.* 2 vols. London: Longman & Co., 1856.

Beamont, William J. *A Concise Grammar of the Arabic Language, Revised by Sheikh Ali Nady El Barrany.* Cambridge, UK: Deighton, Bell & Co., 1861.

Bedford, Arthur. *The Scripture Chronology Demonstrated by Astronomical Calculations.* London, 1730.

Beneke, Chris. *Beyond Toleration: The Religious Origins of American Pluralism.* Oxford: Oxford UP, 2006.

Bentley, William. *The Diary of William Bentley.* 4 vols. Salem, MA: 1905–1914.

Berman, Jacob Rama. *American Arabesque: Arabs, Islam and the 19th-Century Imaginary.* New York: New York UP, 2012.

Bird, Christiane. *The Sultan's Shadow: One Family's Rule at the Crossroads of East and West.* New York: Random House, 2010.

Bloom, Harold. "Introduction." In *Ralph Waldo Emerson, Updated Edition*, ed. Harold Bloom. New York: Chelsea House, 2007: 1–13.

Bloom, Harold. *Where Shall Wisdom Be Found?* New York: Riverhead Books, 2004.

Booth, Robert. *Death of an Empire: The Rise and Murderous Fall of Salem, America's Richest City.* New York: Thomas Dunne Books, 2011.

Bremer, Francis J. *Congregational Communion: Clerical Friendship in the Anglo-American Puritan Community, 1610–1692.* Boston: Northeastern UP, 1994.

Brooks, Mary M., ed. *Textiles Revealed: Object Lessons in Historic Textile and Costume Research.* London: Archetype Publications, 2000.

Brown, Richard D. *Knowledge Is Power: The Diffusion of Information in Early America, 1700–1865.* New York: Oxford UP, 1989.

Buell, Lawrence. *Emerson.* Cambridge, MA: Harvard UP, 2003.

Burstein, Andrew. *The Original Knickerbocker: The Life of Washington Irving.* New York: Basic Books, 2007.

Cameron, Kenneth W. *Ralph Waldo Emerson's Reading.* Raleigh, NC: Thistle Press, 1941.

Campbell, Thomas. *Gertrude of Wyoming and Other Poems.* London, 1814.

Cannon, Garland H., and Alan S. Kaye. *The Arabic Contributions to the English Language: An Historical Dictionary.* Wiesbaden: Harrassowitz Verlag, 1994.

Castell, Edmund. *Lexicon Heptaglotton.* 2 vols. London: Thomas Roycroft, 1669.

Cayton, Mary. *Emerson's Emergence: Self and Society in the Transformation of New England, 1800–1845.* Chapel Hill: University of North Carolina Press, 1992.

Chew, Elizabeth V. "Unpacking Jefferson's Indian Hall" (2009) <http://www.lewis-clark.org/article/3086>.

Child, Lydia Maria. *An Appeal in Favor of That Class of Americans Called Africans.* Boston: Allen and Ticknor, 1833.

Child, Lydia Maria. *Aspirations of the World: A Chain of Opals.* Boston: Roberts Brothers, 1878.

Child, Lydia Maria. "Christianity and Other Religions." *The Index: A Weekly Paper Devoted to Free Religion* 9 (1878): 374–77.

Child, Lydia Maria. "A Few Words about Turkey." *Juvenile Miscellany* 3rd ser. 5 (1833): 310–22.

Child, Lydia Maria. *Flowers for Children.* Boston: C. S. Francis & Co., J. H. Francis, 1854.

Child, Lydia Maria. *The History of the Condition of Women, in Various Ages and Nations.* 2 vols. Boston: J. Allen, 1835.

Child, Lydia Maria. *Hobomok: A Tale of Early Times.* Boston: Cummings, Hilliard, 1824.

Child, Lydia Maria. *Letters from New-York.* London: Richard Bentley, 1843.

Child, Lydia Maria. *Letters from New-York.* New York: C.S. Francis, 1843.

Child, Lydia Maria. *Lydia Maria Child, Selected Letters, 1817–1880*, eds. Milton Meltzer, Patricia G. Holland, and Francine Krasno. Amherst: University of Massachusetts Press, 1982.

Child, Lydia Maria. *The Progress of Religious Ideas, Through Successive Ages.* 3 vols. New York: Charles S. Francis, 1855.

Child, Lydia Maria. "A Tribute to Col. Robert G. Shaw." In *A Lydia Maria Child Reader*, ed. Carolyn Karcher. Durham, NC: Duke UP, 1997: 267.

Chipley, Louise. "William Bentley, Journalist of the Early Republic." *Essex Institute Historical Collections* 123 (1987): 331–47.

Chodzko, Alexander. *Specimens of the Popular Poetry of Persia.* London, 1842.

Christy, Arthur. *The Orient in American Transcendentalism: A Study of Emerson, Thoreau, and Alcott.* New York: Columbia UP, 1932.

Ciabattari, Jane. "Why is Rumi the best-selling poet in the US?" *BBC Culture* (2014) <http://www.bbc.com/culture/story/20140414-americas-best-selling-poet>.

Clarence-Smith, W. G. "The Rise and Fall of Hadhrami Shipping in the Indian Ocean, 1750–1940." In *Ships and the Development of Maritime Technology on the Indian Ocean*, eds. Ruth Barnes and David Parkin. London: RoutledgeCurzon, 2002: 227–58.

Coatsworth, John, Juan Cole, and Michael Hanagan. *Global Connections. Politics, Exchange, and Social Life in World History. Volume 2: Since 1500*. Cambridge, UK: Cambridge UP, 2015.

Commager, Henry Steele. "The Nature of History." In *The Vital Past: Writings on the Use of History*, ed. Stephen Vaughn. Athens: University of Georgia, 1985: 120–29.

Conway, Moncure. *The Sacred Anthology. A Book of Ethnical Scriptures*. London: Trübner & Co., 1874.

Cooke, George W. *Unitarianism in America: A History of Its Origin and Development*. Boston: American Unitarian Association, 1902.

Coxe, Margaret. *Claims of the Country on American Females*. Columbus, OH: Isaac N. Whiting, 1842.

*Cyclopædia of American Literature*. eds. Evert Augustus Duyckinck and George Long Duyckinck. 2 vols. New York: Charles Scribner, 1856.

D'Arvieux, Larent. *The Chevalier D'Arvieux Travels into Arabia the Desert*. London, 1718.

Davis, Stephen. *Atlanta Will Fall: Sherman, Joe Johnston, and the Yankee Heavy Battalions*. Wilmington, DE: Scholarly Resources, 2001.

Dawwānī, Jalāl al-Dīn. *Practical Philosophy of the Muhammadan People. Being a Translation of the Akhlak-I-Jalaly*. Trans. W. F. Thompson. London, 1839.

De Bolla, Peter. *Harold Bloom: Towards Historical Rhetorics*. Oxon: Routledge, 2014.

De Kay, James Ellsworth. *Sketches of Turkey in 1831 and 1832*. New York: J. & J. Harper, 1833.

Dimock, Wai Chee. "Hemispheric Islam: Continents and Centuries for American Literature." *American Literary History* 21 (2009): 28–52.

Dimock, Wai Chee. *Through Other Continents: American Literature Across Deep Time*. Princeton, NJ: Princeton UP, 2006.

Doherty, Robert W. *Society and Power: Five New England Towns, 1800–1860*. Amherst: University of Massachusetts Press, 1977.

Doig, Lesley. "To Have and to Hold? Marital Connections and Family Relationships in Salem, Massachusetts, 1755–1810." In *Commerce and Culture: Nineteenth-Century Business Elites*, ed. W. Robert Lee. Farnham, Surrey: Ashgate Publishing, 2011: 255–84.

Donoghue, Denis. *Reading America: Essays on American Literature*. New York: Knopf, 1987.

Dowling, David. *Emerson's Protégés: Mentoring and Marketing Transcendentalism's Future*. New Haven, CT: Yale UP, 2014.

Du Ryer, Andre, trans. *The Alcoran of Mahomet*, trans. Alexander Ross. London, 1649.

Edwards, Brian T., and Dilip P. Gaonkar, "Introduction." In *Globalizing American Studies*, eds. Brian T. Edwards and Dilip P. Gaonkar. Chicago: University of Chicago Press, 2010: 1–46.

Edwards, Jonathan. *The Blank Bible*, ed. Stephen J. Stein. 2 vols. New Haven, CT: Yale UP, 2006.

Einboden, Jeffrey. "The Early American Qur'an: Islamic Scripture and US Canon." *Journal of Qur'anic Studies* 11:2 (2009): 1–19.

Einboden, Jeffrey. "Emerson's Exegesis: Transcending Symbols." In *Symbol and Intuition: Comparative Studies in Kantian and Romantic-Period Aesthetics*, eds. Helmut Hühn and James Vigus. Oxford: Legenda, 2013: 158–71.

Einboden, Jeffrey. *Islam and Romanticism: Muslim Currents from Goethe to Emerson*. London: Oneworld, 2014.

Einboden, Jeffrey. "'Minding the Koran' in Civil War America: Islamic Revelation, US Reflections." *Journal of Qur'anic Studies* 16:3 (2014): 84–103.

Einboden, Jeffrey. *Nineteenth-Century U.S. Literature in Middle Eastern Languages*. Edinburgh: Edinburgh UP, 2013.

Einboden, Jeffrey. "Ralph Waldo Emerson, Persian Poetry and the German Critical Tradition." Ph.D. diss., University of Cambridge, 2005.

Einboden, Jeffrey. "Washington Irving in Muslim Translation: Revising the American *Mahomet*." *Translation and Literature* 18:1 (2009): 43–62.

Emerson, Ralph Waldo. *The Collected Works of Ralph Waldo Emerson*, ed. Alfred R. Ferguson et al. 8 vols. Cambridge, MA: Belknap Press of Harvard UP, 1971–2010.

Emerson, Ralph Waldo. *The Complete Sermons of Ralph Waldo Emerson*, ed. Albert von Frank. 4 vols. Columbia: University of Missouri Press, 1989.

Emerson, Ralph Waldo. *Dedication of the New Building for the Free Public Library of Concord, Massachusetts, Wednesday, Oct. 1, 1873*. Boston: Tolman & White, 1873.

Emerson, Ralph Waldo. *Emerson in His Journals*, ed. Joel Porte. Cambridge, MA: Belknap Press of Harvard UP, 1982.

Emerson, Ralph Waldo. *The Journals and Miscellaneous Notebooks of Ralph Waldo Emerson*, ed. William H. Gilman et al. 16 vols. Cambridge, MA: Harvard UP, 1960–1982.

Emerson, Ralph Waldo. *The Journals of Ralph Waldo Emerson*, eds. Edward Waldo Emerson and Waldo Emerson Forbes. 10 vols. Boston: Houghton Mifflin, 1909–1914.

Emerson, Ralph Waldo. *The Letters of Ralph Waldo Emerson*, eds. Ralph L. Rusk and Eleanor M. Tilton. 10 vols. New York: Columbia UP, 1939–1994.

Emerson, Ralph Waldo. "Persian Poetry." *Atlantic Monthly Magazine* 1 (1858): 724–34.

Emerson, Ralph Waldo. *Poems*. Boston: James Munroe and Co., 1847.

Emerson, Ralph Waldo. *The Poetry Notebooks of Ralph Waldo Emerson*, eds. Ralph H. Orth et al. Columbia: University of Missouri Press, 1986.

Emerson, Ralph Waldo. "Preface." In *The Gulistan, or the Rose Garden, of Shaikh Sadi of Shiraz*, trans. Francis Gladwin. Boston: Ticknor and Fields, 1865: iii–xv.

Emerson, Ralph Waldo. "Saadi." *The Dial* 3 (1842): 265–69.

Emerson, Ralph Waldo. *The Topical Notebooks of Ralph Waldo Emerson*, eds. Ralph H. Orth et al. 3 vols. Columbia: University of Missouri Press, 1990–1994.

"Emerson's Poems." *The American Review: A Whig Journal of Politics, Literature, Art, and Science* 6 (1847): 197–207.

*Encyclopedia of the Romantic Era, 1760–1850*, ed. Christopher J. Murray. New York: Fitzroy Dearborn, 2004.

al-Farsy, Layla. "Washington Irving's *Mahomet*: A Study of the Sources." Ph.D. diss., University of Wisconsin-Milwaukee, 1983.

*The Felt Genealogy: A Record of the Descendants of George Felt of Casco Bay*, ed. John E. Morris. Hartford, CT: Press of the Case, Lockwood & Brainard Co., 1893.

Finn, James. *Stirring Times: Or, Records from Jerusalem Consular Chronicles of 1853 to 1856*. London: C. Kegan Paul, 1878.

Fisher, Linford D. *The Indian Great Awakening: Religion and the Shaping of Native Cultures in Early America*. Oxford: Oxford UP, 2012.

Flint, James. *Two Discourses: Delivered on Taking Leave of the Old Church of the East Society in Salem, December 28, 1845*. Salem, MA: Observer Office, 1846.

Foley, William E. *Wilderness Journey: The Life of William Clark*. Columbia: University of Missouri Press, 2004.

Follen, Eliza Lee Cabot, ed. *Home Dramas for Young People*. Boston: J. Munroe, 1859.

Fraser, James. *The History of Nadir Shah, Formerly Called Thomas Kuli Khan, the Present Emperor of Persia*. 2nd ed. London: W. Strahan, 1742.

Frothingham, Paul. *Edward Everett, Orator and Statesman*. Port Washington, NY: Kennikat Press, 1971.

Fuller, Margaret. *Margaret Fuller, Critic: Writings from the New-York Tribune, 1844–1846*, eds. Judith M. Bean and Joel Myerson. New York: Columbia UP, 2000.

Furphy, Samuel. *Edward M. Curr and the Tide of History*. Canberra: ANU E Press, 2013.

*Genealogical and Personal Memoirs Relating to the Families of Boston and Eastern Massachusetts*, ed. William Richard Cutter. 4 vols. New York: Lewis Historical Publishing Company, 1908.

Gifra-Adroher, Pere. *Between History and Romance: Travel Writing on Spain in the Early Nineteenth-Century United States*. Madison, NJ: Fairleigh Dickinson UP, 2000.

Gladwin, Francis, ed. *The Asiatick Miscellany*. Calcutta: Printed by Daniel Stuart, 1785.

Goldman, Karla. *Beyond the Synagogue Gallery: Finding a Place for Women in American Judaism.* Cambridge, MA: Harvard UP, 2001.

Goldman, Shalom. *God's Sacred Tongue: Hebrew and the American Imagination.* Chapel Hill: University of North Carolina Press, 2003.

Goodman, Russell. *American Philosophy and the Romantic Tradition.* Cambridge, UK: Cambridge UP, 1990.

Grasso, Christopher. *A Speaking Aristocracy: Transforming Public Discourse in Eighteenth-Century Connecticut.* Chapel Hill: University of North Carolina Press, 1999.

Grégoire, Henri. *De La Littérature des Nègres, Ou, Recherches Sur Leurs Facultés Intellectuelles, Leurs Qualités Morales Et Leur Littérature.* Paris: Maradan, 1808.

Grégoire, Henri. *An Enquiry Concerning the Intellectual and Moral Faculties, and Literature of Negroes,* trans. David B. Warden. Brooklyn: Thomas Kirk, 1810.

Grégoire, Henri. *An Enquiry Concerning the Intellectual and Moral Faculties, and Literature of Negroes.* University [of South Carolina] Libraries Digital Collections <http://library.sc.edu/digital/collections/gregoire.html>.

Gully, Arian. *Grammar and Semantics in Medieval Arabic: A Study of Ibn-Hisham's "Mughni l-Labib."* Richmond, UK: Curzon Press, 1995.

Ḥāfiẓ. *Dīvān-e Ḥāfiẓ,* ed. Parvīz N. Khānlarī. Tehran: Intisharāt-i Khvārazmī, 1983.

Hammer-Pugstall, Joseph, trans. *Der Diwan von Mohammed Schemsed-din Hafis.* 2 vols. Stuttgart und Tubingen, 1812–1813.

Hammer-Pugstall, Joseph, trans. *Geschichte der schönen Redekünste Persiens.* Wien: bey Heubner und Volke, 1818.

Harap, Louis. *The Image of the Jew in American Literature: From Early Republic to Mass Immigration.* Syracuse, NY: Syracuse UP, 2003.

Harris, David. *The Crisis: The President, the Prophet, and the Shah 1979 and the Coming of Militant Islam.* New York: Little, Brown and Co., 2004.

Hayes, Kevin. "How Thomas Jefferson Read the Qur'an." *Early American Literature* 39:2 (2004): 247–61.

Hayes, Kevin. *The Road to Monticello: The Life and Mind of Thomas Jefferson.* Oxford: Oxford UP, 2008.

Hellal, Farida. "Emerson's Knowledge and Use of Islamic Literature." Ph.D. diss., University of Houston, 1971.

Hellman, George. *Washington Irving, Esquire, Ambassador at Large from the New World to the Old.* London: Jonathan Cape, 1924.

Helmreich, Jonathan. *Eternal Hope: The Life of Timothy Alden, Jr.* Cranbury, NJ: Cornwall Books, 2001.

Heron, Robert. *A Collection of Late Voyages and Travels.* Edinburgh: Watson and Co., 1797.

Hill, Amelia. "The New President of Yale College in 1778." *The Connecticut Magazine: An Illustrated Monthly* 5 (1899): 420.

Hischak, Thomas. *American Literature on Stage and Screen: 525 Works and Their Adaptations.* Jefferson, NC: McFarland, 2012.

Hoberman, Michael. *New Israel/New England: Jews and Puritans in Early America.* Amherst: University of Massachusetts Press, 2011.

Hoganson, Kristin. *Consumers' Imperium: The Global Production of American Domesticity, 1865–1920.* Chapel Hill: University of North Carolina Press, 2007.

Holifield, E.B. *Theology in America: Christian Thought from the Age of the Puritans to the Civil War.* New Haven, CT: Yale UP, 2003.

Holmes, Abiel. *The Life of Ezra Stiles.* Boston: Thomas & Andrews, 1798.

Ikhtiyar, Mansur. *Emerson & Persia: Emerson's Developing Interest in Persian Mysticism.* Tehran: Tehran UP, 1976.

Ingraham, Charles Anson. "Personal Characteristics of Washington Irving." *Americana* 14 (1920): 355–56.

Irving, Pierre M. *The Life and Letters of Washington Irving*. 4 vols. New York: George P. Putnam, 1862–1864.

Irving, Washington. *The Alhambra: A Series of Tales and Sketches of the Moors and Spaniards*. 2 vols. Philadelphia: Carey and Lea, 1832.

Irving, Washington. *A Chronicle of the Conquest of Granada: From the Mss. of Fray Antonio Agapida*. 2 vols. Paris: Baudry at the Foreign Library, 1829.

Irving, Washington. *George Washington: A Biography*, ed. Charles Neider. New York: Da Capo Press, 1994.

Irving, Washington. *Journals and Notebooks, Volume IV: 1826–1829*, eds. Wayne Kime and Andrew Myers. Boston: Twayne, 1984.

Irving, Washington. *Letters, Volume III: 1839–1845*, eds. Ralph Aderman, Herbert Kleinfeld, and Jenifer Banks. Boston: Twayne, 1982.

Irving, Washington. *The Letters of Washington Irving to Henry Brevoort*, ed. George S. Hellman. 2 vols. New York: Putnam, 1915.

Irving, Washington. *Life of Mahomet*. London: H.G. Bohn.

Irving, Washington. *Lives of Mahomet and His Successors*. London: G. Routledge & Co., 1850.

Irving, Washington. *Mahomet and his Successors*. New York: George Putnam, 1850.

Irving, Washington. *Mahomet and his Successors*, eds. Henry Pochmann and E. N. Feltskog. Madison: University of Wisconsin Press, 1970.

Irving, Washington. *The Sketch Book of Geoffrey Crayon, Gent*. 2 vols. London: J. Murray, 1820.

Irving, Washington. *The Works of Washington Irving*. Philadelphia: Lea and Blanchard, 1840.

Irwin, John. *American Hieroglyphics: The Symbol of the Egyptian Hieroglyphics in the American Renaissance*. New Haven, CT: Yale UP, 1980.

Jackson, Paul. "Henry Miller, Emerson, and the Divided Self." In *On Emerson*, eds. Edwin Cady and Louis Budd. Durham, NC: Duke UP, 1988: 160–71.

Jahanpour, Farhang. "Emerson on Hafiz and Sa'di: The Narrative of Love and Wine." In *Sufism and American Literary Masters*, ed. Mehdi Razavi. Albany: SUNY Press, 2014: 117–52.

Jefferson, Thomas. *The Papers of Thomas Jefferson, Volume 38: 1 July to 12 November 1802*, ed. Barbara B. Oberg. Princeton, NJ: Princeton UP, 2012.

Jefferson, Thomas. *Thomas Jefferson Papers*, Library of Congress <http://jeffersonswest.unl.edu/archive/view_doc.php?id=jef.00018>.

Jones, Brian Jay. *Washington Irving: An American Original*. New York: Arcade, 2008.

Jones, Jenkin. *Love and Loyalty*. Chicago: University of Chicago Press, 1907.

*Journal of the House of Representatives of the United States: Being the First Session of the First Congress-3rd Session of the 13th Congress, March 4, 1789–Sept. 19, 1814, Volume 5*. Washington, DC: Gales & Seaton, 1826.

Kane, Paul. "Emerson and Hafiz: The Figure of the Religious Poet." *Religion and Literature* 36.1 (2009): 111–39.

Karcher, Carolyn. *The First Woman in the Republic: A Cultural Biography of Lydia Maria Child*. Durham, NC: Duke UP, 1994.

Karcher, Carolyn. "Rape, Murder, and Revenge in 'Slavery's Pleasant Homes': Lydia Maria Child's Antislavery Fiction and the Limits of Genre." In *The Culture of Sentiment: Race, Gender, and Sentimentality in Nineteenth-Century America*, ed. Shirley Samuels. New York: Oxford UP, 1992: 58–72.

Kellow, Margaret. "The Divided Mind of Antislavery Feminism: Lydia Maria Child and the Construction of African American Womanhood." In *Discovering the Women in Slavery: Emancipating Perspectives on the American Past*, ed. Patricia Morton. Athens: University of Georgia Press, 1996: 107–26.

Kelly, George. *Politics and Religious Consciousness in America*. New Brunswick, NJ: Transaction Books, 1984.

Kelly, Howard A. *A Cyclopedia of American Medical Biography*. 2 vols. Philadelphia and London: W.B. Saunders Company, 1912.

Kenschaft, Lori J. *Lydia Maria Child: The Quest for Racial Justice*. Oxford: Oxford UP, 2002.

Klar, Marianna. "Human–Divine Communication as a Paradigm for Power: Al-Tha'labī's Presentation of Q. 38:24 and Q. 38:34." In *Sacred Tropes: Tanakh, New Testament, and Qur'an as Literature and Culture*, ed. Roberta S. Sabbath. Leiden: Brill, 2009: 159–72.

Kronk, Gary W., and Maik Meyer. *Cometography: A Catalogue of Comets*. 5 vols. Cambridge, UK: Cambridge UP, 1999–2010.

Lane-Poole, Stanley, and Arthur Gilman. *The Moors in Spain*. New York: G.P. Putnam's, 1911.

Lathrop, John. "A Sermon, Preached at the Ordination of William Bentley." Salem, MA: Samuel Hall, 1783.

"A Letter of President Dunster to Professor Ravis." *Collections of the Massachusetts Historical Society* 4:1 (1852): 251–54.

Lewis, Franklin. *Rumi: Past and Present, East and West: The Life, Teachings and Poetry of Jalal al-Din Rumi*. London: Oneworld Publications, 2007.

Lingwood, Chad. *Politics, Poetry, and Sufism in Medieval Iran: New Perspectives on Jāmī's Salāmān va Absāl*. Leiden: Brill, 2013.

Litton, Guy. "Gannett's Address at Emerson's Ordination." *Emerson Society Papers* 9.2 (1998): 1, 8–9.

Livingston, Luther. *American Book Prices Current*. New York: Robert H. Dodd, 1914.

Loloi, Parvin. *Hafiz, Master of Persian Poetry: A Critical Bibliography*. London: I.B. Tauris, 2004.

Luedtke, Luther. *Nathaniel Hawthorne and the Romance of the Orient*. Bloomington: Indiana UP, 1989.

Lutz, Cora. "Ezra Stiles and the Learned Jews at Newport." *Yale University Library Gazette* 70:3/4 (1996): 161–69.

Manuel, Frank, and Fritzie Manuel, *James Bowdoin and the Patriot Philosophers*. Philadelphia: American Philosophical Society, 2003.

Marr, Timothy. *The Cultural Roots of American Islamicism*. New York: Cambridge UP, 2006.

Marshall, Megan. *The Peabody Sisters: Three Women Who Ignited American Romanticism*. Boston: Houghton Mifflin, 2005.

Marvin, Winthrop L. *The American Merchant Marine: Its History and Romance from 1620 to 1902*. New York: Scribner, 1902.

Matar, Nabil I. *Europe Through Arab Eyes, 1578–1727*. New York: Columbia UP, 2009.

Mathews, James W. "Fallen Angel: Emerson and the Apostasy of Edward Everett." In *Studies in the American Renaissance, 1990*, ed. Joel Myerson. Charlottesville: University of Virginia Press, 1990: 23–32.

Matteson, John. *Eden's Outcasts: The Story of Louisa May Alcott and Her Father*. New York: W.W. Norton, 2007.

Matthews, Glenna. *The Golden State in the Civil War: Thomas Starr King, the Republican Party, and the Birth of Modern California*. New York: Cambridge UP, 2012.

Matthews, Glenna. *Just a Housewife: The Rise and Fall of Domesticity in America*. New York: Oxford UP, 1987.

Matthiessen, F.O. *American Renaissance; Art and Expression in the Age of Emerson and Whitman*. New York: Oxford UP, 1941.

McCarus, Ernest. "History of Arabic Study in the United States." In *The Arabic Language in America*, ed. Aleya Rouchdy. Detroit: Wayne State UP, 1992: 207–50.

McMillin, T. S. *Our Preposterous Use of Literature: Emerson and the Nature of Reading*. Urbana: University of Illinois Press, 2000.

Merrick, James, trans. *The Life and Religion of Mohammed*. Boston: Phillips, Sampson, and Co., 1850.

Michaels, Joanne. *Hudson River Towns: Highlights from the Capital Region to Sleepy Hollow Country*. Albany: SUNY Press, 2011.

Milton, John. *The Complete Poetry and Essential Prose of John Milton*, eds. William Kerrigan, John Rumrich, and Stephen M. Fallon. New York: Modern Library, 2007.

Mitchell, Colin. *The Practice of Politics in Safavid Iran: Power, Religion and Rhetoric*. London: Tauris Academic Studies, 2009.

Mommsen, Katharina. *Goethe and the Poets of Arabia*, trans. Michael M. Metzger. Rochester, NY: Camden House, 2014.

Morgan, Edmund. *The Gentle Puritan: A Life of Ezra Stiles, 1727–1795*. New Haven, CT, and London: Yale UP, 1962.

Morison, Samuel Eliot. *Founding of Harvard College*. Cambridge, MA: Harvard UP, 1935.

Mostyn, Trevor. *Egypt's Belle Epoque: Cairo and the Age of the Hedonists*. New York: Tauris Parke Paperbacks, 2006.

"The Municipal Seal of Salem." *Historical Collections of the Essex Institute* 8.1 (1868): 3–9.

Murray, Christopher John. *Encyclopaedia of the Romantic Era, 1760–1850: A–K*. New York: Fitzroy Dearborn, 2004.

Niebuhr, Carsten. *Beschreibung von Arabien*. Copenhagen: Möller, 1772.

Niebuhr, Carsten. *Description de L'Arabie: d'après les Observations et Recherches Faites Dans le Pays Même*. Copenhagen: Nicolas Möller, 1773.

Osgood, Joseph B. F. *Notes of Travel: Or, Recollections of Majunga, Zanzibar, Muscat, Aden, Mocha, and Other Eastern Ports*. Salem, MA: George Creamer, 1854.

Oshatz, Molly. *Slavery and Sin: The Fight Against Slavery and the Rise of Liberal Protestantism*. Oxford: Oxford UP, 2011.

Peterson, John. *Historical Muscat: An Illustrated Guide and Gazetteer*. Leiden-Boston: Brill, 2007.

*Pleasant Pastime; or, Drawing-Room Dramas, for Private Representation by the Young*. London: Arthur Hall, Virtue & Co., 1850.

Pococke, Richard. *A Description of the East and Some Other Countries*. 2 vols. London, 1743–45.

*Publishers' Circular and Booksellers' Record, Volume 13*. London, 1850.

*The Qur'an*, trans. Muhammad Abdel Haleem. Oxford: Oxford UP, 2004.

Reid, Ronald. *Edward Everett: Unionist Orator*. New York: Greenwood Press, 1990.

Richardson, Robert. *Emerson: The Mind on Fire*. Berkeley: University of California Press, 1995.

Richardson, Robert. *First We Read, Then We Write: Emerson on the Creative Process*. Iowa City: University of Iowa Press, 2009.

Rosenwald, Lawrence. *Emerson and the Art of the Diary*. New York: Oxford UP, 1988.

Rothschild, Robert. *Two Brides for Apollo: The Life of Samuel Williams (1743–1817)*. New York: iUniverse, 2009.

Ruffin, J. Rixey. *A Paradise of Reason: William Bentley and Enlightenment Christianity in the Early Republic*. New York: Oxford UP, 2009.

Ruiz, Ana. *Vibrant Andalusia: The Spice of Life in Southern Spain*. New York: Algora Publishing, 2007.

Sa'di. *The Gûlistân of Sâdy*, trans. Francis Gladwin. Calcutta: Hindoostanee Press, 1806.

Sa'di. *The Gulistan, Rose Garden of Sa'di*. trans. W. M. Thackston. Bethesda, MD: Ibex Publishers, 2008.

Sa'di. *Lustgarten*, trans. K. Graf. Jena, 1850.

Sa'di. *Rosengarten*, trans. K. Graf. Leipzig, 1846.

Sa'di. *Selections from the Bostan, or the Pleasure-Garden*. Calcutta: C.B. Lewis, 1868.

Said, Edward. *Orientalism*. London: Routledge & Kegan Paul, 1978.

Sale, George, trans. *The Koran: Commonly Called the Alcoran of Mohammed*. 2 vols. London: T. Tegg, 1825.

Salisbury, Edward Elbridge. "Valuable Arabic Manuscripts, at Worcester, Mass." *Journal of the American Oriental Society* 2 (1851): 337–39.

Sandiford, Keith. *Measuring the Moment: Strategies of Protest in Eighteenth-Century Afro-English Writing*. Selinsgrove, PA: Susquehanna UP, 1988.

Schmidt, Gary. *A Passionate Usefulness: The Life and Literary Labors of Hannah Adams*. Charlottesville: University of Virginia Press, 2004.

Selden, John. *Opera Omnia*, ed. David Wilkins. 3 vols. in 6 vols. London, 1726.

Shook, John R. *The Dictionary of Early American Philosophers*. New York: Continuum, 2012.

Smith, Ernest A. *Allegheny—A Century of Education: 1815–1915*. Meadville, PA: Allegheny College History Co., 1916.

Spellberg, Denise. *Thomas Jefferson's Qur'an: Islam and the Founders*. New York: Alfred A. Knopf, 2013.

Sprague, William B. *Annals of the American Unitarian Pulpit*. New York: R. Carter & Brothers, 1865.

Stievermann, Jan. "Emerson's Vision of An American World Literature." In *Emerson for the Twenty-First Century: Global Perspectives on an American Icon*, ed. Barry Tharaud. Newark: University of Delaware Press, 2010: 165–215.

Stiles, Ezra. *Extracts from the Itineraries and Other Miscellanies of Ezra Stiles*, ed. Franklin B. Dexter. New Haven, CT: Yale UP, 1916.

Stiles, Ezra. *Laws of the Redwood-Library Company*. Newport, RI: Samuel Hall, 1765.

Stiles, Ezra. *The Literary Diary of Ezra Stiles*, ed. Franklin Bowditch Dexter. 3 vols. New York: C. Scribner's Sons, 1901.

Stiles, Ezra. "The United States Elevated to Glory and Honor." New Haven, CT: Thomas & Samuel Green, 1783.

Stith, William. *The History of the First Discovery and Settlement of Virginia*. Williamsburg, 1747.

Thacher, John B., and Samuel E. Morison, *Christopher Columbus: His Life, His Work, His Remains as Revealed by Original Printed and Manuscript Records*. New York and London: G.P. Putnam's Sons, 1903.

Thankappan, Nair P. *A History of the Calcutta Press, the Beginnings*. Calcutta: Firma KLM, 1987.

Tholuck, August, ed. *Blüthensammlung aus der Morgenländischen Mystick*. Berlin, 1825.

Ticknor, Anna, and George Ticknor. *Two Boston Brahmins in Goethe's Germany: The Travel Journals of Anna and George Ticknor*, eds. Thomas Adam and Gisela Mettele. Lanham, MD: Lexington Books, 2009.

Tingley, Stephanie A. "'Thumping against the Glittering Wall of Limitations': Lydia Maria Child's 'Letters from New York." In *In Her Own Voice: Nineteenth-Century American Women Essayists*, ed. Sherry Linkon. New York: Garland Publishing, 1997: 1–60.

Toomer, G. J. *Eastern Wisedome and Learning: The Study of Arabic in Seventeenth-Century England*. Oxford: Oxford UP, 1996.

Van Cromphout, Gustaaf. *Emerson's Modernity and the Example of Goethe*. Columbia: University of Missouri Press, 1990.

Vanderburgh, Frederick A. "Oriental Literature." In *The Student's Course in Literature*, ed. Gerhard Richard Lomer. New York: Warner Library Co., 1917: 1–28.

Varg, Paul. *Edward Everett: The Intellectual in the Turmoil of Politics*. Selinsgrove, PA: Susquehanna UP, 1992.

Varisco, Daniel Martin. *Reading Orientalism: Said and the Unsaid*. Seattle: University of Washington Press, 2007.

Varner, Paul. *Historical Dictionary of Romanticism in Literature*. Lanham, MD: Rowman & Littlefield, 2014.

Versluis, Arthur. *American Transcendentalism and Asian Religions*. Oxford: Oxford UP, 1993.

Von Frank, Albert. *An Emerson Chronology*. New York: G. K. Hall, 1994.

Wagenknecht, Edward. *Washington Irving: Moderation Displayed*. New York: Oxford UP, 1962.

Wahr, Frederick B. *Emerson and Goethe*. Ann Arbor, MI: George Wahr, 1915.

Wellman, Joshua, George Chamberlain, and Arthur Wellman. *Descendants of Thomas Wellman of Lynn, Massachusetts*. Boston: A.H. Wellman, 1918.

Whitehill, Walter. *Portraits of Shipmasters and Merchants in the Peabody Museum of Salem*. Salem, MA: Peabody Museum, 1939.

"Will of Dr. Bentley." *New-England Palladium* 50:3 (1820): 1.

Williams, Stanley T. *The Life of Washington Irving*. 2 vols. New York: Oxford UP, 1935.

Winter, Michael. *Egyptian Society Under Ottoman Rule, 1517–1798*. London: Routledge, 2003.

Wright, Conrad. *The Beginnings of Unitarianism in America*. Hamden, CT: Archon Books, 1976.

Wright, Conrad. *Revolutionary Generation: Harvard Men and the Consequences of Independence*. Amherst: University of Massachusetts Press, 2005.

Yohannan, John D. "Emerson's Translations of Persian Poetry from German Sources." *American Literature* 14.4 (1943): 407–20.

Yohannan, John D. "The Influence of Persian Poetry upon Emerson's Work." *American Literature* 15.1 (1943): 25–41.

Yohannan, John D. *Persian Poetry in England and America: A 200-Year History*. Delmar, NY: Caravan Books, 1977.

Yothers, Brian. *The Romance of the Holy Land in American Travel Writing, 1790–1876*. Aldershot: Ashgate, 2007.

Young, Malcolm. *The Spiritual Journal of Henry David Thoreau*. Macon, Ga: Mercer UP, 2009.

# INDEX